1/17/13
$30.00

The American Jury System

Randolph N. Jonakait

Yale University Press

New Haven and London

Set in Adobe Garamond type by The Composing Room of Michigan, Inc.
Printed in the United States of America by Integrated Book Technology.

Library of Congress Cataloging-in-Publication Data

Jonakait, Randolph N.
   The American jury system / Randolph N. Jonakait.
      p.   cm. — (Yale contemporary law series)
   Includes bibliographical references and index.
   ISBN 978-0-300-12463-7 (pbk.)
   1. Jury—United States.   I. Title.   II. Contemporary law series.
   KF8972 .J66   2003
   347.73′752—dc21   2002014241

A catalogue record for this book is available from the British Library. The paper in this book meets the guidelines for permanence and durability of the Committee on Production Guidelines for Book Longevity of the Council on Library Resources.

10 9 8 7 6 5 4 3 2

Contents

Preface

I was nervous. Extremely nervous. I had been practicing law for just two months as a public defender in New York City, and I was about to undertake my first jury trial. Although my job with the New York City Legal Aid Society had given me a month of training before I was let loose in court, I had never seen an actual trial.

The two defendants had been formally charged with "jostling," a crime under New York law that punishes people for unnecessarily putting their hands near or in others' pockets or purses, a crime intended to punish pickpockets. The complaint, however, hardly indicated a light-fingered pair. That legal instrument charged that the two had beaten a person senseless on the Bowery and had taken money out of his pockets.

I knew little about the case other than the single paragraph setting out the charges. New York law did not even require that I be told who the prosecution witnesses would be, much less what they would say. I could do only what I had been taught to do.

In the courtroom before the judge entered, I tentatively called out the victim's name listed in the complaint in hopes that he would talk to me. No response. I said it louder. Still no response. I then called out, "Officer Murphy," who had made the arrests. A man with a gold badge dangling from a breast pocket motioned me outside.

His first words to me were angry. "I worked hard to become a detective. I am *Detective* Murphy, not Officer." He almost spat that last word. He went on to tell me that he had been working a robbery detail when he saw my clients roll a drunk. When I asked where the victim was, the detective confessed that although he had repeatedly been to the dollar-a-night hotel the victim had given as an address, the Bowery resident could not be found.

I entered the bowels of the courthouse to talk to my clients, who were in a holding cell. The two, both much older than the average arrested person, had not made bail. Their "rap sheets" revealed lengthy arrest records, and although I was to see thousands of such criminal records over the years, one of these client's sheets contained an entry I never saw again. Twenty years earlier, he had been arrested for vagrancy in Fort Wayne, Indiana. Although in those days these records seldom reported the disposition of an arrest, this one did. It stated simply, "Put on the bus to Chicago."

One of the defendants moved to the front of the cell and spoke to me through the bars, nervously insisting that he knew nothing about the charges but that he wanted a plea bargain. The district attorney, however, had said that any deal would require both defendants to plead guilty. The other client sat placidly in the far corner of the cell reading a Bible. From there he said firmly, "I'm not pleading guilty. If this was a crime, where is the victim?" When I explained that the charges were not going to be dismissed because of the victim's absence, he just repeated, "If this was a crime, where is the victim? Let's go to trial." And so we went to trial.

I may have thought that a certain majesty or dignity surrounded a jury trial, but the courtrooms on *Perry Mason* and *The Defenders* did not look like this one. Manhattan misdemeanor jury trials were held in small, airless, dingy rooms with humming, dim lights. The smell could never have been captured on television. Part of it came from generations of bodies that had not recently showered; another part came from infrequently applied disinfectant floor cleaners. There were other components, too, but even after years of entering such rooms, I dare not speculate on them all.

The jury selection for that trial is a blur, as are the prosecutor's and my opening statements. The detective testified about how the defendants beat the other man and took his money. In my cross-examination, I suggested that the cop's vantage point did not allow him to see all that he claimed, but mostly I harped on the fact that the supposed victim showed no interest in the case and could not be found. The detective was the only witness.

My summation must have pleased one of my clients, because most of it was variations of "If this was a crime, where is the victim?" The prosecutor responded that justice had seldom seen a more open-and-shut case. The judge then told the jurors the law they were to apply in reaching a verdict, and the jury began to deliberate. Two hours at most had elapsed from the trial's inception.

Perhaps forty-five minutes later, the jury had a verdict. The clerk told my clients to stand and face them. My heart pounded, and I asked myself, "Am I to stand, too?" No one had told me what to do. As I worried whether I was embarrassing myself, the foreman announced the first verdict. I didn't hear it. But when the jury was asked about the second defendant, I clearly heard, "Not guilty."

Relief followed. A few days later, the arresting detective saw me in a courthouse corridor. He extended his hand. "Counselor," he said, "you beat me fair and square." Is that what this jury trial was about? Was it a contest between the cop and me, with the jury as arbiter?

The jury system was starting to seem more complicated and mysterious than I had realized. On the one hand, I thought it possible that my clients had done something like what the cop had recounted, even though I doubted that he had witnessed all he claimed. On the other hand, the state could not prove robbery, and I thought the prosecution was misusing the jostling law against the defendants. According to the wording of the statute, they were guilty, but the acquittal did not seem unjust. Perhaps it was even right.

A few weeks later I was back on trial. Another lawyer and I were defending an English and an Irish immigrant who were charged with assaulting another Irish immigrant. The defense claimed this had been a minor skirmish outside a bar, yet the victim had taken nude pictures of himself indicating that he had received a sound thrashing. Both defendants testified that the victim, not they, had started the fight. The jury acquitted the defendant represented by the other attorney but announced they could not reach a verdict on my client. This seemed nonsensical. The evidence suggested that both or neither were guilty. The other defendant, however, had never been arrested before, and my client had committed an earlier assault. The jury was told that they could not use this prior incident to determine that my client was violent and, therefore, that he had committed the charged crime. Instead, the judge instructed, they should assess how that earlier crime affected the defendant's credibility when he testified that he had not started the fight. Since I was not entirely sure what that instruction meant, I doubted whether jurors could understand it. Even so, when I got over the disappointment of not winning, I realized that the jury's refusal to acquit my client did not seem unjust.

The notion that somehow these trials would have been better without juries did not occur to me. What was the alternative? The only available options were no trial or a bench trial, a trial where a judge without a jury determines whether the accused is guilty. The no-trial alternative meant plea bargaining. Few legal disputes are resolved by trials of any sort. Criminal cases are handled largely by plea bargaining; civil matters by settlement. Trials are not really seen as civilized ways of deciding disputes. Instead, they are threats. If an adversary does not accept the offered terms of resolution, the ominous response is "Let's go to trial." To be an effective trial attorney means not so much to do well in the occasional matter that goes to trial, but instead to be an effective bargainer in the many cases that do not. The ultimate bargaining chip is always a trial. Of course, if an attorney is reluctant to try cases or cannot try them well, the trial threat has little force. Nevertheless, I quickly learned, the major reason for trials is to assure that most cases will end in settlement or guilty pleas.

One of my early bench trials taught me that the system often discourages those who truly want a jury trial. New Yorkers typically dispose of furniture by placing it on the street. Passersby can examine such leavings and take what they want before sanitation trucks haul it off. My client—call him Schwartz—had staked out some abandoned tables and chairs. Another person stated that he had already claimed them and that Schwartz was violating the unwritten street rules of first possession. Shouting and finger-pointing escalated to an altercation. As Schwartz stood his ground, the other person flagged down a police car, and Schwartz ended up charged with assault, theft, and disorderly conduct.

Schwartz maintained he had done nothing wrong. When told that he could plead guilty to disorderly conduct, which is not a criminal violation, and be sentenced to a conditional discharge—in effect, no sentence at all—he vehemently refused and insisted on a jury trial. A jury trial, however, was not easily to be had. Manhattan had only two courtrooms for misdemeanor jury trials, while it had many more to process preliminary matters on felonies and to enter misdemeanor plea bargains. A case would be sent to a jury trial courtroom only if it was clear that both sides were truly ready to proceed. That generally meant that the witnesses for each side had to be present. If they were, however, the case would merely be marked ready for trial. If the jury trial courtrooms were already engaged with other trials, as they usually were, the case would be adjourned to another date, when the process would begin again.

This system often defeated other defendants' desire for a jury. A young man charged with an auto theft, for example, had insisted on a jury trial. In my opinion, he had a respectable defense and stood a good chance of being acquitted. Over a three-month period he tried and failed five times to have his trial scheduled. On each attempt, he had to take off work in order to come to court. His perseverance had cost him a week's wages, and he feared that further time off would cost him his job. When the prosecutor finally told us that if he pleaded guilty, he would get a $150 fine, the young man, who had already lost more pay than that, relented and pled guilty. I do not know if he actually stole the car; there was a good chance he had not. But I understood why, even if innocent, he had said he was guilty.

Schwartz was different. He would have come back forever to have his day in court, but he also had three witnesses—a retired man, a stay-at-home mother, and a young stockbroker. Each had seen the altercation, and each confirmed Schwartz's version. Each had come to the courthouse two times and spent most of the day in a courtroom only to be told that the trial would not go forward that day. When the same result seemed imminent on the third day, the stockbroker told me that he was not sure he would be able to come back again. When I saw the mother nodding in agreement (she had had to hire a babysitter each time she had come to court), I told my client that I thought we needed to go to trial that day. This could happen only if the defendant waived a jury and consented to a bench trial. If he did that, the trial, I thought, would be sent to Judge Logan. I had had hearings and a bench trial in front of him, and he had seemed fair. Judge Logan, however, was already overloaded, and he insisted that my trial be sent elsewhere. It ended up with Judge Wolfe.

Many attorneys, including my supervisor, told me what a mistake I had made. Wolfe was reputed to be short-tempered and vindictive. Wolfe, supposedly, had never seen a defendant who was not guilty, and I was told to inspect my client's footwear. Wolfe, so the story went, had returned home from the opera one night to find his apartment door ajar. He saw a ransacked living room when he heard a noise in his bedroom. There he noticed an open window, and the burglar fleeing up the fire escape. All the judge saw of the miscreant was a sneakered foot. Since then, the judge was hard on every defendant, but especially on those wearing sneakers.

Schwartz, I was relieved to see, was shod in scruffy loafers when we went to trial. His witnesses testified well. I felt confident, but when I gave my summation the judge appeared not even to be listening. Immediately after the prosecutor finished, the judge harshly announced, "Guilty of two-forty-twenty."

Schwartz erupted. Court officers moved to restrain him. I grabbed him and tried to explain as he continued to shout. The judge had found him guilty only of disorderly conduct. The judge had acquitted him of the theft and assault charges, but he had not said so, explicitly. My client thought he had been convicted of the charges against him.

When I finally made Schwartz understand what had happened, he mumbled, "A jury never would have done it like that." The judge then sentenced the defendant to a fine, while a guilty plea would have incurred only the conditional discharge. Perhaps the result would have been the same with a jury, but the outcome had not seemed legitimate to the defendant. Schwartz's anger focused on that one person who had made the decision.

This episode hammered home a lesson that every trial attorney knows. The alternative to a jury is a bench trial, and judges are not dispassionate oracles. They are human beings, and no matter how much they try to transcend their life experiences, they consciously or unconsciously carry them when they don their robes.

I ultimately went on to represent clients charged with more serious crimes and also supervised other trial attorneys. These experiences taught me a fact of life absorbed by most criminal defense attorneys: juries convict most of the time. This truth might have led to my disillusionment with the jury system, but I was repeatedly struck by how seriously jurors take their job. People are plucked from their daily routine and commanded to serve as jurors. Most resent it and have to make sacrifices to come to court. They are asked to make decisions about people they do not know and to assess situations and circumstances they hope never to encounter. It is easy to understand why these ordinary citizens would not care one bit about what they are asked to do. But they do. Whether I have agreed with their decisions or not, I have observed that jurors almost always agonize over making the right decision.

This fact has been highlighted by a few exceptions. The one that upset me the most happened in a robbery trial. A woman had been walking in a poor part of Brooklyn filled with rubble-strewn lots and ravaged shells of structures. Two young men ran up behind her, grabbed her purse, and knocked her to the ground. She saw the two flee into one of the abandoned husks. Her screams brought calls to the police. She testified that she had watched the hiding place of her attackers until the police apprehended the defendant there, and then she immediately identified him as one of the criminals.

Cross-examination demonstrated, I thought, that she had had little opportunity to observe the purse snatchers. They had come up from behind, one on each side of her. She had not looked back, and they had run off in front of her. I tried to show that at best she might have caught a glimpse of the profile of one of them, and although she maintained that she had continuously viewed their hiding place so that they could not have left it without her detection, she had no explanation as to why the police had found only one of the robbers in the building.

The defendant, a teenager, testified that he had simply been hanging out in a neighborhood building when the police arrested him. He swore that he knew nothing about the robbery. The victim's purse was not found.

I then presented what I thought was convincing evidence that the defendant had not been found in the building where the robbers had sought refuge. The victim had firmly identified one location. The police just as firmly said that they had found the defendant elsewhere. Citing official records, I showed that the building where the defendant had been found was located at a considerable distance from the site the victim had pinpointed, with no connections between the two structures.

I argued that the victim was clearly confused and that it was only natural that when she saw the defendant handcuffed in police custody, she identified him as one of the culprits, but the identification was wrong or at least there was a reasonable doubt about whether she was correct. The jury, however, convicted in less than an hour. As the jurors left, I tried to talk to a number of them to try to understand how I had failed. Only one paused. He told me that I had done a good job representing such a clearly guilty person. He then put his hand on my arm, laughed, and said, "We were especially proud of how you were able to make that building move." He looked as if he expected me to chuckle at the joke. When I didn't, he strode away. I was angry, of course, because I had lost, but I was also angry because he had apparently not taken the case or the facts seriously. This was behavior I had seldom encountered in a jury.

Instead, I have found the vast majority of jurors to be diligent and earnest. One juror, for example, sought me in my office the day after returning a guilty verdict. The police had said that while one officer had knocked on an apartment door, another stood out back and had seen the defendant toss drugs out the window. Others besides the defendant, however, had been in the apartment at the time, and the officer who had identified the defendant at the fifth-story window had seen the toss from an oblique angle. The apartment was not the defendant's, and I argued that they had identified the wrong person. At least some jurors agreed, and they announced they were hung. The judge, however, sent them out for further deliberations. The jurors then asked for a clarification as to what "possession" meant. The judge told them that possession as the law defines it is not limited to immediate, physical control. Instead, it includes "constructive possession," meaning that anyone in a place where drugs are present constructively possesses them. I objected, arguing that the law of constructive possession requires knowledge and apparent control of an object. I constructively possess the books on my office shelf even when I am not physically possessing them, but my visitors do not. The judge, however, did not waver, and fifteen minutes later a guilty verdict was announced.

The next day, that convicting juror protested. "I had no choice once the judge redefined possession. I didn't think your client threw out the drugs, but I had no choice after what the judge said. I couldn't sleep last night thinking about that boy."

Because jurors almost always try to reach the right decision, in cases when I've not agreed with their verdict, I do not ask, "What is wrong with you people?" Instead I ask, "What information did I fail to present?"; "What question did I not think to ask?"; "What argument did I neglect to make?" In some cases, I have realized that the outcome was not the result of my failings or those of the jury. Often, the result is ordained by the law as given to the jury.

That conclusion does not mean I was not then concerned with who the jurors were. I, like other trial attorneys, was very much concerned. I had notions about who would make a good juror and a bad juror for each case, and I used peremptory challenges in the service of such notions. We operated with little information about the people being called for jury service and without jury consultants telling us who would make an ideal juror. We would learn age, race, and gender as well as the person's connections with law enforcement and crime victims. We would attempt to infer economic status from information about job, education, and residential neighborhood. We might guess ethnicity from a name. We would try to make assessments from clothing, manner of speech, and such "clues" as a carried newspaper. We would consider hesitancies in answers and eye contact. But usually all this information was only enough for us to categorize prospective jurors into stereotypes. And in the early days of my practice, I lived in a legal world that allowed attorneys to indulge in stereotypes. Race and gender were often the prime pigeonholes. In one trial, for example, eleven jurors had been selected, and both the prosecutor and I had remaining peremptory challenges. Whenever a black person was called for the final seat, the prosecutor challenged; I did the same whenever a white person's name was selected. This continued until one of us exhausted the allotted peremptories. We may have believed in the power of direct and cross-examination and summations, and the importance of what the judge said, but we also believed tremendously in who the jurors were.

In those earlier days, I and others cared about jury selection not merely because we thought that the makeup of a jury might affect their decisions, but also because we knew that what they decided could be terribly important. I was reminded of this fact every time I saw the face of a person behind bars who had been convicted by a jury a few minutes earlier. And I will always remember the person who lept onto a tenth-story ledge after a jury had convicted him. He lost his footing and fell to his death.

By the time I stopped trying cases on a regular basis in the 1980s, I had many views about the jury system. They were not all consistent. The side with the better evidence generally wins jury trials, yet the fact remains that the composition of a jury might be crucial. Jurors are swayed primarily by common sense and logic, but sometimes an emotional appeal is the best tactic. Jurors who are not smart or educated and can't understand complex issues are able to bring their life experiences to the task, which often gives them more valuable knowledge than any judge could have. Juries are generally more to be trusted to get it right than are judges, but juries cannot be trusted in every case.

Since that time, I have gathered more knowledge about juries, which has modified my views and finds its way into this book. I discuss cases from the United States Supreme Court and other tribunals. I present the historical development of the jury system, along with a discussion of how other countries resolve legal disputes. I examine social science studies that explore juries' decision making processes. Perspectives about the jury system from jurors, legal commentators, and the popular culture of fiction, movies, and editorial pages are included.

Experience and study have led me to several central conclusions about the jury system, the bases for which I clarify in this book. The first conclusion may seem trite: the jury system is important. It is important not only to the litigants whose disputes juries decide, but also to a larger society influenced by those resolutions. Juries are also important because of the significant role they play in the American system of government.

The second conclusion is perhaps surprising: the present American jury system works quite well. Juries are much more rational in reaching decisions than many suppose. I have learned that too often, people, including me in my early trial years, overestimate how much influence factors such as the composition of the jury and the quality of the attorneys have on the outcomes of trials. The reality is that the evidence presented to juries is the prime determinant of verdicts, and this is the crucial reason why the system works well.

The third conclusion is that although the jury system works well, it can be made better. Since jury verdicts follow the presented evidence, the most significant way to produce better jury decisions is to improve the information that the jury gets to consider—to improve the evidence presented to the jury.

I hope this book will lead to a better understanding of the jury system, how it works, its significance in American history, its fundamental place in American law and society, and its strengths and weaknesses. Such knowledge might produce an even better jury system.

Acknowledgments

In this book, I describe and analyze the goals, functions, and operation of the American jury system in order to provide a deeper understanding of this institution and why it generally works well. Many people have aided me in this exploration. Among them are my colleague Edward Purcell, who made a valuable suggestion on how to start the project, and other colleagues including Carol Buckler, David Chang, Jethro Lieberman, Stephen Newman, and Donald Zeigler, whose support, discussions, insights, and research suggestions and materials made a big difference. The library staff at New York Law School, always amazingly helpful, provided crucial support for this book time and again. Thanks to all, including Joyce Saltalamachia, Kate MacLeod, Paul Mastrangelo, Sarah Valentine, and Camille Broussard. Many students in my jury seminar and other courses have aided me with their thoughts about the jury system and with their comments about various stages of the manuscript, but most notable was Jessica Cadorine, whose research, writing, and comments advanced my work in many instances.

It is good to have friends, especially Robert Amdur of Columbia

University, who has been supportive throughout this book's gestation period and who then read the manuscript and made valuable comments about it.

I owe much more than a thank you to Harry Wellington. This book would not have been done without him. He suggested the idea to me, helped me in many ways through the various rough patches that occurred, and read the manuscript with a keen eye.

Thanks also to Nancy Moore Brochin at Yale University Press, whose editing vastly improved my book.

In writing this book on the jury system, I also owe much gratitude to two of my professors from years ago, Harry Kalven, Jr., and Hans Zeisel, whose work, discussions, and teaching kindled my interest in the jury system. Those of us who teach can only wish we could be as inspiring as those two were.

Thanks to Amelia Jonakait, who motivates me more than she knows.

Finally, special thanks to G. Miller Jonakait. Mill has always been my best editor and has read several versions of what has been written. Equally important throughout this project, she has made me think, laugh, and smile, and as always, has been a wonderful inspiration.

My gratitude belongs to all these people. The flaws belong to me.

Introduction

No person or committee constructed our jury system. The concept of a jury trial evolved over time, but largely without competition. Because we have nothing to compare it to, we cannot be sure the present jury system is in fact the legal method best adapted to modern conditions. If there is but one housing choice, that structure may evolve through the generations. A dormer may be added; a wall mended; rooms divided; plumbing changed. That evolution may not necessarily produce a successful modern dwelling. The result might be an elegant, functional, sturdy building, but it might also be a monstrosity of ugly proportions, wasted space, and insufficient heating, in which case we should tear it down and try again.

Many think that juries have come down this less productive path and have ceased to serve the modern legal world well. Critics see a jury-rigged affair that seems irrational and dysfunctional. They have made the jury system a subject of parody, ridicule, and bombast. They would accept as correct the characterization of the jury provided forty years ago by Professor Harry Kalven: "We have been told often enough that the jury trial is a process whereby twelve inexperienced laymen, who are probably strangers to each other, are invited to apply law which they will not understand to facts which they will not get straight and by secret deliberation arrive at a group decision. . . . In the forum of armchair speculation, . . . the jury often loses the day." Kalven continues with a quote from the then Dean of Harvard Law School, Erwin Griswold, "But jury trial, at best, is the apotheosis of the amateur. Why should anyone think that twelve persons brought in from the street, selected in various ways, for their lack of general ability, should have any special capacity for deciding controversies between persons?"[1]

The catalog of complaints is thick. Jurors cannot understand the evidence and issues in the complex matters that come to court. Jurors do not understand the law. Jurors disregard the law. Jurors decide cases along racial lines. Jurors do not honestly assess who is at fault or liable, but simply redistribute wealth by moving it from institutions with deep pockets to less fortunate individuals. Jury verdicts are primarily determined not by the evidence, but by the tactics of attorneys, by a few strong-willed and biased jurors, or by hired psychologists and social scientists who determine which jurors to select and how to persuade them. The jury system is too cumbersome and inefficient to decide disputes in the present age. And so on.

Such criticisms are hardly new. Mark Twain's sarcastic invective from 1873 is well known: "We have a criminal jury system which is superior to any in the world; and its efficiency is only marred by the difficulty of finding twelve men every day who don't know anything and can't read."[2] A half century later Charles A. Boston also derided ignorant and incompetent jurors:

> But in a jury, we have raw recruits who could not as a class do well in any one of the many activities which, in civilization, we require from any class in the community. We train recruits to bear arms, we license lawyers, physicians, dentists, midwives, veterinarians, horseshoers and chauffeurs, but, so long as a man speaks any sort of English, can hear, is on the jury list, and has not formed an opinion, he is deemed a competent man to decide disputes in a Court of Justice. . . . It is the residue, men of no great responsibility, men whose occupations do not as a rule develop mental acumen, that are left to serve as jurors.[3]

And today, critics still find jurors crucially ignorant. Professor Albert Alschuler, in more restrained language than his predecessors, concludes, "[T]he public who serve as jurors *are* less educated than the norm, and our skewing of the jury toward the less-informed segment of the population is most evident in the high-profile trials that most shape public impressions of the jury."[4]

That individual jurors do not judge the evidence has also been a constant complaint. Robert Frost supposedly said, "A jury consists of twelve persons chosen to decide who has the better lawyer." Matthew Deady, writing in the 1880s, stated, "The kind of jury trials to which we are drifting in the United States is a gross travesty of that known to the fathers. . . . The trial is converted into a mere game of skill between counsel, in which the chance is largely in favor of the better, if not the sharper, player, without much reference to the law or justice of the case." J. C. McWhorter, writing forty years later in 1923, concluded that only a few jurors truly determined the verdicts: "After all, the jury's verdict is most often the finding of one or two strong or thoughtful men concurred in by the other members of the jury because they have no well-defined opinions of their own. I do not say this in disparagement of the intelligence of the average jury. It is simply the way of all unskilled and untrained men in every walk of life."[5]

Others conclude that it is neither evidence nor truth nor justice but jury selection that decides the case. Professor Alschuler notes, "A familiar wisecrack is that in England the trial begins when the jury is selected; in America, that is when the trial is over." This view is hardly new. Adela Rogers St. Johns writes that her father, Earl Rogers, the famous trial attorney of the early twentieth century, "told law classes . . . that often a criminal case was already won or lost when the twelve jurors sat in the box."[6]

Today the jury's racial composition is often considered crucial, and trial reports habitually catalog how many jurors are white, black, Asian, Hispanic, or Latino, with the obvious implication that these characteristics will determine the verdict. But even in the days when juries were more homogeneous than they are today, similar concerns abounded. Jury selection lore abounds with conclusions about the Scandinavians versus the Italians, the Welsh compared to the Scottish. In 1883, when the larger waves of immigration were yet to come, a commentator bemoaning the fact that jurors often could not agree concluded: "Now-a-days, owing to the comparative mental activity, the development of what may be called an angular individuality, the cultivation of conceit, the absence of a common authority or standard in matters of opinion, particularly in those which often constitute the ethics of a case, the heterogeneous state of society, in many places but recently from the four quarters of the globe and from all conditions of life, there is necessarily such a diversity and contrariety of opinion and predilection in the country upon all topics of interest which admit of dispute, that the chances of unanimity in a jury-room are much diminished."[7]

Indeed, for much of America's history, complaints about the jury system have been fueled implicitly or explicitly by views of ethnic relations. J. Anthony Lukas summarized the scenario one hundred years ago:

> In the [twentieth] century's first decade, America's jury system was in bad odor. Once it had been deemed "the palladium of liberty," the bedrock guarantee of equal justice under the law. But now the eastern and southern European immigrants flooding the cities, and concomitant fears of "mob politics" and public disorder, had set off a chorus of high-minded demands for the system's reform or even abolition. A city jury, warned the *Arena* in 1905, was "frequently corruptible"; plainly put, "you can 'do business' with it, if you have the money." Though a country jury was "rarely corruptible," it was "densely ignorant and stubbornly bigoted." The *Nation* held that "nobody but the criminals and the 'jury fixers' are interested in the continuance of the present state of things. . . . We cannot go much longer picking out imbeciles, knaves and ignoramuses to bring our malefactors to justice."[8]

This summary captures another recurrent criticism. Juries may have served society well in the past, but they are now worthless and old-fashioned. In the nineteenth century, Matthew Deady wrote, "Still in these days of progress and experiment, when everything is on trial at the bar of human reason or conceit, it is quite the fashion to speak of a jury trial as something that has outlived its usefulness." Mark Twain insisted, "It is a shame that we must continue to use a worthless system because it was good a thousand years ago." And at the beginning of the twenty-first century, Professor Chester Mirsky "hopes our dysfunctional adversarial jury trial . . . will become a 20th century artifact."[9]

Many view juries as dangerously outmoded because they fail to understand the important fiscal realities of the day. Juries, according to this view, often damage the country by hampering economic progress. The problem, they say, is caused by both harboring a bias against corporations and feeling compassion for the afflicted. A lawyer wrote in the 1980s, "Sympathy to an injured party, together with a latent hostility to anonymous and rich corporate America and its insurance carriers, often set the stage for enormous verdicts." In 1912, the view was similar. Charles Boston wrote at that time, "[B]efore an average jury in a negligence case a corporation stands less chance of judgment on the merits than an individual, an employer than an employee." Similar concerns go back even further. Morton Horwitz concludes that at America's inception, merchants were not fond of juries, and "one of the leading measures of the growing alliance between bench and bar on the one hand and commercial interests on the other is the swiftness with which the power of the jury is curtailed after 1790." Similar pressures led to "an important institutional innovation that began to appear after 1830—an increasing tendency of state legislatures to eliminate the role of the jury in assessing damages for the taking of land."[10]

Many others, however, hold quite different views. Some believe the justice system favors those with power in society at the expense of the less fortunate. A recent survey found that "forty-seven percent of the American population thinks that courts are ethnically and racially biased and—as if that is not sobering enough—a whopping ninety percent think the affluent and corporations have an unfair advantage in court."[11]

Critics of the jury system also suggest the absurdity of its decision making process, pointing out that no one outside a courtroom would use such a method to decide any important issues. In 1945 the historian Carl Becker labeled trial by jury as "inherently absurd—so much so that no lawyer, judge, scholar, prescription-clerk, cook, or mechanic in a garage would ever think of employing that method for determining the facts in any situation that concerned him."[12]

Many hope that juries will be replaced by a system in which judges or other trained professionals would make all the decisions. Charles Boston, in 1912, concluded:

> [J]udges, as a class, are everywhere regarded as men fitted for the business in which they are engaged, whereas everywhere, except in our bills of rights, juries as a whole are treated as the crudest possible agencies, comparing in some measure with the flip of a coin, the turn of a card, the entrails of a fowl, or a flight of birds, as a means of ascertaining the right. . . . If judges are for any reason not desirable triers of fact, then, at least, the public money would be better spent, public business better expedited, and better results reached if we had standing triers of fact skilled in the art, through experience, and therefore better equipped psychologically for their function.[13]

J. C. McWhorter, writing eleven years later, suggested that tribunals discard juries and replace them with two judges who would have the power to appoint a third. McWhorter reasoned: "It is well known to all lawyers in actual practice that when a case based upon truth and simple justice is presented the wise lawyer searches diligently for some door . . . where he can get to the judge with both law and facts and escape the jury. On the other hand, it is equally well known that every shyster lawyer appearing for a shyster client, relying upon trickery, perjury, fraud, passion or prejudices to win his case, assiduously seeks the jury and avoids the court. The man with a just cause trusts and seeks the court. The man with an unjust cause trusts and seeks the jury."[14]

The cry for professional decision makers continues now often with reference to England, which has largely abandoned civil jury trials, and to other parts of the world where trial by jury is largely unknown. For example, Chester Mirsky, writing in response to a controversial acquittal that he viewed as wrong, states that many "have come to the conclusion that the professional judicial model adopted in civil law countries is worthy of consideration as an alternative. In this model judges are divorced from the competing ideologies of the community (in theory, at least). They are not political appointees, but professionals carefully schooled in fact-finding who are required to rationalize their decisions in detailed, written analyses. . . . It is time to conform American criminal procedure to that of the rest of the world."[15]

And so, the jury system is condemned and vilified, as it seemingly always has been. Why, then, has it survived? The obvious answer is that the jury system endures because it has important strengths. What Matthew Deady said more than a century ago still rings with truth: "An institution of such endurance and far-reaching effect as this—one which has substantially outlived all the political and legal vicissitudes of seven centuries, and been cherished by the English-speaking people of both the old and new world, as the corner stone of their legal procedure, must have something in its nature and composition and thoroughly in accord with the genius of the people, and well calculated to attain the end for which it is designed."[16]

No matter how strong the objections to the American jury system, it is not going away. It is firmly ensconced in our state and federal constitutions, history, and traditions. Juries are required for all criminal trials except those involving the most minor offenses, and no serious movement exists to amend the Sixth Amendment to the federal Constitution (which commands this), to limit the reach of civil juries, or to abolish all civil jury trials. The American jury system will endure. The most important debates are the ones that discuss how to make that system better.

To understand the jury system, one must examine both its strengths and weaknesses. One can begin by cataloging shortcomings and advantages, and also by examining the roles juries play and how well they perform them. Juries do not serve a single purpose but have many functions. Chapters Two through Five explore these roles and discuss how juries further our government of checks and balances; why the jury may actually be a better determiner of disputed facts than the available options; how juries allow for the needed injection of community values into legal decisions; and how juries aid public acceptance of legal determinations.

Chapters Six through Twelve consider the jury's structure: its size, its rules for making a decision, and how jurors are selected. These attributes can affect how well juries fulfill their roles.

The methods by which juries acquire and process information to make their decisions is a crucial component of the jury system. Chapters Thirteen and Fourteen address the presentation of evidence, and Chapter Fifteen discusses how juries are instructed about the law. All three chapters consider the assets and limitations of these processes.

After juries receive instructions about the law, they deliberate. Chapter Sixteen considers these deliberations. Various factors thought to influence verdicts, such as the composition of the jury and the identity and characteristics of the parties, are discussed, as well as how deliberating juries use the proof and the instructions presented to them. One set of verdicts is absolutely final—those acquitting a criminal defendant. The doctrines that produce such finality are considered, along with one of their consequences, jury nullification (the subject of Chapter Eighteen), that is, the jury's power to disregard the law in order to acquit in a criminal case. Other jury verdicts are not always final. Judges may have control over them on appeal and through various procedural devices. I discuss these devices, along with the issue of jury trials in complex cases, in Chapter Seventeen. The finality of jury verdicts in general is the subject of Chapter Nineteen.

Chapter Twenty concludes the book with a discussion of possible reforms for the jury system. Because the verdicts are based primarily on the information presented to the jury, the most important reforms should concentrate on discovering and generating better evidence for presentation to juries.

The jury system's strengths and weaknesses are often intertwined. Consequently, proposed reforms can be sensibly weighed only by recognizing that what strengthens the jury system may simultaneously hurt it. Furthermore, the jury system is part of a larger legal structure. Factors not normally seen as part of that system affect how juries operate, and these must be considered in reform efforts. Conversely, changes in the jury system will also have consequences for the larger legal system, and this, too, must be taken into consideration.

Chapter 1 Overview

The phrase "America's jury system" implies that there is only one. In fact, America has many jury systems. Every state, the federal government, and the District of Columbia has its own courts, laws, legal procedures, customs, and practices. These multiple legal jurisdictions yield multiple jury systems. Even within a single jurisdiction the jury system can vary from one community to another. Moreover, systems for adjudicating criminal cases resemble, but still differ, from those used for civil matters.

All these systems, however, do share enough essential characteristics to make it possible to talk about the American jury system. Nationwide similarities among jury systems are stronger in criminal cases than in civil ones. The Sixth Amendment to the federal Constitution guarantees that "In all criminal prosecutions, the accused shall enjoy the right to a speedy and public trial, by an impartial jury of the State and district wherein the crime shall have been committed." This right to a jury trial does have a limitation. The Constitution says "all," but the Supreme Court has concluded that the Sixth Amendment right does not guarantee jury trials for "petty" offenses. The Court has concluded that crimes carrying a potential punishment of less than six months' imprisonment are presumptively petty, and the accused charged with such a crime is not constitutionally entitled to a jury trial. This presumption can be overcome if additional penalties such as large fines indicate that the legislature intended the crime to be "serious." But at least so far, the Supreme Court has not required a jury trial for any offense that did not authorize a sentence in excess of six months.[1]

Since 1968 this constitutional right to a jury trial has applied to both state and federal criminal trials, which means that the same constitutional standards for trials apply to all criminal cases throughout the country. The same is not true for civil matters. The Seventh Amendment to the federal Constitution guarantees jury trials in civil cases, but this Bill of Rights provision applies only to federal cases. Each state does, in fact, afford jury trials in civil matters, but each state has more latitude in structuring civil jury trials than criminal ones. Consequently, the civil jury systems demonstrate more diversity than the criminal jury systems.

RESOLUTION OF CRIMINAL MATTERS
WITHOUT TRIALS

Jury trials are only one way to resolve legal disputes. In criminal matters, the first level of resolution occurs when a citizen can, but chooses not to, report a crime. For practical purposes, this ends the matter, and while different studies reach different conclusions about the level of underreporting, all concur that many crimes go unreported.

A similar kind of resolution occurs when the police can, but choose not to, bring criminal charges. Law enforcement authorities have wide discretionary powers. Nothing requires them to make an arrest every time they believe they legally can. For example, when the police come upon a boisterous group, they may have probable cause to arrest for disturbing the peace, but often the officers will simply tell the congregants to quiet down and move on. A potential criminal case has been resolved. Citizens have no legal mechanism to force the police to make an arrest, and a police decision not to do so often ends a criminal matter.

Criminal matters are also resolved, in some sense, when a case is not "solved." The percentage of reported crimes that are "cleared" by an arrest varies according to the category of the offense. Roughly two-thirds of homicides lead to an arrest, while only about one-seventh of reported burglaries are followed by an arrest. For felonies—serious cases that carry potential punishments of at least one year—the overall clearance rate is about 20 percent. In short, a large number of criminal matters are "resolved" because no one is arrested for them.

Like the police, prosecutors have a screening function. They do not have to file charges with the court just because the police have made an arrest. A prosecutor may decide not to go forward for many reasons, including, for example, insufficient evidence or the victim's reluctance to press a criminal case. Just as citizens cannot force the police to make an arrest, neither can they force a prosecutor to file charges. How often prosecutors choose not to prosecute an arrested person varies widely not just from state to state, but from locality to locality. The nationwide average seems to be about 10 percent.

Serious crimes pass through yet another filter. About a score of jurisdictions, including the federal courts, require a grand jury indictment for felony prosecutions. The grand jury, a body of ancient lineage, consists of a group of citizens, usually twenty-three, drawn from the community. The grand jurors determine whether there is sufficient evidence for a person to be charged with a felony. To do this, these jurors meet in secret without the defendant being present and hear only evidence presented by the prosecutor. If a majority of the grand jurors believe the evidence is sufficient to sustain charges, an indictment charging a person with a crime is returned. Nearly all grand jury presentations, about 95 percent, result in an indictment.

In most jurisdictions, however, felony prosecutions do not require a grand jury indictment but can proceed by what is called an "information." Generally in these locations a preliminary hearing is required before the prosecutorial information can be filed. This hearing proceeds publicly before a judicial officer; the accused is present and can cross-examine witnesses. Since the purpose is not to determine whether the accused is actually guilty but only whether there is sufficient proof to sustain a charge, the full evidence is seldom presented. The rate of dismissals varies widely and correlates naturally to the screening done beforehand by the prosecutor. On average, less than 10 percent of the cases are dismissed as a result of this kind of preliminary hearing.

Various kinds of pretrial motions may be made after the institution of the charges. These include attempts by the defendant to prevent evidence being presented at trial because it was obtained in violation of the Constitution. If additional information is needed to decide a pretrial motion, a hearing is held before a judge without a jury. Dismissals do result from these pretrial motions, but only in less than 1 percent of cases.

Even after these screening stages, not all remaining cases go to trial. The prosecutor still has the power in advance of a scheduled trial date to dismiss a case. This may happen for any number of reasons as circumstances change and new information develops.

Most criminal cases, however, never go to trial because they are "plea bargained," that is, the defendant enters a guilty plea in exchange for concessions. Those concessions might permit a guilty plea to only one charge when several are pending; it might allow a plea to an offense lesser than the most serious charge; it might have the prosecutor make a sentence recommendation; or in some places, the judge might commit to a specific sentence. The kinds of concessions vary from case to case and from locality to locality. And although in a few places prosecutors claim not to plea bargain, most defendants still plead guilty expecting that sentencing judges will be more lenient with those who admit guilt than with those who force a trial. Guilty plea rates vary around the country, but most cases that survive the initial screenings result in a guilty plea. About 90 percent of the criminal defendants who are convicted plead guilty.

Plea bargaining affects the mix of cases that go to trial. In entering negotiations, the accused's overwhelming concern is with the likely severity of the sentence. He weighs the possibility of an acquittal against the probability that a jury conviction will lead to a greater sentence than if he pleads guilty. Meanwhile, the prosecutor has to consider how much she wishes to use limited trial resources on a particular case as well as the desire to get a conviction that is certain from a guilty plea. The rational plea bargaining parties are thinking along these lines: if the accused is convicted by a jury, he will receive a ten-year sentence, but the likelihood of a jury conviction is 80 percent. Thus, the accused stands a 20 percent chance of being exonerated and having no jail sentence, but an 80 percent chance of getting ten years. The prosecutor has the incentive to offer a plea that will result in a lesser sentence to remove the possibility that no punishment at all will be imposed, and the accused has the incentive to accept the lesser sentence to remove the 80 percent odds of ten years. Plea bargaining, then, is a negotiation over what lesser sentence will be acceptable to both sides. Under these conditions, trials are most likely to result when the parties markedly differ over the chances of a jury's convicting or what the sentence will be if the jury convicts.

If, however, the prosecutor is confident that a jury will find guilt and a ten-year sentence will be imposed, the prosecutor gains nothing by plea bargaining on that individual case. The more certain it is that the accused is guilty, the less reason for the prosecutor to offer a plea. Moreover, as Samuel Gross explains, from the prosecutor's standpoint, "It is obviously sensible to try to restrict trials to cases where the outcomes will be useful—i.e., convictions. If possible, likely losses at trial are avoided through plea bargaining; if not, they may be dismissed even if the prosecutor is convinced of the defendant's guilt. Regardless of their belief in the defendants' guilt, prosecutors focus on the easiest cases—the ones with the best evidence—since those are the cases where their limited resources will have the greatest impact."[2]

Prosecutors want juries to hear clear cases of guilt. They increase their chances of this by dismissing cases or—more often—resolving them through plea bargaining. "Plea bargaining is undertaken after the decision to prosecute has been made. The prosecutor has become an advocate seeking a conviction. If the prosecutor sees weaknesses in his case, his reaction is not to dismiss the case. Instead, he offers a good deal to the defendant. From the prosecutorial standpoint, the most irresistible deals will, naturally, come in the weakest cases—a half a loaf will be better than none. The good deal is often irresistible, and the defendant pleads guilty."[3]

Mandatory sentences also affect which cases go to trial. If there is no or limited sentencing discretion after a conviction, the clearly guilty defendant may not have incentives to accept a plea. For example, some states require that a third felony conviction result in an automatic life sentence (the "third strike" concept), and they prohibit pleas to lesser offenses when the third felony is charged. An accused already convicted twice of robberies may insist on a trial on the new robbery case even if he confessed and was caught in the act. Although he may have little chance of winning the trial, he has little inducement to plead guilty. He is better off hoping for a miracle verdict than admitting guilt, because that guilty plea will still result in a life sentence.

For such reasons, relatively clear cases of guilt often are not resolved by plea bargaining and go to trial. It is not surprising, then, that roughly 60 to 80 percent of criminal juries convict.

The political nature of public prosecutors also affects the mix of cases that criminal juries see. Prosecutors, concerned as they are about public opinion, are less likely to offer a plea bargain and appear to be compromising justice when the case has captured wide public attention. Murder cases often get that sort of notice, especially when the death penalty is at stake. Consequently, a higher proportion of those charged with murder have jury trials than do those charged with other crimes. "Whether it's because prosecutors take weaker cases to trial or because they insist on the maximum penalty, homicide defendants are more likely to face a jury than other criminal defendants. In 1992, for example, 12% of robbery convictions across the country were obtained at trials, of which 8% were jury trials, while 41% of murder convictions were after trial, including

33% that went to jury trial. In other words, since pre-trial sorting does less to winnow homicide cases than other prosecutions, homicide defendants are more likely to face the chancy ordeal of a trial."[4]

Thus, both a rigid stance on plea bargaining and the willingness to take even weak cases to trial increase the rate at which defendants charged with murder go to trial. Consequently, "Prosecutors lose a much higher proportion of murder trials than other felony trials, about 30% vs. 15%. . . . [T]he most likely explanation is that in murder cases they are willing to go to trial with comparatively weak evidence."[5]

Critics often deride plea bargaining for permitting criminals to receive lesser punishments than they deserve. After all, people plead guilty to avoid the longer sentences that a jury conviction would bring. These critics overlook the opposite effect. Since prosecutors are more willing to bargain in weak cases than in strong ones, sometimes defendants who would have been acquitted by a jury are induced to take such pleas. Albert Alschuler states: "The surveys of the 1920s indicated that increased plea bargaining might have led some defendants to plead guilty although they would not have been convicted at trial. As the percentage of convictions by guilty plea grew in that period just preceding the 1920s, both the percentage of convictions by trial and the percentage of acquittals showed a sharp decline. . . . [I]t seems probable that the increased ranks of guilty-plea defendants came in part from defendants who would have been convicted had they stood trial and in part from defendants who would have been acquitted."[6]

BENCH TRIALS IN CRIMINAL CASES

Only about 5 to 15 percent of felony cases actually go to trial. Misdemeanors, which greatly outnumber felonies, see even a smaller percentage going to trial. But not all of these are jury trials. If the charged crime is "petty" and a jury trial is not required, a bench trial is held. A single judge determines whether guilt has been proven. But even when a jury is authorized, many of the cases are still bench trials.

The accused may desire a bench trial for a number of reasons. She may fear that pretrial publicity or the nature of the crime has produced a strong community sentiment against her and that a judge alone will be able to focus on the evidence dispassionately. The accused may plan a legally technical defense or feel that the evidence is so complex that a judge will follow it better than a jury. Prosecutors often favor bench trials because they take less time than jury trials.

When an accused is guaranteed a jury trial, she may not be forced into a bench trial without her consent, but in many places she cannot simply get a bench trial at her own request. In about half the states and the federal system a bench trial occurs only if the prosecutor and the judge also consent. The Supreme Court concluded in *Singer v. United States* that "the Government, as a litigant, has a legitimate interest in seeing that cases in which it believes a conviction is warranted are tried before the tribunal which the Constitution regards as most likely to produce a fair result."[7] In short, the accused has a constitutional right to a jury trial; she does not have a constitutional right to a bench trial.

Bench trial rates vary around the country. They account for about 14 percent of the total federal criminal trials. State comparisons are difficult because states often define "trial" differently. Some label it a "trial" when a jury is sworn or some evidence is presented, others only when a verdict is reached. In addition, some states report data separately for felonies and less serious crimes; some lump them together. Although the data may be limited, however, it seems clear that the rate of bench trials varies tremendously. In a recent year, using the same definition of "trial," bench trials accounted for 2.82 percent of the felony trials in the District of Columbia, but they were 77.38 of the felony trials in Virginia.[8]

While the ability of prosecutors to veto bench trials in only half the jurisdictions might account for some of these differences, it is not a full explanation. Local legal cultures concerning bench trials apparently vary around the country. For instance, in 1997 Philadelphia had 3,781 bench trials and only 640 jury trials.[9] This 86 percent bench trial rate was much higher than for other parts of Pennsylvania even though the law concerning bench trials is uniform throughout the state. Such local variations are not unusual, but the reasons for them have not been fully explored. Nationwide, about 30 percent of state felony criminal trials are bench trials.

ISSUES FOR THE JURY TO CONSIDER IN CRIMINAL CASES

A standard legal maxim states that in a jury trial the judge determines the law and the jury determines the facts. Criminal juries, however, only decide the facts that determine whether a person is guilty of a crime. The definition of "crime" contains a number of parts, or elements, and a jury decides whether the prosecution has adequately proved each of those elements. So, for example, "murder" might be defined as the intentional killing of another person. In deciding whether someone is guilty of that crime, a jury must make a number of factual determinations. Was it the accused who did the killing? Did the accused's action cause the death? If the accused did the killing, did he intend to do it?

While the jury decides facts that determine guilt or innocence, other factual issues are determined by the trial judge. For example, evidence may be excluded from a trial if the accused's constitutional rights were violated in obtaining it, and the determination of these violations often requires the resolution of factual disputes. It may be important and contested whether, for example, the accused was handcuffed when he made a statement. Or it may be important and contested whether the accused consented to a search of his backpack. Such factual determinations may be crucial to the case, but they do not resolve the issue of whether the accused committed the crime. The trial judge will decide them.

Many factual questions that do not resolve guilt can arise besides those concerning these controversial exclusionary rules. Whether the accused's right to a speedy trial has been violated may require deciding the causes of a prosecutorial delay. The evidentiary rules may require determining whether a witness is truly unavailable or whether a statement was made under the stress of an exciting event or whether a lawyer-client relationship existed when something was said. These decisions and many more that do not directly resolve guilt can require a factual determination, and a judge, not a jury, must resolve them.

Perhaps the most important of the nonguilt factual issues are those that concern the sentence of a convicted defendant. A sentencing occurs only when it has already been determined that a person committed a crime. The accused has no Sixth Amendment right to a jury determination of facts that affect only the sentence. The trial judge almost always sentences without the aid of a jury. The major exception is in capital cases, which constitute a tiny fraction of all trials. In 2002, the Supreme Court held that the Constitution requires that juries make the determination of whether the death penalty should be imposed.[10]

When judges sentence, they almost invariably, at least implicitly, make factual determinations. While few convictions result from jury trials, all convictions lead to a sentencing. So it is that judges, not juries, determine the crucial facts in most criminal cases.

APPEALS IN CRIMINAL CASES

A verdict of not guilty is final and ends the case. The prosecutor cannot appeal or otherwise overturn an acquittal. A guilty verdict, on the other hand, is not necessarily the end, because all convicted defendants are entitled to appeal. The overwhelming majority of people convicted after a jury trial exercise this right. Few appellants, however, are successful; nationwide, fewer than one in ten wins in the appellate courts. The successful ones seldom have their cases dismissed but instead are awarded a new trial. Although statistics in this area are notably murky, most who win a new trial are convicted again, through either another trial or a plea bargain.

RESOLUTION OF CIVIL MATTERS
WITHOUT TRIALS

The civil legal process starts when a person or entity decides to seek legal relief or remedy from another person or entity. The person who can seek such relief but does not ends a civil case before it starts. We do not know how often people who may sue do not, but despite the image of Americans as enthusiastic litigants willing to sue at the drop of a bedpan, cup of coffee, or insensitive remark, only a small percentage of potential plaintiffs actually initiate cases. Studies of hospital records, for example, reveal that only about 5 percent of malpractice injuries actually lead to the filing of claims.

The suit itself begins when a complaint is served on the person being sued. This initial pleading sets forth the plaintiff's allegations that her claims entitle her to a specified legal remedy. The defendant responds with an answer, which may deny allegations made in the complaint and may list further allegations of a defense or a counterclaim.

A period of discovery comes after the filing of the pleadings. "Discovery" is the process by which the parties obtain information concerning the suit in advance of the trial. Discovery practices were revolutionized by the adoption in 1938 of the Federal Rules of Civil Procedure, which authorized discovery of a broad range of information. These provisions have been adopted by most states. Discovery has a number of purposes. It helps preserve information that might otherwise not be available at trial. For example, if a witness is unlikely to be available later, the witness's testimony can be taken in advance, preserved, and presented at trial. Discovery also helps clarify what facts are being disputed between the parties, but perhaps most important, "[M]odern discovery allows a party to obtain information that will lead to admissible evidence on the issues that are in dispute. Thus, if an eyewitness to an event is reluctant to talk to a party, that party can require the witness to submit to a deposition, during which the witness, under oath, must reveal her knowledge about the facts. In addition, one party can obtain from the opposing party, relevant facts regarding the case and documents and other items that pertain to it."[11]

Civil discovery is extremely broad. Almost any information can be obtained as long as there is a reasonable chance the information will lead to admissible evidence. In contrast, discovery in criminal cases is severely limited. Parties in criminal cases often cannot obtain all the important information in advance of trial. As a result, surprises and significant gaps in evidence happen much more frequently in criminal trials than in civil ones.

Civil and criminal cases, however, are similar in that few of them actually go to trial. Some civil cases are resolved when a judge determines that no significant factual dispute exists between the parties and that the undisputed facts indicate one of the parties should win, a determination called a "summary judgment." Some trials are avoided because a defendant defaults, that is, the defendant does not appear or otherwise does not properly defend the suit. Plaintiffs may also decide to drop the action or they may not take the necessary steps to bring the case to trial.

Few of the remaining cases, however, do go to trial. Just as guilty pleas end most criminal cases without a trial, settlements out of court resolve most civil cases without a trial. Settlements are agreements reached between the parties that end the case. Typically, plaintiff and defendant agree on some compromise sum of money for the defendant to pay the plaintiff in lieu of having a trial determine the amount. Completely accurate statistics about these trial-avoidance processes are not available, but in one recent year about 760,000 cases that could have gone to a jury trial were disposed of in state courts and about 250,000 were terminated in federal courts. Jury trials accounted for only 1 or 2 percent of these dispositions.

Economic incentives lead to the settlement of many civil cases. Let us say that you sue me. If it is clear to both of us that a jury would find me liable for damages of $100,000, and if it would cost me $30,000 to defend the suit and cost you $30,000 to pursue it, we both have a stake in settling the case for somewhere between $70,000 and $130,000. With such a settlement, I will ultimately spend less and you will recover more than if we force the trial.

Crowded courts also bring pressures to settle civil cases. In some federal courts, civil cases have increased by over 60 percent in the past three decades. Because the public pays for the costs of the courts, more trials means the expenditures of more public funds. Ending a case without a trial reduces the strain on those resources. Hence a judge's job now often includes the encouragement of settlements. Paula Hannaford and her colleagues who study the judicial process note: "Increasingly, judicial productivity is measured by the total number of cases resolved, as compared to the total number of trials presided over. The incentive, therefore, is to get cases resolved as expeditiously as possible. Viewed in this light, a jury trial is the least desirable outcome and a poor reflection on the judge as 'case manager' or 'dispute resolver.'"[12]

The settlement process sculpts the civil cases that do go to trial. The trial cases are, not surprisingly, the most difficult to resolve. Trials occur because one side thinks a jury finding of liability is low while the other thinks it is high or because the two projections of damages differ greatly. In other words, the attorneys have assessed the probable outcome quite differently. Since civil juries get only the cases where the proper resolution is not clear-cut, it is not startling that the liability findings of juries are about equally split between plaintiffs and defendants and that many verdicts receive criticism.

CIVIL TRIALS AS SIGNALS FOR SETTLEMENTS

The rational lawyer looks to jury verdicts to decide whether or how to settle. The attorney tries to assess what a jury is likely to do with the matter if it does go to trial, and he does this by considering past verdicts. Looked at this way, jury trials sit atop a pyramid of cases casting light below. Jury trials do not resolve merely a particular dispute; they also give guidance so that the vast majority of other cases can be reasonably settled.

Attorneys, however, frequently misjudge the damage awards juries will give. Settlement negotiations fail when the plaintiff has asked for more money than the defendant is willing to give. If the parties have been correctly gauging the likely jury outcomes, the actual jury verdicts should generally be above the defendant's final offer and below the plaintiff's last demand. Frequently, however, this is not so. For example, a study of one county's car accident trials found that in 61 percent of the cases, one of the parties received a jury verdict that was worse than a settlement position on the table. In 35 percent of these cases, juries gave plaintiffs less than the defendant's offer, and in 26 percent, plaintiffs received more than they would have accepted at settlement.[13] Other studies reveal results consistent with this one, and indicate that attorneys are poor at predicting jury damage awards. One reason is that attorneys seldom have access to accurate, complete historical information about verdicts on which to base their predictions.

There is no easily obtainable source listing all verdicts. Consequently, attorneys learn about jury decisions from several sources, but all are incomplete and tend to indicate that average jury awards are higher than they are. Only some appellate decisions are published, often omitting the size of any damages award. When damages are mentioned, it is often because they are being challenged as excessive, which can give the impression that the average awards are larger than they actually are.

Various commercial organizations gather and publish data about verdicts. These services differ in scope and comprehensiveness. Most are highly selective, concentrating on unusual cases and awards. As a result, large awards get listed much more often than small ones.

The news media's reporting of "newsworthy" verdicts also gives a distorted picture of jury verdicts. The jury awards reported by the *New York Times,* for example, are about sixteen times higher than the average New York award, and verdicts for plaintiffs are covered twelve times more often than are defense victories, even though New York juries find for defendants slightly more often than for plaintiffs.[14] Once again, the impression is conveyed that jury verdicts award more money than they actually do.

Judges may also supply lawyers with information about jury verdicts, especially as judges increasingly become "case managers" and encourage settlements. Judicial experience with juries varies tremendously, however, and is often quite limited. Federal trial judges hold about ten civil jury trials each year, and many state judges have fewer. Few judges systematically learn about verdicts returned in other courtrooms, and judicial information about jury verdicts is often anecdotal.

Attorneys also ask their colleagues for their advice on potentially acceptable outcomes, tailoring their predictions accordingly. Often, though, this advice is based on poor knowledge of the facts.

Lawyers settle many more cases than they try. One survey of trial specialists found that those with a median of fourteen years of experience had attended a median total of fifty-one trials. This average is probably declining. The number of attorneys has more than doubled over the past several decades, while the number of civil trials has increased only slightly. Because attorneys today tend to have less experience with juries than did attorneys of previous generations, their ability to accurately predict jury verdicts has been seriously hampered.

In short, lawyers do not have good, consistent data about the decisions juries make. The available information often creates the biased perception among these professionals, and the general public, that juries are more sympathetic to plaintiffs—finding defendants liable and awarding large damages—than they in fact are. A goal should be, as Marc Galanter suggests, to improve "the collection and compilation of information about juries and to develop reliable indicators to trace the contours and trends of jury decisions."[15]

THE RIGHT TO JURY TRIALS IN CIVIL CASES

Jury trials resolve only a tiny fraction of civil disputes not only because many cases are dismissed, dropped, or settled, but also because litigants have the right to a jury trial in only a minority of civil cases.

Because the federal Constitution does not require the states to have civil juries, there is no nationwide standard defining when civil parties are entitled to a jury trial. The states and the federal government, however, follow a similar pattern in affording civil juries, a model inherited from England at America's inception. English law broke down noncriminal cases into several categories and had different courts for different kinds of civil actions. Juries were used for suits at common law. The basic concern of the common law was a claim by one person that another had caused him harm and the claimant sought appropriate compensation. If the plaintiff contended that the defendant had dropped a cask and had thereby broken the plaintiff's leg, the suit was at common law to determine if the defendant was liable for the broken leg and, if so, what money was due for medical expenses, lost wages, and so on. If a plaintiff claimed that the defendant had broken their contract, the suit was at common law to determine whether a breach had occurred and, if so, what damages resulted from the breach.

Today, civil juries typically are restricted to matters similar to common-law actions, that is, suits seeking money for harms supposedly caused by the defendant. Many civil matters are, however, different. Disputes concerning estates and domestic relations, for example, do not lead to compensatory damages for the harm one person has caused another. A person seeking a court to order someone to do something other than pay damages is not pursuing a common-law action. For example, my downstream neighbor might be building a dam that would flood my property. I may petition a court to order her to cease so that I can use my land as I see fit. A suit to compel someone to do or refrain from doing something is an "action in equity." These kinds of civil cases that differ from common-law cases traditionally did not afford jury trials, and today judges alone typically decide them.

Actions outside the traditional common-law arena constitute the vast majority of civil cases. State trial dockets are heavily weighted with estate and domestic relations cases, for example, and as a result, juries are not authorized in most state civil trials. Furthermore, even when jury trials are available, the parties may forgo them in favor of a bench trial. As a result, it is estimated that 96 percent of the state civil trials are given to judges without juries, while in federal courts, roughly 55 percent of civil trials go to a judge without a jury.

This, however, does not mean that civil juries are rare, for many civil cases of all sorts are brought. Even though they are present for a minority of the trials, there are still more than 50,000 civil jury trials a year in this country—a reflection of the large number of civil cases brought each year.[16]

The cases civil juries do decide primarily concern issues arising out of injuries from accidents and other causes. From about 60 to 80 percent of state civil jury trials involve such personal injury claims. Contract cases constitute nearly 20 percent of the state civil jury trials, while disputes about real property account for about 3 percent of the jury trials. The mix in federal courts is somewhat different: about 45 percent of the federal civil trials involve claimed injuries to persons or property; contract actions are at stake in another 15 percent of those trials; about 2 percent involve real property claims; about 23 percent concern various federal statutes; and the remainder are disbursed over many issues.

When civil juries operate, they decide more issues than criminal juries do. Civil juries determine the facts and render a verdict on liability just as a criminal jury decides the facts determining guilt. Judges, however, generally decide the remedy, that is, the sentence, in criminal cases, while the civil jury also decides the remedy, that is, what damages the defendant has to pay the plaintiff. In some sense, then, civil juries have more power than criminal juries have.

APPEALS IN CIVIL CASES

As in criminal cases, the jury verdict in a civil case does not necessarily end the legal process. Appeals are possible, and unlike in criminal cases, both sides can seek review from the appellate courts. On the other hand, while almost all those convicted by criminal trials appeal, a lower percentage of losing civil litigants do so. This is partly because indigents convicted of crimes can appeal without monetary cost to themselves. Civil litigants, in contrast, almost always have to ante up on their own, and as a result, some possible appeals are not prosecuted. Furthermore, unlike in criminal cases where plea bargaining stops with a verdict, the jury decision in a civil case does not end settlement discussions. Instead, the plaintiff and defendant often agree after a verdict to a damages figure different from the one set by the civil jury, and the appeal is then dropped.

In addition, the finality of a jury's damages award is not the same as for other jury decisions. Most jurisdictions grant trial judges and sometimes appellate courts power over the size of damage awards. Under this authority, the court can order a conditional new trial by concluding that another trial will have to take place unless the opposing party agrees to a specified change in the damages verdict. *Remittitur,* the reduction of damages, exists in nearly all jurisdictions. *Additur,* the increase in damages, exists in many, but not all, jurisdictions.

IMPORTANT DIFFERENCES BETWEEN CRIMINAL AND CIVIL TRIALS

While criminal and civil jury trials share many essential features, they also have some important differences. One of them has already been mentioned: dissimilar discovery practices make criminal trials different from civil cases.

The trials also differ, however, because the Fifth Amendment, which states "No person . . . shall be compelled in any criminal case to be a witness against himself," protects the defendant in a criminal case against self-incrimination. The criminally accused cannot be forced to testify, and the decision whether to do so rests solely with the defense. As a result, criminal juries often do not hear from the person who will be most affected by the verdict. Parties in a civil case, in contrast, do not have a comparable privilege; even if they do not wish to do so, they can be required by their opponents to testify, and civil juries almost always hear both parties' testimony.

Criminal trials also differ from civil ones by imposing the beyond-a-reasonable-doubt standard of proof. The prosecution wins only if it proves the criminal charge beyond a reasonable doubt. "Beyond a reasonable doubt" places a heavy burden of proof on the prosecution. Jurors should convict only if they have great confidence that the proof of guilt dramatically outweighs other possibilities. If we think of the trial as placing the possibilities of guilt on one pan of a balancing scale with the alternatives placed on the other, a guilty verdict should be returned only when it is obvious to the jury that the scale has plummeted to the prosecution's side. If the scale favors the accused, she, of course, should be acquitted. Most important, if the scale favors the prosecution, but not strikingly so, the accused should still be found not guilty.

Civil cases are usually decided by a preponderance-of-the-proof standard. Whomever the proof favors, however slightly, wins the verdict. If the scale tilts, even minutely, toward the plaintiff, the plaintiff wins; if toward the defendant, even though barely, the defendant wins.

AN OVERVIEW OF A JURY TRIAL

The jury trial begins with the summoning of a group of people as potential jurors and eliciting information from them in a process called the voir dire. Each side in a trial can eliminate people as jurors by exercising challenges, either "for cause," when there is a formal reason to believe that the juror cannot be fair or otherwise cannot serve in the particular case, or "peremptorily," for which no reason need be given, but no potential juror can be dismissed peremptorily because of race or gender. For-cause challenges have no numerical limit, while peremptory ones are restricted. The number of jurors selected varies according to jurisdiction and the kind of case being tried, with juries usually numbering six or twelve, and always large enough so that any verdict is made by a group.

After the jury is selected, the presiding judge may describe some of the basic law and procedures that will apply to the case. This is followed by opening statements, first by the prosecution or plaintiff and then by the defense. These addresses to the jury outline the evidence the parties expect to produce.

The plaintiff or prosecutor then presents evidence through witnesses, documents, or other objects or materials that have importance for the case. Witnesses first respond to questions asked by the party who called them. This is called direct examination. The opposing party then may question the witnesses. This is cross-examination. After the plaintiff or prosecutor presents evidence, the defense can present evidence. When this process concludes, the plaintiff or prosecutor may offer rebuttal evidence.

When the presentation of evidence is complete, each side is allowed to make a closing argument, or summation, to the jury. These statements summarize the evidence and present the inferences and conclusions that a party maintains a jury should draw from that evidence.

The trial judge then gives instructions to the jury. The jurors are to consider the law as the judge supplies it to them, determine the disputed facts important to the action, and then apply that given law to those determined facts in order to reach a verdict. While the line between a question of law that a judge decides and a question of fact that a jury resolves is not always clear, the basic principle remains that the judge defines for the jury the legal principles that are to be used in reaching a verdict. This is done when the judge gives instructions to the jury.

After the instructions are delivered, the jury retires to deliberate in secret. Only the jurors are present during these discussions. In the past, a verdict required unanimity—each and every juror had to agree that a verdict was the right one. Unanimity is still required for criminal verdicts in most jurisdictions, but in a few places for criminal cases and in more places for civil trials, the unanimity requirement has been relaxed. Still, however, jurors never operate by a mere majority principle. A supermajority or consensus is required for all jury trials.

Criminal juries render a general verdict; that is, the jury either convicts or acquits the accused of criminal charges without revealing the grounds or logic supporting the decision. General verdicts are also the most common form of verdict in civil cases. The jury finds for the plaintiff or defendant without disclosing its grounds. In some civil cases, however, the jury might be required to give a special verdict. If so, the judge submits to the jury factual issues to be resolved. After the jury makes its findings about those questions, the judge applies the law to them and enters a decision in the case. Or in a variation, the jury might be authorized to render a general verdict, but also to answer written interrogatories so that the basis of the verdict will be disclosed.

Chapter 2 Checking Abuses of Power

Juries have many functions, and the right to a jury trial became a part of our Constitution to balance and check the powers of governmental officials. This was explained in the Supreme Court case of *Duncan v. Louisiana.*[1]

DUNCAN V. LOUISIANA

Gary Duncan's criminal trial was seemingly insignificant. He was prosecuted in 1966 in Plaquemines Parish, Louisiana, a strip of land rich in sulphur and oil that stretched a hundred miles from New Orleans down both sides of the Mississippi to the Gulf of Mexico. From the 1920s until his death in 1969, Leander Perez was, according to his biographer Glen Jeansonne, the "political boss who held absolute power in Plaquemines Parish to an extent unsurpassed by any parish leader in Louisiana's history."[2] His base of power for most of this time was as district attorney, an office he passed on in 1960 to his son, Leander Perez, Jr. No one held office and no legislation passed without the father's approval. "Perez, who considered lawmakers superfluous middlemen . . . simply drew up laws and inserted them into the minutes of the parish police jury and commission council. . . . He concluded that honest elections were more trouble than they were worth and made sure none was held in his bailiwick. Dead people might have voted in the elder Richard Daley's Chicago and Lyndon Johnson's Texas, but neither place had Babe Ruth and Charlie Chaplin as voters. Plaquemines did."[3]

Indeed, in 1968 a federal court concluded that the number of white people registered to vote in the parish exceeded the number of white adults who actually lived there. In 1962, although more than a fifth of the sparse population was black, 6,906 white people were registered to vote compared to 43 black people.

On August 26, 1966, the federal courts entered an order desegregating the Plaquemines parish schools. Leander Perez was not happy. A dozen years earlier, after the Supreme Court had decided *Brown v. Board of Education,* he announced that he was dedicating his life to the principle of segregation. In the 1960s Perez stated, "Do you know what the Negro is? Animals right out of the jungle. Passion. Welfare. Easy life. That's the Negro. And if you don't know that, you're naive." The spearhead for integration came from communistic Zionists, "to all those Jews who were supposed to have been cremated at Buchenwald and Dachau but weren't, and Roosevelt allowed two million of them illegal entry into our country."[4]

Gary Duncan's nephew and cousin were two of the black students who began attending a formerly all-white school. On October 18, 1966, they were threatened by white students. The twenty-year-old Duncan, a fisherman, married and with a child, was driving by the school after it let out. He saw a group of white individuals standing near his relatives. He stopped, and his cousin and nephew told him that the white people were trying to start a fight. Duncan herded the two into his car and then "touched" or "slapped" a white boy on the arm. A white adult made a call to the sheriff's office. A deputy spoke to Duncan and the other boys and refused to make an arrest.

Three days later, however, the district attorney, Leander H. Perez, Jr., had Duncan arrested for simple battery because of the touch or slap. Duncan requested a jury trial, but Louisiana then limited jury trials to cases where either capital punishment or imprisonment at hard labor could be imposed. Because simple battery in Louisiana was a misdemeanor carrying a maximum sentence of two years, it did not qualify for a jury trial, and Duncan's trial was held without one. The trial judge convicted the defendant and sentenced Duncan to sixty days in the parish prison plus a $150 fine.

In Plaquemines parish, Duncan never had a chance of being acquitted. The judge had set bond at twice the usual level. The sentence was longer than for almost any other battery conviction in the parish. Indeed, local lawyers could not be found to defend him. One of his out-of-state lawyers was arrested for illegally practicing law. A federal court eventually enjoined that prosecution, finding that it "was . . . without basis in law and fact." In another decision, a federal court ultimately concluded that Duncan's trial judge had been "personally hostile to Duncan and . . . altered established principles of criminal procedure in an effort to punish Duncan for his exercise of federally secured rights."[5]

Although this was apparently a minor offense, the Supreme Court latched onto the case to make significant constitutional pronouncements. The first concerned the standards for determining whether states have to conform to the provisions in the Bill of Rights of the United States Constitution.

The first ten amendments to the Constitution by their language apply only to the federal government. The Fourteenth Amendment, however, adopted in the wake of the Civil War, denies *states* the power to "deprive any person of life, liberty, or property, without due process of law." The meaning of that phrase is open to various interpretations, and over time, the Supreme Court has increasingly looked to the Bill of Rights to define the content of the Fourteenth Amendment's "due process clause."

The Fifth Amendment, for example, requires the federal government to pay just compensation when it takes private property for public purposes. The Fourteenth Amendment does not contain this explicit provision about the public seizure of private property, but before the nineteenth century ended, the Supreme Court held that the Fourteenth Amendment's general due process provision incorporated the Fifth Amendment's more specific command. States, therefore, could constitutionally exercise eminent domain only by giving just compensation even though the Fourteenth Amendment did not specifically enunciate this constitutional principle.[6] Three decades later, the Supreme Court took a similar approach and concluded that the Fourteenth Amendment's general due process clause incorporated the First Amendment's specific provisions concerning speech, press, and religion, and thus, the states could not infringe these rights.

By the 1960s, however, the Supreme Court had still not adopted a similar principle for any of the many Bill of Rights provisions concerning criminal trials. The Court had stated only that the crucial criterion for determining when the states had to confer a criminal procedure safeguard was whether "a civilized system could be imagined that would not accord the particular protection." If the imagination could conjure such a civilized system without the procedure, then the Constitution did not require the states to provide it.

In deciding that states had to afford criminal defendants jury trials, the Court in *Duncan v. Louisiana* rejected this earlier test. The previous standard was wrong, the Court concluded, because state proceedings are not merely abstract schemes, "but actual systems bearing virtually every characteristic of the common-law system that has been developing contemporaneously in England and in this country. The question thus is whether given this kind of system a particular procedure is fundamental—whether, that is, a procedure is necessary to an Anglo-American regime of ordered liberty." The question is not, the Court continued, whether a procedure is "necessarily fundamental to fairness in every criminal system that might be imagined but is fundamental in the context of the criminal processes maintained by the American States."[7]

Under the earlier approach, the Fourteenth Amendment did not require criminal jury trials in state courts. As *Duncan* conceded, a fair criminal process could be imagined that did not utilize juries. Indeed, many civilized countries decide criminal matters without juries. But with the inquiry transformed into whether jury trials are fundamental to the American scheme of criminal justice, the Court concluded that history, modern practices, and the core purposes of juries all indicate that criminal jury trials are so essential that the states are constitutionally required to have them.

The *Duncan* Court noted that the generation that framed the Constitution viewed jury trials as an essential component of its freedom. Indeed, jury trials came to America with the English colonists, and every colony provided a right to such trials. Moreover, interference with jury trials met with strident protest. The English Stamp Act allowed some violations of revenue laws to be tried in the colonies without juries, but the colonial Stamp Act Congress of 1765 responded that "trial by jury is the inherent and invaluable right of every British subject in these colonies." As England sought to further limit the colonial right to jury trials, the colonists protested more, and the preservation of jury trials became one of the symbols fueling the Revolution. The Declaration of Independence ultimately protested that the king is "depriving us in many cases, of the benefits of Trial by Jury," and to his "transporting us beyond the Seas to be tried for pretended offenses." Not surprisingly, immediately after independence every state guaranteed jury trials. Before the drafting of the federal Constitution, twelve states had adopted their own constitutions. The only right protected in all of them was the right to a jury trial in criminal cases.

The federal Constitution followed suit. The new nation's charter, in article 3, section 2, guaranteed: "The Trial of all Crimes, except in Cases of Impeachment, shall be by Jury; and such Trial shall be held in the State where the said Crimes shall have been committed." Many, however, criticized this Constitution for not adequately protecting criminal jury trials and other rights. The new country soon adopted the first ten amendments, which included another guarantee of jury trials. The Sixth Amendment states in part: "In all criminal prosecutions, the accused shall enjoy the right to a speedy and public trial, by an impartial jury of the State and district wherein the crime shall have been committed."

Jury trials were fundamentally important at the country's inception. Colonists protested their infringement; all the early states adopted them; the federal Constitution guaranteed criminal jury trials not once, but twice. Furthermore, every state that has since entered the union has protected the right to jury trials in criminal cases. *Duncan v. Louisiana* concluded: "Jury trial continues to receive strong support. The laws of every State guarantee a right to jury trial in serious criminal cases; no State has dispensed with it; nor are there significant movements underway to do so."[8]

The *Duncan* Court built its argument that criminal juries are fundamental to our justice system not merely on historical precedent; it made eloquent reference to the basic legal and societal purposes our juries serve. The widespread use of jury trials reflects "a profound judgment about the way in which law should be enforced and justice administered. A right to jury trial is granted to criminal defendants in order to prevent oppression by the Government." The Court continued that juries can protect society against governmental actors who may use their powers unjustly. "Providing an accused with the right to be tried by a jury of his peers gave him an inestimable safeguard against the corrupt or overzealous prosecutor and against the compliant, biased, or eccentric judge. If the defendant preferred the commonsense judgment of a jury to the more tutored but perhaps less sympathetic reaction of the single judge, he was to have it." Consequently, the Court concluded in *Duncan*, jury trials in criminal cases are fundamental to the American system of justice. The Court held that the Constitution "guarantees a right to jury trial in all criminal cases which—were they to be tried in a federal court—would come within the Sixth Amendment's guarantee."[9]

Some four decades later, many deride juries, but their noise hides the fact that few actually advocate their abolition. Some would like to limit the kinds of civil matters a jury can consider, but no one seriously suggests that juryless tribunals should decide all our criminal cases or even all our civil disputes. There is no movement to repeal the Sixth Amendment's jury trial guarantee. The credible critics are not abolitionists, but reformers.

THE FRAMERS AND PETER ZENGER

Certainly the constitutional generation valued juries precisely because juries did protect against biased prosecutions. The famous trial of Peter Zenger in colonial New York revealed to Americans how a jury could protect against oppression. News of that 1735 case spread quickly via newspapers and correspondence, and a year after the trial, James Alexander, a participant in the proceeding, edited a wildly popular report of the trial. His *Brief Narrative* was reprinted fifteen times before the end of the century.[10]

William Cosby, the greedy and arrogant governor of New York, was at the core of the controversy. He had manipulated the courts by suspending a political enemy as chief justice and replacing him with a more cooperative ally. Cosby was attacked in the legislature, and presumably in homes and taverns, for his actions. But most important for history, he and his cohort were viciously, sometimes amusingly, attacked in *The Weekly Standard,* a paper Zenger printed.

The new, politically acquiescent chief justice tried twice unsuccessfully to convince a grand jury to indict Zenger for seditious libel, telling them, "Sometimes heavy, halfwitted men get a knack of rhyming, but it is time to break them of it, when they grow abusive, insolent, and mischievous with it."[11] Faced with the grand jury's recalcitrance, the governor proceeded without them, ordering Zenger's arrest, and proceeding with "an information" for criminal libel—a method of charging a crime—which did not require grand jury action.

When Zenger's original lawyers challenged the authority of Cosby's handpicked judges to hear the case, the chief justice, after consulting the governor, disbarred them. Soon, however, Andrew Hamilton of Philadelphia, the leading American lawyer of the day, came to represent them.

At trial, Hamilton admitted in open court that his client had published the offending matter, but he contended that the printed material was not false and, therefore, not libelous. The court, however, prohibited the introduction of evidence on this point, and consequently, the highlight of the defense—indeed, the only defense—was Hamilton's address to the jury. After the court ruled that he could not produce witnesses to prove the truth of the publication, Hamilton turned to the jury and said: "Then, gentlemen of the jury, it is to you we must now appeal for witnesses to the truth of the facts we have offered and are denied the liberty to prove; and let it not seem strange that I apply myself to you in this manner, I am warranted so to do both by law and reason. The law supposes you to be summoned out of the neighborhood where the fact is alleged to be committed; and the reason of your being taken out of the neighborhood is because you are supposed to have the best knowledge of the fact that is to be tried."[12]

The jury responded to the appeal and acquitted Zenger. In doing so, they showed future generations how juries could provide a bulwark against an executive's dangerous use of criminal charges. It was an example, however, that only reinforced existing ideas: "That juries provided a constitutional check on executive power was not a lesson any English-speaking person needed the Zenger case to teach—that was why English people loved juries so deeply, and why British North Americans were willing to respond with organized violence when jury trial was interfered with by an assertedly sovereign Parliament in the 1760's and 1770's."[13] The *Zenger* jury did not stand alone. While many in England were convicted of seditious libel during the period, American juries virtually repealed that law by almost always refusing to convict those charged under it.

Colonial juries did not simply check seditious libel charges; they also made the enforcement of despised English trade and revenue laws nearly impossible. Juries often refused to convict. As a result, customs officials and crown officers in America "warned their superiors in England that they would never be able to enforce the trade laws so long as the innocence or guilt of suspected smugglers rested upon the whims of provincial juries."[14] England responded by giving jurisdiction over such matters to judges without juries, which led to the increasingly vociferous complaints that Americans were being deprived of their fundamental right to a jury trial.

JURIES AS A CHECK ON OFFICIALS
OF A REPRESENTATIVE GOVERNMENT

Colonial juries, then, acted as roadblocks to laws regarded as unjust and to judges controlled by the executive. In the new country, laws would be passed by representative bodies. Taxation, and other laws, would come only with representation, and judges would not be under the thumb of the executive. Even with a more democratic government, however, juries were still deemed necessary—indeed, equally important as representative legislatures—for the protection of liberty. Constitutional historian Jack Rakove summarizes, "Americans

[gave] two rights preeminent importance. If the rights to representation and to trial by jury were left to operate in full force, they would shelter nearly all the other rights and liberties of the people."[15]

The constitutional framers' vision of the essential dangers of power and those who wielded it informed this respect for juries. In the era leading up to the Constitution, Americans concluded that the power of those in control, no matter how lawful the apparent authority, had to be limited. "In resisting the British and in forming their own governments, [Americans] saw the central problem as one of devising means to check the inevitable operations of depravity in men who wielded power."[16] Concern over potential domination was widespread. "Power was feared in the eighteenth century, whether it was governmental power, royal power, aristocratic power, or 'mobocracy.' The very existence of power, rather than its abuse, raised concern. All authority was dangerous, but not all power was illegitimate. Only authority checked by procedural rules was 'lawful.'"[17]

This point has been reiterated throughout our history, perhaps no more eloquently than by the attorneys for Lamdin P. Milligan in 1866. During the Civil War, President Lincoln instituted martial law for the trial of civilians in various places. Little controversy surrounded the use of martial law in the border states or where the Confederacy had invaded the North. Lincoln, however, also imposed martial law in Ohio, Indiana, and Illinois, far from the scene of battle, and where the ordinary civilian courts were functioning. Under these controversial orders, military authorities arrested and tried a wide range of people, from those truly aiding the Confederacy to those simply urging an end to the war.

On October 5, 1864, the military commander in Indiana arrested Milligan and others. Milligan was convicted by a military tribunal of conspiracy to free rebel prisoners and aid them in an invasion of Indiana. On May 18, 1865, even though the surrender at Appomattox had occurred six weeks earlier, that court sentenced Milligan to be hanged, a sentence later commuted by President Johnson to life in prison.

In April 1866 as Congress was passing the Civil Rights Act over Johnson's veto and the battle between the legislature and the president over reconstruction intensified, the Supreme Court considered the legality of Milligan's trial. Milligan's attorney, J. E. McDonald, argued that the imposition of martial law had unconstitutionally infringed the right to a jury trial. He conceded that the present time differed from the colonial period. Royal governors no longer could bring criminal charges in this country. The federal judiciary was independent and did not answer to the executive.

Even so, McDonald argued, juries were still absolutely necessary because "judges themselves might not be safely trusted in criminal cases—especially in prosecutions for political offenses, where the whole power of the executive is arrayed against the accused party." Milligan's attorney noted that the Constitution did not change human nature; instead, it recognized it and tried to protect against its excesses. "All history proves that public officers of any government when they are engaged in a severe struggle to retain their places, become bitter and ferocious, and hate those who oppose them, even in the most legitimate way, with a rancor which they never exhibit towards actual crimes. This kind of malignity vents itself in prosecutions for political offenses." The constitutional framers tried "to make the judiciary as perfect as possible, but also to give the citizen yet another shield against his government. To that end, they could think of no better provision than a public trial before an impartial jury." The framers, he said, did not believe that a jury trial was infallible, for "[l]ike everything human, it has its imperfections . . . [but] it is the best protection for innocence and the surest mode of punishing guilt that has yet been discovered. It has borne the test of a longer experience, and borne it better than any other legal institution that ever existed among men."[18] Jury trials, in this view, not only protect against the corrupt executive or corrupt judge, but also act as a check on even the most honorable of officials, because it is only natural that human beings will seek to punish or harm those who oppose them.

The response to such potential abuse was the constitutional system of checks and balances, which could reach the common good even if individuals with power could not always be counted on to work for the general welfare. According to historian Arthur O. Lovejoy, Americans believed that "it [was] entirely possible to construct an ideal political society out of bad human materials—to frame a rational scheme of government, in which the general good will be realized, without presupposing that the individuals who exercise ultimate political power will be severally actuated in their use by rational motives, or primarily solicitous about the general good. . . . [This could be accomplished by] the method of counterpoise—accomplishing desirable results by balancing harmful things against one another." Thus, the jury system took its place as another tier in the American system of checks and balances—one that was denied Lamdin P. Milligan. The Supreme Court in *Ex parte Milligan* unanimously held that the military tribunal had no right to try Milligan because he had not been indicted by a grand jury as required by the Habeas Corpus Act of March 1863, which had suspended habeas corpus during the war. A majority of the Court also stated that the military could not try civilians in locations distant from the war and where the civilian courts were open. While the discipline needed in the armed forces may require trials without juries, the Court held, all civilian citizens where the courts are open "are guaranteed the inestimable privilege of trial by jury." Consequently, Milligan should have received a jury trial.[19]

The essential need for juries as a check on power was further impelled by a shift in early Americans' view of crime. In England, crime was generally seen as a matter between the victim and the criminal. Prosecutions were done not by a public prosecutor, but by the victims or their friends and relatives, who usually had to pay all or most of the costs of their prosecution. Consequently, the poor were unlikely to avail themselves of the power of the criminal courts, and crimes against them were seldom punished by legal means.

A more egalitarian American society, however, concluded that the criminal law should do more than just protect the rich. Society in general is harmed by crime, and the ability to prosecute should not depend upon the wealth of the victim. Since the community as a whole is affected by crime, a community representative should be in charge of prosecution; consequently, public prosecutors came into being.[20]

When crime came to be viewed not merely as a problem between individuals but as a concern for the larger society, the government as a representative of society became an antagonist in the process. This dynamic cast judges in a different light. Even if judges could be trusted to be impartial arbiters when criminal cases were seen as confrontations between individuals, the court, as an instrument of government, could not so readily be seen as disinterested when the government became the prime mover in an ordinary criminal case. Increasingly, a criminal trial was seen not as a relatively equal contest between alleged victim and accused, but as a lopsided battle not only with a specific prosecutor but with the government in general, and the judge was part of the government.

No matter how laws were enacted and no matter how judges obtained and retained office, Americans saw a need to check judicial power. Juries could help do this. As the Supreme Court recognized in *Duncan v. Louisiana,* juries fit into an overall scheme of a government of checks and balances. "[T]he jury trial provisions in the Federal and State Constitutions reflect a fundamental decision about the exercise of official power—a reluctance to entrust plenary powers over the life and liberty of the citizens to one judge or to a group of judges. Fear of unchecked power, so typical of our State and Federal Governments in other respects, found expression in the criminal law in this insistence upon community participation in the determination of guilt or innocence."[21]

Juries are fundamental, according to *Duncan*, not just because of history and not just because they remain in widespread use, but because juries serve crucial societal goals. They prevent governmental oppression by providing a bulwark against unjust laws or unjust prosecutors or unjust judges. But even when laws are fairly enacted, and even when prosecutors and judges are not venal or corrupt, juries are still necessary because the character of human nature indicates that power, especially governmental power, always needs checking. Juries do this.

JURIES AS A CONTINUING CHECK
ON THE PROSECUTION OF ENEMIES

Throughout American history, people have looked to juries to provide relief from laws seen as oppressive. For example, many prosecutions in early Kentucky were for violations of despised revenue laws. Because of the refusal of juries to convict their neighbors charged under these statutes, the laws went unenforced.[22] At later times, Americans turned to juries for relief from other laws they thought unjust, such as those dealing with fugitive slaves, prohibition, and the draft. Violators of certain laws today, frequently involving taxes, the environment, or property, proclaim governmental oppression and seek juries to stand as a freedom-loving barricade by returning acquittals. Although in *Duncan* the Court envisioned juries resisting governmental oppression, their role was seen not so much as nullifiers of duly enacted laws, but as a check on the eccentric or corrupt prosecutor who, using an accepted law, brings unjust charges and against the biased judge who would adjudicate if juries were not used. Gary Duncan's case was a good vehicle for the Supreme Court because Duncan faced exactly such a biased prosecution.

The need for juries as a check on prosecutions continues. A concern over politically motivated trials is always present. In 2000 the sheriff of New York's Suffolk County was under a ninety-count indictment for various corruption charges. The validity of the charges was not clear, but what was certain was that a feud existed between the county's district attorney and the sheriff. "The Suffolk County sheriff has publicly questioned the district attorney's mental stability. He has referred to him as a fascist. The district attorney, in turn, has called the sheriff his sworn enemy. And now the sheriff is accusing the district attorney of using his prosecutorial powers to ruin him simply because 'he hates me.'"[23] One reason for the Sixth Amendment's guarantee of jury trials was a concern about the prosecutions of "enemies," a concern that is always present.

The best fortification against the possible injustices that can result, the framers thought, is a group of ordinary citizens assembled together as a jury.

JURIES AS A CHECK
ON THE CORRUPTION OF POWER

Our government is based on the idea that power, even when exercised by the best, needs to be checked. This view separates the United States from much of the rest of the world and helps explain why we have juries when many places do not. Professor Myron Moskovitz states, "To put it bluntly, Europeans trust authority, and Americans don't. Speaking generally, of course."[24]

The American view is that the need to restrain governmental power may be especially acute in times of crisis, as at the trials of Lamdin Milligan and Gary Duncan, but the need is ever present because judges, being human, have biases. Thomas Jefferson summarized this need: "We all know that permanent judges acquire an *Esprit de corps;* that being known, they are liable to be tempted by bribery; that they are misled by favor, by relationship, by a spirit of party, by a devotion to the executive or legislative power; that it is better to leave a cause to the decision of cross and pile [or heads or tails], than to that of a judge biased to one side; and that the opinion of twelve honest jurymen gives still a better hope of right, than cross and pile does."[25]

In this Jeffersonian view, all people, not just the venal, become affected by the power they wield. Everyone can be tempted by the forbidden, a point made by the wise, old trial judge in James Gould Cozzens's novel *The Just and the Unjust:* "You remember the story of the judge who was offered twenty-five thousand dollars for an opinion favorable to the plaintiff. He threw the man out and when his colleagues sympathized with him over the insult he'd been offered, he said to them: 'Gentlemen, I didn't worry about the insult; you can't insult integrity. What worried me was that he was getting too damned close to my price.' "[26]

Judges can be good people. We can and do have systems to reduce undesirable influences on judges. Nevertheless, the nature of the job affects its holder. Because judges are human, they can be affected by forces that impede neutral decisions and can be tempted by corruption. Juries protect against such human fallibility.

Even Alexander Hamilton, who disagreed with Jefferson over many things, saw juries as a check on judicial corruption. In Number 83 of the *Federalist Papers,* Hamilton stated about trial by jury in civil cases: "The strongest argument in its favor is that it is a security against corruption. As there is always more time and better opportunity to tamper with a standing body of magistrates than with a jury summoned for the occasion, there is room to suppose that a corrupt influence would more easily find its way to the former than to the latter."

Bribing jurors is indeed difficult. Their identity is not known until they are selected at trial. This gives little time to approach them. Perhaps more important, jurors are strangers to the system. Because they come from the community and disappear back into it after the trial, the necessary pathways of solicitation can be hard to discover even if there were time to do so. On the other hand, the identity of the judge is generally known in advance of trial. The judge as a permanent fixture can be studied at some leisure to find approachable avenues. As Hamilton indicated, there will always be more time and opportunity to tamper with permanent judges than with transient jurors.

In addition, the ultimate harm to society is greater when a judge is corrupted than when a jury is compromised. A dishonest juror affects one trial. A crooked judge, however, will hear future cases. Having succumbed once, the odds of yielding again increase. Having acceded, the judge is now vulnerable to blackmail. Thus, the harm of the corrupted judge may continue on beyond one trial.

Juries may diminish the opportunities for bribery and coercion in our trial system, but we cannot know if that is really so. Because we have juries, we cannot know how much judicial corruption there might be without them. Furthermore, when judicial corruption is successful, we do not learn of it, so the extent of the damage is unclear. When such efforts do come to light, however, we tend to hear less about attempts to bribe jurors and more about corrupt judges. "Operation Greylord," for example, led to the conviction of fifteen Chicago judges for bribe-taking and related offenses. Based on what has been revealed historically, at least, we have more to fear from corrupt judges than from corrupt jurors.

JURIES AS A BALANCE TO THE ISOLATION
AND QUALITY OF JUDGES

The Jeffersonian view, however, is not concerned merely with outright corruption. Judges, even when honest, have or develop certain loyalties, views, and biases that will affect their ability to be fair factfinders. Their craft demands respect for the law, and their primary allegiance is to the legal system. A study of the justice system in northern Ireland, where many crimes have been tried without juries, concluded: "When lay triers are involved, the decision-makers are acting as the community, and they can afford to take a wider view of both the merits of the proceedings and the merits of convicting the defendant on the basis of the proceedings. Professional triers of fact cannot take such a wide view of the case. They are accountable, first, to the legal system."[27]

Judges also tend to have or develop a narrower view of a case than does a jury, because judges generally are more loyal to the government. Judges hold permanent state posts. Their selection, which they have sought, occurs through a governmental process. They are paid by the government, and they invariably see themselves, correctly, as an important part of government. Jurors also hold a governmental position and may even receive a stipend from the state, but this is temporary and the money meager. Simply being a juror is unlikely to lead a person to identify with the government.

Furthermore, the best possible people do not always become judges. Judges do not get paid as well as many successful lawyers. Attorneys at the top of the profession usually have to take a significant pay cut to become judges. Indeed, in today's world, even many law school professors' salaries are higher than those of judges. That judicial pay scale deters many of the best lawyers from joining the judiciary.

The pool of possible judges is made yet more shallow by the fact that in this country, perhaps in this country alone, a lawyer must have political visibility to become a judge. This is true not just for the elected judiciary, but also for appointed judges, including federal judges. Federal judges are appointed by the president and confirmed by the Senate. Naturally, the president and the Senate cannot exhaustively survey all lawyers to find the best possible candidates when filling a judicial vacancy. Consequently, being political creatures, they become aware only of people with some political visibility. Such visibility, unfortunately, does not necessarily equate with judicial quality, and many who might be good judges are not considered.

Federal trial judges are appointed for life. This job security helps insulate them from political vicissitudes after they take office. The vast majority of American trials, however, take place in the state courts, and state trial judges are usually selected in a more overtly political fashion and remain subject to more political pressures than do federal judges.

Most states elect trial judges. The American movement toward an elected judiciary began early, partly in reaction to the arrogance of some of the fledgling country's initial judges. Reformers contended that an elected judiciary would allow for public participation in the legal process, check centralized power, and forestall possible judicial arbitrariness. In 1832, Mississippi became the first state to adopt partisan elections of judges. In 1846, New York was electing judges, and the tide rose in that direction. Every state entering the union before 1845 had appointed judges, but by the eve of the Civil War, two-thirds of the states were electing judges to the lower courts and almost as many were electing their Supreme Courts.

The twentieth century saw a movement away from the popular election of judges, but trial court judges are still often elected officials. These elections also narrow the judicial pool, for many who might make good judges do not want to undergo the special rigors of the electoral process.

The problem of attracting quality judicial candidates is exacerbated because the public is seldom well equipped to choose among them. Most in the electorate know little about the qualifications and character of judicial nominees for trial courts. Surveys have shown that 80 percent and more of voters cannot name any judicial candidates for whom they have voted. Indeed, the electorate often pick judges simply by partisan affiliation or ballot position. In reality, then, in many localities it is those who control the political parties' endorsements who effectively pick the judiciary. What Barbara Reed, associate director of the Fund for Modern Courts, has said about New York courts has wider application: "It's all fine and good to say that judicial elections are democratic, but in terms of their practical effects they're not democratic. People aren't getting the whole picture. In effect, they are voting for who the party says are the nominees."[28]

With concerns over these electoral practices, current wisdom suggests we should not elect judges. Appointed judges or some sort of merit selection system seems better, and at least on the surface, elected judges would seem to have less independence than judges who ascend the bench via a different route. Interestingly, however, empirical information does little to support the notion that nonelected judges are better than elected ones. For example, some data suggest that on average, elected judges are more courteous than appointed ones. Other data comparing merit-selected judges with elected ones found merit-selected judges comparable to the popularly picked ones, while another study gave elected judges both the highest and the lowest ratings.

Judges face voters in three ways. Some states have partisan elections of judges. Other states have nonpartisan voting. In the third category, judges are initially appointed by the governor but then face periodic elections for reappointment. Some states have only appointed judges. A brief summary of these different selection methods is impossible because often a state uses different methods to select judges for different courts. Some states, for example, appoint judges to their top courts but elect judges to their trials courts. Others do the reverse, electing the top court judges but appointing judges to the trial courts. Some states have nonpartisan elections for one level of judgeship and partisan elections for another. Some use different methods for different trial courts within the state. For example, some trial judges in New York City are elected in partisan elections; some are appointed by the mayor of New York City; and some are appointed by the state's governor.

The usual method of selecting judges by a merit plan, also known as the non-partisan court plan, or the Missouri Plan, has "a nominating commission composed of lawyers and lay people, which seeks qualified judicial candidates. In theory, it evaluates each candidate on the basis of professional qualifications and recommends the best qualified candidates to the chief executive, who appoints the judge. After serving for a time, the judge runs unopposed in a retention election solely on the basis of performance in office." This method is meant to take the politics out of selection, but governors tend to appoint judges from their own political party. Some commissions know that selecting candidates from the opposite party, in effect, narrows the true list of possibilities and thereby advances the commission members' "political and personal goals. And among the members of the commissions, there are campaigns for selection as commission members that reflect deep-seated tensions between plaintiff and defense bars. Rather than eliminating politics, the forum in which the political battles are played out shifts. Politics, so despised by reformers, is largely eliminated from public scrutiny in a merit selection system, but remains as elite politics. Elite politics, it appears, is far less disturbing to reformers."[29]

The fact is that the quality of our judges, no matter how selected, ranges widely, especially so in the state courts. Judicial scholar Gordon Van Kessel has noted, "The status of state trial judges in America generally is inferior to that of their English cousins. An important reason for this lower position is the fact that most state judges must fight for their judicial positions in the elective process. Subjecting the judiciary to the elective process reduces its status and contributes to its diminished authority."[30]

While our selection processes hardly guarantee that our judges are always the best, perhaps of more concern is that few state trial judges, unlike their federal counterparts, have life tenure, yet most wish to stay in office when their term expires. As a result, consciously or not, judges may make decisions that will help them retain their position. Controversial decisions can lead to waves of popular indignation and fuel the campaigns of challengers for judgeships. Majoritarian pressures, or at least forces perceived that way, can shape judicial decisions. For example, Alabama's trial judges face an election every six years.

These judges had the power to set aside a jury's sentencing recommendations in capital cases before 2002, when the Supreme Court held that juries must determine whether the death penalty should be imposed. The United States Supreme Court has noted the "ostensibly surprising statistics" that in Alabama "there have been only five cases in which the judge rejected an advisory verdict of death, compared to 47 instances where the judge imposed a death sentence over a jury recommendation of life." Justice John Stevens concluded that the reason the override ratio favored the death sentence at ten times the rate of life imprisonment was because elected judges are forced to respond to "a political climate in which judges who covet higher office—or who merely wish to remain judges—must constantly profess their fealty to the death penalty." Not surprisingly, studies have shown that the likelihood of an Alabama trial judge overriding a jury's recommendation of life and imposing the death sentence increases if the decision is made in the year the judge faces an election.[31]

Juries may feel similar pressures from the public, but the effect of those forces is different. Juries are not elected. They are not seeking reappointments. They are not looking for promotions. Jurors' status and livelihoods are seldom affected by their decisions. As a result, juries are much freer than judges to concentrate on the merits of a dispute.

Moreover, if juries were removed from trials, the incentives to influence the selection of trial judges would increase. Judicial elections to certain state courts give an idea of what could happen. Recent efforts to place limits on civil damage awards have spawned many legal challenges in state courts. As a result, business groups and trial lawyers have increasingly tried to influence the elections to state supreme courts, which rule on the legality of those limits. A news report summarizes:

> Millions of dollars in campaign contributions are flowing into races for state judgeships this year, while candidates are testing the limits of ethics rules that forbid them to signal how they might vote on cases. . . . In the new politics, judges sometimes appear as petty as other politicians—and as subject to influence. . . . In a newsletter last fall, for example, the Michigan Manufacturers Association told its members about the importance of the year's State Supreme Court election. The group flatly outlined the group's political goal. In the last election, it boasted that contributions to the manufacturers' political action committee "swayed the Supreme Court election to a conservative viewpoint, ensuring a pro-manufacturing agenda."[32]

Just as judges have attitudes and pressures that affect their judicial decisions, jurors are influenced by their own predispositions. As Richard Lempert has summarized, however, we should have less concern about jurors' tendencies than about those of judges:

> Juror attitudes differ and can cancel each other out. Trial judges hear only one voice, their own. Second, jurors hear one case and then disperse. Judges, in the absence of juries, would hear case after case. If jurors in a case share an attitude so strong that it biases their decision, it is only one case which is affected. If a judge has an attitude so strong it biases her decisions, that attitude can improperly affect a string of cases. Finally, and most importantly, jurors seldom get where they are because of their attitudes. Although lawyers strive to get juries favorably disposed to them, it is hard accurately to discern case-relevant juror attitudes, and no juror can be retained because of a favorable attitude. A juror can only, within the limits of the available peremptory challenges, be rejected because of seemingly unfavorable views. Judges, by contrast, are chosen through a political process in which their attitude may figure prominently. Without the jury, judicial attitudes would be yet more important to decisions in cases, and wealthy repeat player litigants would have reason to spend lavishly to influence the selection of even low level trial judges.[33]

JURORS AS A CHECK AND BALANCE
IN CRIMINAL CASES

All this suggests not merely that judges have views that affect their judgments when it comes to determining facts, but that these perspectives could lead judges to decide cases differently from juries. This proposition, again, is not easily verified. In our system, both judges and juries may make factual determinations, but they do not do so for the same issues. Either we have a jury trial or a judge decides; we do not have a hybrid where simultaneously both judge and jury decide the same case. As a consequence, we do not have data about how, if at all, juries and judges differ when deciding the same factual dispute.

The most famous jury study, however, tried to fill this information gap. In the 1950s, Harry Kalven, Jr., and Hans Zeisel surveyed trial judges asking them, among other things, how the jury decided a case and how the judge would have decided it if it had been tried to the judge without a jury. Kalven and Zeisel's groundbreaking book, *The American Jury*, reported that in their sample of 3,576 trials, juries convicted 64.2 percent of the time, acquitted 30.3 percent of the time, and hung 5.5 percent of the time. Judges cannot hang; they have but two choices. The judges in this sample reported that they would have convicted in 83.3 percent of the trials and would have acquitted in 16.7 percent.

The judge concurred with the jury's acquittal in 13.4 percent of the cases and also agreed with 62.05 percent of the convictions. Thus, in three-quarters of the trials, the judge and jury united on the outcome, and if hung juries are counted as half acquittals, then the judge and jury concurred in 78 percent of the cases.

These numbers, however, mask the ways in which judge and jury disagreed. The disagreements, which occurred 22 percent of the time, were strikingly skewed. The jury acquitted 19 percent of the time when the judge would have convicted, and only 3 percent of the time they convicted when the judge would have acquitted. In other words, as Kalven and Zeisel reported, "The jury's disagreement with the judge is massively in one direction, and the direction is the expected one."[34]

As we have seen, juries exist to provide a bulwark against governmental oppression or at least to act as a check on judges who, because of background, training, and position, are likely to side with the government. If the jury is fulfilling its role, then it should be acquitting more often than judges would. Kalven and Zeisel's data indicate that juries are indeed acting as expected—as a check on the judiciary. Or as the Supreme Court in *Duncan v. Louisiana* concluded when it examined these data, "[W]hen juries differ with the result at which the judge would have arrived, it is usually because they are serving some of the very purposes for which they were created and for which they are now employed."[35]

JURORS AS A CHECK IN CIVIL CASES

The jury as a curb on government, however, may seem only to support juries in criminal cases, where the government is always a party. It would not seem a significant justification in civil cases, where the litigants are usually not affiliated with the government. When one individual sues another, or even when one nongovernmental organization sues or is sued, protection from governmental oppression is not needed, and the fear that judges will instinctively side with the government should not arise. Why, then, do we have juries in civil cases?

The Supreme Court gave its answer in *Colgrove v. Battin*, where, in an opinion by Justice William Brennan, it concluded that "the purpose of the jury trial in criminal cases [is] to prevent governmental oppression . . . and, in criminal and civil cases, [is] to assure a fair and equitable resolution of factual issues."[36] While the criminal jury has the dual goals of curbing official power and providing for satisfactory factual determinations, the Court concluded, the civil jury has but one aim: fair fact-finding. While conceding that the history of the constitutionalization of civil juries differs from that of criminal juries, others conclude that civil juries serve broader purposes than the Supreme Court recognized.

As we have seen, the main body of the Constitution protected juries in criminal cases, and criminal jury trials were further protected by the Bill of Rights' Sixth Amendment. In contrast, the original version of the Constitution does not mention juries in civil cases. The framers justified this absence by contending that a national standard for civil juries could not be specified because the states differed as to what kinds of civil cases required a jury. James Wilson, a signer of the Constitution, defended the omission: "The cases open to a jury differed in the different states; it was therefore impracticable, on that ground, to have a general rule. The want of uniformity would have rendered any reference to the practice of the states idle and useless."[37] These constitutional defenders shrugged off the charge that the constitutional goal was to abolish or limit civil juries. Instead, they maintained, the right to trials in civil cases could be safely left to the legislature, the voice of the people, which would determine when and how civil juries should operate.

The antifederalists, however, vociferously complained about the fact that civil juries were not mentioned in the Constitution, suggesting that the framers' arguments for omitting the institution were disingenuous. The framers' true concern, some thought, was not over the diversity of state practices, but over the specific issue of debt collection.

During the Revolution, many individuals had entered into contracts that required payments at high prices because paper money at the time was significantly devalued. After the war, currency was scarce, and payments at the contract prices were often ruinous for the debtors. Some framers, many have claimed, thought juries were not fully enforcing the contracts and this threatened commercial development. "The harassed debtor . . . could hope that his creditor would be forced to bring suit in the debtor's local court where, under the protection of favorable local laws, the debtor might receive a sympathetic hearing before a jury composed of his friends and relatives."[38] In this context, the Constitution's failure to protect civil juries became one of the strongest of the antifederalist rallying cries. As Professor Charles Wolfram concludes, the "concern for local debtors faced with the threat of suit in federal court, without a jury, was one of the chief motivations for opposition to the Constitution."[39] Civil juries were needed to protect ordinary citizens from their rich and mighty neighbors. Leonard Levy has summarized: "Again and again Anti-Federalists [raised] the contention that without civil jury trials the more powerful and wealthy citizens would control the administration of justice and freely encroach on the common people. Juries were bulwarks against private as well as public oppression. The only agency of government that powerful and wealthy 'oligarchs' could not control was a jury."[40]

The concern, however, was not only with oppression by the rich. Civil juries were necessary for the same reason as criminal juries: to act as a check on the government. They could do this as they could in criminal cases, according to Wolfram, by "guard[ing] against unwanted legislation passed by a misguided legislature" and by curbing corrupt or arrogant judges.[41] Civil juries could also serve as a bulwark against government misfeasance in ways that a criminal jury could not. They could grant damages because of unlawful conduct by government officials.[42]

The check of a jury was especially needed, some antifederalists insisted, because the government was likely to be a party in many civil cases for penalties, forfeitures, and public debts, a prediction shortly to be proved true. For example, in the country's first two decades, 95 percent of the federal civil cases in Kentucky were brought by the government to enforce the highly unpopular internal revenue laws.

The constitutional generation favored civil jury trials not merely because jury verdicts were likely to be more reliable than decisions by judges, but also because civil juries could protect against the powerful, whether they were public officials or private citizens. These views prompted seven of the ratifying states to call for a provision protecting juries in civil cases and for the curbing of a power originally granted to the Supreme Court. Section 2 of article 3 of the Constitution states that the Court's appellate jurisdiction extends to both law and fact. Antifederalists consequently feared that even if Congress authorized jury trials, the Supreme Court, through its appellate powers over facts, could override jury verdicts. Luther Martin said to the Maryland legislature during its ratification debates: "Should . . . a jury be adopted in the inferior court, it would only be a needless expense, since, on an appeal, the determination of that jury, even on questions of fact, however honest and upright, is to be of no possible effect. The Supreme Court is to take up all questions of fact, to examine the evidence relative thereto, to decide upon them in the same manner as if they had never been tried by a jury."[43]

The result was the Seventh Amendment, which both authorized jury trials in civil cases and limited appellate review of jury verdicts. It states, "In Suits at common law, where the value in controversy shall exceed twenty dollars, the right of trial by jury shall be preserved, and no fact tried by a jury, shall be otherwise re-examined in any Court of the United States, than according to the rules of the common law."

The Supreme Court, then, in *Colgrove v. Battin,* overlooked the original intentions of the Constitution when it stated that the only purpose of civil juries is the fair and equitable determination of facts. The Seventh Amendment was also meant to constrain federal judges and to act as a bulwark against oppression by the government and powerful citizens.

Do civil juries actually perform this protective role against the powerful? Data from *The American Jury* indicate that criminal juries act as a check on the government because they decide against the government more than do judges. The same study found that in civil cases, too, judges overwhelmingly concurred (78 percent) with the jury verdict. These disagreements were not one-sided, however; they were almost evenly split. In 12 percent of the cases the jury was more favorable toward the plaintiff than the judge would have been, and in 10 percent of the cases the judge would have been more favorable toward the plaintiff. These data are somewhat incomplete because they do not categorize the parties into groupings such as individuals or corporations. Nevertheless, the study does not support the notion that juries are superior to judges as a check on the powerful.[44]

Kalven and Zeisel's study, however, was done before a general expansion in tort law, especially in products liability doctrine, which permits more individuals to seek large damages from corporations. Even so, recent surveys also cast doubt on the concept of the modern civil jury as a special protection against the mighty. For example, a 1991 survey of Georgia judges showed that almost all agreed with civil juries as often or more often than did the Kalven and Zeisel respondents. In their disagreements with the verdicts, the judges did not see the jury as particularly favoring a party. Instead, 79 percent of the judges "rejected the suggestion that bias in favor of a party was the reason for judge-jury disagreement." Similarly, in other surveys, 80 percent of federal judges and 69 percent of state judges disagreed with the assertion that jurors' feelings about the parties often caused them to make inappropriate determinations.[45]

On the other hand, some data do indicate that judges as a group favor the powerful more than civil juries. For example, in a study, one group of subjects included both mock jurors and judges. They were asked whether it was reckless to send trains over a track that the National Traffic Safety Board had found dangerous. Another group was given the same information plus the fact that an accident had occurred. The researchers were investigating "hindsight bias," the tendency to believe that after an event occurs, it was more foreseeable than people would have predicted. But in his comments on the study, Richard Lempert found something more: "Only 15% of the judges in the foresight condition would have prevented the railroad before the accident from using the tracks . . . , while 37% of the mock jurors would have done so. . . . These differences in foresight condition estimates suggest that [the] judges had values or experiences that differed from those of the citizens who participated in their study. . . . [The judges'] values or experiences may make them more resistant to finding businesses liable for punitive damages or less likely to think that businesses would push to engage in activities that had a high risk of serious accidents."[46]

While it may be unclear whether civil juries act as a special restraint on the powerful, both civil and criminal juries are an important component of our government of checks and balances. Juries provide a bulwark against abuses of power. They act as an essential counterpoise to the overzealous prosecutor and the biased judge. The functions of juries, however, do not end there.

Trials occur because litigants dispute what has occurred. The proceedings require the determination of facts, and juries have the duty of resolving those disputed facts. Justice results only when facts are accurately determined.

Chapter 3 Hammering

Out Facts

Juries determine disputed facts. Did the defendant shoot the victim? Was the plaintiff exposed to asbestos at work? Whose car ran the red light? Although this function is at the core of what juries do, their ability to determine facts accurately is often derided. This derision is fueled partly by the fact that a jury is a group that makes a decision, and group decision making has weaknesses. If "group" is replaced with such a term as "mob" or "committee," the problems and dangers of group determinations become clear. A group may diffuse responsibility, and its members may weigh the matter less fully than they would as individuals. As a result, a group, like the proverbial mob, may have many heads but no brain. A group, many have noted, can be extraordinarily credulous and open to easy domination.

Group decision making can also be inefficient. Bodies of people can take longer to reach a conclusion than an individual would, both because educating a group may be more time-consuming than informing one person and because the individual's decision making process, not requiring the resolution of conflicting opinions, can be quicker than that of a group. American folklore extols the strong individual who makes the final decision: Lincoln confronting his cabinet; Patton moving into battle; Edison deciding the next experiment. By contrast, jokes deriding the inefficiency and results of collective decision making abound.

Perhaps these and other condemnations of groups are frequently valid, but a jury is not just any group. It is a special body with a special task, and its construction as a group actually provides it with special strengths for its assigned job.

GROUP RECALL

A trial is an event, and the jurors collectively are likely to remember more of the trial's evidence than any single person could. Because verdicts are to be based on the evidence, this group memory is a distinct advantage.

Popular culture has recognized this phenomenon. In the movie *Twelve Angry Men,* one juror on a murder trial recalls what the others do not: a key witness had indentations on her nose, indicating that she regularly wore glasses, but she had not been wearing them at the time she witnessed the murder. When this single recollection was shared, all the jurors could use the information in their decision making. Together the group remembered, and was then able to weigh, more evidence than they would have as individuals.

This phenomenon happens regularly in real deliberations. An example is given by Victor Villaseñor, who, after extensively interviewing jurors, re-created the deliberations in the murder trial of Juan Corona, tried in the 1970s for the serial killings of migrant workers in California. As they started to reassemble the evidence, the jurors surprised themselves. It was quickly evident that different jury members recalled different aspects of the testimony. "They were just talking, going over the evidence, and trying to remember what they'd heard and seen during the five months of the trial, and surprisingly they were discovering that, as a group, as a collective memory, they were recalling much more than any one of them individually ever did."[1]

Melvyn Zerman's memoir of his jury service in a murder trial furnishes another instance of an individual memory helping the group make its decision: "[Juror 1:] 'What about [the witnesses'] insistence in their early testimony that it all happened at five-thirty?' Juror 6: 'They didn't have watches.' Juror 1: 'But Detective McKinley testified that when he interviewed Clarissa she at first insisted that she saw Ricky at *five-thirty,* even after he reminded her that the murder was committed at five.' [Zerman commented to himself,] Now how did she remember that? She's brilliant. Juror 6: 'I don't remember that.' Juror 5: 'I don't either.'"[2] This proved to be the turning point in the deliberations, for when the testimony confirmed Juror 1, one of the holdouts switched his vote.

Social science research further confirms that juries bring more informational resources to their tasks than do individuals. In one study, jurors were asked to recall eight items admitted into evidence. Individuals got only about 60 percent right. In groups of twelve, however, a 90 percent chance existed that at least one member of the panel would remember the evidence. While individual memories may have been shaky, the collective recall was better.[3]

This strength extends not just to the number of remembered events but also to the accuracy of recollections. The jury as a group has a self-correcting mechanism for misremembered evidence that an individual acting alone does not have. When one member of the jury recalls evidence erroneously, another will often correct the faulty recollection. In the Juan Corona trial, for example, some time after one of the deliberating jurors described a victim, another juror responded with the grisly recollection: "By the way, Naomi, when you spoke you said that Smith was a nine-fingered man with a beard. According to my notes, *Sample* is the nine-fingered man and Smith is the bearded man, and Sample's is not an old body like you said. Numerous deputies testified that Sample didn't smell and his skin didn't come off in the deputies' hands when they took him out of the grave. Sample's body was fresh. Smith, the bearded man, was old and smelled bad and his flesh came away from his bones."[4] This mattered because receipts given to Corona four days before the discovery of Sample's body were found in Sample's grave. If Sample's body had shown the extensive decay that one juror had thought, then the body had to have been there longer than four days, and Corona's receipts could not have fallen from his pocket while he was burying the victim.

No matter how we rate the objective performance of a jury's collective memory or any other aspect of its decision making, the value of the jury system is best measured against the realistic alternatives. In most instances, the only practical option to a jury trial is a bench trial. The important question, then, is not how juries perform as compared to some ideal standard, but how they compare to a single judge who would decide the case in lieu of a jury. Such comparative data, however, are often lacking. Although much research has been done on the decision making abilities of jurors and those eligible for jury service, judges seldom participate in studies examining how they determine disputed facts. Therefore, the crucial comparisons of judges versus juries depends largely on inference.

Judges are experienced; they are professional; they are knowledgeable about the law and the legal system. It may seem only natural that they are able to recall evidence in a legal proceeding more accurately than are inexperienced, nonprofessional juries. Nonetheless, intuitions about juries and judges should not be accepted uncritically. The data simply do not exist to establish that judges remember more of the presented evidence than does the jury as a group, and there is little reason to accept such an assumption about judges. Judges, after all, are just as human as jurors; their fundamental abilities do not appear to differ from those of the rest of us. Reid Hastie, Steven D. Penrod, and Nancy Pennington, leading researchers who have studied a group's ability to recall more evidence than individuals, conclude that the "group memory advantage over the typical or even the exceptional individual is one of the major determinants of the superiority of the jury as a legal decision mechanism."[5] The group performs better than even the extraordinary individual. In all likelihood, almost always the collective memory of the jury is superior to the individual memory of the most highly qualified judge.

GROUP INTERPRETATION OF EVIDENCE

A jury not only recalls evidence better than an individual, it interprets it better. The value of a piece of evidence is not always obvious. A fact-finder must determine its worth. To do this, the fact-finder first has to assess the credibility of the evidence's source. When a witness states that the defendant was familiar with guns, the fact-finder has to determine if that witness was telling the truth. But even if the witness were telling the truth, the importance of the evidence may still be unclear. The fact-finder must consider the defendant's familiarity with guns and calculate its significance to the case. This process may be a difficult and contentious one because often diverse inferences can be drawn from one piece of information. Professor Robert Burns provides a good illustration: "Did the fact that the criminal defendant had four beers before an accurate shooting of the victim make it more or less likely that he did the killing? Which is the more powerful inference: that the beers lowered his inhibitions, or that they made it less likely that he could have performed the shooting?" In each case one can ask which inference is the "more universal," and then, more important, which inference is the more compelling *under the particular circumstances of this case,* themselves in dispute.[6]

Consider this dramatic example. A man is killed with a switchblade. The prosecution proves that the accused is familiar with switchblades. For most of us, such evidence increases the likelihood that the accused is the killer. In *Twelve Angry Men* one of the jurors is familiar with these knives. He maintains, however, that experienced switchbladers would not have stabbed as the killer did. From this perspective, the murderer, in fact, was unlikely to be versed in the use of this weapon, and the evidence connecting the defendant to switchblades actually reduced the likelihood that he was guilty. The other jurors had not been aware of this possible implication, but the group deliberation forced them to consider it.

This is not merely dramatic license. Real jurors have in essence reenacted the scene. "James Levine, dean of [New York City's] John Jay College of Criminal Justice, . . . said his doctorate was useless as he struggled to decide whether a defendant had intended to pop a man's eye out during a subway brawl, or whether it had been accidental. 'I got educated by a guy who had an education in street fighting,' Professor Levine said of a fellow juror. 'He knew what blows you use to hurt and not hurt. He educated me, with all my degrees.' "[7] As a result, Levine rendered a more fully considered verdict than he would have had he been acting in isolation, as a judge in a bench trial would have.

Examples of this phenomenon abound. In one trial it was clear that the defendant had killed, but not whether the killing was a first-degree murder or some lesser degree of homicide. The deliberating jurors found to their surprise that the relevant evidence had multiple, divergent possible meanings. Hazel Thornton, one of the jurors, wrote in a diary she kept during the trial, "Now we are debating the concept of 'premeditation.' We made a list of supporting and contradicting evidence, and the funny thing is that a lot of the same items are on both lists." A commentator on Thornton's diary stated, "One of the most significant aspects of Thornton's diary is the depiction of the deliberation process when the jurors finally began to discuss the evidence. The thoroughness with which that jury considered each alternative and the breadth of discussion about how to interpret the evidence are truly impressive."[8]

Evidence can have more than one meaning, and when a possible interpretation is not recognized and analyzed, the resulting decision has not been as fully considered as it might have been. Just as a group can recall more evidence than an individual, a group is likelier to recognize and consider more implications of the evidence. Indeed, jurors will often catch the significance of some evidence that the attorneys have not spotted. In one trial, a teenage witness claimed to have seen the defendant commit the murder, but the jurors were not sure whether the witness had truly been at the scene at the time of the crime or only after it happened. Some jurors, however, noticed the implication of a taped statement by the witness. A juror who talked with the attorneys after the case stated, "I do not know if [the prosecutor] recognized immediately how damaging to his case the tape was. (When the defense attorneys first heard it, even they did not appreciate the full significance of Clarissa's remark: 'There were lots of cops around but I couldn't find one.')" The jurors concluded that if she had been testifying about events when police were present, she was describing incidents that happened only after the murder had been committed.[9]

As a group debates competing inferences drawn from the evidence, a related benefit can occur. Not only may an individual in the group be required to consider perspectives and interpretations that otherwise would not have occurred to her, she may also begin to rethink her positions as she is forced to articulate them to others. For example, a juror in the trial of Bernhard Goetz, who shot several youths as they surrounded him on a New York City subway, writes that one of the issues for the jury was whether Goetz had the intent to kill. "There was then a heated discussion, with me arguing that the intent was present as I have believed all along. Searching for a way to convince [another juror], however, I devised an argument that in fact did the opposite, and I wound up deciding that I had been wrong."[10] If the confessional juror had been deciding alone, this reflective process is unlikely to have occurred.

OVERCOMING BIAS AND PREJUDICE

In a similar fashion, a jury decision is more likely to confront and overcome biases and prejudices than an individual determination. The jury selection process, as will be discussed in Chapter Nine, attempts to weed out the obviously biased, with the result that those who sit on juries may be more openminded than the average person. Even so, no one is free of bias. Irrational preconceptions can distort how we see, recall, and interpret information, including courtroom evidence. A judge acting alone, however, will often be unaware of his or her biases and have little chance, therefore, of overcoming them. Such awareness is more likely to be forced on a person in a group because the prejudiced misconceptions may be confronted and corrected by others.

For example, in the Juan Corona trial, one juror had made inferences based on the conclusion that "Corona was unusually neat for a Mexican." A few moments later another juror replied, "In my experience it is not unusual for Mexicans to be neat. My son-in-law is Mexican, Chicano. . . . He works [as a Sacramento cop] at night and he goes to college in the daytime and he studies so much that my daughter has returned to junior college so she can keep up with him. . . . He's an undercover agent. He has long hair. . . . And when he's off duty he's neat, and he's Mexican!"[11]

The group setting can help overcome prejudice in another way. A jury is in essence a small public assemblage of strangers, and many in such situations try to put their best foot forward. Furthermore, in the jury room, jurors are often trying to persuade one another; to be an effective persuader, a juror may find that she will have to try to overcome her own biases. When Melvyn Zerman wrote about his experiences as one of twelve white jurors on a murder trial, he listed the qualities he found in the jurors and concluded that prejudice was the biggest problem. He, however, then concluded, "Ironically, I think now that where the jury is most to be commended was in the painfully conscious effort nearly all of us made to look beyond our prejudices."[12]

This is not to say that jurors are always able to overcome their biases. That is too much to hope from any collection of human beings, but prejudice can be less a determining factor in the group decision making process of a jury than it will be when individuals make determinations alone.

STRENGTH IN DIVERSITY
AND THE NARROWNESS OF JUDGES

The jury as a group is likelier than an individual to overcome prejudices, to recall more of the evidence, and to consider more of the implications of that evidence. Beyond those strengths, though, is another. A group has the potential to transcend the intellectual and experiential limitations of each of its members. A body that has had more life experiences to bring to bear in weighing and interpreting the evidence will be better at those tasks than a more circumscribed body. A heterogeneous assemblage should, therefore, be the best one for overcoming prejudices and recognizing evidentiary possibilities. What might be seen as a weakness—the nonprofessionalism of the jury—turns out to be a strength. This amateur assembly is more likely to bring desired diverse experiences to the evidence than would a collection of professional judges. Indeed, judges may be particularly inept at such assessments because their experiences are often quite limited.

Judges clearly come from a restricted stratum of society. Even today, the judiciary is disproportionately more white and male when compared to the larger society. Most judges are also older than the average age in the community. Few twenty-somethings sit on the bench. In a country where the average salary is under $50,000, judges are uniformly affluent. Judges tend to share a similar educational and work history. In short, judges are different from most of society.

Furthermore, the judicial job itself is isolating. Social intercourse narrows for a judge. Judges should care about the appearances of impropriety, and once the judicial mantle is donned, conversations with friends who are lawyers and others who come before the courts cannot be as freewheeling as before. Judges also become isolated simply because other people often act differently around judges. In many instances, the mere mention of the title "judge" can inhibit behavior in others. A friend of mine once told me, "I was at a child's birthday party with my four-year-old. In walked a judge. All of sudden, I don't know why, I felt that I had to elevate my conversation." My friend, who has had a lot of experiences with judges as a trial attorney, is surely not alone in tending to treat judges differently from "ordinary" people. As a result, the social experiences of judges are often confining.

The unusual way judges are treated on the job is also limiting. They don distinctive clothes that set them apart. They sit on an elevated platform, literally looking down on everybody else and forcing others to look up to them. People must stand when a judge enters the courtroom; they must be quiet because she says so; they tend to laugh at her jokes whether funny or not; they must try to respond respectfully no matter what she says; and so on. Five, ten, twenty years of this dynamic may give the judge a different view of the world than others have, sequestering them even further from more usual perspectives. As Paul Carrington has observed, "Judges are becoming increasingly isolated on the hilltop of class pretense."[13] Consequently, judges are unlikely to have as many life experiences to bring to bear on the interpretation of evidence as would a group that comes from a broader cross section of the community.

It is true that in their courtrooms, trial judges hear many things about the lives of others. This, perhaps, expands a judge's horizons, but the courtroom's contrived world gives little firsthand experience of the situations described. For example, a criminal court judge may frequently hear about police stops and assume that, therefore, he truly understands them. But hearing testimony from a police officer in a well-lit courtroom with clerks, bailiffs, and spectators in attendance and a respectably dressed accused sitting at a defense table can never truly teach someone about the fear, bravado, weariness, and adrenaline the police officer and the apprehended citizen experience on a dark street corner with no one else present. If a judge can really understand such circumstances, it is not from the context of the courtroom but from outside it. The odds are better that someone in a group drawn from diverse segments of the community will have a valuable insight into such a situation than will a judge or even a collection of judges. And when that perspective and other views from the group are shared with one another, the group will have a better chance of correctly assessing the information than will a judge.

Simply put, a judge's experiences are so limited and distinctive compared to those of society at large that a judge is not a particularly good person to interpret evidence when that interpretation depends on ordinary life experiences. A collection of citizens with more diverse experiences—a jury—will be better at recalling the evidence, overcoming prejudices, and identifying and considering the various meanings of the information presented.

GROUP ADVANTAGE IN COMPLEX MATTERS

Litigation today, however, increasingly concerns complex scientific and mathematical matters, from the effects of DNA typing to epidemiological evidence of whether a substance has caused a cancer to a statistical analysis of a company's employment practices to see if it has illegally discriminated. Because evaluation of such evidence does not depend on a commonsense perspective enhanced by diverse life experiences, the advantages of juror over judge seem to disappear. The ordinary juror, perhaps with a year or two of college but no training in the relevant disciplines, may be ill-equipped to handle such information. A judge, who is better educated than the average juror and who may have had the opportunity from repeated trials to have experience with such information, would seem to be the better decision maker. Perhaps, then, while juries tend to decide ordinary cases more effectively than judges, it is judges who are better able to interpret facts involving complex information.

This logic, however, is not supported by any empirical information. Richard Lempert states, "Judges have not cooperated in studies of themselves as they decide complex cases; they seldom participate as subjects in simulation studies and have not done so in studies simulating complex litigation; and they seldom grant interviews in which they explain how they understood the evidence in complex cases."[14] Furthermore, this logic ignores a reality. As Michael Saks points out: "There are these simple facts: Judges are lawyers; lawyers are people who, disproportionately more than most educated Americans, are uncomfortable with quantitative, scientific, and technological information; avoided it as students, and are incompetent with it as adults. By contrast, a well assembled jury containing a high school science teacher, an accountant, or an engineer, should have greater potential than the average judge to understand complex technical or quantitative evidence."[15]

It may be that the average judge deals better with technical information than does the average juror, but this is not the appropriate comparison. The judge must be compared not to individual jurors but to the jury as a whole, and that body often includes people who have a better grasp of the material than does the judge. Kenneth M. Hoyt, a federal trial judge, writes:

> This is not to say that juries necessarily do well in complex cases. All those without technical backgrounds have difficulty in assessing scientific and statistical information, and there is no guarantee that either judges or juries will get it right. In today's culture, jurors bring a high level of problem solving experience into the jury room. A jury panel of twelve persons, more often than not, is composed of persons with an average of fourteen years of formal education and a lifetime of practical experience. The panel includes professionals, business men and women, instructors, and a number of quasi-professional persons. Thus, the jury's ability to take its problem solving skills into the jury room and incorporate them into the deliberative process, debunks the media's notion that jurors are incapable of handling complex civil cases.[16]

Once again, a diverse group making the many kinds of factual determinations that are demanded in court has incredible strengths. A character in Gerald Bullett's novel *The Jury* captures this view of that decision making body. The defendant's loyal friend, who worries that the jury does not know the defendant well enough to recognize his innocence, muses to himself, "In any group of twelve persons you get a few good fellows, don't you?"[17] You also stand a chance of getting knowledgeable ones.

As stated above, juries do not always perform well in complex cases. Those without expertise often find it hard to evaluate scientific and statistical information, and judges and juries may or may not get it right. How are we to assure that the increasingly technical cases heard in the twenty-first century receive a knowledgeable review? Perhaps judges should be specially trained for the task. To some extent such education already goes on. Books have been produced and seminars held to introduce judges to basic scientific and statistical principles. This might make attentive judges more conversant with some technological fundamentals, but, still, compared to the education of scientists or statisticians who testify, this training is unlikely to make judges truly proficient interpreters of scientific and mathematical evidence.

We could, however, develop a cadre of judges with true technical knowledge and let them decide all scientific disputes that emerge in court. This new judiciary would probably do better than existing juries in deciding scientific issues. Even if such new-style judges did exist, however, such a judiciary would have the advantage over juries only in cases involving technical or scientific issues. These are but a small percentage of litigated cases, and juries would still have the advantage in their ability to evaluate ordinary evidence.

Moreover, even in cases with complex evidence, juries might still perform better than technologically trained judges. Specialized education would help with only some of the issues in the cases where it even applied. For example, a person may sue, claiming that a manufacturer's PCBs caused his small cell carcinoma. Perhaps a properly trained person could decide the issue of whether PCBs can cause this disease better than a jury can (and also better than current judges can), but if the technically trained judge does determine that PCBs can cause such harm, a fact-finder might still have to resolve whether the plaintiff did, in fact, encounter the substance, the extent of any exposure, and whether the defendant had produced the particular offending PCBs. Scientific training will not help resolve these issues. Their resolution depends partly upon the question that arises in every case: Is a witness telling the truth?

DETERMINING CREDIBILITY FROM DEMEANOR

Evidence evaluation begins with an assessment of witness credibility. Testimony may be false for a number of reasons. The witness may simply be lying. More probable, however, is that the witness has failed to perceive or remember accurately. If we ask ten people to observe an event, perceptions will differ. If we further ask those people to recall the incident a day, a month, or a year later, those individual recollections will vary. Because our memories and perceptions can be inaccurate, it is to be expected that when people testify, their testimony will contain flaws. Thus, a fact-finder must assess both the likelihood that a witness is lying and the likelihood that an assertion is based on incorrect perceptions and memories.

Some research has been done on people's ability to detect lies. Many of us believe that we are good at translating subtle cues—awkward posture, beaded sweat on an upper lip, hesitations in speech—into a determination of whether someone is lying. Most of us are wrong, however; research indicates that few are good at spotting liars from their demeanor. When asked to detect lies based on demeanor, most people score at chance levels or only slightly higher. Thus, several studies of people trying to determine lies from nonverbal behavior found the majority of those tested scored from 45 to 60 percent, with an average accuracy of 57 percent. Random guessing would have yielded an accuracy rate of 50 percent.[18]

One reason liars are not easily detected is that most people are proficient liars. This is in part because we get so much practice. One study had participants keep a diary for a week of conversations that lasted for at least ten minutes and record lies they told during these exchanges. "The study revealed that lying is a daily life event. On average, people lied almost twice a day or in one quarter of the interactions with others. Of all the people they interacted with over the week, they lied to 34%." Perhaps because people lie so often, research has shown, "there is no typical non-verbal behaviour which is associated with deception. That is, not all liars show the same behaviour in the same situation, and behaviours will differ across deceptive situations. . . . The complicated relationship between non-verbal behaviour and deception makes it very difficult or even impossible to draw firm conclusions about deception solely on the basis of someone's behaviour."[19] The problems of correctly detecting deception at trial are compounded by the fact that lying is easier and consequently harder to detect when the liar has had time to plan the lie.[20]

Research shows that most people are not good at detecting lies, and nothing indicates that we are better at determining when sincere assertions are wrong because of faulty memories or perceptions. Ordinary people are not good truth-determiners from merely observing a person and hearing him speak. Because juries are made up of ordinary people, this seems to damn the use of juries as determiners of fact.

Jurors are amateurs. They come together for a case and then disband. They cannot learn from extensive courtroom experience. Are judges better? They are practiced in making factual determinations; they repeatedly have to decide whether witnesses tell the truth. Judges are professionals. In most areas of life, the trained and experienced perform better than amateurs. By this logic, judges should be better than jurors at determining whether someone is telling the truth. In fact, however, judges are no better at lie detection than are "ordinary" people. Indeed, as a recent research summary states, "Trial court judges . . . demonstrated little more skill at picking out prevaricators than a pipe fitter or bus driver pulled from the street."[21]

Researchers are uncertain whether people can be trained to improve at detecting lies. Studies conflict, some indicating that training people to detect lies improves that ability, others demonstrating that such training actually impairs the ability. Even the favorable studies, however, revealed only limited improvement, increasing accuracy from a paltry 54 percent to a less-than-impressive 57 percent, a very slight move away from the random accuracy rate of 50 percent. Aldert Vrij, a leading scholar on the subject, has concluded that to improve people's ability to discern a lie, more needs to be known about the rare individuals who are good at spotting deception. "Obviously it is only possible to learn from good lie detectors when it is clear which cues they use when they detect lies. Unfortunately, this is still unknown, as hardly any research has been conducted to find out what makes a person a good lie detector. The ability to detect lies is not correlated with gender, age or experience in interviewing. Men are as skilled as women, older lie detectors are not superior to younger ones, and those who are experienced in interviewing suspects are not better than those who lack such experience. Nor is the ability to detect deceit correlated with being confident."[22]

Even if training in lie detection were possible, the traditional education of judges does not include it. Judges go to law schools, which do not teach students how to improve credibility assessment. Courses on contract law, for example, do not include instruction on whether perceptions are accurate; civil procedure does not prepare one to ferret out an inaccurate memory; and property law does not teach a person to tell when a person is lying.

Although trial judges have not been trained to assess credibility, their daily courtroom experience, which can include many credibility assessments, might seem to make them better at such determinations than the average person. This conclusion, however, ignores how often we who are not judges appraise truthfulness. We do so whenever we seek information from a teenage son who is late, inquire of a neighbor about the best route to a restaurant, or ask a spouse how an outfit looks. We also do it, perhaps less consciously, whenever we read a newspaper or watch a news show. The judge is not likely to have more experience than the average person in making such assessments; the judge merely has more experience making them in a courtroom.

It should not be surprising, then, that those whose professions involve the detection of deception are apparently no better at this task than the general public. A summary of studies involving federal law enforcement personnel, federal polygraphers, and police found that most fell in the range of 45 to 60 percent accuracy in lie detection, with an average accuracy rate of only 54 percent. In other words, they do no better than the rest of us in detecting lies from nonverbal behavior. The major difference is that the police are, unjustifiably, more confident than the general public in their assessments.

One of the reasons that we are not good lie-catchers is our frequent failure to receive feedback that facilitates learning. Vrij maintains that people fail to obtain "adequate information as to [whether] their truth/lie judgements are either right or wrong," making learning difficult.[23] Judicial credibility appraisals receive equally limited feedback. Judges may make many decisions about who is telling the truth, but they seldom find out whether their determinations were right. If we had a mechanism to determine whether trial assessments were correct, we would have little need for the trials themselves.

So it is that neither judge nor juror is particularly good at determining credibility from a speaker's demeanor. Once again, however, the diverse assemblage of a jury offers advantages here as it does elsewhere. Research shows "that it is more difficult to detect lies when the liar and lie detector do not share the same ethnic background. . . . [N]on-verbal behaviour is culturally mediated and therefore must be interpreted with a background knowledge of the culture." A witness's ethnicity is more likely to match the background of at least one member of a jury than it will the judge's. Furthermore, if judges are like police detectives in their assessments of liars, the jury provides a further advantage. A study showed that "even though detectives did not successfully identify the liars, the level of agreement among them about who was lying and who was telling the truth was high. Because many detectives made similar decisions, their judgements must have been based on the same cues, or they must have processed the cues in a similar manner." Judges may be similar—not good at detecting liars, but generally agreeing on who is lying. If so, judges as a group will have a systematic bias in credibility assessments. A diverse jury will not share the same partiality among all its members, and the group will have more opportunity to transcend this kind of prejudice than would a judge or even an assemblage of judges.[24]

Decades ago distinguished commentators suggested that our trial process would eventually move away from the traditional analysis of testimony because advances in "psychoanalytical, narcoanalytical and electronic techniques and devices, motivational research and chemistry" would allow greater insight into the human mind, obviating the need for subjective assessments. Despite such predictions, however, infallible credibility appraisals belong only to science fiction, and we must still rely on imperfect human beings to resolve legal disputes. Indeed, even if scientific methods for detecting lies were faultless, the human judging of legal disputes would not end because, once again, outright lying is only part of the reason why testimony might not be the truth. The perfect lie-catcher would still not detect assertions that are faulty because of a mistaken perception or memory. Furthermore, even with an infallible truth machine, we still would need people to make courtroom determinations, for, as we have seen, the meaning of evidence cannot be calculated simply by some objective, quantitative measure. It requires a human being.[25]

CREDIBILITY DETERMINATIONS
THROUGH STORY CONSTRUCTION

The ability to assess witness credibility from demeanor would be crucially important if the jury weighed each individual and piece of information separately and kept a running tally in order to reach a verdict. This atomistic approach would require jurors to immediately appraise the credibility of each witness, placing heavy reliance on witness demeanor.

Jurors, however, do not operate this way. Instead, like the rest of us, they assemble separate pieces of information to form a story. W. L. Bennett and M. S. Feldman describe this holistic approach in their book *Reconstructing Reality in the Courtroom:* "Much of the meaning and, therefore, the interest and importance of social activity depend on who does what, for what reasons, through what means, in what context, and with what sort of prologue and denouement. . . . [S]tories are everyday communication devices that create interpretive contexts for social action."[26]

Organization of information into stories seems to be an almost instinctive, human activity. "Investigators in many different fields . . . have concluded that narrative forms the deep structure of human action. . . . Or, as Barbara Hardy put it, 'We dream in narrative, day-dream in narrative, remember, anticipate, hope, despair, believe, doubt, plan, revise, criticize, construct, gossip, learn, hate and love by narrative.' "[27] We all create, tell, and use stories constantly. When jurors form stories, they do it "first because a story is a handy analytic device for organizing large amounts of information. It serves as a *filter,* a device for reducing a vast array of facts into manageable proportions. Second, it functions as a *framework* for organizing, situating, and interrelating facts. If jurors did not have such a framework, even a crude one, they might find it quite difficult to understand the evidence."[28]

Only through narratives can we order and manage a vast amount of often complex information. Stories organize data, allowing us to make judgments about it. As Norman Finkel notes, the fact that the king in *Hamlet* puts poison in a cup can be interpreted in many ways. "We could construe the poisoning as murder, suicide, accident, or mistake—and these do not exhaust the possibilities. It is only when we set the act within a social context that meaning emerges."[29] Significance is determined by fitting the act into a particular story, and only then is judgment possible.

Jurors transform evidence into stories to organize that information and to be able to make the necessary judgments demanded of them. They do not, however, simply make up stories unrelated to what has happened during a trial. The fact-finders are trying to make sense of the evidence, and *that evidence, consequently, drives the story.*

Trial evidence alone, however, is not sufficient. Too many narrative gaps remain. Jurors need to use their own background knowledge and common sense in addition to the trial evidence to construct meaningful explanations of what they have heard. The result is generally a chronologically organized series of events held together by what the jury thinks are human motives and goals. Hastie and Pennington, who have extensively studied story construction, state, "The story by the juror will consist of some subset of events and causal relationships referred to in the presentation of evidence, *as well as* additional events and causal relationships inferred by the juror."[30]

Attorneys may suggest the string of events, but ultimately the explanation is one constructed by the jurors using the trial evidence. Since, however, evidence can have multiple meanings, a jury may be able to find more than one story to fit that evidence. To make a decision, a juror comes to accept one story as the "best." According to Hastie and Pennington, a story's likely acceptance as the favored one depends on its coverage and coherence. "A story's *coverage* of the evidence refers to the extent to which the story accounts for the evidence presented at trial. The greater the story's coverage, the more acceptable the story will be as an explanation of the evidence."[31]

The coherence of a story depends upon its consistency, plausibility, and completeness. A story should have "in laymen's terms, 'all its parts.'" An account with missing information is suspect, but "completeness also depends on the extent to which a story's component episodes and events are 'glued' together with (usually inferred) beliefs about motives, plans, and intentions. A story in which many interepisode links are missing or attributed to coincidence is less complete and less convincing."[32]

Finally, the singularity of the explanation matters. "If there are multiple coherent explanations for the available evidence, belief in any one of them over the others will necessarily be diminished. If there is a single coherent story, this story will be accepted as the explanation of the evidence."[33] Jurors, of course, do not simply want a story; they want the right story.

Jurors assess witness credibility within the context of the emerging story. Typically, they do not appraise the demeanor of an individual witness and then add or subtract those appraisals from previous determinations of other witnesses. Juries do not do continuous on-line computations. Jurors measure testimony against possible stories. Demeanor, consequently, is not as crucial in judging truthfulness as is the plausibility of what is asserted in light of all the evidence.

For example, juror Mark Lesly reports that during deliberations in the trial of Bernhard Goetz, a fellow juror stated that he did not believe that a witness was telling the truth. Lesly continues, "This was the first time we had discussed the credibility of a witness, and we established then a pattern that we followed throughout: if we decided to disbelieve testimony, we needed a plausible motivation for the witness to lie, or a plausible reason why the witness's recall might be wrong." In doing this, jurors did not examine isolated testimony, but discussed how it fit with other information in the trial. "Our discussion of Christopher Boucher's testimony was focused on its many inconsistencies and the impossibility of some of what he claimed. The most glaring error was the recollection of what Cabey [a shooting victim] was doing when he saw Goetz fire the final shot." Although the witness stated that the victim had not moved, "it was obvious to us that unless Cabey did twist to the right, he could not have been hit at the angle of the bullet that entered his body." As the deliberating jurors considered more of Boucher's testimony, they concluded that for the witness's "account to be correct, there also would have been an audible separation between the fourth and fifth shots, and that separation had not been noticed by *any* of the eight other eyewitnesses who had testified before us. We considered this to be highly improbable, given the circumstances and loudness of the shots." After analyzing more of that witness's testimony, the jurors "agreed that there was a great deal of reasonable doubt as to the veracity of Boucher's testimony. No one really felt that Boucher was lying, but we believed he could have been mistaken about what he thought he had seen."[34]

In assessing this testimony's credibility, the jurors did not view it in isolation with a concentration on the witness's demeanor. Instead, they evaluated the testimony in light of other evidence. That other information led them to develop a story about what had happened in the subway car. Indeed, in this deliberation, the emerging account was artfully articulated by the juror Moseley, who drew cartoon figures and stuck them on a plastic overlay depicting the subway car. He moved them about to indicate how the evidence indicated what had happened. "Moseley's argument was also extremely persuasive, because for the first time he played out the entire scenario. In all of the eyewitness testimony we had heard, everyone had seen only bits and pieces of what had happened. And, because of all the photographs we'd been shown, there was a tendency to think of the whole confrontation as a series of fragments."[35]

Moseley had integrated much of the evidence into a coherent, plausible narrative. Boucher's testimony introduced inconsistencies and implausibilities into that story. The emerging story could be rejected or Boucher's assertions could be disregarded. Not surprisingly, the plausible narrative covering much of the evidence was accepted over Boucher's testimony.

Melvyn Zerman also describes coming to grips with a crucial issue of credibility during the murder trial he sat on: "It was on the fifth day that the crux of the trial stood plainly revealed. The jury would have to decide the fate of a seventeen-year-old boy simply on the credibility of three other teen-agers. There probably would be no other evidence to base a judgment on. How could we determine the truth of what those witnesses were saying when all we had were their words? How could we differentiate between deliberate lies and unintentional lapses of memories or perception?" Eventually Zerman reached the conclusion that the witnesses were not telling the truth, not because of their nonverbal behavior as they testified, but because their testimony could not be pieced together into a coherent whole. He reasoned that the defendant "may be guilty. I'm sure I will never know. But I find the testimony of those three kids so full of contradictions, inconsistencies, gross improbabilities—things I just cannot attribute to a failure of perception and memory—that the state's case sinks like a torpedoed boat."[36]

The trial of Juan Corona for multiple murders of migrant workers also showed how jurors make determinations by weighing evidence against other information to test for coherence, coverage, and plausibility. An important issue in that trial was how a receipt given to Corona had ended up in a victim's grave. The defense established that a garbage dump was a few hundred feet away from the burial site and suggested that the piece of paper had blown from the dump. The jury, however, concluded that this assertion was implausible and not consistent with other evidence. One juror noted that the trial's information established that Corona was neat and hung his receipts from a kitchen nail. "He is not the type of man to have discarded receipts with his garbage in the dump." Another concluded that the receipts were not likely to have blown a distance because "they were folded up when they were discovered in the grave. They were exactly the same as when the Del Pero meat clerk saw Corona fold them and put them in his shirt pocket." Finally, one juror questioned a holdout as they looked at the map of the area: "Now, is it more reasonable that those receipts, folded up as they were . . . blew from here, the garbage dump, along the ground or in the air, and got through all these trees, this orchard, and landed in the grave area two hundred yards away as the man who was burying Sample's body shoveled dirt into the grave? . . . Or is it, Naomi, more reasonable that these receipts, which the clerk at the meat company saw Corona fold and put in his shirt pocket, simply fell out of Corona's pocket as he was working with his shovel, bent over, putting dirt in the grave? . . . Now, the key here, Naomi . . . are the words, 'what is most reasonable.' . . . Reasonably speaking, the only story that makes sense here is that Corona put the receipts in his pocket and they fell out of his pocket at that grave."[37]

The jurors made inferences from the evidence presented, used the knowledge and ideas they had brought with them to the trial, and integrated it all to construct a story that seemed most coherent, consistent, and plausible.

PAYING ATTENTION

Juries also bring a fresh eye to what can be numbingly repetitious to attorneys and judges. In criminal cases, for example, an accused's defense generally is plucked from one of two broad classifications. The first is: "I didn't do it; some other person did it." The second defense admits: "I was involved in the event, but I contest the criminality of my behavior." These broad categories are repeatedly used. Thus: "I did not murder; he attacked me, and I only defended myself." "I did not possess the drugs; the cop is lying and planted them on me." Or, "When I walked out of the store with the unpaid-for dresses in my shopping bag, I was not trying to steal; I put them in there earlier planning to pay for them and had forgotten them—I made an honest mistake."

If one listens to enough trials, most can be stereotypically categorized, and therein lies a danger. When a decision maker views a case as one of many of the same sort, it is difficult for her to pay close attention to its distinctive qualities. When this happens, the notion of individual justice suffers because the case is being decided not on the presented evidence but on remembered patterns.

This can, and perhaps inevitably must, happen to the professional judge hearing testimony day after day. There is little the experienced judge has not already heard. Not so, however, for strangers brought together for just one case. As a result, juries are much more likely than judges to observe each case individually.

In early-twentieth-century England, G. K. Chesterton made similar points after having served on a jury himself. Chesterton realized that for most societal roles we increasingly want trained professionals, and this fueled a cry that experienced jurists should replace the nonprofessional jury. Society, he continued, should also realize that "The more a man looks at a thing, the less he can see it." Chesterton concluded:

Now, it is a terrible business to mark a man out for the vengeance of men. But it is a thing to which a man can grow accustomed, as he can to other terrible things; he can even grow accustomed to the sun. And the horrible thing about all legal officials, even the best, about all judges, magistrates, barristers, detectives, and policemen, is not that they are wicked (some of them are good), not that they are stupid (several of them are quite intelligent), it is simply that they have got used to it.

Strictly they do not see the prisoner in the dock; all they see is the usual man in the usual place. They do not see the awful court of judgment; they only see their own workshop. Therefore, the instinct of Christian civilisation has most wisely declared that into their judgments there shall upon every occasion be infused fresh blood and fresh thoughts from the streets. Men shall come in who can see the court and the crowd, and coarse faces of the policemen and the professional criminals, the wasted faces of the wastrels, the unreal faces of the gesticulating counsel, and see it all as one sees a new picture or a ballet hitherto unvisited.

Our civilisation has decided, and very justly decided, that determining the guilt or innocence of men is a thing too important to be trusted to trained men. It wishes for light upon that awful matter, it asks men who know no more law than I know, but who feel the things that I felt in the jury box. When it is a library catalogued, or the solar system discovered, or any trifle of that kind, it uses up its specialists. But when it wishes anything done which is really serious, it collects twelve of the ordinary men standing around.[38]

Because it is a diverse group, a jury is more likely to recall and thoroughly consider the evidence than is a judge. Because it is a transient group of amateurs, a jury is more likely to pay attention to the evidence than is a judge. Because it is brought together for just one case and then disbanded, the jury's concentration on the evidence is likely to be superior to that of a judge.

A SINGLE-ISSUE BODY

Although they perform state functions, juries differ strikingly from other governmental bodies. Because most such organizations are continuing entities, not single-issue assemblies, considerations other than the merits of an issue can enter into their decisions. Most decision makers, whether overtly or not, have to consider continuing relationships with colleagues, political supporters, lobbyists, media representatives, and the general public. A person may decide to vote a particular way not just on the merits of a particular issue, but for various extraneous reasons. I'll vote the way you want on this issue if you will vote the way I want on another. Even the decision of a life-appointed judge may be influenced, however subconsciously, by how it will be viewed as similar cases arise.

A jury, on the other hand, is a single-issue body. It is brought together to make one decision and then disbands. Because of this, the jury is likely to focus solely on the merits of the case presented. Because the jury vanishes after its verdict, neither its decision nor preliminary discussions need be constrained; most governmental bodies are constrained by how their decisions will affect future ones. Unlike other decision makers, a jury cannot profit from any particular decision. This, too, gives it strength to decide solely on the presented information. As a fictional juror in *Twelve Angry Men* noted, "We have a responsibility. This is a remarkable thing about democracy. . . . That we are notified by mail to come down to this place—and decide on the guilt or innocence of a man; of a man we have not known before. We have nothing to gain or lose by our verdict. This is one of the reasons we are strong."[39]

DECISION MAKING BY CONSENSUS

The jury's focus on fact-finding is reinforced by the proviso that it is authorized to act only when its members reach a consensus. Traditionally, "consensus" meant that all the jurors agreed to the decision. Although this definition has eroded (see Chapter Seven), most criminal juries and many civil ones still operate under the unanimity rule, and those that don't still require a consensus of at least three-quarters of its members.

Few formal governmental proceedings seek to persuade or inform other decision makers. The outcome of congressional votes, for example, is often known in advance, and the public debate rarely affects the result. Because minds are made up before the formal proceedings, members of Congress and senators feel little need to listen to their colleagues, as empty congressional floors regularly attest. Such debates seldom inform; listeners seldom learn. Instead, the "debates" are venting or showboating sessions directed at the folks back home or to the lobbyists in the galleries.

In legislative deliberations, the important discussions are frequently in the informal exchanges that precede the formal debate. Even then, office and hallway conversations are necessary only when it is not clear that one side will win. Once the outcome is evident, the majority does not have to convince the holdouts. When a faction does not have to be persuaded, its views do not have to be considered. Furthermore, these informal colloquies are often one-on-one or involve a mere handful of the total body and do not include all the decision makers at the same time. Consequently, few, if any, of the decision makers will hear what every member of the group may have to contribute on the issue.

Indeed, in many governmental bodies, people often cast a vote without being truly informed on an issue. Some subgroup of the whole, a committee, is often charged with the preliminary consideration of a matter. Others often assume that the committee has fully considered the issue and, depending upon the view of that subgroup, vote in accord with or against the committee's recommendation without fully exploring the matter for themselves.

A jury's consideration of a matter is much different. Under the consensus principle, each juror must come to an individual decision, and only when the requisite number of individual determinations coincide can a verdict be rendered. Individual decisions, however, must be made within a committee of the whole. This jury instruction is typical: "You should not deliberate at any time unless you are all together. It is your duty as jurors to consult with one another and to deliberate with a view towards reaching an agreement if you can do so without violating your individual beliefs. Each of you must decide the case for yourself, but should do so only after a consideration of the case with the other jurors, and you should not hesitate to change your opinion when convinced that it is erroneous. However, you should not be influenced to vote in any way on the question submitted to you by the single fact that a majority of the jurors, or any one of them for that matter, favors such a decision."[40]

A jury is a group, but its judgment is not a group decision in the ordinary sense. Instead, a jury verdict is a collection of distinct, individual decisions. This process does not allow a juror to take shortcuts and simply defer to others. Jurors, themselves, have recognized this important principle. After a long trial and lengthy deliberations in the Juan Corona murder trial, for example, the jury was eleven to one for conviction. The holdout announced that she wished to change her vote to let every one go home. One juror, however, responded, "Naomi, now listen to me. If you vote guilty the way you're talking right now, I for one will not accept your vote. . . . [I]t was an agonizing ordeal for me to change my vote from innocent to guilty, and you're not going to take an easy way out and say you're changing your vote because you're tired or because you want to please us." When the holdout insisted that she could switch, the foreman told her, "[Y]ou can change your vote, but only if you change your opinion and have conviction in your vote." When she then wished to ask the judge about her obligations, the foreman continued, "Naomi, you can't ask the Judge if you can change your vote but keep your own opinions. . . . Now come on, Naomi, let's you and I sit down and talk reasonably."[41]

This traditional requirement of jury unanimity produces a kind of consideration and debate unknown in other governmental bodies, a process that helps force a jury to assess thoroughly the information and its implications. As one juror on the Juan Corona case concluded about the holdout, "She was the best thing that could have happened to a jury. After all, she was making them talk and explain themselves beyond all reason."[42]

A juror has to try to persuade all jurors who disagree with him to his point of view. He cannot do this by offering some incentive unrelated to the case. He cannot offer a vote swap on some other matter. He cannot appeal to the jurors' past decisions. He cannot trot out concerns for upcoming elections. Although exceptions do occur, the juror's only legitimate path of persuasion centers on the presented evidence.[43] Furthermore, since each juror has to be concerned about convincing others, the group's various perspectives and memories about the evidence are likely to emerge for all to consider.

The resulting attempts to persuade will be dynamic. I am unlikely to influence you to adopt my position if I simply ignore what you say. A juror will not be persuasive unless he responds to what the others are saying. Within such a process, all views are likely to be truly considered by the entire body. Such give-and-take does even more. It undercuts rigid dogmatism, for by being forced to listen to others so that rational—hence, persuasive—responses can be made, the persuader puts himself in the position of also being persuaded. As Harry Kalven stated, "It is not merely that twelve heads may be better than one but that a verdict hammered out as a group product is likely to have important strengths."[44]

A jury is a group of laypeople deciding by consensus the facts in a single legal matter. They perform this fact-finding function remarkably well. Because the jury is a group, more evidence is likely to be recalled correctly. Because the jurors are diverse laypeople, the likelihood of understanding all the possible meanings and implications of the evidence is increased. Because the jury is a single-issue body, the jurors are likely to focus solely on the presented merits. Because the jurors must reach a consensus, the various possible perspectives are likely to emerge and be treated with respect. A viewpoint cannot just be ignored, but must be either accepted or refuted. For these reasons, jurors are forced to deliberate, to educate and be educated about the evidence in order to reach a decision. These characteristics of the jury intertwine to help assure a thorough consideration of the information presented at trial, thereby increasing the likelihood that the best verdict emerges.

Chapter 4 Juries and Community Values

Juries exist partly because they are surprisingly good finders of fact. Verdicts, however, often require something more than the simple application of law to determine facts. Often the trial decision maker must give specificity to a broad legal standard in order to resolve a dispute. This process should incorporate community values. Juries also serve this function well.

"FACTS," "LAW," AND VERDICTS

The maxim that juries decide facts and judges decide the law implies a sharp boundary between "law" and "facts." In this view, the contested fact is true or it is not. Furthermore, the law is precise, clear, and comprehensive. It requires no interpretation to be applied to factual determinations. Once the facts are determined, the application of the given law makes the resulting verdict inevitable.

This, however, is a gross oversimplification of our trial system. Verdicts do result from the determinations of such facts and the applications of such laws, but often something more complex is required.

Sometimes even when competing versions of past events have been resolved, the verdict remains unclear because the applicable legal principle is not precise enough to be easily or automatically applied to those determined facts. Instead, the very act of applying the legal norm in a particular situation requires an interpretation of that legal standard. The basic doctrines of personal injury law are the prime example.

Tort law states that a person who acts negligently and thereby causes harm owes damages for the resulting injuries. "Negligence," however, is impossible to define precisely because the ways in which people behave inappropriately to cause injuries are almost limitless. Any attempt to categorize negligent actions would be extremely time-consuming and still incomplete. The law, wisely, does not make such an attempt, but instead employs generalities. As one tort law treatise puts it, "Negligence refers to whether [a defendant] has taken the care of a reasonable person, whether by act or omission, in order to avoid the harms that might foreseeably flow from his actions."[1] The crucial concept—the care of a reasonable person—is hardly an exact formulation that, by itself, can tell us whether particular behavior was negligent or not. That standard cannot be applied to a particular situation without giving it more specific content.

For example, a jury may conclude that the defendant was driving ten miles below the speed limit, the conditions were foggy, and the traffic heavy when the accident happened. Was the driver negligent? The mere finding of these facts does not yield an answer. Someone still has to determine whether the defendant's conduct met the standard of "the care of a reasonable person" under those particular circumstances. The trial fact-finder does this, as indicated by a standard jury instruction: "When I [the judge] use the word negligence in these instructions, I mean the failure to do something which a reasonably careful person would do or the doing of something which a reasonably careful person would not do under the circumstances similar to those shown by the evidence. The law does not say how a reasonably careful person would act under these circumstance; *that is for you to decide.*"[2]

In making the negligence determination, the jury is not simply deciding a question of fact or simply deciding a question of law. Some would call the negligence decision a mixed question of law and fact; others might label it the application of a legal standard to specific facts. However it is categorized, the verdict requires more than a mere resolution of what happened. It also requires a qualitative assessment of the reasonableness of the conduct. The jury in essence must define the appropriate standard of care for a given situation.

Such a determination of standards is akin to, but not the same as, formal lawmaking. While the jury is giving definition to an imprecise norm, the jury's decisionmaking is ad hoc. It may bind the parties involved in the particular litigation, but unlike formal lawmaking, it will not obligate any future litigants or even future juries. The jury's determination of the standard is not published. The jury does not even explain how a reasonable person should have acted under the circumstances. Instead, the jury usually only announces whether the defendant is liable for the injuries, and the jury's determination as to the appropriate standard of care gets silently folded into that verdict. Nevertheless, even though it is determined in the shadows, the definition of the appropriate norm of reasonable care for the particular circumstances is an essential jury function. The jury must not only determine what facts or events occurred, but also measure those facts against a standard to which it must give content.

The same is often true for the damages decision. "Damages," it has been said, "even more than negligence itself[,] is law written by the jury." Damages are not set by a predetermined schedule, but are calculated for each case with the purpose of making the wrongfully injured person whole. This calculation is made by the jury, which is "left free to price the harm on a case by case basis."[3]

Parts of a damages decision, such as medical expenses and lost wages, can require a determination of past events. What medical bills resulted from the injuries? What was the plaintiff's salary before the accident? Other damage components, however, require something different. Because damages can compensate for future losses, the damages determination includes more than assessment of past facts. It can be a prediction or conjecture as to what would have happened had the injury not occurred. Other damages—such as for pain and suffering or the economic losses suffered by a small business owner—have large subjective components, and juries have wide discretion in assessing such damages. In essence, we ask the jury to define and apply the standards by which such components of damages should be measured.

Why does the jury have this job? The system endures at least partly because it is politically expedient not to change it. Even though juries have long held this authority, such responsibility could be stripped from juries and ceded to judges. We could limit the jury's role to the finding of facts. The judge would then use that information to determine whether the actions were negligent or how much damages should be. However, just as a diverse group has advantages over a judge in finding historical facts, a group is also more likely to consider thoroughly all the possibilities of what is reasonable in a particular situation. It will also consider more fully what damages do and do not accrue from a particular injury than will a single judge. Recognizing this, the Supreme Court upheld a ruling permitting a jury to decide a negligence issue even when the parties agreed about the underlying facts. *Railroad Co. v. Stout* concluded that a jury comprising people with varied life experiences can "draw wise and safer conclusions from admitted facts" than a single judge could.[4]

Juries, however, have another advantage when the determination involves standards that require specificity. Alexis de Tocqueville wrote in defense of American civil juries, "Laws are always unstable unless they are founded upon the customs of a nation; customs are the only durable and resisting power in a people." Norms intended to be applied to the entire community should reflect community values, and the norms underlying negligence and damages decisions are meant to apply to us all. The standard of care for a particular situation or the damages for a particular injury should apply equally to anyone in the same circumstances. While the legislature has the authority to set such specific standards, when it has not done so or cannot do so and the determination is left to a trial, the jury, drawn from the cross section of the community, is more representative of the diverse interests of the people than a judge. Hence, a jury is the more appropriate authority than a judge to apply the broad legal guidelines. As Harry Kalven put it, "And that with damages as with negligence itself, the law intends the jury to legislate interstitially, to fill out the vague general formula. On this view the jury's freedom and discretion is not by default but by preference—preference for the community sense of values as the standard by which to price the personal injury." George Priest, a critic of civil juries, has summarized: "In this view, the civil jury is a superior adjudicative institution for defining liability and evaluating damages when complex or conflicting societal values are involved. Many aspects of a factfinder's work in civil litigation require judgments that are in some sense difficult. . . . According [to defenders of civil juries], however, it is not the difficulty of a judgment per se that commends the institution of the civil jury, but the appropriateness of resolving the difficult judgment by the application of broad societal values."[5]

COMMUNITY VALUES IN ORDINARY CASES

Priest, however, has also questioned how often civil juries actually deal with such "broad societal values." Having studied two decades of records of the civil courts of Cook County, Illinois, he concluded that while personal injury trials absorbed approximately 70 percent of the courts' time, most of those cases involved routine injuries, such as a single broken leg or whiplash, while cases involving complex social values such as the valuation of damages for paralysis or the loss of a body part were a distinct minority. Priest concluded, "Chicago civil juries spent 19.62 percent of their time in evaluating damages in cases that arguably could involve complex or conflicting societal values. In contrast, they spent 52.91 percent of their time on routine injuries." Priest then asked, "What good reasons are there for convening twelve citizens to determine damages in the 52.91 percent of civil cases where the most serious injury suffered by the plaintiff was a cut, fracture, strain or bruise?"[6]

One answer is that individual determinations of damages will often be more variable and erratic than a group's decisions. If we ask 120 people individually to assess damages for an injury, we might find that the average award is $50,000, but that the range spans from $1,000 to $100,000. If we give that same information to another 120 people but divide them into ten panels of a dozen each and ask for group determinations of damages, we might still find that the mean award is $50,000, but probably not the extremes found in the individual awards. The range of assessments from the groups is likely to be narrower and less variable than the individual decisions.

Jury studies confirm this effect. For example, in one research effort, the standard deviation—a statistical tool to measure variation in data—from individual damages assessments made before deliberation was more than seven times higher than those from jury verdicts from these same people after they had deliberated.[7] Different juries do not always settle on the same damage awards, but the range of the assessments is not as broad as it is for individual determinations.

Because jury damages decisions are less variable than those made by individuals, there is more consistency. Consistency is, of course, important to the legal system, because the law seeks to have like situations treated alike. Consistency, however, is also important because it promotes predictability. The more consistent verdicts are, the better a knowledgeable person can estimate what a verdict ought to be, and the easier it is for competing parties to agree on an appropriate resolution without trial.

Intuition, however, might lead one to suspect that judges, professionals involved repeatedly with damage awards, should produce more consistency than juries. This hunch has effectively eliminated civil jury trials in England. In 1933, an act of Parliament guaranteed jury trials in civil cases that involved fraud, libel, slander, malicious prosecution, false imprisonment, seduction, or breach of a marriage promise. For all other civil suits, including personal injury cases, the judge was given control over whether a jury would decide the matter. In 1966, an English court concluded that judges would generally give sounder verdicts in civil cases than would juries: "We have come in recent years to realise that the award of damages in personal injury cases is basically a conventional figure derived from experience and from awards in comparable cases. Yet the jury are not allowed to know what that conventional figure is. The judge knows it, but the jury do not. This is a most material consideration which a judge must bear in mind when deciding whether or not to order trial by jury. So important is it that the judge ought not, in a personal injury case, to order trial by jury save in exceptional circumstances."[8]

While juries remain for the trials of serious crimes in England, for practical purposes that 1966 case ended English civil trials for all matters but libel. Its underlying rationale, however, is at odds with existing American law, which holds that there should be an independent determination of damages in each case. Furthermore, the intuition that judges will be more consistent in setting damages is belied by American data. In one study, jurors awaiting jury duty were given a detailed description of an injury and asked to assess damages. The same materials were given to twenty-one senior lawyers, six of whom were former judges. The mean and median awards for both jurors and the legal professionals were about the same, but the individual jurors' range of awards was wider, from $11,000 to $197,000, than was the range given by the legal professionals, which was from $22,000 to $82,000. In other words, although the variability among legal professionals was substantial, it was less than that among jurors. Individual juror assessments, however, are not the proper grounds of comparison. As the researchers noted, "Damage awards are not rendered by individual jurors but by some combination of them, usually twelve or six, who combine their perspectives." With such combined views "the data show that a jury composed of twelve persons would, on average, yield more reliable, that is, less variable, damage awards than a single judge in a bench trial," and the same would also hold true for juries of six.[9]

Even with damages for routine injuries, juries are valuable because they are more consistent in determining the awards than are individual judges, but the value of civil juries for even routine cases goes beyond this. Before the damages issue is reached, liability has to be decided. If the defendant is not found liable, a result that occurs in roughly half the personal injury trials nationwide, the damages issue becomes moot whether the injuries were routine or not. Whatever the injuries, the jury is valuable for that liability decision whenever the determination depends on community values and whenever the evidence is best recalled, interpreted, and resolved by a diverse group instead of a judge.

THE POSSIBLE LEGISLATIVE FIX FOR DAMAGES

Damages are set for each case individually. They are not calculated by using predetermined, fixed schedules, but this practice is not immutable. Legislators could change it by enacting schedules for damages. Or they could set forth benchmark examples prescribing the appropriate damages for those situations and then command that other awards be set in comparison to the legislatively set amounts. The trial decision maker's discretion in setting damages would become more circumscribed, and the present role of juries in setting damages would be diminished.

Workers' compensation laws provide a general example for such a scheme. These laws, which were enacted in all states during the twentieth century, are based on the theory that accidents to workers should be treated like any other cost of business such as the breakage of equipment. Employers are liable for work-related injuries without regard to the employer's or employee's negligence. With the negligence question removed, the major issue becomes whether the injury derives from the job. If it does, compensation is awarded. The size of the award is not difficult because in most cases it is fixed by the workers' compensation statute, which contains detailed schedules of payment for specific injuries. The strengths of a jury add little to this system, and juries do not adjudicate workers' compensation claims.

Such a system does not exist, however, for personal injury claims generally. Workers' compensation laws were enacted because they offer benefits to both workers and employers. When an injury is covered by workers' compensation, it is the sole remedy, and the worker cannot seek additional damages for negligence. The employer benefits by having predictable costs from injuries, for the system requires compulsory insurance, which spreads risk and regularizes expenses. The worker "accept[s] a limited compensation, usually less than the estimate which a jury might place upon his damages, in return for an extended liability of the employer, and an assurance that he will be paid."[10] The essentials here are the elimination of negligence determinations and having insurance coverage that will cover all job-related injuries. So far, no meaningful efforts have been made to extend such a scheme to all possible injuries. Instead, we still rely on individual determinations of negligence and damages to decide when, and how much, compensation is owed for most injuries.

Legislatures could modify this existing scheme and reduce dependencies on juries by leaving the negligence system in place but enacting schedules for damages. Although some legislatures have set limits on various kinds of damages, they have seldom given guides or standards for what damages should be outside the workers' compensation arena. They have not, for example, mandated a compensation amount for the loss of a right arm of a thirty-year-old manual laborer. Legislatures have not set pain and suffering damages for a person who sustained third-degree burns over 50 percent of the body. Such figures could be used not only to award amounts for the particular named injuries, but also as a guide for damages for other harms.

Legislative mandates for damages have not happened for a number of reasons. First, it would be politically difficult. The attempt to set such damages would lead to at least political skirmishing and perhaps open warfare between those who frequently defend tort suits and those who seek to obtain awards. Moreover, legislators might find it unseemly to explain to constituents how they had come to the conclusion that the loss of an eye was worth a particular amount of money. Although some politicians criticize jury awards, many legislators simply find it "more convenient to blame juries for large awards than to try to convince the electorate that the traditional rules of compensation need to be changed."[11] Instead, our system continues to require case-by-case assessments of negligence and damages, and these determinations often benefit from the input of community or social values that a jury provides.

COMMUNITY VALUES AND TRIALS

Negligence cases are the prime example of a decision maker calling upon community values to apply imprecise laws, but they are not the only such cases. Our laws are dotted with such standards, including those assigning criminal responsibility. For example, murder in most jurisdictions includes not only the intentional killing of another, but also killing that results from callous and reckless disregard for human life or when, as some states put it, "the defendant's conduct evidenced a gross deviation from the standard of conduct of a law-abiding person in that situation."[12] Such standards are no more specific than "the standard of care of a reasonable person." Some authority has to determine what is "the standard of conduct of a law-abiding person" for the specific circumstances. Some authority has to further determine what is a "gross deviation" from that standard. Merely determining what historical events took place is insufficient to determine whether a murder occurred. Qualitative assessments of the accused's conduct still have to be made even after the facts have been determined.

Similarly, murder can be reduced to manslaughter when the killing has been provoked, with the usual test asking how a "reasonable person" would have acted under the provocation; a robbery trial issue can be whether an "ordinary person" would have been put in fear of bodily harm by a defendant's actions; and self-defense asks whether the defendant's conduct was that of a reasonable person in the defendant's situation. In each of these situations, the decision maker's job does not end with a simple determination of the facts. Basic facts have to be determined and then qualitatively assessed. As with a negligence determination, imprecise norms that should incorporate societal or community norms have to be applied.

In these instances, like others, the jury is generally a better representative of the community than a judge and is the more appropriate source for the normative assessments that the legislature has left to the trial decision maker. As legal scholar Gary Goodpaster states, "The jury is central to the norm theory . . . because only a body taken from a cross sectional representative group of the community can meaningfully project community norms. In this view, the criminal trial jury is the principal force in shaping and maintaining the structure of the criminal trial, because the jury represents the community, both symbolically and actually, and brings community consciousness, community values and culture into the system."[13]

To some, this view is old-fashioned. In his analysis of juries, Paul Carrington asserts, "America today is far more an aggregation of individuals than a community, and the conception of a verdict as an expression of community morality is simply in most places quaint." Even if Carrington's sociology were correct, however, the law still can require verdicts to incorporate normative assessments even after a fact-finder has resolved the basic facts of what happened. Somebody has to assess the appropriate standards and apply them, and we can expect that "there will be a greater sense of retribution and deterrence where the verdict is closely aligned to the attitudes of the community most directly affected by the offense." Even if the sense of community is not what it once was, the jury will usually be better than the judicial alternative.[14]

COMMUNITY VALUES AND PROOF
BEYOND A REASONABLE DOUBT

The frequency with which juries set norms should not be underestimated. Negligence cases constitute the majority of civil trials, and qualitative judgments about liability and damages are often required in these cases. Some crimes and their defenses also require such assessments, but, in fact, every criminal trial requires the decision maker to make such a determination. A criminal case is never simply about determining the historical facts. The jury has to determine whether the case has been proved beyond a reasonable doubt. The court will define "beyond a reasonable doubt," but that formulation will not, perhaps cannot, be precise enough so that all will agree on how to apply it in a particular case. The decision maker is given but a mere guideline to the meaning of this essential principle of criminal law. The fact-finder is left to give specific content to proof beyond a reasonable doubt within the context of the particular case. Indeed, the definition of reasonable doubt often seems presented in as murky a fashion as possible to give the decision maker wide-ranging discretion in determining what it means.

For example, in the trial of Juan Corona, after days of inconclusive deliberation, the jurors asked the judge to define reasonable doubt again. The court responded by rereading a common definition of that concept: "Reasonable doubt is defined as follows: It is not a mere possible doubt, because everything relating to human affairs, and depending on moral evidence, is open to some possible or imaginary doubt. It is that state of the case which, after the entire comparison and consideration of all the evidence, leaves the minds of the jurors in that condition that they cannot say they feel an abiding conviction, to a moral certainty, of the truth of the charge."[15]

The jurors, not surprisingly, struggled to understand. One of them tried to clarify: "I realize that this definition here at the end is hard to understand because it uses a negative to show a positive. It says . . . that reasonable doubt leaves the minds of the jurors in that state in which they cannot feel an abiding conviction to a moral certainty. But the key here is . . . 'reasonable,' not possible or imaginary. For, before this negative was given, the Judge had said that reasonable doubt is not a mere—why they used the word 'mere' here, I can't understand." After struggling further, this juror concluded, "I've got a headache. . . . It was so clear and then I lost it." Another juror picked up the baton, dropped it, and stated, "As a teacher I'll tell you, to use a negative to try to define something is like saying a horse is a horse because it's not an elephant and, I'll tell you, not only does this tend to mislead, but it's not proper. Oh, I'd like to give those men who wrote these legal books a piece of my mind."[16]

The jurors realized that the case hinged not only on the resolution of conflicting evidence, but also on their subjective reaction to the definition. "They knew that this was at the heart of their dilemma—not so much the actual evidence as the interpretation of the evidence in relation to how the Judge had read the law." Finally, they agreed only when one of the jurors said, "I guess what this all boils down to is that we should use common sense, reasonable common sense, and if we find a man guilty beyond all common-sense questions or reasonable doubts, well, then, that man is guilty by the law."[17]

Even when the charged crime or defense seems to require only an objective determination of what happened and the fact-finder does not have to set a norm for what constitutes wrongdoing, the decision maker still has to answer subjectively the most important question in a criminal trial: Has the charge been proved beyond a reasonable doubt?

"Beyond a reasonable doubt" cannot be defined precisely in the abstract, but can be determined only as it is applied in a specific context. The practical application of the "beyond a reasonable doubt" standard should reflect community standards. A jury, once again, can often do that better than a judge. At least, the jury tends to do it differently. Kalven and Zeisel's study concluded that in 11 percent of the instances when judges disagreed with the jury verdict, the jury had a more generous view than the judge of what constituted reasonable doubt.[18] The jury system has many reasons for existing, and one of them, as Laura Levenson has said, is that "by ensuring that community voices will be injected into the decisionmaking process, the jury trial serves the very practical purpose of ensuring greater respect for the verdict because it is based on community standards rather than on abstract notions of the law."[19]

Chapter 5 Abide the Issue

In Stephen Vincent Benet's *The Devil and Daniel Webster,* when Daniel Webster sets forth to battle the devil for the New Hampshire farmer's soul, Webster asks for a trial. Mr. Scratch hesitates, and Webster shouts, "Let it be any court you choose, so it is an American judge and an American jury. Let it be the quick or the dead, I'll abide the issue."[1]

Having the public abide, or accept, the issues resolved by our judicial system is crucial. A prime societal function of the court system is to provide for an orderly and peaceful way of settling disputes. The larger society wants individuals to use the courts instead of resolving their conflicts in the streets. We want disputants and others to accept court determinations so that the dispute ends and is not continued outside the courtroom. This public acceptance does not always occur, but examples of that rejection are noteworthy precisely because they are so rare. Overwhelmingly, the public accepts the results of the legal system. As Benet's Webster indicates, juries help ensure that.[2]

JURIES AND THE ACCEPTANCE OF VERDICTS

A community is more likely to accept verdicts when the decisions reflect or incorporate societal norms. The jury, as both the symbolic and actual representative of the community, is more likely to render verdicts based on widely accepted standards than are other authorities. The shared responsibility of a jury verdict also aids its acceptance within the community. When a single judge makes a legal determination that produces dissatisfaction, the discontent centers on that individual decision maker. The displeased can see the outcome as resulting from one person's whims, caprices, prejudices, stupidity, or lack of common sense. With the shared accountability of a jury's decision, however, the locus of any discontent is more diffuse and, consequently, less intense.

The fact that juries are composed of "amateurs" also promotes the acceptance of verdicts and dissipates dissatisfaction. The professional judge is a fixture. She will be there after the verdict is handed down and, therefore, can be a visible target for the disgruntled. The jury, however, comes almost mysteriously out of the community and flows back into it after the determination is made. In an important sense, the jury ceases to exist the moment it renders its verdict. More than a hundred years ago, Matthew Deady, despite his many criticisms of the jury, said much the same thing:

> Trial by jury helps to maintain the credit and authority of the court, by joining with it, for the time being, a respectable body of the people, whose presence and co-operation tend to identify the public and non-professional element of society with its proceedings, and make them in a sense their own; and by relieving it from the difficult and invidious task of passing upon questions of fact involving the motives, intentions, and integrity of parties and witnesses, it thereby shields it from the rancor and distrust of those who are discredited or prejudiced by the proceedings before it. A court is a bright and permanent mark for the arrows of disappointed litigants and professional envy and malice. But a jury has only a momentary existence, and is almost intangible. At the call of the law it comes forth from the people, hears the parties, gives its verdict, and passes away—is resolved into its original elements. In a free country, the losers must always be allowed to grumble, but the dissatisfaction with the action of the jury is not aimed at anyone in particular. It discharges itself in the air, and passes off as harmless as sheet lightning.[3]

Because juries are such a fixture of our legal system, we take many of their strengths and benefits for granted. It certainly is easy to overlook how well the jury system promotes acceptability of trial outcomes. One has to try to imagine a world of trials without juries, a world where all trials would be to the kinds of judges we now have. In the 1990s, many thought the verdict in O. J. Simpson's criminal trial was wrong. For them, the decision led to outrage, editorials, and jokes. Despite all the criticism of the outcome, however, society did accept it. Imagine, however, what would have transpired if the trial judge alone had rendered the not guilty verdict; imagine all the other controversial trials and the public reaction to them if a single judge had made each decision. We could expect similar outrage, editorials, and jokes—but now focused on the particular individual who had made the decision and who would be in a position to make similar determinations in the future. Would the public accept that judge's next controversial verdict?

Zechariah Chafee, Jr., in his classic study, *Free Speech in the United States*, examines a situation in which something like the eradication of jury trials did occur. In 1919, California created the new crime of criminal syndicalism aimed against the radical labor organization, the Industrial Workers of the World (IWW). This crime made it illegal not only to engage in acts of violence to accomplish "a change in industrial ownership or control, or effecting any political change," but also to teach or justify such doctrines, to publish material advocating such doctrines; or to organize or knowingly belong to a group advocating such doctrines. Criminal prosecutions followed, but juries typically refused to convict.[4]

Unhappy with the plethora of jury acquittals, the attorney general responded by getting an injunction against the IWW prohibiting that organization and its members from committing acts of criminal syndicalism. While criminal trials require juries, proceedings for violations of injunctions are actions in equity tried to a judge without a jury. In essence, then, California was trying people for crimes but depriving them of a jury and forcing them to submit to a bench trial. Chafee responded:

> Sooner or later we shall pay the price. In a jury trial, the responsibility is distributed. It does not all fall on the judge. The accused is convicted by men from the street, not very different from himself except in their freedom from crime. The jury takes up the slack, as it were. [With a single judge], there is nothing to take up the slack. The judiciary, the most delicate part of our political machinery, is subjected to a terrific strain when it is made to do unaided, and in highly controversial cases, work fitted for the rougher mechanism of the criminal law. . . .
>
> Experience has proved it wise that the public should have a fairly direct share in those functions of government that intimately affect the life of the average man; for instance, taxation, which may only be initiated by the branch of the legislature closest to the people, and punishment, which must be inflicted by a jury. . . . The use

of the injunction to put men in a prison without a jury trial for reasons that seem insufficient to a considerable body of their fellow-citizens is liable to produce a resentment that may eventually sweep away some judicial powers that had better be preserved, along with what can be spared.[5]

James Gould Cozzens's novel *The Just and the Unjust* offers another example of how the jury system protects the legal system generally and the judicial power in particular. A big-city drug dealer has been kidnapped and killed in a rural county. The jury convicts the defendants only of second-degree murder, but the facts seem to indicate that a first-degree murder with an automatic death sentence was the correct result. The verdict, however, has undeniable elements of justice. The FBI seems to have brutally beaten a confession from one defendant. The defendants may actually have been opposed to the killing done by another who is now dead. Whether a death sentence, even if legally required, was appropriate for this crime is ambiguous.[6]

In Cozzens's scenario, after the verdict has been reached, the central character, the assistant district attorney, disappointed with the jury's decision, talks with his father, a respected judge. The father states:

> The jury protects the Court. It's a question how long any system of courts lasts in a free country if judges found the verdicts. It doesn't matter how wise and experienced the judges may be. Resentment would build up every time the findings didn't go with current notions or prejudices. Pretty soon half the community would want to lynch the judge. There's no focal point with a jury; the jury is the public itself. That's why a jury can say when a judge couldn't, "I don't care what the law is, that isn't right and I won't do it." It's the greatest prerogative of free men. They have to have a way of saying that and making it stand. They may be wrong, they may refuse to do the things they ought to do; but freedom just to be wise and good isn't any freedom. We pay a price for lay participation in the law; but it's a necessary expense.[7]

The judge's point has a corollary. If resentments build up against a judge for his verdicts, that judge's decisions will inevitably be affected by these feelings. The jury, more easily than a judge, might be able to bend the law to reach a just result; also, the jury, with its shared responsibility, may often be more able than a judge to make the legally correct, but difficult, decision that will bring opprobrium from the community.

It is hard, especially when it is unpopular, to find a person guilty when there are severe consequences for the accused. It is hard, especially when it is unpopular, to exonerate a person who may be a criminal. It is hard, especially when it is unpopular, to tell one person that he must give his money to another. It is hard, especially when it is unpopular, to do the opposite—to tell, for example, the mother of the child born with a birth defect that she and her son will not receive the compensation from the company that manufactured a drug she believes caused the deformity. Correct, but unpopular, decisions may be made more easily by a group with shared responsibility than by an individual acting alone, especially when that group largely disappears after the decision and the individual has a continuing position requiring her to make other difficult decisions in the future.

Juries protect judges from the resentments that would naturally result if those governmental officers made all trial determinations. Consequently, our court system is perceived to be more legitimate than it otherwise would be. Juries also legitimate the legal system by being able to render decisions judges could not and by rendering unpopular verdicts that may be correct. Indeed, sometimes those in the system insist on jury trials for almost precisely these reasons. The trial of Bernhard Goetz provides an example.

Goetz claimed he was defending himself when he shot four men on a New York City subway in 1984. The case garnered inordinate interest because it encapsulated issues about urban crime, race and racism, gun control, self-defense, and vigilantism. Shortly before testimony was to begin, George Fletcher reports, the defense offered to plead guilty to two felony charges in a way that "would have seemed to vindicate Goetz in his confrontation with the four youths, and yet satisfy the public interest in condemning and deterring violent conduct on the subway. But the District Attorney refused the deal. It was too important, in his view, to try the case and let a jury of ordinary New Yorkers resolve the issues."[8]

The importance of the jury's role in helping to legitimate the legal system cannot be overstated. Even if we disregard what the data, evidence, history, and logic have shown—that juries are better finders of fact than judges; produce less variable verdicts than judges; succeed better at incorporating community values into verdicts than judges; and provide a needed buffer against professional government officials—juries fill an important role simply because they make verdicts more acceptable. This promotes a crucial function of the legal system: the peaceful resolution of disputes. What has been said about juries determining awards for pain and suffering can be more forcefully generalized to the entire jury system: "If there is no difference between jurors and professionals, the jury verdict may have the advantage of providing a sense of procedural justice and legitimacy to the award."[9]

A sense of procedural justice has a further benefit. We can hardly expect enthusiastic approval of a trial's outcome from litigants who have lost, but a trial heard by a jury may help them countenance the result. Social science research shows that people are more likely to accept a negative decision when they have had a fair hearing, or at least one they perceive as fair.[10] For most people, fairness requires a neutral arbiter, and because juries are perceived as fairer than judges—who are professional, government decision makers—society tends to view jury verdicts as more fair than judicial ones.

Only a few studies have examined the idea that jury trials lead to the ready acceptance of verdicts. One such study interviewed tort litigants, some of whose cases had been resolved by trial and the rest by settlement reached between the parties without a trial. Both groups expressed satisfaction with the results, but "litigants whose cases had been decided at trial were more satisfied with the procedural aspects than were litigants who had settled. . . . [T]rial litigants were more likely to see their proceedings as dignified and careful."[11]

The fact that juries make verdicts more legitimate, however, can be a mixed blessing. When a legal system is not seeking honorable goals, the jury can lend legitimacy where none should be granted. A colonial trial provides an example. In controversial and grossly unfair trials in New York in 1741, both whites and blacks were charged with conspiring together to commit arson and other crimes to aid a slave rebellion. Although the law required that only the whites receive jury trials, all those accused did. One historian concludes that the slaves were also given jury trials so that the outcome would not rest on the shoulders of a few officials. "Citizens would share the burden of judgment and be involved from case to case. That promised the judges and prosecutors a measure of insulation against charges of proceeding arbitrarily. . . . The decision of the king's men to have jury trials then was self-serving. It promised to strengthen their hand [and] protect them from public criticism."[12]

We can fault the jury system in such circumstances, but the problem is not with juries per se. Juries can never be expected to be much better, or worse, than the society that produces them. A society that is pervasively racist or otherwise corrupt is unlikely to produce fair juries. Justice, in this case, however, will not be improved by eliminating juries. Government officials who would make decisions in the absence of juries come from the same milieu and are not more likely to make fair decisions. The authorities of colonial New York conducted reprehensible investigations and trials, and they desired the verdicts the juries rendered. Elimination of the jury system would not have led to fairer results. And, without this system, those opposed to the manifestations of a corrupt society may too easily focus their discontent on the government officials making the decisions instead of where it truly belongs. Because juries are likely to be seen as embodying societal values, the jury system can have some worth even when producing unjust results, for the likelihood will increase that the discontent will focus where it should—on those societal values.

HOW JUDGES AND JURORS VIEW JURIES

The notion that juries lead to public acceptance of trial outcomes may seem ludicrous in light of the public's typical reaction to juries. Juries are called inconsistent, irrational, biased. A jury trial is no better than flipping a coin. Juries decide cases because of attorneys' theatrics. Trials are determined by high-powered and high-priced consultants who know how to stack a jury to guarantee the desired outcome. Criticisms like these are legion, making one wonder whether the legitimizing function of the jury really works. Although critics of juries are easy to find, critics of the trial judiciary as an institution are comparatively rare. The trial bench generally commands much respect. Would this be so if juries did not exist? Michael Saks concludes: "No doubt judges would eventually be viewed by the public as inconsistent and irrational if juries were not there as lightning rods to protect the judges. What appears in the surveys to be a 'problem' [of jury criticism] may actually be a measure of the jury's success in its lightning rod function. Were the public's eternal displeasure with juries translated into eventual abolition of the jury, very soon no one would be more distressed by that turn of events than judges."[13]

Judges may realize this, at least instinctively. Trial judges, who are in a position to develop an informed and objective opinion, strongly support the jury system. In surveys, more than three-quarters of judges view civil jury trials as a fundamental procedure that must be kept. Furthermore, as we have seen, judges not only generally agreed with jury verdicts, they also "give their civil juries high marks for their process of decision making. . . . In [one] study, the judges average rating for the reasonableness of juror questions was 5.8 on a scale of 1 (very unreasonable) to 7 (very reasonable). [Another] study reported that over 98% of state and federal judges believe that jurors usually make a serious effort to apply the law as they are instructed. . . . Over two-thirds of the respondents disagreed that jurors too often fail to apply the law because of comprehension problems. . . . Seventy-nine percent of the survey respondents rejected the suggestion that bias in favor of a party was the reason for judge-jury disagreement and 92% rejected jury miscomprehension as the reason for the disagreement."[14]

Few judges advocate major jury system reform. "It is something of a para-dox," says Valerie Hans, "that judges are even more supportive of retaining the civil jury's powers than the public, since the jury's role is to represent the public in the courtroom."[15]

Judges may appreciate juries not only because they act as a lightning rod and generally legitimate the judicial process, but also because "juries shoulder some of the judges' responsibility for adjudication [and] . . . [j]ury verdicts can insu-late judges' rulings at trial from effective appellate review."[16] Perhaps, however, as Michael Saks points out, the main reason judges view juries more favorably than the public is that judges have "the advantage of comparing their own judgments about a case with the verdict returned by the jury. When they find the juries' verdicts usually are the same as, or not unreasonably different from, their own, they find validation not only in their own thinking about the cases, but in the jury's as well. We might wonder what the public would think of the jury if it could observe them as judges have the opportunity to observe them."[17]

Perhaps many would come to the conclusion that distinguished trial judge Budd G. Goodman reached: "We live in an imperfect world and the jury sys-tem is our imperfect attempt to deal with that world. The best we can do is to try to find twelve citizens, imperfect as they are, to listen, observe, consider, dis-cuss, and reach the best verdict, the fairest verdict, they know how, given their imperfections. That is the most we can ask, and to my unending surprise, by whatever route they travel, juries by and large arrive at substantial justice."[18]

We might also wonder how the public would regard jurors if more people saw juries as the jurors themselves have seen them. Alexis de Tocqueville saw the jury as vitally important to America not so much for its judicial role in deciding particular disputes, but in its political role. The widespread use of juries, espe-cially in civil cases, which affect many aspects of society, "contributes power-fully to form the judgment and to increase the natural intelligence of a peo-ple. . . . I do not know whether the jury is useful to those who have lawsuits, but I am certain it is highly beneficial to those who judge them; and I look upon it as one of the most efficacious means for the education of the people which society can employ."[19]

George Priest, in contrast, doubts whether juries serve this educative func-tion simply because so few people actually become deliberating jurors. By his calculations, even in a year with high trial activity, only 14,000 out of a popula-tion of over 5 million in Cook County, Illinois, served as jurors. Even if a ripple effect were to triple the educative function of jury service, only a small percentage of the polity would be affected by it. On the other hand, although no accurate records are kept on the number who serve on juries each year, estimates are that about 2 million people annually respond to jury summonses and that about 1 million or more serve.[20]

Priest's point, however, still has validity. Only a minority of adults can claim that their view of the jury system comes from their own jury service. In one survey only 6 percent of respondents said the source of their beliefs about juries came from their personal experience as jurors. In another poll, only 23 percent stated they had served as jurors. What is striking, however, is the reaction of those who have served. The supposed common reaction to a jury service summons is unfavorable. People expect the experience to be distasteful or at least a waste of time. Yet surveys of those who have served overwhelmingly indicate that former jurors have confidence in the jury system. Indeed, a significant majority of respondents indicate that their impression of juries was favorable after jury service. One researcher concludes that the "simplest explanation for the more favorable reaction of trial jurors to jury service is that participation stimulates a commitment to [a] specific jury and its verdict that is powerful enough to include the system as whole."[21] James Gould Cozzens has another explanation for why citizens have respect for the trial system once they have become jurors: "[The jurors] could joke about the law, and speak of it disrespectfully; and say that there was no justice, or that the rich could get away with murder, or that political influence was what counted; but, in fact, they never believed it. It could not be true because they had the final say. When they swore that they would well and truly try and true deliverance make between the Commonwealth and the prisoner at the bar, they meant it."[22]

Those who are plucked from the community and required to do the duties of a juror, perhaps quite amazingly, generally have increased confidence in the legitimacy of the trial system. This reaction alone cannot make the system legitimate or the system's verdicts acceptable, but it contributes to those desired results.

WHY JURY TRIALS IN AMERICA
BUT NOT EVERYWHERE

If juries are so valuable, why are they nonexistent in so much of the world? England does retain jury trials for criminal matters, but civil juries have been largely placed in the dustbin. Civil matters in countries governed by civil law—many of the European, South American, and Asian nations whose law is derived not from England but from continental Europe—are determined solely by judges. But even in these civil law countries, many have recognized the value of lay participation in criminal matters. While the composition of the trial courts is not the same in each nation, the criminal courts often consist of one to three professional judges and a group of lay judges, usually called "lay assessors," who generally outnumber the professional judges. In some countries and for some charges, only professional judges, usually a panel of three, adjudicate. This body, whether a mixed group or only professional judges, together decides all questions of law and fact.

The reasons for the different systems are many and complex, for adjudication systems are born of and reflect a country's history and society. American culture has multiple strands, which often compete. One thread, which is stronger in the United States than in most other places, is a faith in local community rule and a distrust of government officials. We tend to believe that we should be made to obey only those laws that we, ourselves, would have been willing to make and are willing to enforce and not laws that were simply imposed from above. As Americans, we tend to think that we can make decisions at least as well as politicians and bureaucrats. In some sense, we think it is only a happenstance that they are there and we are not. We may be conflicted about this, but an American lodestar, often expressed during election seasons, is that ordinary people can make wise decisions—indeed, often better decisions than can elites who are out of touch with the people. Our distrust of authority results in a government with fragmented, perhaps often inefficient, power.

Juries remain our most enduring expression of a bedrock American principle: we can, and should, put our trust in the wisdom, knowledge, decency, and common sense of ordinary Americans. Juries stand against the notion that some are suited to rule and others to be ruled, against the cult of the expert and the elite. The strengths of the jury system fit in with much of the American character and American mythology. Melvyn Bernard Zerman's description of his own jury experience captures this notion:

> The decision each one of us made was determined by much more than what we heard and observed in the courtroom. The influences on that decision included all the values and experiences and hopes and suspicions and ideas and ideologies that we carried into the jury room as unseen baggage. What [the prosecuting attorney] cited as our "sophistication" he would have been better advised to call our humanity, and it was not only inevitable, it was proper that this humanity, with all its strengths and failings, be brought to bear on the matter.
>
> Strengths and failings our jury had in abundance. We were not a highly educated

group. . . . But almost all of us had basically sound judgment—common sense, if you will. A good many of us had compassion and even more had patience. A few of us were articulate, a few analytical and highly logical in our thinking. . . . We also had our share of ignorance, selfishness, and extreme egotism. . . . Certainly the twelve of us did not comprise any kind of elite. . . . We would be more appropriately characterized as "salt of the earth" types than as eggheads hatched in sociology, law, or political science. . . . But in saying all this, we have neglected the salient point: The hallmark of the jury system is the ordinariness of the people in the jury box.[23]

The seriousness and effort that juries bring to their deliberations are all the more amazing because these ordinary people are asked to decide a matter that will have little effect on them. According to Zerman:

> We were, above all else, a responsible, almost extravagantly serious group. . . . Right from the start all of us were united in one belief at least—that we had been chosen to perform a formidable, indeed fearful, task, and to it we had to apply whatever wisdom we possess. . . .
>
> To paraphrase Bernard Shaw's Eliza Doolittle, the difference between an ordinary man and a juror is not how he behaves, but how he's regarded. This, it seems to me, is the key to the success of the jury system in criminal trials. If a person, whatever his background, knows that much is expected of him—no less than helping to determine the course of someone else's life—in all probability that person will strive with all his capability to be wise and just and compassionate, to stretch himself beyond his foibles and his prejudices. One thing you can be sure of: he will not forget that the stakes are high.[24]

Here is one of the central tenets of America, one that time and again has been proven to contain much truth. When a crisis occurs, we can, we should, and we do expect much of the ordinary citizen, and without the support of the ordinary person, the crisis will not be satisfactorily resolved. A trial does not impress like war or the aftermath of a natural disaster, but every trial in essence is a mini-crisis. There is a conflict needing resolution with much at stake for the disputants. The American jury system ultimately rests on the notion that especially in a crisis we should not defer to a government official, but we should, and can, expect much of ordinary citizens, and the good of our society requires that ordinary citizens support what happens. Law should not be left to the lawyers; judgment should not be left to the judges. Thus, our jury system endures.

The many rationales discussed in the foregoing chapters tell us why a jury—a group of laypeople determining by consensus facts and related matters in a single legal proceeding—might be a good way to make certain legal decisions. The justifications, however, do not define the specifics of a jury. How large a group must a jury be? How much consensus is needed? Who are the laypeople who constitute a jury? The jury has long endured, but it has not remained a static institution, and the answers to these questions have not stayed the same. We turn to these and related issues as we discuss jury size, unanimity, and juror selection in the following chapters.

Chapter 6 Jury Size and
Jury Performance

In 1968 *Duncan v. Louisiana* held that the right to a jury trial in a criminal case is fundamental and that the same right applies in both state and federal prosecutions. The federal courts had but a single model for a jury trial. A jury consisted of twelve people who had to reach unanimity in order to render a verdict, as the Supreme Court had said two years earlier. The right applied to trials of any federal crime that was not "petty," which was defined as a crime carrying a possible penalty of more than six months.1

The states, in contrast, had diverse models for juries. Some states employed juries smaller than twelve; some did not require juries to be unanimous in their decisions; and although all states guaranteed jury trials, they varied concerning the kinds of crimes to which this right applied. Indeed, Louisiana law at the time of *Duncan* illustrated all these complexities. Jury trials were guaranteed, but only for crimes that carried sentences of death or hard labor. If not, the trial went to a judge without a jury. If the crime permitted, but did not require, a sentence of hard labor, the accused was entitled to a five-person jury with a unanimous verdict. If the crime required a punishment of hard labor, a twelve-person jury was required, but only nine of the jurors had to agree to reach a verdict. If the crime was punishable by death, the jury was twelve and the verdict had to be unanimous.

After *Duncan*, the Supreme Court began to consider whether the different state forms of jury trials were constitutional. The process began in 1970 when the Court in *Williams v. Florida* held that a jury of six passed constitutional muster. In doing so, the Court abandoned its precedent of *Thompson v. Utah*, set at the end of the nineteenth century.

THOMPSON V. UTAH

A Mr. Thompson was charged in the Utah territory with calf-rustling. He was tried and convicted in the territorial courts by a jury of twelve, as federal law dictated, but his motion for a new trial was granted. This second trial was held in the state court because by then Utah had gained statehood. As the Utah constitution permitted, this jury had only eight people. In 1898 the case made its way to the Supreme Court, which first noted that the Sixth Amendment right to a jury trial applied in the territorial courts and that, whatever the normal powers of the state, any trial for a crime committed before statehood had to provide a jury consistent with the federal constitution. The Court stated that the federal jury trial right required a jury constituted as it was in the common law of this country and England. This, *Thompson* concluded, was a jury of twelve acting unanimously. "[T]he wise men who framed the constitution of the United States and the people who approved it were of the opinion that life and liberty, when involved in criminal prosecutions, would not be adequately secured except through the unanimous verdict of twelve jurors. It was not for the state, in respect of a crime committed within its limits while it was a territory, to dispense with that guaranty simply because its people had reached the conclusion that the truth could be as well ascertained, and the liberty of an accused be as well guarded, by eight as well as by twelve jurors in a criminal case."[2]

WILLIAMS V. FLORIDA

Seventy years later the Supreme Court again considered the issue of jury size. This Court found that *Thompson's* basic approach was wrong. *Williams v. Florida* agreed that the common law required juries of twelve, but the Court went on to state that "there is absolutely no indication in 'the intent of the

Framers' of an explicit decision to equate the constitutional and common-law characteristics of the jury."[3] Instead, the Court concluded that no one could now know precisely what the framers meant by a jury trial.

Rather than searching history for the constitutionally required number of jurors, *Williams* concluded that a jury's characteristics should be defined by the function that the framers envisioned for juries: the prevention of governmental oppression. *Williams* continued, "Given this purpose, the essential feature of a jury obviously lies in the interposition between the accused and his accuser of the commonsense judgment of a group of laymen, and in the community participation and shared responsibility that results from the group's determination of guilt or innocence." Differently sized bodies could serve these functions, but "the number should probably be large enough to promote group deliberation, free from outside attempts at intimidation, and to provide a fair possibility for obtaining a representative cross-section of the community."[4]

The Court, citing but a few experiments and mostly using its own instincts, concluded that juries of six would little affect how well juries performed. The Court intuited that the change in community representation between juries of six and twelve "seems likely to be negligible," and while juries of six might be less likely to hang than juries of twelve, this "seems unlikely to inure perceptibly to the advantage of either side. . . . And, certainly the reliability of the jury as a factfinder hardly seems likely to be a function of its size."[5] The Court concluded that the twelve-person jury was merely "a historical accident." A jury of six, the Court held, is constitutional.

STUDIES OF JURY SIZE

Williams engendered a storm of controversy by concluding that halving the historical jury would not affect group deliberations and community participation. Scholars quickly produced a flurry of studies about how size affects jury performance. Three years after *Williams,* however, that research did little to alter the Supreme Court's view of smaller juries. In 1973 *Colgrove v. Battin* held that six-person civil juries did not violate the Seventh Amendment's right to juries in civil cases. Consigning its discussion of the studies to a footnote, the Court noted that since 1970, "much has been written about the six-member jury, but nothing that persuades us to depart from the conclusion reached in *Williams.*"[6]

In 1978, however, while reviewing Claude Ballew's misdemeanor obscenity conviction by an Atlanta jury of five, the Court took more note of the scholarship regarding jury numbers. The Court now stressed that social science studies showed smaller juries had a negative effect on deliberations. "The smaller the group, the less likely are members to make critical contributions necessary for the solution of a given problem. . . . [M]emory is important for accurate jury determinations. As juries decrease in size, . . . they are less likely to have members who remember each of the important pieces of evidence or argument. Furthermore, the smaller the group, the less likely it is to overcome the biases of its members to obtain an accurate result. When individual and group decision-making were compared, it was seen that groups performed better because prejudices of individuals were frequently counterbalanced, and objectivity resulted."[7]

These studies also showed that accuracy decreased and inconsistency increased with smaller panels. Moreover, because juries generally hang because one or two jurors hold out against the remainder favoring conviction, the decrease in hung juries resulting from a smaller jury size disproportionately harms criminal defendants by increasing the conviction rate. Finally, the Court noted, smaller juries will not represent the community as well as larger ones. "If a minority viewpoint is shared by 10% of the community, 28.2% of 12-member juries may be expected to have no minority representation, but 53.1% of 6-member juries would have none."[8]

Although these data suggested that the assumptions underlying the acceptance of six-person juries were wrong, the Court did not overturn its earlier decision. Instead, without "pretend[ing] to discern a clear line between six members and five," the Court reaffirmed that six-person juries were constitutional but held that juries of less than six were not.[9]

Research on how size affects jury performance has continued. The studies consistently show that larger juries are more likely to contain minority members, recall more of the evidence, spend more time deliberating, and bring more informational resources to those deliberations than are six-person juries. Just as individuals render more variable decisions than groups, juries of six produce more variability than do juries of twelve. In civil cases, studies generally agree, smaller juries show an increased variability in damages, with a higher average award.[10]

THE ECONOMIES OF SMALLER JURIES

The benefits of smaller juries seem obvious. They are more economical than larger bodies. A jury of six takes up the time of fewer citizens than a jury of twelve, and trials will be shorter. Six people will deliberate less long than twelve. Smaller bodies produce fewer hung juries. Six jurors can be selected more quickly than twelve.

These economies, however, can be overstated. A jury of half the traditional size does not, in fact, result in a trial taking half the time. There is a reduction in the time it takes for jury selection, but the reduction is seldom dramatic. The selection process almost always includes questions and comments directed at the entire group of prospective jurors, and it takes as much time to address six in this fashion as twelve or twenty or any other number. Jury deliberations of six do not take half the time of twelve. Moreover, jury selection and deliberation are but components of a trial that also includes preliminary instructions to the jury, opening statements by all parties, direct and cross-examination of witnesses, closing statements, and final jury instructions. Smaller juries do not affect these procedures at all. In fact, studies reveal that smaller juries bring no significant economies to trials.[11]

Smaller juries produce more variable verdicts, and these have costs. Because increased variance makes outcomes harder to predict, settlements are less likely, and, therefore, the demands for jury trials can increase. Paul Carrington suggests that it "is therefore imaginable that the . . . rules reducing jury size are a deft shot in the . . . foot, that the reduction in the size of jury intended to save time and money actually increases the number of trials, and that the cost of the additional trials more than offsets the saving achieved by having fewer jurors."[12] In addition, the increased variability of small jury verdicts might also mean a rise in the number of acquittals. Michael Saks explains: "Because criminal trial verdicts are . . . skewed (with around eighty percent of verdicts favoring the prosecution), the error-generating effects of reduced jury size will be asymmetrical. More cases that would have been convictions by twelve jurors will be moved into the acquittal column by six jurors than the other way around. In short, more errors of erroneous acquittal will occur than of erroneous conviction."[13]

At first glance, it may not be apparent that Saks's conclusion is correct, but assume that smaller juries would produce a verdict different from that rendered by a larger body 10 percent of the time. Twelve-person juries convict much more often than they acquit. The rates vary around the country, but we will use Saks's figure of 80 percent. Out of every hundred trials with twelve jurors, then, eighty will end in conviction, and, ignoring hung juries for the moment, twenty juries will acquit. With a 10 percent variance in smaller juries, of those eighty convictions, the six-person body will convict only seventy-two times and will acquit 10 percent, or eight times. Of the twenty acquittals with the twelve-person juries, the smaller bodies will also acquit eighteen times, but now also convict twice. Thus, if the larger juries were producing eighty convictions, the six-person juries would produce only seventy-four.[14]

LITTLE MOVEMENT TO INCREASE THE SIZE
OF SMALLER JURIES

Perhaps because they recognize the drawbacks of smaller juries, many jurisdictions still retain traditionally sized juries. Criminal trials in most places do require a jury of twelve, at least for trials of felonies. The majority of states and the federal government, however, now permit juries of fewer than twelve to decide civil cases.

Those who have studied jury size almost uniformly oppose the smaller-sized bodies.[15] Because the savings produced from the smaller juries do not seem to be significant and the smaller size causes jury performance to suffer, it seems only natural that a movement to return to larger juries would be strong. Even so, in most places where six-person juries are used, there have been few serious attempts to restore larger juries. Why this is so has been little explored, but Paul Carrington provides a cynical explanation: "Despite these many serious questions about the political wisdom and practical efficacy of the half jury, there has been little stir outside the academy with respect to these issues. The eagerness of judges to embrace the half jury demonstrates a thin allegiance to the political values that gave rise to the Constitutionalization of the institution. The calm acceptance of the changes by the trial bar demonstrates that its allegiance to the institution is tactical; as long as the transformation of the institution does not diminish the importance of the members of the bar in the process, they seem willing to accept whatever comes."[16]

If smaller juries were enlarged, however, not all agree that twelve is the right number. On the one hand, Carrington states, "While the number [twelve] is not a magic one, a group of that size is small enough to be responsible and large enough to speak with representative authority."[17] Others call for more research: "An obvious response to these changes [resulting from smaller juries] would be to increase the jury's size. This should not be accomplished by enshrining in the Seventh or Fourteenth amendments any particular number of jurors. Instead, it should result from a process of experimentation that better informs us about the relevant effects and trade-offs of jury panels of different sizes."[18]

THE SUPREME COURT'S FAULTY INTUITION

Juries can be, and in some places are, smaller than six. In concluding that halving the traditional jury would not significantly affect how juries perform, the Supreme Court cited only a few empirical studies without probing their validity. Instead, it relied almost entirely on its own instincts. Competent studies, however, show these judicial assumptions to be wrong. In other words, the justices did not know what they were talking about.

This may be surprising, but it should not be. Few Supreme Court judges have had much contact with juries. The bar, like almost any human institution, has its own hierarchy. As a general rule, the less a lawyer deals with "common people," the more prestigious the position she holds. The lawyer involved with mergers and acquisitions stands on a higher rung than one dealing with personal injuries or crimes. Supreme Court justices do not represent a cross-section of the bar. They generally come from the bar's elite, and this gentry seldom has much experience with juries. Because the Supreme Court's intuitions about juries do not come from any depth of experience, they should not automatically be trusted.

There is, of course, a broader point here. Supreme Court justices are educated and thoughtful. If this group's intuitions about juries should be viewed skeptically, surely suspicion is also in order for the views of many others about the jury system, no matter how smart, prestigious, or knowledgeable, when those opinions are based only on intuitions, assertions, and anecdotes and not on extensive experience or serious study.

Chapter 7 Unanimity and

Hung Juries

Juries traditionally have had to reach unanimous agreement to render a decision. But why? Most governmental bodies operate according to a majority principle and speak with multiple voices. Judges write dissenting opinions; losing legislators castigate the majority and issue minority reports.

The unanimity requirement seems to have developed in fourteenth-century England. The jury was to pronounce the truth, and there was only one truth. If all jurors did not agree to a verdict, then a truth was not being declared. Or as Leonard Levy states: "The rule of unanimity may have originated . . . because the test was the voice of the country and the country could but have one voice. . . . A unanimous verdict . . . , which was regarded as representative of the country, an expression of its sense, carried a supernatural weight."[1]

A desire for certainty in trials persists to this day. When a court renders a two-to-one decision or a congressional committee renders a split vote, we cannot help but think that a different panel or another election could change the results. Such decisions have limited definitiveness; they are part of a continuing process in which the future might bring a new outcome. Dissenting voices tend to undercut the finality and, hence, the acceptance of a decision because another day a differently constituted body might reverse it.[2]

In contrast, with a unanimity requirement, juries must speak with one voice. The result appears authoritative and final. Such authority serves the public good, because the greater the apparent agreement, the more likely it is that the litigants and the public will accept the jury's decision.

STATUS OF THE UNANIMITY REQUIREMENT

Despite the unanimous jury's long history, the Supreme Court in 1972 stated that unanimous verdicts are not constitutionally required. Oregon had convicted two men by jury votes of ten to two and eleven to one, and Louisiana had permitted a nine-to-three conviction. As it did when concluding that juries smaller than twelve were permissible, the Court in reviewing the nonunanimous verdicts concluded that tradition or history does not control. It stated, "Our inquiry [into the constitutionality of those verdicts] must focus upon the function served by the jury in contemporary society." The majority stressed that "the essential feature of a jury obviously lies in the interposition between the accused and his accuser of the commonsense judgment of a group of laymen." The Court then asserted: "A requirement of unanimity, however, does not materially contribute to the exercise of the commonsense judgment. . . . [A] jury will come to such a judgment as long as it consists of a group of laymen representative of a cross section of the community who have the duty and the opportunity to deliberate, free from outside attempts at intimidation, on the question of a defendant's guilt. In terms of this function we perceive no difference between juries required to act unanimously and those permitted to convict or acquit by votes 10 to two or 11 to one."[3]

A bare majority of the Court adopted this position. Justice Harry Blackmun, who was in the majority, wrote separately and stressed that the Court was approving verdicts only where "a substantial majority" had to be convinced and stated that a verdict by a seven-to-five vote, rather than nine to three, "would afford me great difficulty."[4] As a result, subsequent courts and commentators have concluded criminal verdicts must command supermajorities of at least nine to three in order to be constitutional.

Having decided that juries could have fewer than twelve members and that twelve-member juries did not have to return unanimous verdicts, the Court soon had to face the inevitable question of whether small juries had to be unanimous. In 1979 *Burch v. Louisiana* held that a six-person jury was constitutional only if its verdict were unanimous. The Court's rationale was murky. The best the Court could muster was that "having already departed from the strictly historical requirements of jury trial, it is inevitable that lines must be drawn somewhere if the substance of the jury trial right is to be preserved."[5]

Despite the Supreme Court's ruling, however, today only two states permit nonunanimous verdicts in felony cases.[6] The demand for a clear and unified voice in felony cases would appear to hold sway.

Civil cases present a different picture. Nonunanimous civil juries have been around since 1879, when California permitted civil verdicts by a three-quarters majority. Utah followed in 1892, and shortly thereafter Kentucky and Missouri joined the movement toward nonunanimity. By the mid-1970s over half the states allowed for nonunanimous verdicts in civil cases. The federal courts, however, while permitting the parties to agree to a nonunanimous civil verdict, otherwise still require unanimity. Today, only fourteen states along with the federal courts require unanimous verdicts in civil jury cases.[7]

Unanimous verdicts encourage a thorough review of the evidence and generate authority and finality for verdicts. Most jurisdictions require unanimity in felony trials. Opponents of unanimity, however, suggest that the requirement for unanimity leads to irrational compromises, long trials, and hung juries. Are they correct?

UNANIMITY AND COMPROMISE VERDICTS

Justice Lewis Powell, concurring in the decision to permit state criminal juries to be nonunanimous, said, "[T]he rule that juries must speak with a single voice often leads, not to full agreement among the 12 but to agreement by none and compromise by all, despite the frequent absence of a rational basis for such compromise."[8] For example, the majority of jury members may believe that a defendant who has raised a claim of self-defense is guilty of murder, while the others do not think she committed a crime at all. To reach a unanimous agreement, the jurors may agree on a unanimous verdict of manslaughter even though none of the jurors truly think that is the correct verdict. If a nonunanimous verdict had been permitted, the compromise might not have been needed.

No data indicate precisely how often compromise verdicts occur in criminal cases, but civil cases may see more. In the traditional civil trial, both liability and damages issues are heard and decided in one proceeding, leaving considerable room for juror negotiation. One juror may believe that the defendant is liable for the plaintiff's damages of $100,000; another may believe that the defendant should not be held liable at all, and, therefore, the plaintiff should recover nothing. The possible compromise is an agreement to hold the defendant liable but to award damages somewhere short of $100,000.

Studies of trials that have divided the liability and damages phases into separate, "bifurcated" trials that determine liability in one proceeding and damages in a separate proceeding do indicate that civil juries reach compromise verdicts in unitary trials, which decide both issues in one proceeding. As might be expected, liability findings are lower in bifurcated proceedings compared to unitary trials. If liability is found, however, the average award is higher.[9]

Juries, especially in unitary civil trials, may compromise to reach a verdict. Although studies have not been done examining how nonunanimous verdicts actually affect compromises, nonunanimous verdicts would naturally seem to decrease the compromise rate. That, however, is not a compelling reason for abandoning unanimity. Other changes, most notably bifurcations, will tend to reduce compromises without losing the benefits of unanimous jury verdicts.

MAJORITY VERDICTS AND SHORTER TRIALS

Nonunanimous juries might produce more economical trials by shortening the deliberation time. Certainly, the length and costs of trials are important issues. The *Los Angeles Times* reported in 1998 that the average daily cost of running a Superior Court in that city was about $9,500, which included supplies and salaries of judges, prosecutors, public defenders, and staff.[10]

In earlier times, the relative costs were lower because trials were shorter. At the beginning of the nineteenth century, some courts would hold twelve trials in a day, and in the 1890s it was not unusual for six trials to be completed within that span. A 1922 study found that the Cleveland courts normally completed several trials daily. In the middle of the twentieth century, however, the average trial lengthened. In 1953, the average felony jury trial in Los Angeles lasted 3 days; in 1964 it was 3.5 days; in 1968, 7.2 days; and in 1998, according to the *Los Angeles Times,* it was 14 days. In the District of Columbia, the average felony trial went from 1.9 days in 1950 to 2.8 days in 1965. In 1968, 26 percent of federal civil trials were completed in a day. Twenty years later only 14 percent were. In 1968, only 75 federal civil trials lasted 10 days or more. Two decades later the number was 359.

A host of factors cause longer trials. The law has become more complicated,

or at least the judicial instructions to juries have become longer, forcing length-
ier deliberations. Evidence law has been liberalized, permitting more evidence
to be presented. Proof has become more complex with the increased use of experts. Current court rules often allow more parties and more issues to be joined
together into one case than in years past, making trials more complicated.
Modern business practices often generate more records than previously, leading
to the availability of more evidence. Especially in civil cases, rules have allowed
parties to discover more information from their opponents and elsewhere, and
this, too, has led to the increased production of trial evidence. More attorneys
now bill by the hour than in an earlier era, which may be an incentive to pro-
long trials.

Deliberation time, too, has increased. Deliberations had to be quick when
several trials were held in a day. The cause of lengthened deliberations is clearly
not the unanimity requirement, which was almost always in effect for those by-
gone, rapid jury verdicts. It should not be surprising, then, that nonunanimous
juries have not been shown to lead to significantly shorter trials. Furthermore,
while short deliberations were once common and expected, today brief deliberations are often suspect. In the O. J. Simpson murder trial, some saw the jury's
quick decision as an indication that the jury did not fully and fairly consider the
presented evidence.[11] If shortening trials is the goal, remedies other than abandoning unanimity are needed.

UNANIMITY AND HUNG JURIES

In a number of high-profile trials in the 1990s, juries could not reach unanimous agreement, fueling concern over hung juries. Because the modern movement for nonunanimous juries has aimed primarily to reduce the number of
hung juries, these trials led to claims that the hung jury rate was too high and
proliferating. There were also concerns that deadlocked juries were increasingly
caused by the irrational juror—often a member of a racial minority—who refused to follow the law.[12]

Little data exist, however, to support the claim of increasing hung juries or
their putative causes. In part, this is because court systems as a routine matter
do not catalog hung juries. Courts generally report final dispositions—verdicts, settlements, guilty pleas, and dismissals—and because a case does not
end with a hung jury, it is not a final disposition.

The reporting problem is further complicated by the fact that a uniform definition of "hung jury" does not exist. If five defendants are tried jointly in one

trial and the jury convicts four and hangs on one, some jurisdictions would record this as a hung jury, while others would label it a conviction, and still others would record four convictions and one hung jury. Similarly, when one defendant is charged with a number of crimes in a single trial, many jurisdictions will consider only what happens to the most serious charge. Others will call it a hung jury if the jury could not reach a result on any count. If a jury convicted a defendant of a bank robbery but deadlocked on possession of a switchblade found in the family car when the accused was arrested, many jurisdictions would label the outcome a conviction and others would call it a hung jury.

Without addressing these methodological difficulties, Kalven and Zeisel's 1950s study of cases reported a hung jury rate of 5.5 percent. Some think the study inaugurated "the conventional wisdom that a hung jury rate of 5 percent is the norm—and that rates exceeding this indicate a problem." In contrast, a 1975 study in California found a 12.2 percent hung jury rate, varying from 5.1 percent in one county to 21 percent in another. Twenty years later, however, that California rate had not increased. A 1995 California report found "a strikingly similar pattern across the two decades. . . . These statistics are notable for several reasons. The first is that high levels of hung juries are not a recent phenomenon in the California courts. . . . The second is that hung jury rates in excess of 10 percent—twice the usual quoted 5 percent rate—appear regularly. Third, there is a great variation from year to year and from court to court." Part of the reason for these apparently high rates—and perhaps the only one—is that the California study adopted the broadest possible definition of a hung jury, as one that is "unable to agree upon a verdict with respect to one or more defendants and one or more charges."[13]

Information about hung juries has recently begun to improve as the National Center for State Courts has collected data about them. The center reports, "From 1980 to 1997, the total federal hung jury rate varies only 0.8 percent, from a low of 1.2 percent of all jury trials in 1985 and again in 1988, to a 17-year high of 2.0 percent in 1992."[14] Federal civil juries hung at about one-third the rate of criminal juries, and criminal hung juries varied from a low one year of 2.1 percent to a high of 3.0 percent. The difference between the rates in criminal and civil trials may be due in part to the fact that the burden of proof differs in civil and criminal cases, and also because federal civil juries typically have six members while federal criminal juries have twelve. Although both bodies must be unanimous, it is easier to get that agreement from the smaller group.[15]

What is most striking about the data on federal hung juries, however, is not the difference between the civil and criminal rates, but how low and stable both are. While many jurisdictions have permitted nonunanimous, six-person juries in civil cases, presumably to decrease the number of hung juries, the federal civil courts *even with unanimous juries* have hung jury rates below 1 percent.

The state data are more fragmentary. The National Center for State Courts has obtained statistics on hung juries from about thirty cities and counties around the country for a three-year period, but the sources are not uniform, sometimes coming from the courts, sometimes from prosecutors' offices. Furthermore, the data are not derived from a uniform definition of "hung jury."[16] Nevertheless, the survey revealed an overall average hung jury rate of 5.2 percent, varying from 1.5 percent in Oakland County, Michigan, to a high of 14.8 percent in Los Angeles. The study also reviewed all the dispositions during an eighteen-month period in New York State and found hung juries occurred 2.8 percent of the time throughout the state, varying from 0 percent in thirty-eight of the sixty-two counties to 18.8 percent in one county.

Part of the reason for the difference in reported rates stems from the small number of cases tried in some places. For example, that 18.8 percent frequency reflects three hung juries out of only sixteen trials. Obviously the rates would plunge or escalate with just a slight change in either the number of hung juries or the number of trials. And, again, the variations may stem from different definitions of "hung jury." Absent a uniform definition, it is virtually impossible to know precisely how hung jury rates vary around the country.

The variability is also due in large measure to local differences in the kinds of cases that are tried by juries. For example, in one county, 71 percent of the cases disposed of one year ended in a guilty plea, while 18 percent were dismissed. Eight percent of the cases had bench trials, while only 3 percent of the dispositions were jury trials, and the hung jury rate was 4.8 percent. In a contiguous county, 93 percent of cases ended with a guilty plea; 1 percent was dismissed; 1 percent went to a bench trial; and 5 percent had a jury trial. The hung jury rate was 0.6 percent. These different disposition patterns make it likely that the characteristics of the jury cases in the two counties differ, making meaningful comparisons of their hung jury rates difficult.[17]

Case characteristics do affect hung jury rates. Kalven and Zeisel's study found that when judges classified cases as clear-cut and easy, only 2 percent of the juries hung, but when the cases were labeled close, 10 percent of the juries hung. Thus, if some jurisdictions do truly have a higher hung jury rate than other places, the reason may be simply that more of their jury trials are more difficult to decide than those in other places.

In sum, then, available information does not indicate an increasing problem with hung juries. The information available for federal trials shows a long-term, stable pattern of infrequent hung juries. The California data remain consistent over a two-decade span, and the national figures, even though they must be treated cautiously, indicate that hung jury rates are much as Kalven and Zeisel found them almost a half a century ago. Consequently, those who have studied the data in detail conclude that the information "does not support the belief that hung jury rates in criminal cases are a widespread problem."[18]

REDUCTION OF HUNG JURIES
THROUGH MAJORITY VERDICTS

Although hung juries may not be an increasing, pervasive problem, eliminating the unanimity requirement can still reduce the number of them. Kalven and Zeisel cataloged the last vote of hung juries and concluded that if a jurisdiction permitted verdicts by ten to two votes, the percentage of hung juries would decrease by 42 percent because the final minority consisted of one or two holdouts in 42 percent of deadlocked juries. In other words, if it can be assumed that a ten-to-two vote with unanimity required would still have occurred if the decision rule permitted a verdict with two dissenters, a hung jury rate of 5.6 percent as Kalven and Zeisel found would be reduced by 42 percent to 3.2 percent.[19]

Even if the reduction is small, however, the decline throughout the country might seem to produce significant economies. For several reasons, however, the savings can be overstated. Not every hung jury results in another trial. Some are settled or plea bargained after the jury has hung, and the burden of these cases is small compared to those that are tried again.

Furthermore, eliminating a retrial that would have produced a different outcome from the majority vote in the first trial cannot automatically be counted as a savings. If a hung jury vote is ten to two for a murder verdict or ten to two that a bus company is totally liable for an accident, for example, elimination of a second verdict that would have found the defendant not guilty or guilty only of manslaughter or that the bus company was not liable is not an unmitigated economy. The subsequent verdict may indicate that the majority vote in the first trial was not the best outcome, and that the unanimity requirement had actually prevented a mistaken verdict.

Information about what happens after a jury deadlocks is scant. One study of hung juries conducted by the Los Angeles public defender's office found that over a three-year period, 1.6 percent of the county's felony jury trials ended in a hung jury with an eleven-to-one split for conviction. Only a third of those cases were tried again, with 58 percent of those retrials resulting in a conviction, 19 percent in an acquittal, and 23 percent in yet another hung jury.[20] Permitting ten-to-two jury verdicts would have prevented new trial costs for only the 0.35 percent of hung juries that were retried. On the other hand, 42 percent of those retried were not convicted even on a second try. The savings on new trials resulting from nonunanimous verdicts would hardly have been an unalloyed positive for those defendants.

This information also casts doubt on the notion that eleven-to-one-for-conviction hung juries are usually caused by a deranged holdout. Note that while a majority (58 percent) of the second Los Angeles trials cited above resulted in a conviction, many (42 percent) did not. These cases apparently presented close, hard issues for resolution even though the initial juries were split eleven to one. Indeed, while one might assume that an eleven-to-one vote is tantamount to unanimity, Kalven and Zeisel's study showed that hung juries—including eleven-to-one hung juries—occurred only when there was a substantial minority at the beginning of the deliberations even if only one holdout remained at their end. When the first ballot had a minority of three or less, the hung jury rate was a scant 1 percent. When four or more were in the minority on the first ballot, the hung jury rate was 15 percent. Kalven and Zeisel concluded:

> According to [one] notion, juries hang not so much because of the objective situation of the case, but rather because once in a while an eccentric juror will refuse to play his proper role.
>
> The [information] shows that juries which begin with an overwhelming majority in either direction are not likely to hang. It requires a massive minority of 4 or 5 jurors at the first vote to develop the likelihood of a hung jury.
>
> If one may take the first ballot as a measure of the ambiguity of the case, then it follows that the case itself must be the primary cause of a hung jury.
>
> But the substantial minority need exist only at the beginning of the deliberations. During the process it may be whittled away. . . . Nevertheless, for one or two jurors to hold out to the end, it would appear necessary that they had companionship at the beginning of the deliberations.[21]

THE *TWELVE ANGRY MEN* SCENARIO

One of the arguments in favor of unanimity arises from the scenario in which the small minority is pitted against the majority, permitting the possibility that the small number will hold sway. American drama has, in fact, immortalized the lone juror who convinces the majority of the rightness of his position. The situation depicted in *Twelve Angry Men* in which an initial holdout (played by Henry Fonda and Jack Lemmon in different movie versions and by countless more in school and community theaters) eventually convinces the other eleven to change their minds is, however, rare in reality. Kalven and Zeisel found that in almost all cases deliberations bring the minority in line with the majority views, with the initial minority seldom prevailing. "[I]n the instances where there is an initial majority either for conviction or for acquittal, the jury in roughly nine out of ten cases decides in the direction of the initial majority. Only with extreme infrequency does the minority succeed in persuading the majority during the deliberation." Others have corroborated this conclusion, suggesting further that it requires three or more jurors in the minority position to change the majority view. With criminal cases, then, majority verdicts overall will not be much different from unanimous ones, but, of course, even if only 5 percent of the verdicts would be different, many trials throughout the country would be affected.[22]

Even if nonunanimous verdicts do not change outcomes dramatically, they do tend to change the nature of deliberations. Nonunanimous juries deliberate for shorter periods of time than do their unanimous counterparts. Members of small minorities in majority juries participate less than they do in unanimous juries. Nonunanimous juries discuss both the law and evidence less than do unanimous bodies. Mistakes about the evidence and the instructions are corrected more frequently in unanimous juries. Talkative jurors talk more in nonunanimous juries, and nontalkative jurors contribute more in unanimous bodies. Nonunanimous juries recall less evidence.[23]

Perhaps most important, majority jurors in trials not requiring unanimity have less confidence in their own verdicts. Naturally, the holdouts are negative about the quality or outcome of deliberations, but the majority are also affected. Reid Hastie reports that "jurors from both majority and holdout factions have lower respect for their fellow jurors' open-mindedness and persuasiveness under the nonunanimous decision rules." Michael Saks concludes, "Apparently, at the end of the day, the existence of dissenters left even the majority with some lingering doubts that it had reached the right verdict."[24]

If tomorrow nonunanimous juries became the order of the day, there would be some benefits, but several drawbacks. Nonunanimous juries might reduce slightly the number of deadlocked juries. The final verdict pattern would not be precisely the same as with unanimous juries, but, at least in criminal cases, it would not change dramatically. Nevertheless, some verdicts would be altered, and although this would constitute a small percentage of cases, the absolute numbers of affected parties would be substantial. Jury dissatisfaction with its own deliberative process and its outcome should also be a significant consideration. "[B]ecause respect for the institution of the jury is a critical condition for public acceptance of jury decisions, the lower postdeliberation evaluations of the quality of their decision by jurors in nonunanimous juries and the larger number of holdouts who reject the jury's verdict under these rules greatly diminish the usefulness of the majority rule jury as a mechanism for resolving legal disputes."[25]

Furthermore, certain majority verdicts present particular problems concerning acceptance. Lisa Kern Griffin states, "Ultimately, unanimity supports the legitimacy of the verdict, particularly if majority verdicts break down along racial lines. A high profile case resolved by a majority verdict of 10–2, if those two members of the jury were of the same race as the defendant, would be greeted by both the court and the public as an illegitimate decision."[26] Roger Parloff makes the same point even more forcefully.

> A conviction or acquittal in a highly publicized, racially sensitive case obtained by white jurors outvoting black jurors could be literally an incendiary event, especially in a state that had only just recently switched to using nonunanimous juries. Some blacks might see the verdict as unjust not only because of disagreement with the outcome, but because the verdict had been achieved by means of a process that allowed the input of black jurors to be disregarded and circumvented. Such critics would charge, in fact, that the nonunanimous system had been designed with precisely that invidious goal in mind, and that it had been devised in deference to white fears that black jurors could not be trusted to exercise their civic duty, and to white intuitions that their own assessments of police credibility were intrinsically superior to black jurors' assessments of police credibility.
>
> Worst of all, the critics who would angrily denounce the new system in such vituperative terms would be precisely and undeniably right.[27]

Hung juries do not present the problem some portray, but if their reduction is a desirable goal, nonunanimous verdicts aid that goal only slightly, and at a significant price. Such verdicts produce only a tiny decrease in deadlocked juries at the cost of damaging the quality of the deliberations and harming the legitimacy and acceptability of verdicts as well as altering the outcomes of some trials.

Chapter 8 The Vicinage

The selection of a jury begins when people are summoned to the courthouse as potential jurors. Then a particular jury is picked from those who were summoned. Those summoned almost invariably come from the community of the trial, a requirement with ancient roots.

COMPURGATION, ORDEALS, AND BATTLES

Before the institutionalization of jury trials, dispute resolution in England depended on processes requiring supernatural intervention— proof by compurgation, ordeal, and battle. Compurgation required the accuser and accused to swear oaths. Compurgators, or oathhelpers, were enlisted in their behalf to vouch for these oaths. Their number depended upon the gravity of the case. If an accused could assemble the required number of compurgators, he was acquitted. In a society that believed false oaths would elicit divine wrath and whose communities were small enough to ensure that the integrity of its members was well known, this method of proof was not completely illogical. Although it was not formally abolished in England until 1833, compurgation fell from favor during the Middle Ages, presumably because principals were allowed to select their own oathhelpers and people could often be found who did not fear godly retribution from false oaths.

Proof by ordeal also depended upon supernatural intervention. The ordeal by fire generally required the accused to pick up a red hot iron. If he remained unharmed, it could only be because he had been protected by the Deity, who would protect only those who were blameless. Thus, an unburned hand established innocence, while raw flesh proved guilt. Similarly, in the ordeal of water, a person was plunged into a pool. If he sank, it indicated that God's pure water had accepted him, and he was not guilty. The "innocent" then had to hope for the intervention of ordinary mortals to rescue him before drowning.

Proof by ordeal also disappeared early.[2] Partly this was from the suspicion that in a few notable instances innocence was obtained not by heavenly intercession but through collusion with the trial masters. Perhaps more important, however, this system depended upon the clergy, whose official presence was necessary to ensure divine intervention, and in 1215, the Council of Lateran forbade priests to participate in proof by ordeal.

A trial by battle was a duel between accuser and accused. An accused could plead not guilty by throwing down a glove and declaring that he would physically defend himself against the charge. If the accuser wished to pursue the accusation, he picked up the glove and weapons were chosen. If the accused were vanquished or killed, God was assumed to have foreordained the result and the loser was adjudged guilty. If the accused won, however, or if he simply kept the fight going from dawn until dusk, he was acquitted.

The battle system, even when it had credence, had severe limitations. Not all were expected to participate. Women, the maimed, and the elderly were exempt. Furthermore, the system became corrupted when "litigants" were allowed to choose representatives to replace them, and professional battlers (not labeled "lawyers") came into existence.

As the limitations of these earlier methods of proof were recognized, they were increasingly replaced by another method of adjudication, a trial by jury. By the thirteenth century, this jury system had become the principal method of dispute resolution. While bearing similarities to our present system, however, it had some striking differences.

EARLY JURY TRIALS

Early English jurors were not originally assembled to hear evidence or have information presented to them. Instead, they were brought together to render a verdict based on their own knowledge. In small, intertwined communities, jurors were expected to know about the dispute or at least about the disputants, and this information formed the basis for a jury's decision. These self-informed juries had to be drawn from the dispute's locality—from the "vicinage"—because only local people would have the requisite knowledge to decide the matter.

Over time, these early juries were transformed from bodies deciding solely on the basis of their own knowledge to ones who heard witnesses and rendered verdicts based on evaluations of what those witnesses said. Such a change had an administrative advantage. Jurors were now easier to find. The eligible pool expanded because a juror no longer had to have specific knowledge concerning the dispute; the juror only had to evaluate the presented information. With this change, a crucial feature of the modern jury was born. Juries were no longer selected for what they already knew of the conflict, but on the promise or assumption that they would impartially evaluate the information presented to them at trial.[3]

The need for a community-based jury would seem to have declined. Nevertheless, a jury of the vicinage remained a bedrock principle in America.

THE VICINAGE REQUIREMENT

In January 1769, the English parliament passed laws permitting persons accused of treason in the colonies to be transported and tried in England. The fledgling Americans vehemently protested. The Virginia legislature quickly responded by stating that "sending such Person, or Persons, to Places beyond the Sea, to be tried, is highly derogatory of the Rights of British subjects; as thereby the inestimable Privilege of being tried by a Jury from the Vicinage, as well as the Liberty of summoning and producing Witnesses on such Trial, will be taken away from the Party accused." In 1774, the first Continental Congress declared: "That the respective colonies are entitled to the common law of England, and more especially to the great and inestimable privilege of being tried by their peers of the vicinage." The Declaration of Independence condemned King George "for transporting us beyond the Seas to be tried for pretended offenses."[4]

Not surprisingly, then, the drafters of the United States Bill of Rights sought to ensure local jurors. They could not simply adopt existing colonial practices, however, because those practices varied considerably. Although in New York, for example, a trial by the vicinage was essential, the procedures elsewhere were often less demanding. In early Virginia, by contrast, all trials were held in Jamestown, and the jurors were selected from there even when Jamestown was not the vicinage of the crime.[5]

Concerned that the term "vicinage" was too vague and that a requirement that jurors come from the county in which the offense was committed was too impractical or expensive, the drafters of the Bill of Rights adopted compromise language. The Sixth Amendment guarantees a trial "by an impartial jury of the State and district wherein the crime shall have been committed, which district shall have previously been ascertained by law." The first districts created by Congress generally coincided with state boundaries. As a result, jurors in federal trials (except for capital crimes, which by statute required jurors from the local county) could be selected from a broad area.[6]

States today, however, have a narrower notion of vicinage. In both civil and criminal cases, state jurors are generally selected from the county or smaller area where the case is tried. Because federal districts encompass more than a single county, federal juries are usually drawn from a broader geographical area than are state juries. Even so, both federal and state juries, in an important sense, are drawn from the locality of the dispute.

ADVANTAGES OF COMMUNITY JURORS

Local juries endure partly for administrative reasons. It is generally more convenient and economical to hold trials where a dispute originated and to get jurors from nearby. In addition, local juries tend to be the best fact-finders. Those from the local community more readily understand the evidence and see its possible interpretations. As a New York City resident, for example, I have greater understanding of how people enter and leave subway cars at rush hour than would a resident of, say, Sheboygan, Wisconsin. Sheboyganites no doubt have more knowledge about their own Bratwurst Day. Thus, local jurors are more likely to understand localized references in the evidence. "[J]urors of the vicinage are more likely to be familiar with the setting in which the incident occurred, and the mannerisms and colloquialisms of the people involved, facilitating intelligent comprehension and evaluation of the evidence being presented. If jurors are purposely summoned from a community unrelated to the [dispute] so as to insure ignorance of the geographical and cultural setting in which the incident occurred, they are likely to misinterpret the evidence, or not to understand certain evidence, or to become confused about the evidence, precisely because of the lack of knowledge of the context of the incident."[7]

Another reason for local juries is that the consequences of a trial often fall most heavily on the trial's community. When a person is removed as a criminal or is allowed to return to the community having been found not guilty, for example, the neighbors are affected. Because a community-based jury may have a higher stake in making a correct decision, they may pay closer attention to the proceedings. Similarly, the consequences of prosecutorial or judicial actions fall most heavily on the communities where the judges and prosecutors have power. If those officials need to be checked, the local community is in the best position to rein them in. Finally, a community is more likely to accept a verdict if representatives of the community have made the decision.

Although local juries have many benefits, in some instances they may not be ideal. Especially when a litigant is not a member of the community where the dispute has occurred, representatives of a distant community might better understand the evidence produced. Consider the following famous example: "Professor Lon Fuller once discussed the danger that jurors called to judge a sailor charged with threatening another with bodily harm would not understand the mores of the waterfront and would attribute too much to testimony that the defendant had said in the past that he would 'stick a knife in [someone's] guts and turn it around three times.' . . . To be able to evaluate statements of witnesses, a jury needs sufficient knowledge of the witnesses' worlds to place their statements in context."[8] Thus, the New Bedford sailor charged with a crime in a New Bedford bar gets a New Bedford jury. If, however, that sailor is vacationing in Utah when the threat occurs, he will still have a local jury, but it will be from Utah, and that body might not readily understand the parlance of the waterfront.

The drafters of the Constitution showed concern for such out-of-state civil parties by providing "diversity jurisdiction" in federal courts. The Constitution gives the federal courts power to determine cases when a citizen of one state sues the citizen of another state. Although Congress has imposed limits on this jurisdiction—most notably requiring that a minimum amount of money be in controversy, now set at $75,000—a suit, even if it concerns only state law, can be heard in federal court when the parties are citizens from different states.

Diversity jurisdiction, however, affects the selection of the judge more than of the jury. If a California citizen sues a New Yorker in New York, and if the case remains in state court, a New York State judge will preside and the jury will consist of New Yorkers selected from the county of the suit's location. If the same case is removed to the federal court in New York, a federal judge will preside at trial, but the jury will still consist of New Yorkers. Diversity jurisdiction does not require jurors to come from both California and New York.

The jury-of-the-vicinage requirement does sometimes undermine public acceptance of verdicts. For state trials, the "vicinage" generally means the county where the trial is located. This may generally be a good criterion for determining the community from which the jury should come, but it is not always a perfect device. Assume, for example, a situation in which a county is overwhelmingly white. A minority leader who has been protesting discriminatory housing practices is arrested for committing a shocking crime. The jury-of-the-vicinage requirement means that the jury will be drawn only from the heavily white county. That jury may be perfectly fair and competent. But if it convicts, its verdict may well be perceived as suspect. Such suspicion might be lessened if the verdict is rendered by a jury drawn from a community beyond that of the crime.

Community passions can also make a jury of the vicinage problematic by pushing jurors to base their verdict not only on the presented evidence and instructions but also on information and feelings gathered outside the courtroom. Courts can, and occasionally do, order litigants and lawyers not to discuss a pending case. But although some countries prohibit the press from reporting on pending cases, the First Amendment prevents such a broad preemptive remedy. Furthermore, the Sixth Amendment grants the accused the right to a public trial, and the First Amendment grants the public and the press the right of access to criminal trials. The right to a public trial is not absolute, but the strong presumption of open courtrooms is difficult to overcome. As a result, most trials and pretrial hearings are open to the press.[9]

Potential jurors, then, may have read or heard about the case outside the courtroom. The most common procedure under these circumstances is simply to question potential jurors about their knowledge of this pretrial information. The goal might be to find jurors who are not familiar with it, because people who are not aware of the publicity cannot be affected by it. If, however, the information has been of general interest and widely circulated, the pool of people oblivious to it will be distinct. Studies show that such a group is likely to be less educated and to hold lower-status jobs as compared to the general public. Seating jurors who are unaware of publicity may yield a jury untainted by prior knowledge, but also a body that may be less representative of the community and lacking in the diversity that furthers good jury deliberations.

Jury trials do not require ignorant jurors; fair trials need, as the Sixth

Amendment commands, "impartial" jurors. Impartiality demands that jurors decide the case on the presented evidence and instructions. Prior knowledge can conflict with impartiality, but it does not have to. The question is whether the potential juror is willing to learn at trial and base a decision on that information or whether the prior knowledge will affect the verdict. Although a person may know about the case, she can be an impartial juror if she is able to decide solely on the trial presentation.

The Supreme Court has held that protracted questioning about the effect of pretrial publicity on impartiality is not required. Instead, it is constitutionally satisfactory merely to find out whether prospective jurors are familiar with pretrial reports, and if so, whether they can set preconceived ideas aside and decide the case on the presented evidence.[10]

Many courts, however, go beyond these constitutional minimums and permit extended questioning of potential jurors in highly publicized cases. It is not clear, however, whether such a lengthy process affects the trial's outcome. In a study with mock jurors exposed to prejudicial newspaper stories, one group was given a superficial voir dire and the other group received an extensive, probing interrogation and a detailed instruction from the trial judge to disregard newspaper accounts. The two groups did not differ in their verdicts, suggesting that the prolonged interrogation had no discernible effect.[11]

Furthermore, there is no guarantee that even an extended voir dire about pretrial publicity will uncover what prospective jurors do and do not know. For example, the holdout in the Juan Corona multiple murder trial revealed during deliberations that the defendant's brother was an admitted homosexual, had attacked a prosecution witness, and fled to Mexico. The other jurors were amazed because no such evidence had been presented at trial. The holdout stated that she had gathered this information from a detective magazine read months before the trial. One juror responded:

> "[T]hey asked us during the voir dire if we'd read about the Corona case before they accepted us as jurors."
>
> "Yes," said Naomi, "they asked if we knew anything about the Juan Corona case which would prejudice us but they never asked"—she smiled—"if we knew anything about his brother Natividad. Now, I'll tell you, in the magazine it said his brother was a homosexual, and [a witness] said these are homosexual murders and so it only makes sense."[12]

Similarly, a pretrial survey about a highly publicized New Jersey trial found that most people in the community had fixed opinions about the case, but only a small minority of prospective jurors admitted to any predisposition, suggesting that not all were telling the truth.[13]

Furthermore, when jurors pledge to set aside previously acquired information, they are promising to accomplish a difficult, perhaps impossible, feat. It is difficult to compartmentalize the mind in order to ignore absorbed information. Promises to do so may have limited effect, because the use of the information may be subconscious. A survey of jury-eligible citizens questioned about two controversial cases found that the better-informed people tended to find the government's case compelling, but these same people did not perceive themselves as being biased against the defendants. The researchers concluded that the well-informed prospective jurors may not have been able to respond objectively to questions concerning their own impartiality.[14] Indeed, most mock jury studies show that those exposed to damaging information outside the courtroom convict at a higher rate than those not exposed to the news stories.

Pervasive pretrial media coverage presents a legal conundrum. Little can be done to hinder the publicity, and the search for jurors oblivious to the news reports results in a less-educated, less-representative jury. On the other hand, we can doubt jurors' good-faith pledge of impartiality. Another remedy, however, is possible: a change of venue.

CHANGE OF VENUE

Venue and vicinage are related, but different, concepts. Venue is the place where a trial is held, which is normally the location of the event that is the subject of the litigation. If an alleged murder or act of malpractice took place in Dane County, for example, then the venue for the murder or malpractice trial is Dane County. Vicinage, as we have seen, requires that jurors be drawn from the community where the trial is held—in this case, Dane County.

Occasionally, however, because of pretrial publicity or other causes of prejudice, the normal location will not yield an unbiased jury. Selecting the jurors from another community may provide a fairer trial. A change of venue, that is, moving the trial to another locality, and drawing the jurors from the new location may be necessary to provide an impartial trial.

Because a criminal defendant is normally seen as having the right to a jury of the vicinage, venue cannot be changed against a criminal defendant's wishes. But neither can it be changed simply because a defendant requests it. His right to a jury of the vicinage is not one he may simply waive whenever he thinks it would be in his interest to do so. Instead, he must show why a venue change is needed.

The mere fact of pretrial publicity is not sufficient to justify a venue change. The accused must show that there is "reasonable likelihood" that a fair jury cannot be selected. In rare situations, a court might assume such prejudice when massive media coverage has so saturated a community that picking an impartial jury seems unlikely. More frequently, however, an accused must do more than point to damaging news stories to get a venue change. Using polls or by voir dire he must show that a large percentage of jury-eligible citizens have been exposed to the publicity and that many of them have concluded that the accused is guilty as a result. Even with extensive publicity, however, a sufficient number of jurors usually pledge impartiality, and a jury from the community can be empaneled.

Venue changes are rare. Courts recognize that local communities have a legitimate interest in resolving cases, and any motion to change venue must overcome the presumption favoring the original locality. Finally, venue changes are rare because often they simply would not matter. Media attention today is seldom restricted to one community. A changed venue may do little to get a fairer jury. Because some notable trials in large cities have received changes of venue, the public believes this is a routine procedure. In fact, changes of venue happen very infrequently and occur primarily in small, rural areas where community interest may be intense but significant publicity has spread no farther than the county border.[15]

Community-based juries, then, are embedded in our legal system. Even so, calling juries community-based does not define who from the community is eligible to be a juror and how they are selected. And this definition has not remained consistent over time. In fact, the definition of eligibility has expanded steadily until today juries are the most diverse, the most democratically representative of any of our government institutions.

Chapter 9 The Most Diverse of Our Democratic Bodies

Although our juries come from the community, historically not every member of the community could be a juror. Just as the right to vote was once restricted in this country, so, too, was jury eligibility. When the Constitution was adopted, every state limited jury service to men; all but one of the states required jurors to be property owners or taxpayers; three permitted only white individuals to serve; and one disqualified atheists. Roughly the same limitations were placed on voting. Soon, however, the franchise began to expand as property qualifications were dropped or diluted. Over time, jury eligibility followed with a similar expansion. By the second half of the nineteenth century people who were eligible to vote generally could serve on juries. Jury pools expanded from a propertied class to the inclusion of all adult white male citizens. Others, however, were still excluded.

THE FORMAL INCLUSION OF BLACK JURORS

Up until the Civil War, only six states formally permitted black people to vote. Not surprisingly, this minority group did not then serve on juries. The first black jurors were apparently two who served in 1860 in Worcester, Massachusetts.[1]

The Fifteenth Amendment, enacted following the Civil War, gave black people the right to vote, but the Civil War amendments said nothing directly about jury service. In 1880, however, the Supreme Court in *Strauder v. Virginia* held that a state statute expressly prohibiting black people from jury service violated the equal protection clause of the Fourteenth Amendment. Black people could not be legally excluded from the jury rolls because of their race, but the Court's opinion also suggested how black and other perceived undesirables could be kept off juries. While proscribing race, the Court concluded that a state could "prescribe the qualifications of its jurors. . . . It may confine the selection to males, to freeholders, to citizens, to person with certain ages, or to persons who have educational qualifications. We do not believe the Fourteenth Amendment was ever intended to prohibit this. . . . Its aim was against discrimination because of race or color."[2]

Many jurisdictions, especially in the South, found ways to adopt qualification requirements to prevent black people from becoming jurors. As late as the 1950s, black people occasionally served on juries in the large southern cities, but almost never in southern rural areas.

WOMEN JURORS

Strauder held that although juror eligibility could not be limited to white people, it could be restricted to men. Along with the movement for women's suffrage, however, came a movement to permit women to be jurors. As women won the right to vote, they often were permitted to serve on juries as well. Utah, in 1898, was the first state to allow women jurors, followed by Washington in 1911 and Kansas in 1913. An expanded right to vote, however, did not automatically grant jury eligibility. Wyoming and Colorado granted women the right to vote in the nineteenth century but did not permit women to serve on juries until the 1940s.

This pattern remained even after ratification of the Nineteenth Amendment in 1920 granted women the right to vote throughout the country. Some states automatically expanded jury eligibility to include women after the right to vote was granted, while others did not permit women to serve until decades later. Various reasons were given for not having women jurors. Some opponents supposedly wished to protect women from the "corrupting influences" of trials, while others argued "that women were, for a variety of reasons—emotionalism, inability to sustain logical and rational argument, prior commitment to domestic chores—less capable than men." Such arguments were expressed in a North Carolina flier opposing women's suffrage on the grounds that women voting would lead to women's jury service. The tract asserted that in Washington, where women could vote and be on juries, women jurors were separated from their families and had not been allowed to attend their children stricken with the measles. It went on to state "that at almost every term of court language is used and incidents recited from the witness stand that grate on the sensibility of all refined men present. Profanity, obscenity and the detailed narration of the immoral acts and doings of the lowest type of humanity are brought out in all their revolting nakedness. . . . Men of the South, do you like this prospect for your wife, your daughter, or for the women who may become your wife?"[3]

Even after women had become eligible for jury service, they often received distinctive treatment. For example, a 1921 Oregon law required that "in all cases in which a minor under the age of eighteen years is involved, either as a defendant or as complaining witness, at least one half the jury shall be women." On the other hand, a 1949 Massachusetts law empowered judges to exempt women from jury service when they would "likely . . . be embarrassed by hearing the testimony or by discussing [it] in the jury room."[4]

The most common form of special treatment, however, was to award women an exemption from jury service based on their sex alone. A 1937 New York statute granting women jury eligibility created exemptions from jury duty that could be claimed by "a clergyman . . . officiating as such . . . ; a practicing physician, surgeon or surgeon dentist having patients requiring his daily professional attention, a licensed pharmacist . . . a person belonging to the army, navy or marine corps . . . ; [a] captain, engineer, or other officer, actually employed upon a vessel . . . ; [an] attorney . . . regularly engaged in the practice of law . . . ; a duly licensed embalmer . . . ; a woman."[5] Some states went further and did not just provide an exemption that had to be claimed, but instead permitted women to serve on juries only if they volunteered for service. As late as 1961, when women could serve on juries in forty-seven states, they had to volunteer in nineteen of those forty-seven in order to be eligible.

This situation has changed. The roots of the changes go back to the 1940s when the Supreme Court concluded that the jury pools from which federal trial juries were selected had to represent a fair cross section of the community.[6] This led the Supreme Court in 1946 to invalidate federal jury selection procedures that excluded day laborers[7] and women. Justice William O. Douglas, writing for the Court, stated:

The thought is that the factors which tend to influence the action of women are the same as those which influence the action of men—personality, background, economic status—and not sex. Yet it is not enough to say that women when sitting as jurors neither act nor tend to act as a class. Men likewise do not act as a class. But, if the shoe were on the other foot, who would claim that a jury was truly representative of the community if all men were intentionally and systematically excluded from the panel? The truth is that the two sexes are not fungible; a community made up exclusively of one is different from a community composed of both; the subtle interplay of influence one on the other is among the imponderables. To insulate the courtroom from either may not in a given case make an iota of difference. Yet a flavor, a distinct quality is lost if either sex is excluded. The exclusion of one may indeed make the jury less representative of the community than would be true if an economic or racial group were excluded.[8]

The Sixth Amendment did not then apply to the states, and in 1961 the Supreme Court upheld a state system in which women were eligible for juries only if they volunteered. The Court noted that the community roles of women were expanding but went on to state that "woman is still regarded as the center of home and family life. We cannot say that it is constitutionally impermissible for a State, acting in pursuit of the general welfare, to conclude that a woman should be relieved from the civic duty of jury service unless she herself determines that such service is consistent with her own special responsibilities."[9]

ADOPTION OF THE FAIR
CROSS SECTION REQUIREMENT

In 1968, however, *Duncan v. Louisiana* held that the Sixth Amendment applied to the states. Seven years later in *Taylor v. Louisiana* the Court confronted Louisiana's jury selection system, which did not disqualify women from service but required them to file a written declaration of their desire to serve.[10] As a result, less than 10 percent of potential jurors were women. The Court, with only Justice William Rehnquist dissenting, held that this system denied the defendant his right to a jury trial as constitutionally guaranteed by the Sixth Amendment. *Taylor* first noted that federal jury pools had to be representative of a cross section of the community:

> We accept the fair cross section requirement as fundamental to the jury trial guaranteed by the Sixth Amendment and are convinced that the requirement has solid foundation. The purpose of a jury is to guard against the exercise of arbitrary power—to make available the commonsense judgment of the community as a hedge

against the overzealous or mistaken prosecutor and in preference to the professional or perhaps overconditioned or biased response of a judge. This prophylactic vehicle is not provided if the jury pool is made up of only special segments of the populace or if large, distinctive groups are excluded from the pool. Community participation in the administration of criminal law, moreover, is not only consistent with our democratic heritage but is also critical to public confidence in the fairness of the criminal justice system. Restricting jury service to only special groups or excluding identifiable segments playing major roles in the community cannot be squared with the constitutional concept of jury trial.[11]

The Court concluded that women constitute a sufficiently large and distinct group so that their systematic exclusion from jury pools violated this fair cross section requirement. Although Louisiana may have been able to point to some rational reason why its volunteer system made sense, this was not sufficient to save those procedures.

The States are free to grant exemptions from jury service to individuals in case of special hardship or incapacity and to those engaged in particular occupations the uninterrupted performance of which is critical to the community's welfare. . . . A system excluding all women, however, is a wholly different matter. It is untenable to suggest these days that it would be a special hardship for each and every woman to perform jury service or that society cannot spare *any* women from their present duties. . . . The states remain free to prescribe relevant qualifications for their jurors and to provide reasonable exemptions so long as it may be fairly said that the jury lists or panels are representative of the community.[12]

The Court stressed a limitation of its ruling. It was not holding that the trial juries themselves must satisfy the fair cross section requirement. "Defendants are not entitled to a jury of any particular composition; but the jury wheels, pools of names, panels or venires from which juries are drawn must not systematically exclude distinctive groups in the community and thereby fail to be reasonably representative thereof."[13]

Four years later *Duren v. Missouri* added clarification. The Court held that a violation of the fair cross section requirement was established when a defendant showed: that the representation on jury pools of a distinctive group in the community was not fair and reasonable in relation to the numbers in the community; that "this underrepresentation was due to systematic exclusion of the group in the jury process"; and that the state had not shown "a significant state interest" to justify the exclusion. Missouri had permitted women to decline jury service by claiming an exemption on the jury summons. As a result, while women constituted 54 percent of the community, they accounted for only 15 percent of the jury pool. The state could not justify this underrepresentation by merely claiming a childcare concern. Justice Byron White, writing for the Court, stated "that a State may have an important interest in assuring that those members of the family responsible for the care of children are available to do so," but an exemption would have to be "appropriately tailored to this interest."[14]

THE REACH OF THE FAIR
CROSS SECTION REQUIREMENT

The fair cross section requirement has produced a dramatic change in how our juries are selected, and understanding its reach is important. First, as *Taylor* made clear, the requirement does not apply to individual trial juries. From a practical standpoint, this limitation is necessary. A group of six or twelve will almost always fail to represent all the characteristics of the community.

Instead, the fair cross section requirement is a mandate that the people who are brought to the courthouse from which the trial juries are selected—variously referred to as the jury pool, venires, the array, talesmen—should fairly represent the community. While applying only to this phase of jury selection, the requirement, however, has obvious effects on the entire selection process. The best way to ensure that jury pools represent a fair cross section of the community is to have the list of jury-eligible people represent a fair cross section and then randomly bring people from that list to the courthouse. And, of course, trial juries selected from skewed jury pools have little chance of fairly representing the community. If the pools contain a fair cross section of the community, the likelihood of having representative trial jurors increases.

The *Taylor* ruling applies only to criminal trials, but civil trials are also affected. Governments do not create separate jury lists for civil and criminal cases; instead jury pools for both kinds of cases come from the same source, using similar procedures. The fair cross section requirement for criminal cases has also meant that civil juries will be selected from pools that fairly represent the community.

The fair cross section requirement does not require the representation of every imaginable societal segment. Instead, the group must be "large" and "distinctive." We know that women are covered, as are racial groups, but it is not clear what other slices of the community must be fairly represented. The defining test is hardly precise, but for a group to qualify for the requirement, it must be identifiable, and its underrepresentation must affect the jury's ability to act as a check on governmental oppression and to preserve public confidence in our criminal justice system. Courts have found Mexican Americans, Native Americans, and Jews to be such groups for the fair cross section requirement, but not other groups such as blue-collar workers or young adults.

The jury pool does not have to mirror the community demographics precisely. Instead the underrepresentation of a group must be large enough to raise questions about the fairness of the jury selection. Little doubt exists when, for example, a community includes 50 percent women but only 10 or 15 percent of the jury pools consist of women. Nonetheless, no precise standard has been set to determine when underrepresentation is significant enough to violate the fair cross section requirement.

In addition, the underrepresentation does not violate the Sixth Amendment if it results from exclusions narrowly tailored to serve legitimate societal interest. As the Court suggested, for example, the state may validly be concerned about child care. An exemption for all women to serve this purpose is too broad because not all women have child care responsibilities. An exclusion that permits those people caring for children to be exempted from jury service, however, is narrowly tailored to serve the appropriate goal. This exemption will probably allow more women to be excused from jury service than men. Women, as a result, may be underrepresented on jury pools, but this, and other appropriately drafted exemptions and exclusions, does not violate the fair cross section requirement.

Finally, the lack of a fair cross section has to result from a "systematic" exclusion. This does not require showing an intent to discriminate or exclude. The equal protection clause of the Fourteenth Amendment also protects against disparate treatment of distinctive groups, but equal protection requires proving that the government or a government official intended to discriminate against a group. In the jury schemes considered in *Taylor* and *Duren,* no official prevented women from being eligible for jury service, and no proof showed that the legislatures were intending to exclude women in enacting the juror selection schemes. The equal protection rights of women may not have been violated. Even without the intent to discriminate, however, the systems in place requiring women to volunteer or permitting them an automatic exemption led to the underrepresentation of a distinctive group. Thus, there was a systematic exclusion that violated the accused's right to jury pools containing a fair cross section of the community.

The fair cross section requirement comes close to placing on the government an affirmative duty to provide jury pools that accurately reflect the community. This represents a huge change from the historical practices of jury selection in this country.

THE IMPACT OF THE FAIR
CROSS SECTION REQUIREMENT

The most obvious effect of the fair cross section requirement is that jury pools now include groups that were once excluded. African Americans must be included in the venires; so do women. Not only do they have to be represented, they must be represented in numbers that correlate to their numbers in the community. One recent survey of eight major cities showed that about 53 percent of those called for jury duty today are women. The degree of racial diversity, not surprisingly, varies more from place to place, but it too indicates a significant change from earlier practices.[15]

The fair cross section requirement has also spawned another fundamental reform. For much of our history, no matter how broad or narrow the definition of juror eligibility, the pools were not randomly picked from the eligible group. Instead, government officials individually selected potential jurors from those eligible. The usual method of selecting a jury venire was that when a case was about to go to trial, the trial judge would order the sheriff to produce a stated number of potential jurors at the courthouse. The sheriff was left to his own devices concerning how he selected these potential jurors. Especially in small communities where the government official might be aware of the views of different citizens, the sheriff could have a great effect on the case's outcome by consciously skewing his selection process.[16]

Most often the nonrandom selection of the jury pool, not surprisingly, aided the prosecution, but occasionally the opposite was true. For example, in the 1880s Jesse James's brother, Frank, a southern sympathizer, was tried for murder and robbery in Missouri, where feelings about the Civil War were still strong. The sheriff was ordered to empanel one hundred potential jurors. The prosecutor claimed this pool was stacked against the state. Certainly it was striking that all one hundred were Democrats, and the jury did acquit.[17]

Even in jurisdictions where potential jurors were randomly summoned from rosters of those eligible for service, those rosters themselves often did not constitute a fair cross section of jury-eligible citizens. This was especially true in places that used a "key-man" system to gather the jury lists. Political and civil leaders such as the head of a service organization, the chamber of commerce, or other community bodies supplied names of potential jurors, usually people the key-men knew. This system was supposed to produce higher-quality jurors than would a more inclusive jury list. That may have been so, but it often produced "white, comparatively affluent, better-educated jurors who very much resembled the profiles of the key men making the selections. In the South the key-man method managed for years to virtually eliminate blacks from serving as jurors."[18] Many states and the federal courts have abandoned this method, but the key-man system is still used in about 30 percent of the states. Now, however, with the fair cross section requirement in place, the jury lists compiled by these key-men must fairly represent the community.

The fair cross section requirement has also affected the discretionary powers held by jury commissioners to compile jury lists. These are outlined in Linda K. Kerber's description of Florida practice: "'In the selection of jury lists,' the 1949 statute read, 'only such persons as the selecting officers know, or have reason to believe, are law-abiding citizens of approved integrity, good character, sound judgment and intelligence, and who are not physically or mentally infirm, shall be selected for jury duty.' This discretion was widely used for keeping blacks off juries. Charged with finding black men of 'integrity, good character, sound judgment and intelligence' in a segregated state in which whites assumed that none of these qualities were characteristics of blacks, jury commissioners throughout the South regularly placed in jury pools the names of a handful of black ministers, funeral directors, and perhaps a shopkeeper or two, and assumed that the entire African-American community was therefore represented on the jury."[19]

The jury commissioners' powers were used not just to reduce the number of black individuals in jury pools. The discretion could also eliminate those who seemed to threaten mainstream values. For example, in the 1940s Los Angeles jury commissioners interviewed prospective jurors to eliminate those with "a wrong conception of government or law enforcement."[20]

Once the states had to comply with the fair cross section requirement, many of them abandoned such vague juror qualifications because they impeded representative jury pools. A state can retain nebulous restrictions on jury service, but now if their administration leads to underrepresentation of distinctive groups, the government must show that the exclusionary practices are no broader than necessary to serve a valid governmental interest.

SPECIAL JURIES AND THE FAIR
CROSS SECTION REQUIREMENT

The fair cross section requirement has also cast doubt on the constitutionality of special juries. The term "special jury" has no precise definition but has generally meant trial jurors with some special qualification. Some early English and nineteenth-century American courts, for example, used juries restricted to merchants in commercial disputes. A related example was the ancient "jury *de medietate linguae* (literally, 'of the half- tongue')—to which foreign defendants would have been entitled. Half of the jury would be citizens of the state where the case was tried, while the other half would be foreigners. The notion was not merely to facilitate communication, but also, as expressed by a defendant in a seventeenth-century English case, to secure jurors 'of my own country, that may be able to know something how I have lived hitherto.' "[21]

A third example was slightly different. The English common law had few qualms about executions but balked at hanging pregnant women. To determine whether the condemned's claim of pregnancy was valid and the execution should be postponed, a jury consisting entirely of married women or widows who had experienced childbirth would inspect the prisoner to determine whether she was truly pregnant.

These special forms of juries died out a century or more ago, yet one version of the special jury persisted much longer. New York, for example, permitted a "blue-ribbon" jury when that was deemed necessary for a fair and impartial trial or the case had special "importance or intricacy." From the regular jury pool, the jury commissioners, after conducting personal interviews, prepared a smaller list of potential jurors who were deemed specially able. The trial jury was then selected in regular fashion from this subset, who were generally more affluent and educated than other potential jurors. The Supreme Court upheld the constitutionality of this procedure in the 1940s, but that was before the states had to comply with the fair cross section requirement.[22] In 1965 New York repealed its authorization for blue-ribbon juries.

Proposals for special juries, however, are still sometimes floated. One version asks "for racial or ethnic quotas for certain types of juries." Some proponents "make the explicit argument for adapting the historical *de medietate* practice to modern trials that promise to be racially charged. Others argue for racial quotas in order to give reality to the 'jury of peers' and thereby to secure a fair trial."[23] These proposals, however, have not progressed beyond some legal literature. No legislature has made any serious move to adopt them, partly, perhaps, because selecting one portion of a trial jury from one jury pool and the rest of the jury from another one would seem to run afoul of the fair cross section requirement.

Another suggestion for special juries would require express educational requirements or expertise for jurors in certain kinds of complex cases. The proponents of such special juries do not advocate a jury *pool* limited to prescribed qualifications. Instead, because the fair cross section requirement does not apply to individual trial juries, they propose that the best qualified from a representative jury pool could be selected to provide blue-ribbon jurors. Jury selection procedures today do not mandate such an approach, but it can be implemented with the parties' consent.

Even if we could find ways to have specially qualified juries, many still doubt their wisdom. While there may be an intuitive plausibility to the claim that more educated jurors will perform better in certain complex cases, the matter has been little studied, and even highly educated people often misunderstand basic scientific and statistical principles. Studies have shown that jurors with more schooling do deliberate longer and recall more of the evidence and instructions, but these benefits accrue as long as some jurors have college degrees. On the other hand, blue-ribbon juries are more homogeneous than are regular juries, and this loss of diversity can harm deliberations. As we have seen previously, "Varied life experiences, perspectives, and values in the group may result in a more wide-ranging discussion and increased understanding of the behaviors involved."[24]

Complex trials usually involve a mix of issues at least some of which benefit from diverse perspectives. "For example, in a serious automobile accident in which defendant negligence is at issue, there may be substantial variation across communities in beliefs about the appropriate uses of the public streets. Urban areas may have norms encouraging the use of streets as areas for play or general congregating that are uncommon in affluent suburban areas. An awareness of such subcultural differences may be important in making judgments about the plaintiff's negligence. The capacity of a blue-ribbon jury to make sensible judgments on issues of negligence may be seriously eroded in such a case, even if its ability to deal with statistical evidence about future wage losses or the testimony of forensic experts in accident reconstruction is enhanced."[25]

There could be more experimentation in selecting blue-ribbon juries in some complex cases, but it should not simply be assumed that such a body will be better. Careful research and monitoring is needed to see how such juries actually perform.

IMPLEMENTATION OF THE FAIR
CROSS SECTION REQUIREMENT

The apparently simple mandate that jury pools must represent a fair cross section of the community is often hard to achieve. The obvious method is to compile a list of all in the community eligible for jury service and then randomly select groups from this register to be potential jurors. The compilation of all jury-eligible citizens, however, can be difficult. Federal census, income tax, and social security records might yield such a roll, but federal law limits the use of this information, and these sources cannot be used to compile jury pools.

Instead, the list of registered voters usually serves as the starting point for assembling the names of potential jurors. Registered voter lists, however, do not contain everyone eligible for jury service. Only 60 to 80 percent of those eighteen years old or over are registered in most places, and those percentages have been dropping. The nonregistered voter is more likely to be a minority, less affluent, young, or one who moves frequently. Consequently, drawing jury pools solely from voter lists may not yield a true cross section of the community. Some challenges to the exclusive use of such lists to assemble potential jurors have been successful.

Many jurisdictions now supplement the registered voter rolls with other sources. New York, for example, also uses lists of state taxpayers, licensed drivers, and public assistance and state unemployment recipients. Washington supplements voter lists with the register of licensed drivers and state-issued identification cards. Other places have utilized local censuses, telephone books, city directories, and lists extracted from property taxpayers and hunting and dog licenses. In addition, the inclusiveness of jury lists has expanded as many places have ended or narrowed exemptions from jury service, and now doctors, lawyers, firefighters, undertakers, and others find themselves as prospective jurors for the first time.

Even a comprehensive compilation of those in the community, however, does not guarantee that jury pools will represent a fair cross section. The next step usually is to mail a questionnaire to those listed to ascertain their basic qualifications for jury service. They will be asked such things as their ages, citizenship, ability to comprehend English, and felony convictions. Finally, from those who are deemed eligible for jury service, groups are summoned to the courthouse at a particular time to be prospective jurors.

Not everyone, however, responds to these questionnaires and summonses. Mail is misdelivered, more often, studies have shown, in poor neighborhoods than in affluent ones. People move, and their mail is not always properly forwarded. Many forget or simply refuse to respond. Jury service is not always high on a list of favorite activities; one recent survey indicated that 25 percent of those eligible for jury duty would try to find some way to avoid the service.[26]

Avoidance of jury service is not a recent phenomenon. In colonial New York, it was often difficult to find the requisite number of jurors, and those who did not appear were routinely fined. In the 1873 trial of Boss Tweed for corrupt activities in New York City, about a hundred men were summoned for jury duty, but only twenty-eight showed up and the rest were fined. If those avoiding jury service could be found for the purpose of exacting fines from them, it might seem that ways could have been found to compel jury service. Instead, fines paid by the wealthy often allowed them, in effect, to buy their way out of jury duty. As one commentator notes, from 1870 to 1940 there were numerous complaints that the affluent were avoiding jury service, with the result that influential segments of the populace were losing faith in verdicts.[27]

The present problem of jury avoidance varies greatly from locality to locality. A recent North Carolina survey found that in some counties, close to half those summoned simply did not appear. A jurisdiction may address this problem by repeat mailings, but little more than that is usually done.[28] As long as jury boxes do get filled, jury officials generally think they have better things to do than to track down the stay-at-homes. Judges, especially those who face election, are unlikely to hold obdurate jurors in contempt with the attendant publicity this might produce. And lawyers and litigants are concerned that people too much coerced into jury duty will be hostile and bad jurors whose efforts to listen and deliberate carefully will be suspect. Jury service can generally be avoided today by simply refusing to respond to the questionnaire or summons.

Instead of pursuing the recalcitrants, more jurisdictions have been trying to deal with jury avoidance by removing some of the unnecessarily onerous aspects of jury service. One of the most frequent complaints about jury service is the apparent waste of potential jurors' time. In the past, for example, those summoned often had to sit at the courthouse for a week or more even if they did not make it on to a jury. Now it is common for people to be called for only one or two days, and if they are not selected for a jury, they are dismissed. Other localities have allowed jurors to be on phone alert and summoned to the courthouse only when a jury is about to be empaneled. Such an apparently mundane problem as parking can deter jury service, and child care is an issue for many. Certainly, improving the conditions of jury duty should be a continuing goal.

The fair cross section requirement, although not always perfectly implemented, has worked a great change in the composition of our juries. The result has been the presence of more minorities and women, but it goes beyond that. The more inclusive jury lists have brought better representation on many fronts. Jury pools now mirror the community better than before on such characteristics as income, age, education, and occupation, as well as on race and gender. The modern jury is now "the most diverse of our democratic bodies. After courts began to interpret constitutional mandates . . . to require that women and minorities be included on juries, the demographics of juries changed dramatically at a pace far exceeding the diversification of legislatures, executive branches, or the judiciary." Some may applaud this trend in juries, but its increased democratization may also have fueled distrust. Robert Burns concludes, "[I]t is clear that the trial, the jury trial in particular, is under attack at this point in our history. The reasons for this are complex[, but] . . . it is no accident that the level of hostility to the trial has risen during a period [roughly the last thirty years] when Congress and the Supreme Court have quietly democratized the jury, bringing perspectives to this important institution that had long been unrepresented."[29]

Chapter 10 Challenges for Cause

The assembly of a jury pool representing a fair cross section of the community is merely the first step in selecting a trial jury. The actual trial jurors have to be picked from this group, and they are not merely a random selection from the jury pool. The lawyers and judge in each trial select a jury through the exercise of for-cause and peremptory challenges. This chapter considers the process of finding out information about prospective jurors, the voir dire, and the procedure to excuse jurors who will not be impartial—challenges for cause. (The next chapter will discuss peremptory challenges.)

VOIR DIRE

A trial begins when an array of potential jurors is brought to the place of trial. The trial judge may greet this group with some introductory remarks telling them the basic nature of the case, an estimate of how long the trial is expected to last, and who the parties and lawyers are. Then the voir dire begins.[1] The prospective jurors are questioned to find out whether they will be impartial in the particular case being tried and to obtain additional information that attorneys may use in exercising peremptory challenges.

Jury trials do not require this voir dire. Great Britain does without it. Voir dire questioning and peremptory challenges have been abolished there, with potentially important consequences: "An accused can still challenge jurors for cause, but without the opportunity to question prospective jurors which is available to American lawyers, the ability of a barrister both to detect and to establish bias are severely limited. Unless the barrister or the defendant is aware of a reason for suspecting a juror's impartiality, or the juror volunteers such information, the juror will be permitted to sit. The resulting jury may be more democratic, in that it is the undiluted product of random selection, but whether or not its members are biased is virtually impossible to determine."[2] In America, however, every trial includes some voir dire questioning. It is constitutionally required in criminal cases in order to meet the Sixth Amendment requirement that jurors be "impartial."

These constitutional requirements, however, are minimal. Potential jurors do not have to be questioned individually but can be asked in groups, for example, whether pretrial publicity has prejudiced them. The Constitution leaves it to the trial judge's discretion whether inquiry about specific grounds of possible bias are necessary. For example, in 1973 in *Ham v. South Carolina,* the trial judge refused to ask specifically about possible prejudices concerning the defendant's facial hair. Although this was a time when beards commonly evoked strong negative feelings, the Supreme Court stated, "Given the traditionally broad discretion accorded to the trial judge in conducting *voir dire* . . . and our inability to distinguish possible prejudice against beards from a host of other possible similar prejudices, we do not believe the [defendant's] constitutional rights were violated when the trial judge refused to put this question."[3]

The Constitution requires only that potential jurors be asked generally about their ability to be impartial. The major exception is when racial issues are central to a criminal case. Specific questions about racial prejudice must then be asked, but even so, no more than perfunctory questions about race addressed to the entire panel are constitutionally necessary. Extensive questioning of individuals is not. Furthermore, the requirement to inquire about racial prejudice arises only when race "permeates" the case, and the mere fact that the crime is an interracial one does not give rise to the constitutional duty to voir dire about racial bias.[4]

That the Constitution requires little voir dire questioning does not mean that most trial courts permit only a minimal inquiry. On the contrary, many— probably most—trial courts would permit more than what is constitutionally required. The result is a wide variation in practice from jurisdiction to jurisdiction and from trial court to trial court on voir dire questioning in both civil and criminal cases.

The basic forms of voir dire themselves vary widely. The chief difference centers on whether the attorney or the judge is the primary interrogator. In about one-third of the states and the federal courts, the trial judge has the discretion to conduct the questioning or permit the attorney to do so; in another third, the attorney has the main control over the process; and in the remainder, the court examines the prospective jurors with the attorneys supplementing the questioning.[5]

The form of the voir dire does matter. When attorneys do the primary questioning, for example, the process takes longer, a significant consideration. One study found that the voir dire process constituted 40 percent of the total trial time, and lengthy jury selections provoke some of the loudest criticisms of the jury system.[6]

Part of the reason the voir dire process takes more time when attorneys control the process is that they often use it for purposes other than gathering information about prospective jurors. They also seek to indoctrinate, socialize, and educate prospective jurors. Stephen Phillips, who wrote about a New York case he prosecuted, explains:

> An attorney will ask essentially rhetorical questions of jurors, the purpose of which is not so much as to elicit an answer as to make those listening think about and accept the attorney's view of a particular problem. For instance, I would ask a juror whether he felt he could convict Richardson of the gun-possession charge even though I could not physically produce the weapon in court. After explaining that the law did not require the actual gun itself to prove my case, I would ask the juror if he had ever thrown a rock into the ocean or a lake. The person would answer yes, and then I would ask whether the fact that this rock could not be recovered would create any doubt that in fact it had been thrown. Of course the answer would be no, and then I would explain that the same principle applied to the gun charge. If the evidence presented at the trial persuaded the juror that Richardson had possessed the gun, its absence from the courtroom did not mean that the defendant was innocent. The purpose of these questions was not to discover the juror's prejudices, but to make a point that might help the jury to convict. It was an opportunity to neutralize a possible weakness in my case—even to turn it into an advantage. I was laying a foundation for arguments that I would be making later.[7]

The trial judge has wide discretion in allowing this sort of questioning. Moreover, how well this aspect of voir dire actually educates or indoctrinates the jurors is open to intense debate. Some see such tactics as embarrassingly condescending, but attorneys when given the chance frequently use them.

The form of the voir dire also affects how much information is elicited about the potential jurors' impartiality. In some questioning, jurors are asked general questions, such as, "Is there any reason why you cannot be fair and impartial in this case?" This, in effect, requires the potential jurors to volunteer possible grounds of bias and produces fewer responses than do questions about specific areas of possible partiality, such as, "Has the pretrial publicity led you to believe that the accused is guilty?" Similarly, potential jurors are less likely to concede bias when they are addressed as a group than when they are questioned individually. A Canadian case where a father was charged with sexually abusing his daughter and the jurors were asked as a group whether they could be impartial provides a notable example. The jurors apparently all nodded affirmatively. The defense attorney, however, thought there was some hesitancy in the responses and convinced the trial judge to question the potential jurors individually. During this procedure, three potential jurors conceded that they could not be impartial, and a mistrial was declared. "In the subsequent retrial, . . . [t]he jurors were questioned individually out of the presence of the rest of the prospective jurors. . . . [O]f 27 jurors questioned 13 (or 48%) stated that they could not be impartial."[8]

Potential jurors can abuse the system at this point. Those who do not wish to serve may claim bias simply in order to be excused. Sometimes these admissions flood the court, as in the notorious trial for murder of radical labor leader Bill Haywood at the turn of the twentieth century: "The difficulty was that many talesmen, not wishing to serve but knowing they didn't have grounds to be excused, could simply claim an opinion hardening into bias, which would assure them quick passage back to the ranch. Indeed, so may talesmen were eager to confess that their minds were made up that reporters regarded the process as farcical. 'God's truth, but they were liars!' wrote a man from the *Denver Post.* 'They came in and sat in the vacant chair, one by one, and perjured themselves blatantly, freely and eloquently.' "[9]

Indeed, one commentator has stated the most common reason for dishonesty during voir dire is to avoid jury service. There is, however, little that can be done about it. Seymour Wishman, trial attorney and author, notes, "If a juror knows the right excuse and is willing to insist on it in the face of the judge's intimidation, it is easy to avoid serving on a jury. All a person has to say is that he can't hear or see well, or he has to be home to feed his kids, or that he hates criminals or that he loves them, and that juror can be off the case."[10]

Claims of bias by potential jurors are, in fact, not the usual problem. Failure to report bias is a bigger problem. Most of us want to appear fair-minded and find it difficult to say publicly that we are biased. Jurors learn what answers will result in their removal, and many feel that giving those responses is akin to failing a test and being censured by the trial judge. The usual result is that admissions of bias decline significantly as the voir dire proceeds. In one case, for example, "in which a black defendant was tried for the murder of a nineteen-year old white woman. . . , [f]our of the first nine people questioned said that they could not be impartial. Of the remaining fifty-two, only one admitted to bias."[11]

Who asks the questions matters. Judges elicit fewer reports of bias than lawyers do. "In terms of prime purpose—uncovering overtly biased jurors— lawyer-conducted voir dire, according to most studies, is markedly superior to judge-conducted. The most frequently discerned reasons: One, lawyers, because of their superior knowledge of the case, ask better questions, on the whole, than do judges; two, jurors tend to be in awe of judges or fear them and may try to impress them with a 'fair-mindedness' that sharp questioning from an attorney would disprove."[12]

How questions about bias are asked also matters. Because successful challenges for cause extend the jury selection process, many judges indicate that lack of bias is the correct response. To speed things along, "judges often ask questions designed to secure declarations of impartiality, and then treat these declarations as conclusive."[13]

For example, a legal rule in criminal cases states that the accused does not have to testify and further that this refusal cannot be used against her. This goes against our commonsense way of proceeding in other contexts, and the voir dire frequently asks prospective jurors whether they will hold it against an accused if he does not testify. Some jurors indicate hesitancy about accepting this principle. A trial judge hearing such a response could grant a for-cause challenge, but most often the juror's reaction brings further inquiries. The manner of that inquiry can be crucial. The judge may say in an intimidating manner that this principle against self-incrimination is required by our law. The judge then asks, "Surely you can be fair and follow the law, can't you?" Most potential jurors have respect for judges or at least can be cowed by them, and few people want to confess unfairness or an inability to follow the law. The juror often responds by agreeing with the judge and stating that she can obey the law, thereby eliminating the grounds for a for-cause challenge. Colorado Judge Morris Hoffman's satirical comments highlight the problems inherent in this practice:

"I sympathize with lawyers when one of my bone-headed colleagues (it's never me) says something like, 'Well, counsel, you make a good point arguing that Juror Jones is biased because she was in this same kind of car accident last week, but she said she can be fair. You'll just have to use one of your peremptory challenges.' . . . Voir dire tends, especially when it is judicially administered, to be a hollow mockery. . . . [F]or that potential juror who was asleep and gave the wrong answer, there is what I call the Lazarus syndrome. You rehabilitate that juror by saying, 'When you said you would be unfair you really thought I meant fair because you didn't hear me very well because the acoustics in the room were temporarily bad.' "[14]

Comparable moments occur often in jury selection, and not all judges seek to exercise their powers of resurrection. Many respectfully question the potential jurors, trying to discover whether they will be biased. But because the trial judges have great discretion in how they proceed and there is wide variation in how they exercise this power, the result is a great difference from case to case in the number of jurors who confess bias.

No matter how it is done, however, most who have studied the practice conclude that our voir dire process is not particularly good at flushing out those who will not be impartial.[15] Nevertheless, some feel that it is the best we can do: "Some judges believe that the voir dire merely gets at the most superficial information about a juror, and that only an in-depth examination extended over a period of months could offer even a chance of flushing out a potential juror's hidden antipathies. Others feel that as long as our society wishes a system of trial by jury, the voir dire is the only practical approach, and is therefore worth spending at least some time on it."[16]

It may be, however, that although the voir dire is not particularly effective at finding the possible biases of potential jurors, the process still serves valuable purposes. For example, in one study, jurors who had been peremptorily challenged were asked to remain and observe the trial as if they had been selected jurors. In addition, the summoned jurors who had not been asked questions during the voir dire were also asked to observe the trial. The study found that overall, those peremptorily challenged voted about the same way as the selected jurors, while the those who had not undergone the voir dire voted disproportionately for guilt. The study concluded that juries composed of those without the voir dire would have convicted in every case, while the real juries convicted five times, acquitted six times, and hung once. The reasons for the differences among the jurors could not be fully explained, but the researchers suggested that the voir dire process itself may make jurors behave differently.

"The personal questioning that occurs during the voir dire and the willingness of the attorneys and judge to retain a juror may leave an impact on the sitting jurors that was not experienced by the . . . jurors [who were not voir dired.] This voir dire process may impress upon the jurors the importance of their task and may enhance their awareness of their duty to decide the case fairly and impartially."[17]

HARDSHIP EXCUSALS

Sometimes voir dire elicits the report that a potential juror would have to endure special hardship to serve on the jury. A person may be taking care of an invalid; a long planned trip is about to begin; a student may have final exams; pressing problems at work may need immediate attention. The trial judge has wide discretion in excusing potential jurors for hardship, but almost always the longer the trial is projected to last, the more people will ask for excusal. This can affect the representativeness of the jury, for the requests do not cut equally across demographic lines. Those with higher incomes and more education claim hardship more often; consequently, jurors on longer trials are more likely to be unemployed or retired, female, without a college education, and unmarried than are jurors who serve on shorter trials.

No reliable statistics have been kept on how many potential jurors are excused for hardship, but the number can be high, partly because the court and attorneys are wary of empaneling jurors who are forced into making a great personal sacrifice to serve. One trial lawyer states: "Often as many as half the panel are excused because they claim some pressing personal or business reason that will conflict with their service. By and large, such excuses are accepted uncritically by all concerned. Neither [defense attorney nor prosecutor] had any desire to keep an unwilling juror imprisoned in the jury box for many weeks. Such a person would seethe with hostility, and his ultimate actions would be unpredictable."[18]

CHALLENGES FOR CAUSE

The voir dire information may also indicate that a potential juror cannot be impartial. A husband, for example, should not sit on the jury when his wife is suing for damages, and most states statutorily forbid relatives of the parties or others directly involved in the case from being jurors. Such statutes usually also list some other specific grounds for disqualifying a potential juror—for example, if the person has served as a juror in some related matter or the person will serve as a witness in the impending trial.

Bias, however, can have many causes. As we have seen, as a result of pretrial publicity a potential juror may have formed such a firm opinion of the case that he cannot decide the matter solely on the presented evidence and instructions. A potential juror may be a stockholder in the company being sued or work for one of its stores. Or he may have such a high or low opinion of the police that he cannot fairly evaluate a testifying officer's credibility. Or he may believe a law is wrong and cannot follow the judge's instructions. Because not all the possibilities can be categorized specifically, a juror can also be excused for cause under a general standard, such as, the juror "has a state of mind that is likely to preclude him from rendering an impartial verdict based on the evidence adduced at trial."[19]

The attorneys can, thus, challenge for cause any potential juror who they believe cannot be impartial. When this occurs, the trial judge must determine whether the potential juror should be excused. United States law considers the trial judge, who has seen and heard the voir dire, to be in the best position to determine whether a challenge for cause should be granted, and it gives the trial judge broad discretion in deciding whether in these and myriad similar circumstances potential jurors should be excused.[20]

There are few data on how often challenges for cause are granted, but a typical estimate is that perhaps about one in twenty jurors is excused for cause. This generalization, however, masks the fact that the decisions are often difficult and trial judges vary greatly in their proclivity to find the requisite cause. Differences in the exercise of this judicial discretion are one reason the number of successful challenges for cause can vary considerably from courtroom to courtroom.

THE DEATH PENALTY, CHALLENGES FOR CAUSE, AND VOIR DIRE

The death penalty has raised special issues for challenges for cause. Many people, of course, are opposed to capital punishment. Some find it impossible to make a person subject to the death penalty even if the case has been proved beyond a reasonable doubt. Such potential jurors can be excused no matter how the sentencing issue is decided. Other capital punishment opponents maintain that they can fairly judge guilt or innocence, but they could not impose a sentence of death. Jurors have the responsibility of determining sentence as well as guilt or innocence. This is a two-step jury process. First, a jury determines guilt or innocence. If the jury finds the accused guilty of a crime for which a death sentence is possible, that jury, after hearing more information about the appropriate sentence, determines whether capital punishment should be imposed. This situation allows death penalty opponents to impartially determine guilt, but not to impartially determine a sentence if guilt is found.

The Supreme Court has held that potential jurors can be removed from such juries if they could never return a death sentence, but they cannot be excused simply because they "expressed scruples" against the death penalty. To be removed for cause, however, a juror does not have to make it absolutely clear that he would not impose a death sentence. Rather, the issue is whether the person's views "would prevent or substantially impair the performance of his duties as juror in accordance with his instructions and his oath." The potential juror who cannot impartially consider the death sentence can be removed for cause. If the same jury considers both guilt and the sentence, the excusal of such a juror means not only that he will not help determine the sentence, he will also be excluded from the process of determining guilt, even though he may be able to do that impartially.[21]

Critics of this process contend that in attempting to get impartial jurors for sentencing, we produce juries biased on the issue of guilt. Those who find it difficult or impossible to impose the death penalty may not only see capital punishment differently; they may also tend to see issues that affect the determination of guilt differently from those who can deliver a death sentence. Studies have attempted to show that so-called death-qualified juries are more likely to convict than are juries comprising people both for and against the death penalty. The defendant in *Lockhart v. McCree* relied on this research, contending that a death-qualified jury deprived him of his constitutional right to an impartial jury for the determination of guilt.[22]

The Supreme Court rejected the argument. The Court first noted that death-qualified juries do not violate the fair cross section requirement and reaffirmed that that mandate applies only to jury pools and not trial juries. Consequently, it does not affect the use of either for-cause or peremptory challenges. Furthermore, the fair cross section requirement applies only to distinctive groups, such as "blacks, women, or Mexican-Americans" and not to "groups defined solely in terms of shared attitudes that would prevent or substantially impair members of the group from performing or substantially performing one of their duties as jurors."[23]

The Court continued that even if it were shown that death-qualified juries are "somewhat more 'conviction-prone,'" the accused's right to an impartial jury to determine guilt is not violated. The Court stressed that the jury that convicted was in fact impartial because all the selected jurors had pledged to decide the case on the presented evidence and instructions. "[E]xactly the same twelve individuals could have ended up on his jury through the 'luck of the draw,' without in any way violating the constitutional guarantee of impartiality."[24]

A solution to conviction-prone, death-qualified juries would be to have separate juries decide guilt and the sentence. The guilt phase could include all who could impartially determine whether the accused committed the crime. If this jury found the defendant guilty, then a second, death-qualified jury would be empaneled to decide the punishment. This process has costs, however, for, as the Court concluded in *Lockhart v. McCree,* "much of the evidence adduced at the guilt phase of the trial will also have a bearing on the penalty phase," and such proof would have to be produced twice. Consequently, the death-qualified jury deciding both issues "serves the State's entirely proper interest in obtaining a single jury that could impartially decide all of the issues."[25]

Potential jurors who would automatically impose the death penalty for a particular crime present a related problem, because the Supreme Court has held that the death penalty cannot be a mandatory punishment—the conviction for a certain crime cannot automatically lead to a death sentence. Instead, capital punishment can only be an option, and the sentencing authority must exercise discretion in determining whether capital punishment should be imposed. Death penalty statutes vary, but generally they require the prosecution to prove specified aggravating factors about the crime (the method of committing the crime was especially heinous), or about the accused (the accused will be dangerous in the future). The defendant then has the opportunity to present mitigating information. The sentencing authority must weigh all this evidence in determining whether the particular person should be put to death.

Any person who would impose capital punishment merely because an accused has been convicted of a certain crime and without weighing the other information should be removed for cause. That "automatic-death-penalty" jurors can be challenged for cause helps prevent the possibility that a death-qualified jury is conviction-prone. In practice, however, the two challenges do not entirely balance out. More automatic-death-penalty jurors make it on to capital cases than capital punishment opponents. Thus, in a study of jurors who had actually sat in capital cases, half responded that death is the only acceptable punishment for certain kinds of murder, while only about 5 percent thought that death is always inappropriate for those crimes. Either view should have disqualified them from service. The researchers concluded: "It thus appears that a sizable number of persons that qualify for service as capital jurors after the attorneys and the trial judge question them fail to appreciate or personally accept the principle . . . that the death penalty is never the 'only acceptable' punishment for a capital offense. . . . Jurors' responses . . . appear to reflect a predisposition toward seeing death as the right punishment. . . . If neither the judge nor the attorneys detect this predisposition during voir dire, the jury will contain members who are especially prone to take a stand for death prior to, and irrespective of, evidence and arguments at the sentencing stage."[26]

The present practice of having one jury decide both guilt and sentence in death penalty cases is constitutional. This does not mean it is wise. Its chief benefit is that it reduces costs. As two commentators have concluded, however, "the burden the state would incur if it were required to seat both types of jurors through trial and replace them at sentencing does not seem particularly significant. Given the *possibility* of bias and lack of community representation that otherwise results, it would seem that this burden should be borne."[27]

Chapter 11 Peremptory Challenges

Peremptory challenges are the last step in jury selection. They are exercised by the parties after the rulings on the challenges for cause. Peremptory challenges require no showing of bias. As long as they are not used to exclude potential jurors solely on the basis of race or gender, they can be used without explanation.

Challenges for cause, because they help assure an impartial jury, are unlimited in number. Every biased person, no matter how many are revealed, should be excused for cause. The number of peremptory challenges, for obvious reasons, is always limited, and that number varies from jurisdiction to jurisdiction and by the kind of case being tried. In federal criminal trials, for example, each side has twenty in capital cases and three in misdemeanor trials. For other felonies, the prosecution has six and the defendant ten. In New York the numbers are equal for both sides, but vary from three to twenty depending on the category of the case. Although numbers vary, peremptory challenges exist for all civil and criminal jury trials.

The method of exercising peremptories also varies. A common jury selection practice picks twelve from the assembled potential jurors.

These twelve undergo voir dire questioning. Challenges for cause are then made. If, say, two are excused, the prosecutor may use peremptory challenges on any of the ten remaining. If he uses one, the defendant may peremptorily challenge any of the remaining nine. If the defendant excuses three, the remaining six would be sworn in. Six more people would then be called, and the process would start anew with, in some places, the defendant having to use peremptories first on the even rounds, until the requisite number of jurors and alternates were sworn.

In this system, the attorneys do not know who the replacement will be when a juror is challenged peremptorily. The challenge in some sense is a gamble that the substitute will be better than the juror excused. By contrast, in the "struck jury" system, jurors are questioned and challenges for cause are exercised until the panel equals the size of the jury *plus* the total number of peremptory challenges for both sides. If the jury is twelve and each side has ten peremptory challenges, a group of thirty-two is assembled after the challenges for cause. Then the parties exercise their peremptories to reduce the body to twelve. This method takes more time, but because all the potential jurors have been questioned when peremptories are exercised, a party is always able to exclude those most objectionable to her.

"SELECTING" A JURY

Whatever the system, the hallmark of peremptory challenges has been a grant of unfettered and unexplained discretion to the parties. As long as they have peremptories remaining, they can exclude whomever they wish. By using this power, an attorney is said to "pick" a jury. This is a misnomer. A lawyer cannot pluck out an individual for service; she can only exclude. Her power is to *deselect*.

Attorneys, however, believe that by their wise use of peremptory challenges, favorable juries will result. A great deal of lore exists about how to exercise peremptory challenges. This lore is based primarily on stereotyping. Potential jurors are categorized into groups that are thought to have different tendencies in judging cases. Some of these groupings are made according to occupation. Bankers, for example, are said to be good for prosecutors and civil defendants. Daily wage earners are bad for defendants in income tax prosecutions. Butchers, with a forbearance for blood, have little hesitation in convicting criminal defendants. Teachers are sympathetic to civil plaintiffs and criminal defendants, and so on. Sometimes the stereotypes contradict each other: accountants believe in order and are good for prosecutors; accountants are trained in exacting standards of performance and will find a reasonable doubt where others would not. Ethnic stereotyping abounds. Irish Americans are forgiving and have a sense of injustice; German Americans believe in law and order; black people from West India will feel superior to black people born in the United States, and so on. Attorneys may catalog people into those who are churchgoers and those who are not. Some attorneys have notions about the significance of such things as beards, bow ties, obviously dyed hair, or the kind of reading material a potential juror is carrying.

PEREMPTORY CHALLENGES AND REPRESENTATIVE JURIES

Peremptory challenges can sometimes be in conflict with the goal that juries be representative of the community. For example, when challenges are driven by a negative perception of a group, fewer members of that group will be on a jury. If bankers are out of favor with criminal defense or plaintiffs' attorneys, fewer bankers will serve. Although the Supreme Court has ruled that peremptory challenges do not conflict with the fair cross section requirement, the persistent use of peremptory challenges to exclude a particular group from a jury can nevertheless make a verdict seem less trustworthy and therefore less acceptable. The trial of Dan White is an illustration.

A jury acquitted Dan White of murdering San Francisco Mayor George Moscone and Supervisor Harvey Milk and convicted White only of the lesser crime of voluntary manslaughter. Harvey Milk was one of the first openly gay elected officials in the country, and the crime seemed to be motivated at least partly by anti-gay sentiments. Jury composition became an issue:

> No openly gay or lesbian jurors served on White's jury apparently because of a deliberate effort by the defense to exclude lesbians and gay men. As a result, a perception of homophobia tainted the trial and verdict. . . . . The anger culminated in a riot at San Francisco City Hall that, in an enduring image, left a string of police cruisers ablaze. . . . Lesbians and gay men believed that they had been deliberately excluded—because of their sexual orientation—from the jury considering the case of the man who assassinated the most significant gay political leader in history up to that time. If sexual orientation represented a dividing line qualifying or disqualifying citizens for jury service, then lesbians and gay men were not equal under the justice system and had no reason to have confidence in its judgments.[1]

Such tension between the use of peremptory challenges and the need for representative juries increases when a frequent litigant, such as a district attorney, consistently uses her peremptories to eliminate members of a disfavored group. African Americans have been so treated by prosecutors. Throughout much of our history, even when black individuals made it onto jury pools, prosecutors disproportionately peremptorily challenged them so that their overall presence on juries was minuscule. As reported in the 1960s Supreme Court case of *Swain v. Alabama*, not only did the prosecutor use his challenges to exclude all the black candidates from the jury, prosecutors in the county consistently used their peremptories similarly.[2] Although the county had a significant number of black residents, apparently none had served on a jury for the preceding fifteen years.

This was not an aberrant practice confined to Talledega, Alabama. To a greater or lesser extent it existed throughout the country. Even when prosecutors did not consider black people as a group to lack the mental or moral capacity to be good jurors, they still tended to exclude them. Just as defense attorneys challenged bankers, thinking that they were likely, by their identification with the established social order, to be pro-prosecution, prosecutors challenged black individuals on the assumption that they would tend to be pro-defense jurors. This was true as late as the 1970s in a place as socially and politically liberal as Manhattan. Even there, prosecutors disproportionately used peremptory challenges to exclude black people. A New York City prosecutor of the time captured the generally prevailing practices: "Traditionally, prosecutors have attempted to keep blacks off juries on the theory that they will be predisposed to acquit. Conversely, defense attorneys have tended over the years to seek out black jurors."[3] A juror's diary during a 1970s New York City trial confirmed the prevailing practice. "By peremptory challenge, [the prosecutor] dismisses every black woman and every black man. There are about eight blacks in our group of forty and all but one of them are called into the jury box before I am. A few are obvious challenges: two people who live near the scene of the crime and know the area well, a man whose wife was recently arrested for trespassing (but soon released), a woman who admits that the state would have to prove the defendant guilty beyond *any* doubt before she would vote to convict. But others, particularly a very conservatively dressed black businessman, seem the epitome of white-middle-class values. They are the targets of [the prosecutor's] challenges all the same."[4]

At first glance it might seem that the tendency of adversaries to use racially motivated peremptories would cancel each other out. That, however, was not the usual result. If, for example, each side had ten peremptory challenges in selecting a twelve-person jury, and black individuals made up 25 percent of the jury pool, no black person would be likely to make it onto the jury if each side exercised its peremptories based only on race. A total of thirty-two qualified people would be needed to select the jury if all twenty peremptories were used. Of the total group, eight would be black. Because the prosecutor had ten challenges, he could exclude them all, and the resulting jury would be selected from the remaining twenty-four white people. Indeed, the defense attorney could not use race as the sole criterion for his challenges because it would have been clear that he could not eliminate all the white people. From the beginning of jury selection, the defense would have had to distinguish among them, trying to eliminate the least favorable.

In my own experience in the New York trial courts, prosecutors only occasionally used race as the sole criterion for peremptories, but it was almost always a significant factor. The result was that the number of black people who served on juries was less—often significantly less—than their representation in the jury pools. Although the black population must have fair representation on jury *pools*, jury pools do not decide cases. Black people, however, were not represented proportionately on the trial juries that actually did decide cases. This situation existed as long as peremptories could be used for any reason without explanation.

PEREMPTORY CHALLENGES AS A VIOLATION
OF EQUAL PROTECTION

The world of peremptory challenges changed in 1986 when the Supreme Court decided *Batson v. Kentucky*. That case and later ones found that although excluding potential jurors because of their race did not violate the fair cross section rights of the litigants, peremptory challenges exercised on racial grounds violated the equal protection rights *of the jurors*. The principle was expanded in 1995 to forbid peremptory challenges based solely on gender. The Supreme Court forbade criminal defense attorneys and all parties in civil litigation, as well as prosecutors, from using peremptories in these discriminatory ways. In other words, the *Batson* principle applies to all jury trials in the United States.[5]

Articulating the *Batson* rule is straightforward, but determining *Batson* violations is often difficult. The Supreme Court has mandated that a three-step analysis must be employed. First, the party claiming a violation must establish that the practices used during jury selection—the pattern of exercising peremptories and the nature of the voir dire questioning—could support the inference that the challenges were used to exclude a group protected by the equal protection clause. A group to be protected has to be "cognizable." Race and gender clearly define such groups, and the Supreme Court has also indicated that Latino jurors cannot be discriminated against in the use of peremptory challenges. Beyond that, however, the Court has not indicated which, if any, other groups gain protection under *Batson.* The possibilities are legion. Are Italian Americans a cognizable group under *Batson?* Are Jews or Jehovah's Witnesses or gays? The lower courts have considered many such claims, with inconsistent results. Beyond race and gender it is simply not clear whether other groups are protected.

If the possibility of apparent discrimination is established, the proponent of the peremptory has to come forward with a nondiscriminatory explanation for the challenge. The court at this second stage merely decides whether the offered explanation is nondiscriminatory. It makes no determination on the persuasiveness or even on the plausibility of the explanation. As the Court stated in a case claiming racial discrimination, "At this [second] step of the inquiry, the issue is the facial validity of the prosecutor's explanation. Unless a discriminatory intent is inherent in the prosecutor's explanation, the reason offered will be deemed race neutral."[6]

The Court's cases indicate that "neutral" here is broadly defined. In *Purkett v. Elem,* the prosecutor's explanation for an apparently discriminatory challenge was that the juror had long, unkempt hair, a mustache, and a beard. The Court concluded that this explanation was race-neutral, for those characteristics are not peculiar to any race. In *Hernandez v. New York* the Hispanic defendant's attorney objected to prosecutorial peremptories excluding Spanish-speaking Hispanic potential jurors. The prosecutor explained that he was excusing those whose questioning indicated to him that "they would be hard pressed" to accept the court interpreter's translation of Spanish-speaking witnesses. The Court held that this explanation was a neutral one. It "rested neither on the intention to exclude Latino or bilingual jurors, nor on stereotypical assumptions about Latinos or bilinguals. The prosecutor's articulated basis for these challenges divided potential jurors into two classes: those whose conduct during *voir dire* would persuade him that they might have difficulty in accepting the translator's rendition of Spanish-language testimony and those potential jurors who gave no such reason for doubt. Each category would include both Latinos and non-Latinos. While the prosecutor's criterion might well result in the disproportionate removal of prospective Latino jurors, that disproportionate impact does not turn the prosecutor's action into a per se violation of the Equal Protection Clause."[7]

Many have contended that such decisions permit any half-witted attorney, even if intending to use peremptories in a forbidden manner, to concoct explanations that will be deemed neutral. One Illinois court, listing reasons that had been accepted as race-neutral, stated:

> [W]e now consider the charade that has become the *Batson* process. The State may provide the trial court with a series of pat race-neutral reasons for exercise of peremptory challenges. Since reviewing courts examine only the record, we wonder if the reasons can be given without a smile. Surely, new prosecutors are given a manual, probably entitled, "Handy Race-Neutral Explanations" or "20 Time-Tested Race-Neutral Explanations." It might include: too old, too young, divorced, "long, unkempt hair," free-lance writer, religion, social worker, renter, lack of family contact, attempting to make eye contact with the defendant, "lived in an area consisting predominantly of apartment complexes," single, over-educated, lack of maturity, improper demeanor, unemployed, improper attire, juror lived alone, misspelled place of employment, living with girlfriend, unemployed spouse, spouse employed as school teacher, employment as part-time barber, friendship with city council member, failure to remove hat, lack of community ties, children same "age bracket" as defendant, deceased father and prospective juror's aunt receiving psychiatric care.[8]

A neutral explanation, however, does not end the analysis. It merely kicks things into the third stage. The court does not have to accept a nondiscriminatory explanation, but must determine whether the proffered reasons were a pretext for forbidden discrimination. The Supreme Court has stated that "implausible or fantastic justifications may (and probably will) be found to be pretexts for purposeful discrimination." In *Hernandez* the Court stated, "If a prosecutor articulates a basis for a peremptory challenge that results in the disproportionate exclusion of members of a certain race, the trial judge may consider that fact as evidence that the prosecutor's stated reason constitutes a pretext for racial discrimination."[9]

On the other hand, the explanation does not have to be sensible to satisfy *Batson*. *Purkett v. Elem* stressed that a "legitimate reason" for an apparently discriminatory peremptory challenge "is not a reason that makes sense, but a reason that does not deny equal protection."[10]

Although courts do find neutral explanations pretextual, such conclusions are rare. One study found that discrimination was shown in only 15 percent of claimed *Batson* violations. Another study found that the claims of improper use of peremptories on gender grounds were much less frequent than racial ones, with about 20 percent of the gender claims succeeding. Another concluded that "a prosecutor who wanted to rebut a prima facie case of illegal discrimination in jury selection did not face a significant challenge." This has led one commentator to conclude, "Only the most overtly discriminatory or impolitic lawyer can be caught in *Batson's* toothless bite and, even then, the wound will be only superficial."[11]

Two kinds of pressure push judges toward accepting the offered grounds even when the reasons are insincere. First, labeling the explanation a pretext is tantamount to calling the lawyer a liar and, worse, a bigot. Even judges find it difficult to make such a charge. The difficulty is compounded because judges are often friendly with the lawyers practicing in front of them, especially those who appear frequently.

The potential remedies for a *Batson* violation present problems. The claim that peremptories are being used discriminatorily against black people, for example, usually comes only after a disproportionate number of black candidates have been dismissed. The remedy when the violation is found may seem obvious: seat the improperly challenged jurors. That, however, is often difficult because those dismissed jurors may have already been sent home or selected for other juries. The jurors may simply not be available.

The only other remedy that seems sensible is to start the jury selection over so that the new jury will be formed in a nondiscriminatory manner. Judges resist this option. It is costly in both dollars and time, and a judge's institutional inclinations are against incurring more expense. Furthermore, this remedy is not much of a punishment for the offending attorney. He is not forced to accept jurors he did not want and can hope that the new panel of jurors, by the luck of the draw, will suit him better. Once again, the forces on the judge push her not to find the explanation pretextual.

Finally, the Supreme Court has indicated that the trial judge is in the best position to determine whether the explanation is pretextual, but it has given little guidance on how trial courts should accomplish this. Nevertheless, some factors have been widely used by lower courts in determining whether explanations are pretextual: the stated reasons are unrelated to the case; the challenged juror was not questioned thoroughly; questions to support the explanation were asked only of the challenged juror, but not of others; the characteristics of the challenged juror that support the explanation were shared by others who were not challenged. If, for example, the attorney asks only Latinos whether they can accept a court translator's interpretation but does not seek to find out who else understands Spanish, challenges to the Latinos will more likely be considered a pretext. If bearded black individuals are excused but bearded white people are not, the chances of a pretextual finding increase.

THE EFFECT OF *BATSON*

It would be naive to think that *Batson* has ended the use of discriminatory peremptory challenge. The studies indicating only rare violations of *Batson* should be treated gingerly. First, these studies generally consider only reported cases, yet most trial decisions are not published. Normally only appellate decisions are reported, and many *Batson* rulings do not get appealed. Prosecutors cannot appeal following a criminal trial, and parties who have been found to have violated *Batson* but still win at trial will not appeal the ruling. The data simply do not exist to indicate how often trial courts rule that peremptory challenges have been used unconstitutionally.

Even if those data did exist, however, the impact of *Batson* could not be measured solely by the number of violations found, for no doubt *Batson* has changed behavior, and those modifications are difficult to measure. Before *Batson* attorneys could legally use peremptories to exclude a racial group; now it is a constitutional violation. Cynicism about lawyers is rampant, but many (perhaps most) in fact do try to obey the law. Consequently, since *Batson* some attorneys who may have used peremptory challenges in a discriminatory manner in the past do not do so today.

Batson may have a positive effect even on the unscrupulous lawyer. I may not want black individuals on the jury, but challenging them all will lead to a *Batson* claim. I may be able to concoct a neutral-sounding reason for their discharge, but I have to be careful in doing so. If my pretextual explanation for excluding a black candidate is that I do not trust bearded people, I may later, to preserve the pretext, have to use a peremptory on a bearded white person whom I wished to keep. If I do challenge the white person, I not only may lose a juror I want, but I will also be exhausting my challenges sooner than I otherwise would have and may have to accept the next called jurors no matter what their race. These factors will make even biased attorneys think twice about exercising challenges solely on racial grounds. Indeed, one of the ways to mask racial discrimination is for the attorney to permit some African Americans on the jury so that most can be excluded.

Mark Cammack's conclusion about *Batson* seems the fairest: "[T]here is no reliable evidence that the *Batson* limitations on the peremptory challenge reduced or eliminated the underrepresentation of minority groups on juries. . . . Nevertheless, the rule has likely had a positive impact in improving jury diversity. Most attorneys probably take the prohibition against race- or gender-based peremptories seriously, and even though it is fairly easy to concoct a pretextual race- or gender-neutral reason, not all attempts by attorneys to justify their challenges are accepted."[12]

In fairness, another factor requires consideration. Attorneys selecting juries may indulge in racial or gender stereotyping, but few lawyers do it to denigrate a minority or a gender. Lawyers are trying to win cases. If they exclude women or blacks, it is because they think those exclusions will increase the likelihood of trial success. Voir dire questioning, as we have seen, varies greatly. If it elicits little more than occupation, preexisting knowledge about the case or parties, and an affirmation that the potential jurors can be impartial, the lawyers will know little about the individuals called for jury service. A good part of the attorneys' knowledge is based on what is readily observable, including the gender and apparent ethnicity of those called. Under such circumstances, race and gender, consciously or not, will affect the decisions on peremptories. If I am selecting a jury in a robbery case, and I know little about you other than that you are female and black, and that you work on a construction crew, generalizations about women, African Americans, and construction workers will drive my decision as to whether you would be a good juror for my client. *Batson* tells me to individualize my peremptory challenges and not to base them solely on race and gender, but with such limited information, those surface characteristics, no matter how noble my intentions, will invariably be a large component on which I base my decision. The more information I have about potential jurors, the greater the chance that the role of race and gender will decrease in my jury selection. Stereotyping declines with an increase in individual knowledge about prospective jurors.

Recently I was called for jury duty, and I spent some of my time talking to and observing those also summoned. As conversations went on, I realized how differently I perceived some of these people than I would have as an attorney picking jurors after the typical voir dire. One, for example, was a white man in his mid-thirties. He was a captain in the New York City fire department. This information, the kind obtained during typical voir dire questioning, would have led to my knee-jerk assumption that he would identify with law enforcement, especially in the kind of case to which we were called—that of a young black man who had allegedly committed a burglary and resisted arrest. My assumptions about this juror, however, became more confused when I saw that he was reading *The New Yorker* and carrying a book on art history. During a break we chatted, and I learned that he was raised in a small town and had moved to New York after graduation from college. He was taking some graduate courses in both psychology and business, and he talked passionately about the need for minority firefighters in many New York City neighborhoods. As part of his work, he had helped investigate claims of wrongdoing in the department, and he stated that he had learned how hard it was to know for sure from an investigation what had really happened. None of this information had come out during a rather perfunctory voir dire. The defense attorney peremptorily challenged him, and he was excused. I probably would have, too. With some of the additional information, however, I might have felt differently about him; I might have seen beyond the stereotypes that the surface information conveyed to me and seen a complex person.

PRETRIAL INVESTIGATIONS
OF PROSPECTIVE JURORS

Not surprisingly, lawyers feel that they can use peremptories more effectively when they better know the jury pool. Attorneys may have several other sources of information besides the voir dire questioning. In many places, a list of those about to be called as jurors is made public or furnished to the litigants. In some cities, companies using these lists do some research and will, for a fee, provide basic information about the potential jurors. The parties can also collect information about those who have been summoned, but they cannot communicate in any way with those called, nor, according to ethical standards, can the investigation be "vexatious or harassing."

The Internet has made such information-gathering easier, but it was occurring well before this modern technology existed. For example, in the murder trial of labor leader Bill Haywood at the beginning of the twentieth century, the lawyers "were amply equipped with precise intelligence gathered during the massive effort both sides had expended to compile the preferences, affiliations, and dirty little secrets of hundreds of potential jurors. Both sides had sent small armies of scouts into the countryside posing as insurance men, encyclopedia salesmen, and other itinerants."[13] In the trials of Henry Thaw for killing architect Stanford White in 1907 and 1908, once a person was identified as a potential juror, "detectives in the employ of the District Attorney and of the defense, began searching investigations into his life, his habits and his reputation and general standing in the community."[14] In the trial of Bruno Hauptmann for kidnapping and killing the baby of Charles Lindbergh in 1932, when "the list was published of the 150 talesmen from who the twelve jurors would eventually be chosen, orders [from the prosecution] went out for them to be thoroughly (but secretly) investigated."[15] Accounts from some of the New Jersey State Police troopers indicate the extent of the investigations:

> Trooper Sawyer was sent to Weartsville to investigate one of the talesmen, Jonathan Voorhees. "On the pretext of trying to locate a man formerly of Weartsville, Mr. Voorhees was engaged in conversation. . . ." Two days later Trooper Genz was in the back room of Cutter's Drug Store when Voorhees came into the front shop. "I told Mr. Cutter to engage him in conversation and lead up to his view about the state convicting Hauptmann. I could hear them talking from where I was standing and Mr. Voorhees stated that he had not made anything definite in his mind as yet." Genz made informers of a Mrs. Yandell and the local doctor, by the name of Anderson. "Mrs. Yandall will obtain any information she can for us and turn same over." Dr Anderson, asked to comment on Mrs. Verna Snyder, was equally obliging. "Anderson thinks that she would make an honest juror, but is not too sure if her husband would turn her against the State Police because he has been arrested a few times for disorderly conduct."[16]

Prosecutors, with ready access to some information, are the parties most likely to compile data about potential jurors. "Because members of the prosecution staff may have conducted earlier trials involving members of the same panel, the prosecution may be able to compile information on the voting habits of particular jurors. The prosecution will likewise have more ready access to the arrest and conviction records and other government records relating to the prospective jurors. Moreover, the prosecution may utilize the services of local police or the FBI in acquiring background information."[17]

Detailed investigations of potential jurors, however, have never been routine matters. Not all jurisdictions make available advance lists of those summoned to jury service, and of course, these investigative efforts are costly and therefore generally limited to well-financed parties with much at stake.

INFORMATION FROM VOIR DIRE

In most trials, the voir dire remains the prime source of information about jurors. Not surprisingly, attorneys often desire a detailed and lengthy questioning period, and since *Batson,* they can argue that it is necessary to comply with the Supreme Court requirements to avoid challenges based on race and sex. An extensive voir dire, however, makes a trial longer and costlier, and judges often seek to keep the questioning as short as possible.

We saw in Chapter Ten that the voir dire was not a particularly good process for discovering bias, partly because people resist acknowledging their unfairness. The voir dire process is also often ineffective at uncovering information that will help in the exercise of peremptory challenges. This stems in part from the fact that any voir dire invades the privacy of the potential juror, and the more detailed the questioning, the more invasive it is. Should a person have to tell a stranger in front of others how old she is; what magazines she reads; or how often she attends a place of worship? Should people have to talk about their divorces, their sons in jail, or their speeding tickets if they don't want to? In a voir dire, they may have to.

Many prospective jurors become tight-lipped under such circumstances, often failing to mention germane information. One study asked jurors who had just rendered a verdict questions that paralleled those during voir dire. The study concluded that 39 percent of the interviewed jurors had not given pertinent responses during the voir dire, which had directed questions at the jurors in a group. D. W. Broeder concludes, "The most common way that jurors deceive is by withholding relevant information, the way [a prospective juror] did in not responding to the judge's question about whether or not he had ever been a defendant."[18]

Just as prospective jurors are more likely to admit bias when questioned individually, they are more likely to be forthcoming about other sensitive subjects when addressed separately. Often, however, questions are not asked of each person but are put to a group simultaneously. Have any of you been in a car accident? Have any of you been a victim of a crime? Those who have an affirmative response are supposed to, in effect, volunteer. Numerous impulses can affect this split-second decision. The raised hand will lead to further questioning, placing this person at the center of attention among several dozen strangers, a position that makes many uncomfortable. Often it will seem that others before who had responded affirmatively were peremptorily challenged. Apparently they gave the "wrong" answer. The information sought may be the kind that a person does not want widely known. The prospective juror, not unreasonably, can feel that she will probably not be selected anyway, so there is little reason to volunteer this ordinarily private information. And sometimes the voir dire question itself is so subjective that it encourages the prospective juror to interpret the question to suit himself.

Recently, I was voir dired with other prospective jurors. We were asked as a group by the trial judge, "Have any of you had any dealings with the police that would affect your ability to be impartial in this case?" Now, I have had many varied experiences with the police. I have been a practicing attorney with many police contacts. Some of my students have been in law enforcement. My academic work has brought me in conflict with forensic scientists working for the FBI and other laboratories. I have received traffic tickets, some of which I thought were unjust. As a teenager, I was questioned about a stolen car. When my family, friends, and I have been victims of crimes, the police responded. Shortly after a bombing, the FBI made inquiries of me about a tenant who might have had connections with a terrorist group. Some of these encounters flashed through my head in the moments after the question was asked. I also felt that with what was already known about my background, it was unlikely I would be selected. I knew that talking about some of these matters would make me uncomfortable. Should I have volunteered any of it? I thought of myself as someone who could be impartial, and none of those experiences would change that. I did not raise my hand.

The traditional voir dire also produces limited information because often attorneys will shy away from pressing potential jurors about sensitive topics. Lawyers seek to develop rapport with jurors, and the voir dire affects this. Asking potential jurors invasive questions in open court may offend jurors who are selected, and this can lead to circumspection by the attorneys. One commentator concludes, "Attorneys simply do not ask questions or employ techniques that are effective in detecting or eliminating prejudice, concentrating instead on educating and indoctrinating prospective jurors and ingratiating themselves to the panel." Studies confirm the inefficacy of the typical jury selection questioning. The conclusions of a study interviewing 225 posttrial jurors done a generation ago remain valid: "[V]oir dire was grossly ineffective not only in weeding out 'unfavorable' jurors but even in eliciting the data which would have shown particular jurors as very likely to prove 'unfavorable.'"[19]

JUROR QUESTIONNAIRES

Because of the limitations of the traditional voir dire, the courts have increasingly come to use questionnaires filled out by potential jurors. This improves efficiency. All jurors can supply information at the same time outside of court. Attorneys can also review the responses in advance of the voir dire and use the trial's oral questioning to home in on key areas revealed by the questionnaires.

Besides promoting a more efficient process, questionnaires can also reveal more information. Written answers are frequently more forthright than oral ones. With questionnaires, jurors have more time to think about their responses. Respondents are not being asked to volunteer private information publicly, and they are less likely to withhold relevant facts when responding to specific written questions.

In addition, questionnaires often probe more deeply than the voir dire. The considerations that restrain the attorney from offending jurors with in-court questioning are fewer, because the attorney is not directly linked to any question. Potential jurors may be offended by the written questions, but they will not so easily be able to direct anger at one of the adversaries. Consequently, more searching, often personal, questions may be asked—and answered—in the written form.

Although the information a questionnaire can garner may help reduce reliance on stereotypes in jury selection, it also leads to problems. The more potential jurors are asked probing questions, the more their privacy is invaded. Jurors' privacy has not been a prime concern in the trial process. Lawyers may not wish to offend jurors, but when ways are found to elicit information without producing a backlash against one particular party, lawyers naturally will seek more invasive answers. The judge, perhaps, should be concerned about juror privacy, but her main duty is to make sure that the trial is fair and efficient. When information can be obtained that might make the trial fairer and proceed more quickly, the judge's inclinations may permit the compilation of material without much consideration of its effects on jurors. No one's chief function in court is to act on behalf of the jurors, and not surprisingly their privacy, at least until recently, has been little considered.

The expanded use of jury questionnaires, however, has now drawn some concerns, perhaps prompted by the form used in the highly publicized 1990s trial of O. J. Simpson. A juror who was selected but later dismissed during the trial states that it consisted of 79 pages, 28 parts, and 294 questions. The questions ranged from age, race, gender, marital status, and occupation to impressions of the major participants and discussions about the case. Other questions were even more personal: "What do you think is the main cause of domestic violence?" "How would you feel if a close family member or relative married someone of a different race?" "Did you vote in the June 1994 primary elections?" "Have you ever provided a urine sample to be analyzed for any purpose?" "Do you believe it is immoral or wrong to do an amniocentesis to determine whether a fetus has a genetic defect? Please explain." "What accomplishments in your life are you most proud of?" "Please name the three public figures you admire most." "How do you feel about being a juror in this case? Please explain." Working quickly and seldom elaborating on the answers, it took the juror, surrounded by groans from his colleagues, four hours to complete the questionnaire. He adds, "While we were filling out the questionnaire, one comment came up over and over again: 'This is so personal.' You could hear it muttered all about the room."[20]

A few jurors have rebelled against such information-gathering. For example, Dianna Brandborg filled out most of a 110-item questionnaire given to her as a prospective juror, but she refused to answer queries about her political views, family income, medical care, reading material, car, volunteer work, and membership in clubs and other organizations. The judge explained that the information was sought "mainly to give [the attorneys] an idea of what kind of person you are where they can make an intelligent decision in whether or not to exercise one of their peremptory challenges." Even so, she maintained that this was the kind of information that she would tell no one and refused to give the answers. The trial court held her in contempt and sentenced her to three days in jail and a $200 fine.[21]

A federal court eventually concluded that if a juror raises privacy concerns, the trial court should seek the sensitive answers in a closed proceeding and seal the resulting record. Because Brandborg was not offered that closed proceeding, her contempt citation was set aside. The court, however, also made clear that if the trial court considers the questions appropriate, the juror's privacy rights have to give way and the juror has to answer.[22] As questioning becomes more intrusive, we can expect that potential jurors will further resent the selection process. And as the public identifies with those jurors, the resentment may translate into further distrust of jury trials.

More than feelings about juror privacy, however, fuels the distrust of such extensive information-gathering. A deeper concern is that this kind of information will make attorneys too good at selecting jurors. Parties are entitled to impartial jurors, and increasingly detailed information about potential jurors may further that goal by helping to ferret out bias. Ultimately, however, the party would like not simply to remove those who have some prejudice against him but to have jurors that actively favor him. Detailed information about prospective jurors makes it seem possible for the attorney to shape the jury so that it will be inclined toward his client; it helps cement the popular notion that trials are won by selecting the "right" jurors.

This issue strikes at the heart of the jury system. If jury selection, and not the evidence, is the prime determinant of a trial's outcome, the principle upon which trials are based is undermined. No longer the societal forum in which facts are accurately and justly determined, they become instead a place where stereotypical bias and knee-jerk assumptions hold sway. The public perception that jury composition determines outcome, whether true or not, erodes the acceptability and legitimacy of verdicts.

In some ways, the extensive information about potential jurors moves us back to earlier times. Through much of our history, especially in small towns, the jury pool was sufficiently limited so that lawyers could know or find out more about potential jurors than modern investigative devices are now likely to uncover. On the other hand, lawyers then simply used seat-of-the-pants intuition to assess the data, and the competing attorneys' efforts often seemed to cancel each other out to produce a pretty good jury. This, however, was before the birth of the modern jury consultant industry.

Chapter 12 "Scientific" Jury Selection

Jury consultants promise the use of social science methods to help attorneys win cases. They offer several kinds of services. Consultants may advise the attorney on what evidence to present and how to present it. Mock juries, for example, may be assembled to study the effects of different courtroom strategies. "Shadow juries" may be formed to watch the actual trial and to give their feedback on the proceedings. Jurors may be interviewed after verdicts to hone techniques for future, related trials. Such services have drawn few comments, but claims by jury consultants that they can help a party "scientifically" pick a favorable jury have received much attention.

The 1971 trial of the "Harrisburg Seven" highlighted the role of consultants in helping to select juries. Philip Berrigan, a well-known Catholic priest who opposed the war in Vietnam, and six others were charged with a host of crimes, including conspiring to destroy selective service records and to blow up heating tunnels in Washington, D.C. Many venues were considered for the trial, but the government chose Harrisburg, Pennsylvania, a city regarded as conservative and unsympathetic to anti-war activists. Jay Schulman, a Columbia University sociologist, offered his services to the defense. Schulman designed and supervised a survey of over one thousand people in the Harrisburg area asking about attitudes concerning religion, education, government, and war resistance. A computer analysis of the results allowed the defense to produce profiles of the kinds of jurors who would be most or least sympathetic to the defendants, information that was then used in the exercise of peremptories. Perhaps most important is that some of the conclusions seemed to contradict the prevailing wisdom as to who would make good and bad defense jurors. Although the government spent more than $2 million on the prosecution, the trial ended with a hung jury on the most serious charges. Proof of principle seemed established; the methods apparently worked.

As word of these jury selection practices spread, the use of jury consultants increased. One Boston trial lawyer is quoted as saying, "No self-respecting trial lawyer will go through the process of jury selection in an important case without the assistance of highly paid trial consultants." A New York attorney echoes, "It's gotten to the point where if the case is large enough, it's almost malpractice not to use [them.]"[1] Not all who try cases, however, agree. Noted attorney Gerry Spence has said:

> I never use a jury consultant. Some try to create the profile of the juror most likely to stand with you, but there is no such person—not in the real world. A person who matches the profile will quickly be stricken from your list when you discover that she winces whenever *you* walk past her, or he wants to bash in your head because he is threatened by you. The ideal juror is like an automobile manufacturer who makes a seat that should fit everyone but fits no one. I say to jury consultants, if you want to choose the jury, then you try the case. You cannot pick a jury for me any more than my mother could pick my wife. You can only pick the jurors *you* like, the ones with whom *you* resonate—if, indeed, you resonate especially with anyone.[2]

Jury consultants are in fact used in only a tiny fraction of jury trials, and even though they came to prominence in high-profile criminal trials, about 80 percent of the consultants' practice today is in civil cases.[3]

EFFICACY OF JURY CONSULTANTS

Jury selection experts attempt to determine who among potential jurors will be most and least receptive to a client's case, and they devise strategies to pick and challenge those jurors. The Harrisburg trial provides a model for how it might be done. A community survey may attempt to find what demographic characteristics correlate most strongly with support for the client's case. Such a survey is akin to a political poll revealing that certain demographic characteristics—age, income, educational levels, religion—correlate with support for a particular candidate. A community survey will poll jury-eligible people to see if correlations can be found between demographic and attitudinal characteristics and support for a client's case. Then jury questions are formulated to identify those characteristics. Psychologists and other social scientists may also be retained to observe jury selection and to rank potential jurors on personality scales for such attributes as authoritarianism or to look for cues divined from their body language.

Jury consultants, like many other people trying to make a living, claim great success for their work. "Leading practitioners of jury science boast they can predict trial outcomes before the evidence is heard with over 90% certitude."[4] If the claims are true, jury trials are in trouble. When verdicts can be controlled merely through manipulation of jury selection by social scientists, there is little point to jury trials. The problem is compounded by the fact that jury consultants are expensive. The minimum for meaningful work has been put at $50,000, with extensive services going as high as $500,000. Few litigants can afford this, and as a result the wealthy may be able to, in effect, buy favorable verdicts.

But are the consultants' claims accurate? Are they worth their cost? In the Harrisburg case it was assumed that nationwide the college-educated were more likely to be opposed to the Vietnam war than were those with less education. The community survey, however, found that liberal college graduates tended to leave the Harrisburg area and that the remaining college-educated would be poor jurors for the defense. Consequently, contrary to prevailing wisdom, the defense sought less-educated jurors. In fact, the college-educated in the United States generally were *not* the group most opposed to the war. As James Loewen carefully explains, while some might have thought that more education brought more opposition, polls in 1966, 1968, and 1971 showed that those with only a high school education opposed the war more than did college graduates and that those with only a grade school education were even stronger opponents.[5] Published, nationwide Gallup polls would have led to the same jury selection strategy that was used by the consultants.

The rate of success claimed by consultants must be put in perspective. "[I]f half of all jurors are expected to vote for conviction, simple guessing or coin flipping would yield a 50 percent accuracy rate. And if 80 percent of the jurors prefer conviction, either in a single case or across cases, an 80 percent accuracy rate can be achieved by always predicting conviction."[6] Thus, the jury consultant's predictions in a criminal case are meaningful only to the extent that they better an 80 percent accuracy rate if juries generally convict at that rate, for anyone with the basic knowledge of conviction rates could achieve an 80 percent accuracy.

Most important, however, jury consultants have published almost no data to support their claims, and other social scientists are highly dubious of their assertions. Social science studies have consistently found that *the overwhelming determinant of verdicts is the evidence presented to the jury.* Much research has been done trying to find correlations between the race, gender, age, economic status, political views, and other characteristics of jurors and their verdicts. Although every finding is not precisely the same, one conclusion is consistently reached—verdicts cannot be predicted accurately simply by knowing the makeup of the jury. Studies have shown that if we provide different people with the same evidence and examine the differences in their verdicts, only 5 to 15 percent of the variations can be connected to demographic and personality variables, with 85 to 95 percent of the variance accounted for by other factors. The presented evidence is much more important in determining the outcome.[7]

Even modest correlations between juror characteristics and verdicts, however, can sometimes be important. "With a jury pool one-half favorable and one-half unfavorable, an attorney acting on a completely random basis would correctly classify one-half of the jurors. If, however, a survey reliably found a five percent variance in verdicts attributable to attitudinal and personality measures, successful use of that data would raise the attorney's performance to sixty-one percent of the jurors. With a fifteen percent variance, performance would increase to sixty-nine percent."[8]

These numbers, however, are a best-case projection unlikely to be achieved in the real world of jury selection. First, one attorney alone does not select the jury. It is an adversarial process, and both sides are trying to eliminate unfavorable jurors. No matter how well an attorney does in classifying favorable jurors, she does not act alone. For example, in the case chronicled in Jonathan Harr's *A Civil Action,* where jury consultants had been employed, jury selection took six days, and both sides had exhausted their peremptories on the fifth. "In the end, . . . most of those chosen were essentially compromise candidates. . . . The lawyers really did not know much about any of these people. Superficially, at least, it wasn't the jury of [the plaintiffs' attorney's] dreams, and it wasn't [the defense attorneys'], either. The judge, of course, was aware of this. He brought the proceeding to a close by telling the lawyers, 'You're not entitled to a jury of your liking. You're only entitled to an impartial jury.' "9

Not only does the adversary system have a leveling effect on getting a favorable jury for one side, but the modest correlations between juror characteristics and outcomes have so far yielded little useful information to be used in jury selection. That is because most often the correlations have been discovered not in advance of trial, but in hindsight. Demographic and attitudinal information is collected from mock jurors who are then given the evidence. After they state what verdict they think appropriate, analysis is performed looking for correlations between jury characteristics and the different outcomes. In one study with twenty or more variables of juror characteristics, five were found to correlate with the verdicts, accounting for only 11 percent of the variance. So far, however, predictions have not had notable success, and, of course, predictions are what is necessary for jury selection. Reid Hastie has said, "The predictive power of [juror] characteristics invariably [turns] out to be subtly dependent on specific aspects of the particular case for which they proved valid. Due to their subtlety, prospective identification of any of these factors under the conditions that prevail before actual trials remains doubtful."10

Although the research consistently casts doubt on jury consultants' claims, defenders of the practice offer a proof-is-in-the-pudding argument: lawyers use the services of consultants, and their use is increasing. "In drawing inferences as to the efficacy of trial consulting, we must give due notice to the fact that law firms and in-house counsel look increasingly to consultants for pretrial preparation, jury selection, and trial strategy, notwithstanding the absence of any guarantee of victory and the pricey cost of the services. Perhaps the most revealing indicator of trial consulting efficacy is the sizable fees attorneys and their clients are willing to spend for the services."11

Few attorneys, however, are well versed in social science literature. Most know little about the empirical studies, and no doubt many users of consultants are just indulging in a modern version of Pascal's wager: "It can't hurt. Maybe it can help. If the client can afford it, why not?" For example, Harr's *A Civil Action* recounts the case concerning the claim that dumped chemicals caused cancer in Woburn, Massachusetts. Jerome Facher, the attorney for one of the defendants, agreed to contribute $25,000 for a poll of potential jurors, only to find out that 80 percent thought large corporations should ordinarily be held responsible for damages from toxic wastes and that 77 percent who knew of the case thought the corporate defendants were liable.

"I didn't need to pay twenty-five thousand dollars to be told that," Facher grumbled.
A few weeks later, [an attorney for the other defendant] had called again, this time to inform Facher that they planned to stage a mock trial and watch several panels of "jurors"—people selected at random off the street—deliberate from behind one way mirrors. Facher had refused to contribute. "I wouldn't pay another nickel after those pie charts," he said. "I think it's pissing money away." Facher later estimated that the jury research had cost Cheeseman's client at least a hundred thousand dollars. "The gold-plated defense," Facher called it in disgust. "Some clients think that the more money you spend, the harder you're working."[12]

There are many attorneys who no doubt feel differently and would attest to the merits of jury selection by consultants. Nevertheless, a "large body of systematic empirical work has called into question the efficacy of both traditional and scientific jury selection strategies. In general, the demographic characteristics, personality traits, and general attitudes of jurors have weak and unreliable effects on verdicts." This echoes the statements of others: "In effect, no research has provided that social scientific methods can be a powerful aid to attorneys in the task of detecting juror bias."[13]

CONCERNS ABOUT JURY CONSULTANTS

"Scientific" jury selection methods, whether successful or not, do raise concerns. Although the presented evidence determines verdicts in the vast majority of cases, individual juror attributes seem to have some effect on outcomes. Over time the importance of these predispositions may become better understood, with important ramifications for jury selection. Moreover, even with modest correlations between juror characteristics and outcomes, if the adversarial system fails and one party knows more about these effects, jury selection could yield a skewed jury. Finally, while juror characteristics may little affect ordinary cases, the extraordinary trial may be different. In trials that garner lots of attention, such as those with political implications or when celebrities are involved, special, case-specific biasing factors may be at work that good community surveys and carefully constructed questioning of potential jurors may uncover. Indeed, even notable skeptics of "scientific" jury selection in typical trials concluded that the O. J. Simpson trial "may be an example of a case in which jury selection did help cause the verdict." Of course, even if jury selection matters only on the margin and jury consultants can affect a small percentage of cases, in a jury system as large as ours, those margins do encompass a lot of cases.[14]

Certainly, a growing popular impression is that jury composition determines outcome. Until recently, the public showed little interest in the individual identities of jurors. Press reports of noteworthy trials from earlier times contained little or no discussion about the characteristics of the individual jurors. Today such information is common. Jury consultants contribute to this perception by offering to increase the odds of winning dramatically no matter what the strength of the evidence may be. They claim to be "scientific." They claim greater success in selecting favorable jurors than any lawyer could do using seat-of-the-pants hunches. By implication, their advice cannot be offset by an adversarial attorney; it can be balanced only by the work of a comparable jury consultant. The inexorable conclusion is that whoever has the better jury consultant wins. This in itself undermines public confidence in the deliberative process. But because few among us understand the "scientific" methods underlying the process, it seems driven by some dark face operating with the use of some secret database. Such a paranoid vision of the process further undermines confidence in the resulting verdicts and the entire enterprise.

Such views are pervasive enough that jury consultants are among the chief villains in bestselling fiction. John Grisham's 1996 book, *The Runaway Jury*, revolves around tobacco litigation. The judge and all the lawyers are unethical and corrupt. The lawyers blackmail, bribe, and compromise jurors in hopes of getting their verdict, but are outwitted by a conspiratorial couple. In his own way, the young man of the pair is just as corrupt as the others. He contrives a way to get on the jury and then manipulates the jury's decision. In this swirl of corruption, none are more evil than the jury consultants, one of whom

> was Carl Nussman, a lawyer from Chicago who no longer practiced law but instead ran his own jury consulting firm. For a small fortune, Carl Nussman and his firm could pick you the right jury. They gathered the data, took the photos, recorded the voices, sent the blondes in tight jeans into the right situations. Carl and his associates flirted around the edges of laws and ethics, but it was impossible to catch them. After all, there's nothing illegal or unethical about photographing prospective jurors. They had conducted exhaustive telephone surveys in Harrison County six months ago, then again two months ago, then a month later to gauge community sentiment about tobacco issues and formulate models of the perfect jurors. They left no photo untaken, no dirt ungathered. They had a file on every prospective juror.[15]

One can only hope that few readers see the corrupt and unethical behavior that occurs in the book as usual practice, but for this kind of novel to receive attention, the conduct must at least be seen as an extension of the plausible. Surely many believe that one way—perhaps *the* way—to win a trial is to shape and manipulate (and maybe bribe and coerce) the jury. In another fictional account of jury tampering, *A Jury of Her Peers,* by Jean Hanff Korelitz, a jury consulting firm, for hefty fees, offers unique services to politically ambitious prosecutors. The firm kidnaps mentally unstable homeless people and programs them with drugs. They go to court and take jury summonses from those wishing to avoid service. Their programming makes them seem acceptable to the defense, but they, in fact, will vote only for conviction. While the book is hardly realistic, the dark implication that people can be robotically programmed to produce a desired outcome reveals the distrust engendered by jury consultants. Jessica Cadorine explains, "For the novel to have any impact on the reader (the novel is not science fiction) the reader must believe, at the very least, some trial consulting firms probably do use unethical tactics to tilt juries toward one position or another. Korelitz's novel is a fantastic example of such unethical and illegal behavior, but it probably does reflect distrust and wariness on the part of the public about the behavior of some consulting firms."[16]

REFORMS FOR JURY CONSULTANTS

Concern over the perceived power of jury consultants has led to suggested reforms. The most strident calls for their elimination: "We want to eliminate these consultants because: They undermine our confidence in the criminal-jury system by making the jury selection process appear unfair, and in some cases be unfair. They intrude into the lives of people who are simply fulfilling their civic duty. They institutionalize a system of unequal justice making it far more difficult for the People to prosecute wealthy defendants successfully. They make it far more likely that the side with money, either the prosecution or the defense, rather than the side with justice, will prevail."[17]

Even if the profession could do all these things, it cannot simply be banned. Consultants are not doing anything different from what attorneys regularly do; they just claim to do it better and more scientifically. Attorneys attempt to assess community attitudes, although that may merely be by reading local newspapers, listening to radio call-in shows, or talking with neighborhood barbers. An attorney tries to devise voir dire questions that will elicit potential biases and provide information for the exercise of peremptory challenges. Even without jury consultants, attorneys have regularly sought the advice of colleagues and others on the best use of peremptory challenges. Finding a line that would separate permissible aid from the impermissible is futile.

On the other side of the argument, the activities of jury consultants could be used to obtain fairer trials. Good, extensive surveys of community opinions are valuable in determining those rare situations when the venue should be changed. And if better voir dire questioning can bring out biases that otherwise would remain hidden, a more impartial jury will be empaneled.

Other changes short of abolition, however, should be considered. Some suggested reforms attempt to blunt the apparent competitive advantage jury consultants give by requiring that some of their information be shared with the opposition. Parties are entitled to seek out information that might help their case, but they are not necessarily entitled to a proprietary interest in the information they collect. Parties often have to share evidentiary material, such as documents or the names of witnesses they have uncovered, with their opponents. Elaborate rules of discovery exist because we believe that a trial is more likely to get at the truth when the affected parties have access to the same information. When the material is available to all, something like a free market exists in which the information's strengths and weaknesses, its implications and limitations, can be exposed, allowing the most valid conclusions to emerge. With the shared information, the attorneys might both be able to eliminate prospective jurors who would favor the other side, with impartiality as the result. Furthermore, if such information had to be entered into the court record, the community could more readily learn what consultants really do and how they do it, and jury consultants' effects on verdicts could be better gauged. Finally, if the information had to be shared, the advantages of the rich who hired the consultants would be partially balanced.

The work of jury consultants, however, does not fit into the existing discovery doctrines because it is not evidentiary material, and courts have not forced disclosure of consultants' data. This follows the generally accepted principle that a party does not normally have to disclose information it has developed on its own about potential jurors. Prosecutors, for example, have been able to keep confidential the information they have about how prospective jurors have decided previous cases.[18] The doctrines that might prevent disclosure of survey data, however, are not written in stone. They were created by courts and legislatures, and courts and legislatures could change them. Rules could be enacted that would permit the disclosure of some of the consultants' information, but such dictates, so far, have not been forthcoming.

Instead, the approach to jury selection consultants is now strictly adversarial. Parties can use them whenever they decide to, and their information does not have to be shared. Not everyone, however, has the resources to employ consultants. Indigent criminal defendants have asked courts to appoint jury consultants for them, and on very rare occasions this has been done.[19] Such cases, however, should not be seen as harbingers of a trend. Resources for the defense of the poor are often incredibly limited. Even if an accused is able to get the services of an attorney who is competent and not overworked, money to hire investigators, forensic scientists, and psychologists has been almost impossible to find in many places. The routine appointment of jury consultants for indigent defendants is simply not a realistic possibility.

Another set of reforms would limit the information that jury consultants rely on. Some propose following Great Britain and Canada, which forbid pretrial investigations of jurors. Others simply suggest keeping jury lists confidential until the eve of trial, as many jurisdictions now do, so that extensive investigations of potential jurors will be impractical. Advance jury lists, however, can promote fair trials by aiding the determination of whether jury pools truly represent a fair cross section of the community. Moreover, pretrial investigation can shorten voir dire and provide confidence in the answers obtained there.[20]

Because jury consultants often rely on extensive voir dire questioning and questionnaires, some reformers have sought to limit both.[21] Such a proposal has costs, for, as we have seen, the less information attorneys have about potential jurors, the more attorneys have to rely on gross stereotypes in the exercise of their peremptories, and the likelihood increases that jurors will be excused on what are in reality race-based and gender-motivated challenges. In what has become a conundrum, more information about the jurors helps satisfy the goals of *Batson* while simultaneously permitting jury consultants to operate.

THE ELIMINATION OF PEREMPTORIES

The difficulty of enforcing *Batson* and the dangers presented by jury consultants have led to the most radical suggestion: eliminate peremptory challenges, a position Justice Thurgood Marshall advocated in *Batson*. This is a radical solution because peremptory challenges are an ancient part of jury trials and were well-established when the country was formed. The federal courts and every state provide for some form of peremptory challenge in every jury trial. Even so, the Constitution apparently would not prevent their elimination. The Supreme Court has said that peremptories were "essential to the impartiality of the trial," but it has also stated time and again that the Constitution does not require that the parties be allowed to exercise peremptories. "[P]eremptory challenges are a creature of statute and are not required by the Constitution."

Apparently peremptories could be abolished, and Justice Marshall does not stand alone in advocating abolition.[22]

In their critiques of peremptory challenges, federal District Court Judge H. Lee Sarokin and Colorado District Court Judge Morris B. Hoffman both urge their elimination. Sarokin with G. Thomas Munsterman stresses that attorneys use peremptories in their attempts to construct not an impartial jury, but a *partial* jury. They note that the selection process is both expensive and time-consuming, that public confidence in the courts is undermined when potential jurors are excused without reason, and ask, "What could be fairer than a group of jurors drawn by lot from a panel that represents a fair cross section of the community and subject only to valid challenges for cause?"[23]

Morris Hoffman suggests that the true driving force for peremptory challenges ended with *Batson*. While there may have been many reasons why peremptories became institutionalized in America, "there can be no doubt," says Hoffman, "that the single most significant factor in extending the life of the peremptory challenge in the United States was its use as a tool to perpetuate the racial purity of juries. Now that that battle has been lost by the states, it is time to retire the peremptory challenge." The present process, Hoffman contends, is filled with irrationalities that undermine the public's confidence in our trials.

> The most obvious, and in some ways most important, dimension to the problem of the peremptory challenge is that it reflects a deep distrust of prospective jurors wholly inconsistent with the trust we repose in sitting jurors. . . . I worry about the message we are sending to that inevitably biased juror. "Go ahead, act on your bias. We are all biased, and none of us can resist acting on those biases. So go ahead and act on yours. After all, you passed the test of peremptory challenges." . . .
>
> [W]hat lawyers are really doing when they exercise peremptory challenges is making crass and, by definition, unjustifiable generalizations about large classes of jurors. In this sense, the proposition that black jurors will not convict a black defendant is no more offensive than the proposition that jurors who wear pocket protectors are pro-prosecution. Neither our rules of evidence nor even our most basic ideas of due process tolerate such preposterous propositions, and it is amazing that we tolerate them in the selection of jurors. . . . *Batson* teaches that some irrational stereotypes are constitutionally permissible, and some are not. . . .
>
> At worst, these homegrown theories are our old friends racism, sexism, and class hatred all dressed up in [modern] psychobabble. At best, they are animus-free nonsense, but nonsense nonetheless. In either case, the daily infliction of these theories on our citizen jurors is exacting a palpable cost in lowered public confidence in the quiet rationality of our jury system.[24]

Although Great Britain abolished peremptory challenges in 1988, no American jurisdiction has made any serious steps in that direction. This is partly so because while trial judges may wish them gone, trial lawyers desire them. The attorneys' devotion to the practice may not seem logical, for if peremptories were eliminated the strategic balance between the parties would apparently not be changed. Furthermore, no hard information supports the notion that a lawyer's exercise of peremptory challenges truly matters. Or putting it more colorfully, as Judge Hoffman has, "Really, don't you [trial lawyers] have to admit . . . that the decisions you make in exercising peremptory challenges are a bunch of hooey?"[25]

Be that as it may, lawyers love peremptories, and according to Hoffman, a basic reason that they do is because "they are fun."

> Peremptory challenges are a combination of psychiatry and palm reading, which probably overlap greatly anyway. We just love to judge people, and we love to predict the unpredictable. "You're fair; you're not. You think you are so smart trying to hide your bias, but I detected it. You're with us; you're against us. . . ." I think one of the reasons peremptory challenges are so fun is precisely because they allow "trafficking" . . . in this kind of drivel. It's drivel, but it's fun drivel. I think many opponents of peremptory challenges are ineffective because we focus on the drivel part and not on the fun part. It's the fun part that we are going to have to talk lawyers into giving up, and that's not going to be easy.[26]

Hoffman may have a point. Something more is going on, and Michael Saks hints at it in his summary of the efficacy of jury selection practices: "[I]f social science jury selection methods cannot usually be much help except on the margin, what about lawyers selecting juries the old fashioned way, by relying on their intuitive judgments? The available evidence is that, at least for most lawyers, that is an even less effective road to a favorable jury."[27] The key to why attorneys wish to retain peremptories may be in that phrase, "at least for most lawyers." Many trial attorneys do not suffer from immodesty, and the majority may believe that they are among a small group of attorneys who exercise peremptory challenges with more finesse than their opponents. They believe that they are among the select whose skill or intuitions give them an advantage, and not surprisingly they do not desire to surrender the benefit handed to them by peremptories.

There are, however, important reasons to maintain peremptory challenges beyond attorneys' arrogance or playfulness. Peremptories continue to have an important role in producing fair trials and building confidence in verdicts. We might assume that trials would be fairer without peremptory challenges because for-cause challenges would remain to remove the biased. Without peremptories, however, for-cause challenges would not work as effectively as they now do. If a lawyer senses that a potential juror has a bias but has not admitted it, he may press that juror during the voir dire. Sometimes such vigorous questioning demonstrates the absence of impartiality, and the person is removed for cause. A fairer jury results. Such in-depth questioning, however, can be offensive to the prospective juror. Many people bristle at the suggestion that they cannot be fair, and a probing voir dire can convey the notion that the lawyer is skeptical about an individual's claim of impartiality. If the inquiry does not yield grounds to remove the juror for cause, the attorney is in a dilemma. The juror has not been excused, but the questioning has antagonized her. The usual response now is to peremptorily challenge that person. The abolition of peremptories, however, removes that safeguard, and attorneys would become more hesitant to lay the groundwork for a challenge for cause. As a result, without peremptories, more biased jurors would make it on to the jury. Barbara Babcock states it well: "The peremptory challenge is the insurance that makes genuine inquiry into juror bias possible."[28]

Moreover, "the peremptory endows the litigant with a role in the process, thus promoting in Blackstone's words 'a good opinion of the jury the want of which might totally disconcert him.' "[29] Sometimes that role is to pay attention to and act upon one's own intuitions. Common sense indicates that we are often correct in thinking a prospective juror may not be neutral, although partiality cannot be established in a legal sense. I once tried a minor drug case in Manhattan. A potential juror gave his name and then stated that he was the editor of what many would regard as a pornographic magazine whose scant copy often seemed to praise drugs and denigrate the police. He, however, steadfastly maintained that he could follow the law, be impartial in any kind of criminal trial including a drug case, and fairly evaluate a police officer's testimony. The court had no reason to excuse him for cause, but to the surprise of no one, the prosecutor excused him peremptorily. In another case a client of mine was charged with selling drugs to an undercover police officer whom I would contend was mistaken or lying. I encountered a potential juror who was the father of an undercover police officer doing the same kind of work. He touted his fairness including his ability to impartially judge a police officer's testimony. He could not be excused for cause; I peremptorily excused him.

Even when a potential juror professes impartiality, good reasons may exist to think the person is at least unconsciously biased. Observers of those trials of mine were hardly shocked that those potential jurors were excused. Many, no doubt, thought the trials were fairer without them. Peremptory challenges do not always damage the appearance or substance of fairness; they can also make trials substantively fairer.

In addition, although peremptory challenges may antagonize citizens, they can deflect hostility away from judges. "When a prospective juror has told the court that he or she can be impartial, rejecting this assurance and excluding the juror for cause is likely to seem insulting. In this situation, the peremptory challenge has permitted both judges and prospective jurors to save face. Judges have resolved doubts against exclusion, relying on the peremptory challenge to correct their errors and to do so without explicitly rejecting the jurors' protestations of impartiality."[30]

Peremptories have a further beneficial role. Sometimes a potential juror is peremptorily challenged because he is seen as the type who will be stubbornly contrary or erratic. Such "three-dollar-bill" people, as Albert Alschuler labels them, will not add a useful perspective to the deliberations, but simply make agreement harder to reach. Peremptories often weed out such extremes. In England, one consequence of the abolition of peremptories was a concern that hung juries would multiply, which brought some of the pressure for the relaxation of the unanimity requirement there. Indeed, some who wish to abolish peremptory challenges in this country recognize that hung juries would probably increase unless unanimous verdicts are abandoned and the benefits brought by unanimity are forgone.[31]

Finally, and perhaps most important, the abolition of peremptories will increase the power of trial judges in jury trials. With peremptory challenges gone, challenges for cause would be the only removal mechanism. Trial judges, as we have seen, have great control over whether for-cause challenges are granted. Today that power is diluted by the use of peremptory challenges. If peremptories were abolished, the authority of the judge to mold the jury would increase tremendously. The judge would have essentially unchecked power to fashion the jury, and consciously or not, judges will often produce less than truly impartial juries. Our system of checks and balances teaches us to be on guard about such situations. Barbara Babcock raises this essential point:

> [The] total elimination of the peremptory challenge is ill-advised as it would focus jury selection entirely on the challenge for cause. The judge alone—in a series of highly discretionary, practically unreviewable decisions—would then be permitted to shape the jury in every case. But under the Constitution, the jury trial is guaranteed precisely because our tradition is not to trust the unilateral actions of judges. In

particular, the jury is meant to offset the class bias and elitism that characterizes the judiciary, yet we can hardly expect judges to find "cause"—i.e., incipient bias—in jurors who reflect their own image in background or outlook.[32]

Part of the reason that judges oppose the continuation of peremptories while attorneys steadfastly support them is because of the often natural tendency for those with authority to desire even more control. Concentrating power in judges may not be inherently bad, but our traditions and common sense tell us to be wary of such trends, and the movement supported by judges to abolish peremptory challenges is an attempt to give judges more power.

A COMPROMISE POSITION

Because there are compelling reasons for protecting peremptories, perhaps a compromise position ought to be sought. Instead of abolishing them completely, their number could be sharply limited. This could both promote the goals of *Batson* and reduce the probability that attorneys and their consultants could sculpt a jury to achieve a biased result. If, for example, the parties had but three challenges to select a twelve-person jury, the attorneys would be unlikely to exercise the peremptories solely on racial and gender grounds, for their challenges would be quickly exhausted. As more of the disfavored group were called, some would inevitably be sworn as jurors. If a minority group constitutes 25 percent of the pool and three of the first twelve prospective jurors are that minority, the attorney would have to think hard about eliminating them simply because of their ethnicity. The other side would probably challenge some of the remaining nine, and some might be excused for cause. The odds would be high that more minorities would be called and they could not be challenged. Meanwhile, the attorney would have no peremptories for the non-minority jurors even when they seemed unfavorable. Attorneys would quickly learn that most often even if a group were disfavored, distinctions among members of that group would have to be made and the least disfavored ones allowed to be sworn. In other words, the attorney trying to best serve her client would have to make individual distinctions among the group, and this is precisely what *Batson* seeks.

Furthermore, with fewer challenges, attorneys would also have little ability to shape a biased jury. The attorney would have to think carefully about using a precious peremptory to remove a seemingly neutral juror in hopes of getting a favorable one, because this would quickly exhaust the challenges. Even if an unfavorable one were subsequently called, the attorney might not be able to exclude him. Instead, lawyers would have to husband peremptories to guarantee removal of those who appear worst for their client, leaving little room for the active shaping of the body. The result should be a desirable jury, one with the most apparently partial people removed, but not one shaped by an attorney into being predisposed toward one side.

Meanwhile the affirmative benefits of peremptories would remain. The parties would have exercised some control over the selection process, thereby promoting acceptance of the outcome by both the litigants and the public. The parties would retain the ability to probe for a for-cause challenge. And a check would remain on the trial judge's power to shape the jury.

Slashing the number of peremptories, however, will not be easy to accomplish. Trial attorneys are devoted to them, and if they had their druthers, they would have more. Lawyers will not be lobbying for fewer peremptories, and although peremptories have been widely discussed in *Batson*'s wake, legislatures have done little to reform the process. The matter of peremptories has been left to the courts, but because in most jurisdictions the number of peremptories has been set by legislative enactments, the courts do not have the power to limit their number. Thus, although limitation may be a good idea, and certainly experimentation with curtailment is desirable, little progress in that direction is apparent.

On the other hand, there is already now great variation in how many such challenges a party is entitled to. As we have seen, their number varies from jurisdiction to jurisdiction and often within a state by the kind of action being tried. I have tried cases where I had twenty peremptories and cases where I had three. I can attest that the strategic use of peremptories is much different where they are numerous compared to where they are sharply limited. Unfortunately, good studies of how curtailed peremptories affect jury selection and the resulting fairness of trials have not been done. They certainly would be welcome and might be a needed spur for reform.

Chapter 13 The Adversary System

The jury is a passive receiver of information. We may take this aspect of juries for granted, but it is one of the main characteristics that separates juries from other decision making bodies. If a child is thought to have eaten cookies before dinner, the parent does not determine the facts by merely receiving information the child chooses to present. Instead, he peers into the cookie jar to see if cookies are missing; he inspects hands and mouth for telltale signs of melted chocolate chips; he asks questions. If a plane crashes, investigators do not proceed solely on data others choose to present. Instead, they go to the crash site to inspect; they question witnesses; they seek out and examine cockpit voice recorders; they consult experts; and so on.

When I want to learn about the jury system, I pick books to read; I seek court statistics; I go to the courthouse to observe juries in action; I talk to those called to be jurors; and so on. Juries do not employ these active methods; they wait to be told things.

Normally we would rebel at making decisions based solely on the information that others choose to present us. When we want knowledge, we usually have a hand in pursuing it. It seems artificial and condescending for someone else to restrict our access to information. Nevertheless, such a decision making method is at the core of our jury system. Consequently, jurors are put into an extraordinary position, one they are unlikely to encounter elsewhere in their lives. They are responsible for making a decision, but they do not have control over the information upon which it is based. Jurors are informed through the adversarial presentation of evidence, which is now a central component of our jury system.

THE RISE OF THE ADVERSARY SYSTEM

Juries originally decided disputes using their own knowledge of the matter. That method disappeared long ago, but juries did not then immediately become dependent on the adversary system for weighing the evidence; instead, they relied heavily on judges.

At the beginning of the eighteenth century, a criminal defendant charged with a felony—except for treason trials, where lawyers were allowed—could not have an attorney to assist in the development of the facts. Defense counsel could present legal arguments, but he could not offer evidence, examine or cross-examine witnesses, or address the jury in opening or closing statements. If these were to be done, the accused, unaided, had to do them. The justification was that because the accused knew the facts best, a defense through a skilled intermediary would only impede justice. Prosecutors, who were often the crime victims themselves, could have counsel, but in practice generally neither side had a lawyer. Instead, the judge played a central role in eliciting and presenting evidence.

The judge was the chief interrogator of witnesses. His inquiries extended to the accused, who, even if he had a privilege against self-incrimination, could not really refuse to answer, because, unrepresented by counsel, he had to speak to make a defense. Consequently, many trials were essentially duels of wit between the defendant and the judge.

Few trials, however, featured vigorous questioning. Little information was elicited from the witnesses, and even less of that information was challenged. By today's standards these trials were exceedingly short. Indeed, the common-law felony trials of 1700 are barely recognizable to the modern eye:

> Criminal trials in the early eighteenth century were typically very brief, no more than half an hour on average, including the jury's deliberation and the announcement of their verdict. Not a great deal of evidence was introduced. The facts at issue were normally presented orally by the victim of the offense, supported by witnesses who, like

the victim, gave their evidence briefly and generally under the questioning of the judge. The judge acted as examiner and cross-examiner—although the defendant and jurors could ask questions and often did so by blurting them out, procedure was in that regard rather chaotic. The judge's intention was to present defendants with the evidence they would have to counter to maintain their innocence. Defendants had an opportunity to question each witness in turn and to reply to the evidence, supported by witnesses to the facts and to the character. Accused felons were not allowed counsel, but had to speak entirely for themselves.[1]

This system began to change around 1730, when, for unknown reasons, the prohibition of counsel was breached, but the breach was only partial. Defense counsel still could not address the jury or argue the facts. But—and this was crucial—attorneys were increasingly allowed to question witnesses. Limited to this tool, defense attorneys soon became skilled cross-examiners, and cross-examination began to transform the trial process. Cross-examination was "a mechanism that offered the broadest latitude for the development of persuasive proof with a minimum of restriction. Through cross-examination, defense counsel could present his theory of the case, refute an opponent's claims, develop favorable proof, discredit opposing witnesses, and generally advance his client's position before the jury." The significance of the expanded role of defense counsel cannot be overstated. As J. F. Stephen said a century later, the rise of lawyers for the accused was "[t]he most remarkable change" that occurred in English criminal procedure.[2]

When judges controlled the trials, they may have asked some questions, but challenging examinations were rare. Now defense counsel saw a probing interrogation as his role.

> For the most part [judges] took the evidence as they found it and sought to have it enlarged upon only to clarify the case to be answered, rather than necessarily to discredit it. . . .
>
>   By the 1780's at least, defense counsel had come to have a different view of the evidence presented against their clients, a different view of the prosecution witnesses, and certainly a different view of their own role in the trial from that of the judge. They had come by then to see themselves as the defendant's advocate. Even if the scope for that advocacy was limited, their cross-examination of the prosecution witnesses could make a significant difference for the accused they defended.[3]

As the attorneys gained power through cross-examination, judicial power decreased. In 1700, English judges had the central courtroom role. A hundred years later, judges were largely passive in regard to the evidence, and defense advocates were the dominant force in trials.

The changes were so significant that, in effect, a new trial system was created. Before defense cross-examination, English trials were judge-dominated inquests. During the eighteenth century, trials increasingly became adversarial, and by the early 1800s criminal trials in England were true adversary affairs.

The adversary system may have arisen even sooner in America. Defense counsel was the precipitating factor for the English change, and America guaranteed an accused the right to counsel before England did. In any event, even before the Revolution, adversarial trials in the colonies can be found, and they soon became firmly ensconced in the new United States.[4]

The adversary system, of course, is now a central foundation of courtroom procedure in the United States. Indeed, the Supreme Court has repeatedly stated that the Constitution's Sixth Amendment grants those accused of crimes a right to an adversarial process, and even if a similar constitutional right does not directly apply in civil cases, the adversary system is also entrenched in noncriminal trials.[5]

PARTISAN PRESENTATION OF EVIDENCE

With the adversarial process, juries receive information selected, managed, and controlled by the parties and their attorneys. Jurors do not get the evidence from a neutral source committed to presenting all the information or establishing the truth. Instead, the jury has to construct the truth out of competing partisan presentations.

That accurate facts and fair verdicts can and do emerge from such adversarial displays of information and argument is not as illogical as it may seem. A committed champion will often discover and challenge more evidence than will a neutral performer. As an attorney, I am ethically and psychologically committed to having my client prevail. This gives me an incentive to seek out all the information favorable to my client's position, an incentive a neutral seeker of evidence would not have. Similarly, as an advocate I will probe my opponent's information to find its gaps and other shortcomings, and will probably see them more often than a disinterested person would. The competitive nature of the adversary system also means that a party cannot merely present any story he desires to tell. He will have to make sure that it is supported by the evidence, for if it is not, his opponent will quickly pounce on its shortcomings.

"[T]he advocacy ethos presupposes an 'invisible hand' theory of competition . . . premise[d on the theory] that when two advocates vigorously oppose each other in an effort to do their best for their client, rather than with the aim of discovering truth, they inadvertently serve the systemic goal of truth-finding."[6]

The theory is that because of the competition and incentives built into the adversary system, the fullest presentation and best analysis of the relevant information will result. Many who analyze the adversarial process make analogies to free market economics. "This incentive system is similar, of course, to other free enterprise concepts that govern economic thinking. The notion is that people who stand to gain or lose from a transaction are likely to be motivated to act more effectively than those who are indifferent to the transaction."[7]

Not everyone, however, sings the praises of the adversary system. Just as the market economy has reformers and critics, so, too, does the adversary system. Critics frequently point out that most of the world's courtrooms use neither the adversary system nor the jury system.

TRIALS IN CIVIL LAW COUNTRIES

In many countries whose law is not derived from English common law, commonly referred to as "civil law countries," noncriminal matters are handled much differently than they are in America. Judges, not juries, make all determinations of law and fact, and, although attorneys are involved, there is not an adversarial presentation of evidence. Indeed, there is not even a "trial" in the American sense of the term.

A group of judges, often three, decides the case. One judge presides at the earlier stages where evidence may be presented, motions and rulings on procedure are made, and the areas of agreement and disagreement are worked out. If there is testimony, the presiding judge elicits it by asking witnesses to recount what they know. This narrative is rarely interrupted except for periodic summaries dictated by the judge to a clerk. After the narrative is complete, the judge, sometimes in response to suggestions by the attorneys, may question the witness to further develop the testimony. The collective bench's decision is based not on live testimony, but on the presiding judge's summaries as well as other written materials and counsels' arguments. Some civil law countries have found this method of adjudication with its many meetings to be inefficient and have been moving toward a single, comprehensive hearing. Even so, judges, not juries, still make the decisions, and a judge, not the attorneys, is responsible for developing the evidence.

Criminal matters in civil law countries, on the other hand, do culminate in a trial and in many places do have lay decision makers. Nevertheless, the procedures differ significantly from American ones.

The first stage is an extensive pretrial investigation, undertaken in some countries by a judge and in others by a public prosecutor. Both judge and prosecutor are civil servants insulated from the political process. The investigating officer controls the nature and the scope of the investigation. He questions the suspect and witnesses, including those suggested by the suspect. The investigating officer's duty is to gather all the relevant information and determine whether criminal charges should be brought. If the findings support charging the suspect with a crime, the evidence is summarized and compiled into a complete written record, and this dossier is forwarded to the trial court. Because the defendant has access to the entire dossier, she can learn the full extent of the case against her before trial.

The composition of the trial court varies from country to country and by the seriousness of the charge within a country, but the courts typically consist of up to three professional judges and a group of lay judges, called lay assessors. When included, the lay assessors usually outnumber the professional judges. In some countries and for some charges, however, only professional judges—usually a panel of three—adjudicate. This body, whether a mixed group or confined only to professional judges, together decides all questions of law and fact. If the defendant is convicted, the adjudicative group pronounces the sentence along with the guilty verdict.

The lay assessors are selected differently in different countries and sometimes for different categories of cases. In some places they are selected at random from the general population and sometimes appointed by officials, generally not just for one case, but for a fixed term of years during which they may adjudicate a dozen trials or so annually. The parties to the case have no role in selecting the lay judges.

The professional judge presiding at the trial is familiar with the dossier, but the other professional and lay judges are not, and only the evidence presented in open court is considered in adjudicating the charges. Such proof is taken without the kind of technical evidence rules that exist in American courts, and its order and development are controlled by the presiding judge, not by the prosecutor or defense counsel.

The trial generally begins with a statement from the defendant. The accused does not have to speak, but most do. This is partly because silence sometimes can be taken as corroboration of guilt; partly because the right to silence has to be asserted in front of those who will judge the defendant; and partly because the determination of guilt and sentence both come from the same proceeding. Silence at the trial could mean that the defendant gives up the chance to mitigate punishment, and few are willing to take that risk.

The accused does not merely respond to questions, but first has the opportunity to present a coherent narrative presenting her version of the events. After this, she is questioned, primarily by the presiding judge, who is prepared for this task by becoming familiar with the dossier. The presiding judge then decides what other witnesses to call. These witnesses, too, present information largely without interruption followed by questioning, primarily by the presiding judge. Although counsel may suggest questions and lines of inquiry, the trials proceed with relatively passive attorneys and an active judge.

The verdict does not have to be unanimous. If the requisite votes for conviction (often two-thirds) are not garnered, the defendant is acquitted. Unlike an American jury, this panel cannot stalemate. The trial court's decision consists of a detailed, written report discussing the evidence, including the testimony of each witness, and explaining the court's findings of fact and law as well as the reasons for the sentence if there has been a conviction. This opinion serves several functions. Because the professional judge has to write such a judgment, he naturally has an incentive to develop the evidence fully and carefully during the trial. The written analysis also allows a higher court to review both the factual and legal conclusions reached by the trial court, and both sides can appeal a decision on guilt and the sentence.

This summary does not fully describe any single country's justice system, but contains the elements common to many. Certain crucial differences from American trials are evident. First, while laypeople may have a role in adjudicating criminal matters, the trials do not include juries as we know them. Second, civil law criminal trials do not use an adversary procedure where attorneys acting on behalf of the parties have primary responsibility for developing and attacking the evidence. Instead, in civil law countries judges have the duty of impartially getting to the truth and are the active participants in developing the evidence.[8]

EFFECTIVENESS OF THE ADVERSARY SYSTEM

Critics point out that the judicial systems of much of the civilized world do not use the adversary system, and also that it is not widely used to gather knowledge or make decisions outside courtrooms. On this point, the distinguished jurist Max Frankel said:

We proclaim to each other and to the world that the clash of adversaries is a powerful means for hammering out the truth. . . . That the adversary technique is useful
within limits none will doubt. That it is "best" we should all doubt if we were able to
be objective about the question. Despite our untested statements of self-congratula-
tion, we know that others searching after facts—in history, geography, medicine,
whatever—do not emulate our adversary system. We know that most countries of
the world seek justice by different routes. What is much more to the point, we know
that many of the rules and devices of the adversary litigation as we conduct it are not
geared for, but are often aptly suited to defeat, the development of the truth.[9]

Part of this criticism is beside the point. Many disciplines have methods that
are not used elsewhere, and surely there are also many differences between history, geography, and medicine and the European court systems. Nevertheless,
the assertion that the adversary system serves truth well is mostly an article of
faith. Indeed, although we may be able to study which processes litigants and
others *perceive* as more fair, conclusions about the comparative abilities of different judicial procedures to ascertain the truth seem unverifiable.[10]

Studies have produced inconsistent results. While some research suggests that
adversarial processes tend to produce more relevant evidence than do nonadversarial procedures, Franklin Strier maintains, "[I]n empirical studies, those acting
as adversary system attorneys generally did not differ in their diligence from those
acting as inquisitorial system attorneys, except when the original distribution of
facts was unfavorable to one party. Nor was the claim that the adversary system
results in more facts being presented to the factfinder substantiated."[11] Others
looking at the same information, however, find reason to praise the adversary
process because it tends to protect the weakest. "Psychological experimentation
has shown that an advocate working in an adversarial context who finds his client
at a factual disadvantage will spend significant effort to improve his client's position. This is to be contrasted with the behavior of the advocate working in an
inquisitorial setting who will seldom undertake an extensive search for better evidence to bolster a weak case. The adversary process appears to encourage advocates to protect parties facing an initial disadvantage and hence to improve the
overall quality of the evidence upon which adjudication will be based."[12]

INDIVIDUAL AUTONOMY AND
CHECKS AND BALANCES

There are, then, reasons to both attack and defend the production of evidence
by the adversary system, but the system remains entrenched because it serves

other functions apart from the quality and quantity of proof produced. As with peremptory challenges, the adversary system may be entrenched partly because it is fun for the attorneys. Lawyers not only dig for evidence, they also plot strategies for the development of persuasive stories from that evidence, work on oratory for addressing the jury, and sharpen their wits for cross-examination. Lawyers trying cases feel important and useful. They are the stars of the proceeding, in a limelight they do not enjoy when judges are responsible for the collection and development of the evidence. Lawyers' egos aside, however, the adversary system serves other more important functions as well.

Because attorneys are, in a real sense, extensions of the litigants, the adversary system cedes control of the litigation to the client, and the attorney has to serve the client's purposes. Robert Burns explains:

> [T]he factual theory of the case is determined in part by the client's objectives, and the lawyer is bound to present the theory that is most consistent with the client's objectives. Client control of the key factual theory of the case, toward the establishment of which an effective advocate will rigorously marshal everything, is a feature of the Anglo-American trial system that is strongly at odds with its Continental cousins. . . . On the Continent "the law" as interpreted by the judges ultimately determines what the relevant factual questions are, and hence what the "ultimate facts" can be. Nothing so ephemeral, so political, so individual as a given party's "objectives" should interfere with that process.[13]

The lawyer advises on what course to take, but it is the client who chooses. The presented evidence is a collaborative effort "in which the story that the client claims to be true is confronted by the lawyer's judgment about what is factually plausible and morally compelling."[14]

The litigant has an advocate whose ethics and desire for professional satisfaction and success require the litigant's cause to be championed. Because the party controls the factual theory of the case and his representative is responsible for the evidence to support it, if this fails to persuade, in an important sense, the litigant has no one to blame but himself. This increases the likelihood that the litigants, and thereby the public, will accept the outcome. It confirms the individual's autonomy vis-à-vis the state. The verdict is not some official dictum controlled by the state; it is the result of a struggle between litigants and their lawyers. "[A] trial advocate may and often must make the most impolite or embarrassing suggestions, even if they are offensive to the powerful. By the law of professional responsibility, the client's interests supersede every code of silence. This enforced brashness is enormously important and deeply antiauthoritarian. . . . The parties' control of what story to tell, of what fact to put in issue, is an important bulwark against the invulnerability of One Big Story."[15]

Thus, the adversary system serves as an important check on the government. It prevents a government official from deciding what proof is important and from fashioning it into a factual theory that will affect the lives of litigants. Instead, the adversary system gives the power to those who will be most affected by the outcome—the parties.

Judges with authority over the evidence too often lose objectivity.[16] During the McCarthy era of the 1950s, Kenneth Graham maintains, congressional committee proceedings revealed the dangers when development of the evidence and the conclusions to be drawn from it were combined in one body. "[C]ommittee members determined what evidence to seek, whether or not it was admissible, and what it proved—thus combining in the committee functions that under the Sixth Amendment are divided among counsel, court and jury. This combination of functions allowed the committee to intimidate witnesses who did not perform as desired." An adversarial presentation cannot only overcome these dangers, it can dilute undesirable prejudices; research indicates that "adversarial procedures are more effective than nonadversarial (inquisitorial) procedures in counteracting decision makers' . . . biases."[17] Others have pointed out that the adversarial process can preserve the impartiality of the decisionmaker: "If the judge is assigned the task of making factual inquiry, both theoretical analysis and empirical data suggest that her biases are likely to be intensified and her decisions opened to prejudicial influence. This loss of neutrality is arguably as significant a problem as any skewing caused by party control."[18]

Juries also serve as an important check on and balance to governmental power. The adversary system interacts with the jury system to serve this function:

[I]f the jury and not the judge makes the decision about guilt or innocence, the lawyers remain free to argue to the judge as zealously as they like about the issues of law without fear that if they alienate the judge, they will thereby influence a determination on the issue of guilt or innocence. The adversary system has resulted, therefore, in a practice of criminal defense that is characteristically more vigorous than that displayed by lawyers in European systems that function without vesting final authority in a jury of laypersons. . . . [T]he distortions of competition are less serious than the potential for corruption when the power of judgment is concentrated in a judge who, like the inquisitorial judge of the European past, claims the final word on the accusation, the facts, and the law. If, as Lord Acton said, power corrupts and absolute power corrupts absolutely, the safest way to run a criminal trial is to bifurcate the power of presenting the evidence between prosecution and defense and to divide the power of decision between judge and jury.[19]

LAWYERS AND THE ACCEPTANCE OF VERDICTS

The adversary system can helpfully protect against governmental abuses of power and can aid the acceptance of verdicts, but its reliance on lawyers can undercut the legitimacy of trial outcomes. Lawyers are the stars of the trial process. Almost nothing happens without their initiation or participation. Characters with such a central role, it is natural to think, must be central to the trial's resolution, and certainly lawyers ostentatiously proclaim that they crucially affect what a jury does. Such "beliefs are promoted in the trial advocacy literature, are passed along from experienced attorneys to newcomers to the profession, and seem to be quite persistent." It has been easy to see a verdict not as the product of the persuasive force of the evidence, but as controlled by the lawyers' abilities and performances. Even academics, normally temperate in their comments, can conclude, "Juries are shamelessly but routinely manipulated by trial attorneys." What Kalven and Zeisel noted a generation ago remains true today: "[I]t is one of the more popular assumptions about the jury that it tends to 'try the lawyers,' that, unlike the judge, it is susceptible to the skill and rhetoric of trial counsel and that he may well be a major determinant of the jury's decision. The very legends of the bar's heroes, of the Erskines, the Choates, the Darrows, imply that lawyers of their caliber would make a decisive difference in any case."[20]

The influence of attorneys on jury verdicts, however, is greatly overstated. That effect has seldom been studied, partly because it is almost impossible to do so, but the research that does exist tends to show that lawyers seldom play a central role in the outcome. For example, one of the few attempts at a rigorous examination of the issue concludes that "the existing empirical literature . . . does call into question the assumption that reactions to lawyers are pivotal." The study found that deliberating jurors spent little time discussing the lawyers, but when they did, the comments were closely intertwined with the evidence and tended to deal with substantive points. The researchers also found that jurors' beliefs about the case were not irrevocably set at the trial's beginning when lawyers made their opening statements, but instead the jurors' feelings about the outcome evolved as the evidence unfolded, indicating that jurors were influenced much more by the presented proof than by the attorneys' characteristics and performances.

[O]ne theme in these findings is individual [attorney] attributes like style or personality do not seem to matter as much as is suggested in the trial advocacy literature. A
second theme is that jurors pay more attention to substantive aspects of the trial—
the nature of testimony by witnesses and how they withstand cross-examination.
The importance of substantive aspects of the testimony, combined with the greater
observed willingness to respond to evidence, suggests the possibility of substantial
influence by attorneys. But it suggests that such influence will not flow from rhetor-
ical flourishes or pleasing appearance or attractive personality, but rather from *the
skill of the attorney in making substantive choices about what types of witnesses and evidence to present, and his or her skill in implementing those choices.*[21]

Lawyers may wish it otherwise, but the information drawn from witnesses,
documents, and objects—that is, evidence—is the primary determinant of
jury verdicts, not lawyerly performances. Common sense indicates this even
without research. Throughout this country, prosecutors win more than they
lose. Prosecutors may feel like hotshots because they prevail about 80 percent of
the time, but many in the defense bar are former prosecutors. The skills of the
lawyers do not change with their move from the prosecution to the defense
table. Because the conviction rate remains in the prosecutors' favor even as the
composition of the prosecutorial staff changes and even as former prosecutors
become defense attorneys, the imbalance in verdicts cannot be explained by the
abilities or performances of attorneys. It is caused by something else, and that
something else is *the evidence.* Prosecutors overwhelmingly win because they
have better cases than defense attorneys, not because they perform better in
court.

Although it may be a myth that lawyers make a great difference in jury verdicts, it is a deeply held one. "Its persistence may come from the natural human
inclination to overestimate one's own importance and the absence of a strong
and deep empirically-based research literature which contradicts this view. In
addition, the limited availability of effective feedback mechanisms by which
lawyers learn to assess their own performance more accurately may also perpetuate the belief in lawyer influences."[22]

While it may not be the shadow of her smile or the cut of his suit that carries
the day, lawyers do, however, matter. The adversary system depends on the attorneys, and if that system is to serve its legitimate functions, lawyers must perform in accordance with its goals. If each adversary does her appropriate job,
the evidence and factual theories will be well presented, and that presented evidence will drive the deliberations and the resulting verdict. The crucial concern for lawyers and the jury system should be the possibility that the compet-

ing attorneys are mismatched. The adversary system requires competent counsel, each equally striving to present favorable evidence for its side and to reveal weaknesses in the evidence from the opponent. When the advocates perform unequally, the adversary system breaks down, damaging the jury's ability to render a proper verdict.

The impact that the disparate quality of counsel has on a trial is, of course, also hard to study. We have little data on this issue beyond that collected by Kalven and Zeisel, who surveyed judges and reported that in 76 percent of cases before them the judges considered the attorneys of equal quality. In 11 percent, they found defense counsel superior, and in 13 percent they found the prosecutors superior. After comparing jury verdicts with judges' opinions, Kalven and Zeisel concluded that an imbalance in attorney quality may affect one trial in ten.[23]

If the imbalance in attorney quality affects only 10 percent of the trials, factors other than comparative lawyer performance influence the vast majority of verdicts. Nevertheless, 10 percent represents a large number of trials. Indeed, in instances where innocence has been clearly established after a conviction, one of the chief causes of the wrongful convictions has been inadequate defense counsel.[24]

The fact remains, however, that lawyers' performances skew jury outcomes in only a small percentage of cases. What is not taken into account in this assumption about the importance of attorneys is the truly essential role of the presented evidence.

Chapter 14 Presentation of Evidence

Attorneys cannot present any information they desire in any way they like. Ethical rules, for example, generally forbid a lawyer from presenting a witness that the lawyer knows is lying. Even without ethical strictures, however, the adversary system militates against using perjured testimony. The opponent has a great stake in exposing the lying witness. If that exposure succeeds, the party calling the perjuring witness will no doubt suffer greatly. As long as there is a significant chance that the perjury will be exposed, an attorney is unlikely, with or without the ethical rules, to call a witness knowing that he will lie.

The ethical rule, however, restricts the attorney only from presenting a witness she *knows* will lie. The attorney may think the testimony is implausible; the attorney may be suspicious of its veracity; the attorney may even believe that it is a lie. Nevertheless, an attorney may ethically present it because she does not *know* it is a lie. Such knowledge generally can come only when the witness himself confesses that it is a lie. This is rare.

TRIAL STRUCTURE

Whatever the effect of this and other ethical rules, attorneys are restricted by the trial structure and elaborate rules of evidence that regulate what information is presented to the jury and how that information is presented. The structural rules are so ingrained that little thought is given to how they might affect juries. Indeed, through fiction, drama, and news reports, most of us are familiar with basic trial procedure.

After the jury is selected, the attorneys make opening statements to the jury about what they hope to establish in the trial. The prosecutor or plaintiff puts on its case. That party calls witnesses. Witnesses take an oath and then testify by responding to questions asked by the party who called them. When this direct examination concludes, the opposing side gets to cross-examine, that is, to ask questions of that witness to show the limitations, ambiguities, or falsehoods of his or her testimony.

Although typically, oral testimony predominates at trials, a party is not limited to producing witnesses. Physical objects can be presented to the jury. These could consist of contracts or letters or the murder weapon or anything else that could have a bearing on the matter in dispute. The party also might present demonstrations or experiments or pictures or other things that could illustrate the theory of the case.

When the prosecutor or plaintiff completes the presentation of his case, the defense presents her witnesses, physical evidence, or demonstrations. At the conclusion of the defendant's case, the prosecutor or plaintiff has the opportunity to present evidence that rebuts what the defense has presented. The defense can then rebut the rebuttal.

Once the presentation of evidence concludes, each side addresses the jury in closing statements or arguments in which the adversaries try to demonstrate to the jury why their presented evidence indicates their side ought to win. The judge then instructs the jury about the applicable law. Finally, the jury retires to deliberate in secret and returns to render its verdict.

The trial structure not only has the jury operating on passively received information, it also forces a jury to assimilate material in other unusual ways. One party proceeds with its entire case before the other side goes ahead, even when there are several contested issues. This seriatim method means that information on a particular point is not presented in a continuous stream, but in a disjointed manner with other evidence intervening. For example, a prosecutor on a murder trial may contend that the defendant had a motive to kill, had access to the murder weapon, and was seen in the vicinity of the murder near the time of its occurrence. The defendant may contest all these issues. While it might seem most rational to present all the evidence about each contention together, that does not occur. The information about a motive might be presented on day one by the prosecutor and on day four by the defense, with the prosecutor's proof about access and vicinity intervening. In a more complex trial, the intervening time between the presentation of all evidence on the same topic might be weeks or even months.

The proof not only comes in fits and starts, it comes in the unusual form of responses to advocates' questions. Witnesses are put in a strange position. They take an oath to "tell the truth, the whole truth, and nothing but the truth," but they are never allowed to narrate fully and freely what they know about the accident or murder or whatever the trial is about. Instead, witnesses are required to answer only the specific questions put to them. Even at the end of a witness's examination, we do not say, "Is there anything else you would like to add or was there anything left out of your testimony?" Witnesses may be required to tell the truth, but not the whole truth. It is purely happenstance if they do.

Once again, the method of eliciting proof is not one that jurors encounter in their normal lives. We do not normally receive information only through a question-and-answer format. If we are contemplating buying a house, for example, we might ask someone we think knowledgeable, "What's the neighborhood like?" We would expect the person to freely relate information about the locality, and we might interject or follow with questions to probe or prompt or clarify. A trial does not present testimony this way. Witnesses are not allowed to give a narrative of what they think is important; they are restricted to answering questions.

This limitation is especially striking because studies suggest that questioning alone is not the best way to elicit the fullest information in the least distorted way. The preferred method is what we often do instinctively—allow a person to give a free, uninterrupted report about the topic of interest and only then ask questions to remove ambiguities, fill in gaps, and test whether knowledge has been exhausted.

Witnesses in European trials commonly present testimony in such fashion, but we do not employ this method in our jury trials primarily because the witness granted such freedom may too easily say something that the rules of evidence (discussed later in this chapter) do not permit. When a witness is limited to responding to questions, however, the question itself often indicates that legally doubtful material is about to be elicited. The opponent of this evidence can object after the question and before the answer, and if the judge agrees that the objection is valid, then the witness can be prevented from divulging the improper material. With free-flowing narratives, the objection can come only after the cat is out of the bag, and the jury will hear things it should not. Consequently, although in our daily lives we collect information through unimpeded reports clarified by questioning, a jury receives information through a method almost never encountered outside the courtroom.

EVIDENCE LAW

The prohibition on narratives implies that trial witnesses are not allowed to say everything they know about a case; indeed, modern evidence law often precludes witnesses from testifying about certain matters. Evidence law before 1800 was concerned primarily with the formal requirements necessary to have documents presented to the jury and with the disqualification of witnesses. Grounds for disqualification were plentiful. The early courts seemed to view almost every potential witness as so likely to perjure themselves that they had to pass stringent criteria in order to qualify. The witness had to believe in a Supreme Being who rewarded truth and punished lies; if not, the witness could not take a meaningful oath and could not testify. Those who had been convicted of crimes, assuming they were not hanged, lost many rights, including the right to testify in trials. Children were disqualified, and so were those believed to be mentally deranged. Most important, those with an interest in the case could not testify because of the concern that this stake would conflict with the required duty to tell the truth. This prohibition extended to the criminal defendant. Both to prevent marital discord and because spouses were seen as a single unit, if one spouse was interested in a case and was, by virtue of that interest, disqualified, then the other spouse could not be a witness either. On the other hand, when a person was allowed to become a witness, few restrictions were placed on the testimony itself.

Over time this situation changed. Various grounds for disqualification disappeared, so that today virtually anyone who has personal knowledge that might aid the jury can testify. But as the notion of widespread witness incompetency diminished, the law became increasingly concerned with what witnesses were allowed to say.

Modern evidence law is premised on an inclusionary principle. It defines relevant evidence as any information that could logically have an impact on the trial's factual issues. All relevant evidence is admissible—that is, a jury can hear it and consider it when they deliberate to render a verdict—unless some other rule, doctrine, or law makes that relevant evidence inadmissible. Many rules, however, exclude relevant evidence. These rules tend to serve two purposes. One purpose is to promote a desired social good. The "exclusionary rule" that prohibits the introduction of evidence obtained from an unconstitutional search or seizure is an example. The banning of this evidence from trials is meant to deter law enforcement officers from committing such illegal searches or seizures in the future, but the cost is that the quality of information presented at trial is diminished.

While the idea of excluding evidence to affect police behavior has been roundly criticized, similar rationales permeate evidence law. The constitutional privilege against self-incrimination, for example, exists to prevent the government from employing various coercive interrogative techniques. Other privileges exclude important information from trials in order to protect relationships that are considered private. For example, evidence law extends a privilege to the information shared between a patient and a psychiatrist. Even when what passes between them could have great importance to a trial, the jury will not hear it.

Another example would be a suit concerning whether a product is unreasonably or dangerously defective. Many might consider it useful to know whether and how that product had been changed since the accident. Evidence law, however, generally forbids a jury from learning this information under the theory that if "subsequent remedial measures" can be used against those who improve products after accidents occur, they will make fewer such improvements. Because society as a whole would suffer if such evidence were presented to juries, a rule prohibits its admissibility at trial.

Exclusionary evidence rules are designed to protect society and the individuals in it, but they exist for another reason as well. Some doctrines rest on the notion—extraordinary at first glance—that depriving the jury of pertinent data might actually increase the chances that the resulting verdict is correct. For example, we often think it useful to learn about someone's past traits or behavior. If you were running a company hiring drivers, you would want to know the driving records of job applicants. You would, no doubt, be more likely to hire the one with a perfect driving record rather than the one whose life was checkered with traffic tickets and accidents. Surely, most of us would be less likely to socialize with someone if we knew he had been arrested for violent behavior, and we would hesitate to lend our belongings to a neighbor who was known to be dishonest or careless. Nevertheless, when a person is in court for allegedly causing an accident or committing a crime, the jury is not allowed to hear about that person's past bad behavior. The law restricts evidence about a person's character or past tendency to act in a certain way if the purpose is to show that the person acted consistently with that character or with that tendency at a particular time. That the defendant was reckless before cannot be used to show that he was reckless in this instance. That the defendant committed robberies in the past cannot be used to show that she committed this robbery.

Jurors are not allowed to learn about such past behavior because they might make an unfair determination on that basis that a party is "bad." Imagine that two pedestrians crossing the street in the same way are hit by cars being driven in an identical manner. Experience teaches that if the fact-finder learns that one pedestrian has been convicted of several crimes, tortures dogs, and drives recklessly, that pedestrian will be less likely to win a favorable verdict. The distinguishing information indicates nothing about fault in this particular case, yet the fact-finder will be influenced by that information. The law, however, commands that the two pedestrians, whose fault or lack of fault in causing the accident was the same, should be treated equally. In the cause of equal justice, proof about the prior behavior of both pedestrians should be kept from the jurors.

The situation becomes more difficult, though, when the information might be relevant to a correct legal outcome but could also simultaneously distort a juror's judgment. Consider, for example, the case of a driver involved in an accident. If the jury finds out that the driver has often driven recklessly in the past, two outcomes are possible. Common experience teaches us that a person who frequently drives carelessly is more likely to drive carelessly another time than is a person who has a spotless driving record. On the other hand, experience also teaches that if two drivers were driving with equal caution and are therefore equally liable for an accident, information that one of them often drives recklessly will make it less likely that he will get a favorable verdict. A fact-finder hearing about past misdeeds might judge a person on his past behavior rather than on the conduct that occurred at the time of the accident. The proof of prior recklessness, then, gives information that can both aid and distort consideration of a proper verdict. An evidentiary rule generally excludes such evidence. It is based on the principle that sometimes excluding relevant information can increase the likelihood of a correct verdict.

The hearsay rule, another crucial evidentiary doctrine, also has at its source a belief that keeping some information from the jury can lead to a fairer verdict. This rule is based on the premise that jurors can most meaningfully assess a person's information when that person can be cross-examined in front of them. Without the opportunity to test the testimony's limitations and ambiguities, its true worth can be easily misjudged. The basic concept, then, holds that witnesses can tell the jury what they have personally and directly perceived, but they cannot relate what someone else has told them. If the witness to an accident does not testify, but rather someone else is allowed to tell the jury what that eyewitness said about the accident, the jury would not have the benefit of any cross-examination of the eyewitness. Without that cross-examination, the evidence will not be truly tested. The law says secondhand testimony should not be relied upon in reaching a verdict and generally prohibits witnesses from telling the jury what others have said. Such evidence is hearsay.

This hearsay rule is hardly airtight. Some three dozen exceptions to it exist under the theory that some kinds of hearsay are likely to be reliable or necessary and ought to be admitted. The basic principle, though, remains; hearsay evidence is prohibited because fairer judgment is rendered when witnesses can be cross-examined.

Finally, judges have wide discretion in determining what information jurors will receive. Many evidence doctrines are not so much rules that truly define admissible evidence as they are guidelines to be employed by judges. For example, evidence rules permit experts to testify if their evidence can aid the jury. Federal evidence doctrine, however, maintains that expert testimony can help the jury only if that testimony is based on good science or other competent grounds. Before the jury can hear the expert, the judge must determine whether the proposed testimony is likely to be sound. "Good science," however, has not been defined so precisely that all reasonable people will agree that adequate grounds for an expert's testimony have been demonstrated. The trial judge is allowed to make this determination, and as long as the judge is not unreasonable in doing so, her ruling will be upheld.

Indeed, in an important sense, almost no evidence gets admitted without discretionary review by the trial judge. The law recognizes that many pieces of evidence, even when there is no specific rule covering them, are like character evidence in that the information is simultaneously relevant to a proper decision, but also has the potential to lead a jury to make its decision on an improper basis. A basic evidence rule commands trial judges to balance the importance of such evidence against the possibility that it will distort the verdict. They are to exclude it whenever "its probative value is substantially outweighed by the danger" of its detriments.[1] On a regular basis, then, judges have to exercise discretion in determining what information goes to the jury.

EVIDENCE, ACCURACY, AND CONSISTENCY

The evidence presented to the jury is the primary determinant of verdicts. We cannot expect verdicts to be better than the information the jury gets to consider. Therefore the doctrines that affect the presentation of evidence are crucial components of the jury system. Not only is the information presented in a way that we do not ordinarily encounter, as we have seen, it may often be incomplete. The attorneys may not present all the relevant evidence, and the evidence may be precluded by rules that prevent jurors from hearing it. If a verdict is wrong, it may not be because of the jury, but instead because of the methods used to inform the jury.

The variability of jury verdicts among similar cases may, therefore, stem from the evidentiary process. Even if two trials involve precisely the same facts, it is highly unlikely that the evidence would be presented in exactly the same way. Different attorneys may discover different evidence, and even if they possessed the same information, they might make different strategic choices about how or whether to present it. They may conduct direct examination and cross-examination of witnesses differently. Also, although evidence rules are similar throughout the country, they differ in details by jurisdiction. Even with identical rules, many of the admissibility decisions will rest within the discretion of the trial judge, and two judges are unlikely to coincide precisely on how they exercise their discretionary powers. Thus, the same evidence will probably not be admitted in different trials. Finally, the same witness testifying about precisely the same subject will almost never give exactly the same testimony from one trial to the next. In short, the methods by which juries are informed guarantee that the evidence presented will differ from one trial to the next.

Variability is inherent in the jury system; we cannot expect one collection of decision makers always to render the same verdict another would based on the same evidence. But our methods of presenting evidence to juries actually encourages variability.

JUROR NOTE-TAKING

If we think a verdict is wrong, we should not assume that the blame lies with the jury or with the lawyers. We must also examine how jurors get their information. We are unlikely to see radical changes in these methods, because the adversary system is constitutionally required, firmly entrenched, and time-tested.

Nevertheless, recent reforms have attempted to change some aspects of how jurors get their information.

The most common reform permits jurors to take notes. Juror note-taking had long been discouraged, perhaps dating "from the time when illiteracy was common. Courts then may have feared the few literate jurors would exert disproportionate influence on the others."[2] Some people say that note-taking will distract jurors from observing witness demeanor and listening to the testimony. Notes, these critics suggest, are often inaccurate or incomplete, may be misleading, and are ultimately unnecessary because jurors will have available, either through audio recordings or court reporters' transcriptions, an accurate verbatim account of all testimony. Perhaps most important, critics remind us, not all jurors will take notes, potentially giving the note-takers a dominant position during the jury deliberations.

On the other hand, many people learn best by taking notes. The good college student takes notes during lectures. Doctors make notes in files. Indeed, even judges and lawyers can be observed taking notes during testimony. Recognizing the prevalence of note-taking, the law in most places today is not as rigid as it once was and grants the trial judge discretion to permit jury members to take notes.

Studies of note-taking have indicated that the majority of jurors, given the opportunity, take notes and would do so again. Jurors reported having minimal problems with the notes taken by their colleagues. One study in federal court, however, where jurors were randomly assigned to a trial in which they were either permitted or prohibited from taking notes, produced a surprising result: "[J]urors allowed to take notes reported feeling less well informed than jurors who were not allowed to take notes, and they reported it was difficult to reach a verdict."[3] On the other hand, judges in this study, who were asked to report their views about the legal correctness of the jury verdicts, reported no difference between the juries who had been allowed to take notes and those who were not. Little indicates that note-taking aids the objective performance of juries, but virtually no data indicate that taking notes harms jury performance either. Because jurors often want to take notes, it makes little sense to stand in their way. Perhaps the most sensible system is this, suggested by William Schwarzer: "The decision whether or not to take notes should . . . be left to individual jurors. Only those who are comfortable with it will take notes, and to prevent those jurors from doing it may make them feel that an already difficult job has been made even harder. The judge should instruct that each juror's notes are only for his or her personal use and should not be read or given to anyone else."[4]

QUESTIONING OF WITNESSES BY JURORS

While the trend permits note-taking, the questioning of witnesses by jurors remains restricted. There are several reasons for this. It conflicts with the adversary system's principle that the lawyers are best situated to determine what and how information should be presented. The questioning juror may inadvertently and inappropriately lose the desired neutrality by pursuing a particular theory. The questions could be unnecessary because they will be answered by later witnesses or because they are not legally germane to the case being tried. Jurors may become resentful if their questions are not allowed, and no doubt some will not be asked because they will violate the rules of evidence. Direct questions to a witness may create antagonism between the witness and the juror. Because of such concerns, many courts adamantly prevent jurors from asking questions.[5]

On the other hand, juror questions have obvious benefits. A federal judge has stated:

> Common sense tells us that some jurors at some time during the trial will not understand some of the evidence being offered: it may be the meaning of a word, the significance of an exhibit, or a part of an answer lost in a moment of distraction. . . . A juror who becomes confused early in the trial may miss the significance of later evidence. Such a juror will not be an effective participant in the deliberations and may be dominated by those who claim to have understood the evidence.
>
> Lawyers cannot clear up juror confusion or lack of understanding if they do not know it exists. And even if the case is well tried, jurors may have questions.[6]

Certainly jurors often want to ask questions. Melvyn Zerman's comments about his jury service capture the feelings of many jurors: "Juror 6 and I agreed that at various moments we have had almost uncontrollable urges to shout out our own questions at the witnesses." Jurors can also feel resentful when they are denied the opportunity to seek clarifications and information. During the deliberations in the Juan Corona trial, for example, the jurors became restive in the face of their inability to ask questions: "We're dealing with a one-way conversation and everyone knows that a two-way conversation is certainly superior. . . . We should be able to talk until our whole question is understood."[7]

A study found that 80 percent of jurors wished to ask questions and that half still had unanswered questions at the end of the case.[8] At least some of the time, jury questioning could make a difference. Steven Phillips writes about a robbery case he prosecuted. The two eyewitnesses had mentioned that the robber was wearing a hat. This seemed an incidental fact to the attorneys. Phillips did not have the witnesses describe it, and the defense asked no questions about it. The deliberating jurors, however, had concerns: "It was reasoned that a wide-brimmed hat could have hidden the robber's features and cast doubt upon my witnesses' identification. In point of fact, the hat in question was a beanie, and would not have disguised the robber. But the jury had no way of knowing this, and it disturbed them. Had they been given the opportunity to question the witnesses, one of the jurors undoubtedly would have sought a description of the hat, and the answer would have made their deliberations easier. In some cases, such questions can make the difference between a guilty verdict and an acquittal."[9]

Most jurisdictions, however, do not permit juror questioning of witnesses or lawyers, and even in the few that do, severe restrictions are placed on the practice. Jurors are generally told that they should ask questions only for clarification and not to develop theories of their own, and they should limit their questions to important points. They should wait until the witness has completed testimony, and if their question goes unanswered, to write the question down and pass it to the judge. Jurors are instructed that the judge may not necessarily ask the question and they are to draw no inferences if it is not posed. If it is asked, the jurors are not to weigh that evidence more heavily than other proof. Not surprisingly with such restrictions, not many jurors ask questions.

The effect of jury questioning is not entirely clear. Some studies have found little value in the questioning, while others have found that jurors become more attentive when they know they can pursue this avenue of inquiry. Furthermore, some studies indicate that jurors who are allowed to ask questions feel more informed, believe the deliberative process is better, and ultimately have more confidence in their verdict.[10]

Even if juries are allowed to ask questions, however, it will do little to change the jury from being a primarily passive body. The limited questioning permitted a few juries does not begin to approach the freedom with which we are allowed to seek information in other areas of life, such as the probing we might do if our teenager arrived home late, or if a friend gave us a stock tip, or if we were seeking employment in a new company. In those circumstances, we could ask many uncensored and unfiltered questions, and the responses might immediately elicit other queries. We might actively seek a conversation or dialogue, something forbidden even to those jurors permitted to ask questions. Depending upon our natures and our level of concern, we could also seek other sources of information. We might call the parents of our son's friends or check the mileage on the car; we might ask for annual reports or the history of our friend's other recommendations; we might seek out feedback from former and present employees at the new company, and so on. Compared to other investigative activities jurors engage in, this limited ability to question will never make them more than passive receivers of information.

Nor should it be otherwise. Because jurors are ordinary citizens brought together for one case, there is little choice other than to have someone else present the evidence. The jurors certainly cannot be expected to collect it themselves. It takes a great deal of effort to obtain the information upon which a case is based. Jurors are not trained in such information-gathering, nor would they have the time to undertake this task. Furthermore, juries are too large to take such an active role. With six or twelve people directly asking all the questions that might occur to them plus the additional time to weed out impermissible inquiries, trials would become unmanageably long and unfocused. The reforms that have been tried may continue, but there will continue to be heavy restrictions on jurors' abilities to ask questions. The lawyers will continue to be the primary presenters of the factual information and the arguments about it.

JURY QUESTIONING OF EXPERTS

Routine questioning by jurors may indeed be impractical, yet expert testimony presents a particular situation in which extensive questioning by jurors might prove valuable. Experts offer information that is outside the normal experience and common sense of the fact-finders. Not surprisingly, juries and judges often have difficulty grasping and assessing such material, and they will often find themselves unsure of what the expert is presenting. Under such circumstances, it may be essential for fact-finders to question the experts. Judges do often question experts. Whether in a bench trial or in a pretrial hearing on the admissibility of the evidence or for some other reason, good judges often directly ask experts questions to clarify the information. Such questioning often leads to further questions, and something like a real conversation between the judge and the expert can develop. If judges, who may have heard similar expert testimony in the past and who are generally better educated than the average juror, feel the need for direct questioning of experts, then surely jurors will, too.

The judge, however, is allowed to ferret out the desired information by direct, extensive questioning. Jurors, in contrast, do not get this opportunity. Even in places where juror inquiry is permitted, questions must be formally submitted in writing, thus precluding an active exchange between juror and expert.

It is easy to see the potential benefits from increased juror involvement with expert testimony. Any dangers that normally exist from juror questioning are largely irrelevant. When a juror is trying to understand an expert, who is a trained witness, it is much less likely than with other testimony that a juror will seek to learn prejudicial, inadmissible evidence. Permitting jurors to be more active in seeking information from expert witnesses may prove useful.

Chapter 15 Instructions

Jurors do not search out the evidence; neither do they seek out the law that is to be applied to the case. Rather the trial judge instructs them about the legal principles that are relevant to the case. These instructions are a crucial part of a trial. Jurors may reach erroneous verdicts because they ignore the law or do not determine the facts correctly, but errors are inevitable if the jurors do not understand the applicable law. Even though comprehension of the judicial instructions seems essential, jurors often are unable to understand certain instructions. So what is the nature of these instructions? What effect do they have on verdicts? What reforms of the process, if any, are sensible?

INSTRUCTIONS REGARDING THE
STRUCTURE OF THE TRIAL

Instructions given to a jury may be broken down into two categories. One set concerns the substantive law the jury is to apply in deciding a particular case. These might include a legal definition of murder or medical malpractice. Traditionally these instructions have been given just as the jury begins its deliberations. But other kinds of instructions are given at various times during the trial and provide for the jury the overarching legal framework for the trial. For example, jurors will be told that they should consider only the evidence presented at trial and not other information. They will be told that what a judge or an attorney states is not evidence and that the attorneys' opening and closing statements and questions are not evidence. Evidence, they are told, consists only of a witness's answers to questions, documents and other physical objects that the judge admits into evidence, and stipulations between the parties. To help ensure that the jurors consider only the presented evidence, jurors will be told to restrict their behavior outside the courtroom during the course of the trial: they should not talk to anyone about the case; they should avoid news coverage about the trial; and they should not otherwise seek out information about the matter. The jurors will also be told they should keep an open mind throughout the presentation of evidence and not to discuss the trial with the other jurors until formal deliberations begin.

Such instructions are fairly straightforward. A few of them, however, present problems. Some are difficult not because they cannot be understood, but because they seem to conflict with basic human nature. So, for example, jurors are told to shun relevant information that comes from outside the trial. This can be difficult, especially during long, highly publicized trials. It is only natural to be curious about what is being reported about an event that is absorbing one's own life, and not all individuals can resist the curiosity. In the Juan Corona mass murder trial, Matt, a juror, confessed that he found it difficult to avoid reading his morning newspaper.

> All his life he'd read the dailies. . . . Sure, he knew the Judge told them every day they were not to read papers or listen to the radio or watch TV but hell, the Judge only meant that in connection with the Corona case. Man was an animal of habit, and he wasn't about to change his habits overnight just because somebody told him to. So all trial long Matt had read his papers every day. . . . Only he had always kind of skipped over those headlines that mentioned Corona, or mass murder, or more confusion in the prosecution's case. . . . Those headlines were catchy, and often so misleading that in spite of himself a few times he'd read a whole article concerning the Corona case.[1]

Jurors do not always insulate themselves from information outside the courtroom. What if judges and not juries were the sole determiners of fact? Would they be less susceptible to media coverage than juries? Probably not. After all, judges, too, are human. Few judges might admit that they had been exposed to media coverage during a trial, but surely it happens. Indeed, judges may assume that their training and professionalism will make it easy for them to disregard such extraneous information, an attitude that might make them less vigilant than the average juror in avoiding news coverage. Furthermore, the jury system offers a safeguard that a judge acting alone does not have. If a juror in deliberations offers media gleanings, others might indicate that such sources are improper, as did happen in the Corona deliberations. Studies confirm that when inadmissible evidence is mentioned in deliberations, other jurors point out that such evidence should not be considered. While this may not stop individual consideration of the information, it prevents open discussion of the material.[2]

On the assumption that early discussions may lead jurors to draw conclusions before all the evidence is heard, jurors are also told not to discuss the case before deliberations begin. A person who gives an early opinion may begin to skim the evidence, concentrating only on the aspects that confirm her voiced hypothesis. Furthermore, premature discussions may involve only some of the jurors, and all of them should be included in the deliberation process. A classic British murder mystery captures the reasons for the admonition to shun premature deliberations. Over lunch during a trial, some jurors begin to solicit views on a case when another juror states: "'I say,' he said. 'You know, I don't want to interfere, but do you think that's quite wise? Wouldn't it be better if we didn't discuss it at all until we'd heard the other side? It's so likely that in conversation we shall begin to take sides, and there we are, making up our minds on only part of the evidence. Honestly, I do think we'd better talk about something else.'" That juror later reminds himself (and the reader), "The essential principle of British justice was that both sides should be heard and their evidence weighed in full by every member of the jury. It would be a failure in his duty if he made up his own mind before all the evidence which they had heard had been dissected and commented on by the jury as a whole."[3]

Experience teaches, however, that the injunction to hold discussion until deliberations begin is frequently violated. Such patience goes against human nature. Being social creatures, people naturally, perhaps compulsively, want to share their opinions about the events they are all observing and will have to judge. There is a strong impulse for the jurors to sound out one another on various matters before the evidence is concluded. Juror memoirs indicate that such conversations happen often. "In the jury room and as we leave the courthouse," Melvyn Zerman writes, "we are starting to disregard the judge's admonition not to discuss the case. There are no discussions in which we all join, but there are conversations involving two or three jurors, one of which I am part of, others of which I overhear."[4]

Discussions within small groups is typical. The judicial instruction not to discuss the case until deliberations begin has the effect of restraining exchanges involving the full group, but not smaller subgroups.

Jurors, then, often disregard the judge's admonition and discuss in inappropriate venues. Even so, they do seem to grasp that the point is to keep an open mind until all the evidence is heard. A juror in General William Westmoreland's libel suit against the CBS television network captures the predominant mood: "We were careful not to try to influence each other, but we couldn't help but discuss some of our feelings. . . . I wonder what other jurors think. No one has discussed opinions. We have been quite careful to heed the judge's words. We discuss the case, but it's mostly to clarify terms and to tidy up questions on notes."[5]

These jurors are not atypical. One survey indicates that half the juries studied had at least one member who engaged in conversations about the case before deliberations began.[6]

Why give an order that will be violated? Some maintain that abandoning the admonition can actually bring a benefit if it is coupled with expanding questioning by jurors. Earlier discussion combined with questioning could allow jurors to clarify ambiguous evidence.[7]

Only Arizona has formally allowed jurors to discuss matters before deliberations. Even when given this chance, however, only some juries engage in predeliberation discussions. The jurors themselves are concerned about making premature decisions, often expressing concern that preliminary discussion will "compromise their ability to make an independent judgment about the evidence."[8]

To analyze the change, Arizona randomly permitted some juries predeliberation discussions while the others were instructed not to engage in them. Those who were permitted the discussions reported that they were very useful in helping them understand the evidence. Even so, no other data confirmed that they actually understood the evidence better than the juries who had been instructed not to discuss. Both groups reported that they understood the evidence well, and judges thought that both comprehended the issues equally. The jurors permitted discussion reported less uncertainty at the beginning of deliberations, but no differences in verdicts were detected between the groups. Both reported equal satisfaction with their verdicts.

Surprisingly, the group permitted early discussions reported more contentious deliberations and less unanimity on the final ballot. This did not translate into a greater incidence of hung juries, perhaps because the reform was allowed only in civil cases and Arizona permits a civil verdict by a three-quarters vote. The researchers caution that such reports indicate the difficulties that might arise in states requiring civil unanimous verdicts or in criminal trials, which require a higher standard of proof.[9]

Overall, permitting discussions before deliberations did not have significant consequences. The study notes, "The results of the field experiment fulfill neither the fondest hopes nor the worst nightmares of supporters and critics of the trial discussions jury reform."[10]

"LIMITING" INSTRUCTIONS

A jury often learns information that is not admissible according to the rules of evidence. For example, a witness reveals that the defendant has insurance to cover any damages set by the jury. The fact of insurance coverage is not admissible evidence because it neither helps establish the defendant's negligence nor speaks to the level of damages incurred by the plaintiff. But a jury learning that the defendant is covered by insurance might think, consciously or not, that a finding against the defendant has few repercussions for her because she will not have personal liability for payment. This information about the insurance, even though it is inadmissible, increases the likelihood of finding the defendant liable. The standard response to the common situation when a jury learns inadmissible, but prejudicial, information is for the trial judge to tell the jurors that they must disregard it.

A related predicament exists. Under the rules of evidence, some evidence is admissible, but its use is circumscribed. For example, the prior convictions of a criminal defendant might be relevant to the trial because criminals are often recidivists. If the accused committed a crime before, it is more likely that he committed a crime again. Evidence law, however, decrees that prior convictions are not to be used this way because jurors may tend to convict merely because of those past misdeeds without fully examining the evidence about the crime in question. It may be too easy to convict someone merely because he appears to be a bad or dangerous person.

In assessing testimony, however, jurors have to determine whether a witness is telling the truth. Most of us believe that some people are more likely to lie than others, and convicted criminals may lie more often than others. Anyone who testifies may be asked about her prior convictions to aid the fact-finder in determining whether the testimony is the truth. When an accused testifies, then, the law permits the jury to consider prior convictions in assessing the likelihood that the accused is telling the truth on the witness stand, but it does not permit the jury to use the evidence to conclude that she is simply a criminal who committed yet another crime. When the accused is asked about her prior convictions, the court gives what is called a "limiting instruction" telling the jury the permissible purpose of the evidence and also telling them they should not use it in the impermissible way.

Instructions to disregard evidence or to use it in a limited way are extremely difficult to obey. In the first situation, jurors are ordered to ignore information, an inherently difficult task. It is akin to being asked the time, hearing a clock chime twelve, and then being told not to use the chiming clock in giving an answer. Some jurors sense the futility of being told to disregard testimony. Hazel Thornton's diary of her jury experience states that a witness testified that he and the defendant, charged with murdering his parents to get their money, "dreamed of a 'Billionaire Boys Club' (this was stricken from the record, like we can actually forget these things)."[11] Indeed, validating her sarcasm, some jurors mentioned the "Billionaire Boys Club" during the deliberations.

Studies confirm that information cannot be disregarded on command. Indeed, an instruction to disregard may highlight the matter, increasing the likelihood that it will become mentally embedded. Psychologists have commented on Thornton's diary: "Most empirical evidence suggests that jurors are not only generally incapable of disregarding inadmissible statements, but that they are even more influenced by them after being admonished by the judge. . . . Thus when a judge instructs jurors that they must disregard inadmissible testimony, it is quite possible that the jury will consequently pay *more* attention to that piece of testimony than if they had received no admonition."[12]

In one study, for example, mock jurors considered a civil car accident case. Half were told that the defendant had insurance; half were not. Half of the former group were instructed to disregard the insurance coverage and half were not. The award for damages from those told about insurance but nothing more was about 10 percent higher than from those who had not heard about the coverage. Those told to *disregard* the insurance, however, awarded about 39 percent more. In another study involving a criminal case, mock jurors were told that the defendant had a knife. Some were simply told that this information was inadmissible evidence, while others were told that it was inadmissible and were told to disregard it. "Researchers discovered when the mock jurors were admonished not to consider the evidence, they considered it more than those who were simply told that the evidence was inadmissible." Studies also reveal that jurors often are unsuccessful in following instructions limiting the use of evidence to a particular purpose.[13]

In this heavily researched area, many studies confirm that jurors, despite instructions to the contrary, use inadmissible evidence or use evidence inappropriately in reaching verdicts. Michael Saks provides a partial inventory of these findings:

> (a) When informed about defendant's witness's prior crimes for the permissible purpose of evaluating credibility, jurors use the information for the impermissible purpose of inferring the likelihood that the defendant committed the currently charged crime. (b) Mock jurors have been found to use the strength of evidence of liability to help them assess compensatory damages. (c) And to use evidence of punitive liability to judge compensatory liability. (d) When accomplices escape, jurors are more lenient toward the defendants who were caught. (e) Mock jurors deciding rape cases based their verdicts in part on the race, physical attractiveness, sexual history, and respectability of the victims. (f) There is evidence of greater leniency toward defendants who are of low status, who are attractive (unless the attractiveness has been used to accomplish the crime), whose [social-economic status] is higher, and who are not wearing prison garb or being attended by armed guards. (g) Studies of civil cases find that more attractive plaintiffs, white plaintiffs, and plaintiffs with higher family status, are awarded more in damages.[14]

These frequently replicated findings would appear to raise serious questions about the legitimacy of the jury system. We do not want legal decision makers who cannot follow specific legal injunctions. But we should consider whether *anyone* could follow legal instructions. Jurors try to comply, but we ask them to perform what may be impossible. Once information has been absorbed, few of us can trace all the ways it can influence. We can strive to compartmentalize our minds or expunge the information, but that is difficult or impossible to do. These instructions simply fly in the face of human cognitive processes. Yes, inadmissible evidence can still influence jurors. Whom would it not affect?

There is no reason to believe that the judicial alternative is any better. Judges, too, are human and can be swayed by inadmissible evidence. In one study both judges and jurors were exposed to inadmissible material. The researchers concluded, "The standard argument in favor of judges is that, due to their training and experience, the judges should be better able than the jurors in their ability to set facts aside. However, the judges who were exposed to the inadmissible material were no better able to disregard the evidence than the jurors."[15] Research does not support the contention that judges can limit their verdicts to the admissible evidence any better than jurors can.

The best way to reduce the effect of inadmissible evidence is not to replace the jury but to prevent inadmissible evidence from reaching them in the first place. The jury system's structure is part of the solution. "[A] judge can be the gatekeeper who prevents certain inadmissible information from ever reaching the jury, thereby insuring that the jury's decision is kept free of such influences."[16] Judges might be tainted, but juries could be pure. Judges should be seeking in advance of trial to know more about the problematic evidentiary areas than they do now, so that fewer rulings are made after jurors have heard inadmissible testimony.

Stricter enforcement of ethical rules would also be useful. Attorneys are not supposed to knowingly elicit inadmissible evidence before a jury, but today such behavior is almost never penalized. Typically, the only consequence is that the jury is told to disregard the impermissible material. This may produce only a hidden smile from counsel.

PATTERN INSTRUCTIONS

Instructions are also hard to follow because too often they are phrased in nearly incomprehensible language. This is the situation with many of the instructions given to jurors right before they deliberate.

The trial judge may instruct the jury about general legal principles at the trial's inception and give limiting instructions during the evidence-taking phase of the trial, but traditionally she presents the main body of instructions that the jury is to use in reaching its verdict immediately before that body retires to deliberate. These instructions can be lengthy, covering a lot of legal ground. They will include general principles that apply to all trials. They may repeat earlier instructions such as limitations on the use of evidence. The judge will also state the general principles that apply to the broad category of cases like the one being tried. If it is a criminal trial, it would include the information that a criminal conviction is warranted only if the prosecution proves every element of the charged crime beyond a reasonable doubt. The instructions will then go on to the more specific legal principles of the case. The judge, for example, will give legal definitions of murder or medical malpractice. The instructions will cover legal issues raised by this particular case. If, for example, there is a claim of self-defense, the judge will define it. Finally, the jurors are told that if they have questions about the evidence that was presented, they can view the documents or other materials that have been admitted or have the testimony read back by the court stenographer and that if they have questions about the instructions, they can request further clarification from the judge.

Traditionally, the judge presented these instructions orally, generally reading them from what are called "pattern instructions," a set of directives used by all trial judges in that jurisdiction. Such uniformity did not always exist. In the early nineteenth century, judges, using their own words, drafted the instructions, explaining the law in everyday language. In an age that lacked the technological means to reproduce such instructions for all the jurors, and when many jurors were not fully literate, they were always given orally.

This changed as lawyers began to suggest instructions to the court. The requested instructions were often in legalistic language, and as judges selected from the growing smorgasbord of offerings, the instructions became longer and more complicated. The instruction process became increasingly idiosyncratic, varying greatly from judge to judge and from trial to trial, undermining the ideal of uniform justice. Appellate courts began to scrutinize instructions more closely, and reversals for faulty instructions increased.

In the 1920s, a movement began in New York to standardize instructions, and in 1938, the judges of the Superior Court of Los Angeles County prepared a *California Book of Approved Jury Instructions,* containing instructions that had been upheld in an appellate case. The movement for model instructions mushroomed. Today books of pattern jury instructions are available for almost every jurisdiction, and in several states, the use of approved pattern instructions is required.

Whether pattern instructions are mandatory or not, trial judges favor them. These instructions simplify their task. They do not have to draft instructions for each case or have to select from the attorneys' submissions, which in the past had often been a subtle attempt to slant what the jurors were told. Lawyers also like pattern instructions. With them, they no longer have the time-consuming task of submitting a complete set of instructions to the judge. Furthermore, with the existence of pattern instructions, attorneys know from the beginning what those instructions will be and can present their cases with these in mind.

Their chief attraction, however, is that they are virtually reversal-proof. When they are used, they are unlikely to be successfully challenged on appeal. So, although the jury is the immediate audience, the instructions are really aimed at the appellate courts, and the judge giving instructions is speaking not so much to a group of lay decision makers as to other judges. Instructions that might be clear to those trained in the law, however, are often incomprehensible to jurors. The problem is compounded by the fact that pattern instructions typically are drafted by committees of lawyers and judges. Committee products of any sort are often justly derided, and lawyers, at least when producing legal documents, are not known for their felicitous phrasings. Also, because instructions will have to apply to many cases, they often contain general, abstract terms that seem muddy when applied to a particular dispute.

Not surprisingly, then, jurors often do not comprehend pattern instructions. They do not ignore them, however; they try gamely to understand and apply the information within them. One study showed that jurors can spend as much as a fifth of their deliberation time discussing the law, and they feel that these efforts pay off. Individual jurors believe that they personally understand the instructions, but, tellingly, they also believe that many of their colleagues on the jury do not.[17]

> Jurors in one survey were asked to indicate whether they understood most of the law, part of it, or not very much of it. Eighty-seven percent said they had understood most of it, while less than 1 percent said they did not understand much of it. Similarly, in a second survey, 81 percent of the jurors agreed that they found the judge's instructions easy to understand. . . . Yet when the jurors in one of these same surveys were asked about the understanding of their *fellow* jurors, 45 percent indicated that they thought fellow jurors did not understand the instructions.[18]

Jurors may believe that they understand the instructions, but research suggests that they do not. Many studies designed to examine juror comprehension of instructions consistently show "that jurors do not understand a large portion of the instructions presented to them. It is common to find over half the instructions misunderstood, and even the most optimistic results indicate that roughly 30% of the instructions are not understood."[19]

The problem sometimes stems from the difficulty of the concepts, no matter how they are phrased, but often "the difficulty appears to lie not in conceptual barriers to understanding but in the way the instructions are written."[20] Instructions too often use unclear terms and befuddling syntax. Here, for example, is a standard instruction on "contributory negligence," an important concept in many torts cases:

> You are instructed that contributory negligence is the failure by the plaintiff to use reasonable care for his own safety just before and at the time of the occurrence in question, which failure proximately causes the injury of which plaintiff complains.
>
> You are instructed that everyone is responsible, not only for the result of one's intentional acts, but also for an injury occasioned to another by one's want of ordinary care or skill in the management of one's property or person, except so far as the latter has, acting intentionally or by want of ordinary care, proximately contributed to the resulting injury.[21]

Got that? I went to law school, and yet I have had to read that passage several times to understand it. Even then, "proximately" gives me trouble. Outside the field of law, I do not believe I have ever uttered or heard it, and even those with wider vocabularies than mine might have trouble determining what it means in this context. My handiest dictionary gives multiple definitions for "proximate": "1. next; nearest. 2. closely adjacent; very near. 3. fairly accurate; approximate. 4. next in a chain of relation." Even if the word were familiar to me, it is not clear which of its differing meanings I am to use. "Next" and "approximate" are not exactly the same concepts.

This instruction is not unique in its difficulty, and it is not surprising that jurors do not always comprehend such abstruseness. Such instructions cry out for simplification and clarification.

CLARIFYING INSTRUCTIONS

Many instructions could be rewritten to increase comprehension. Some basic principles should be widely implemented to eliminate commonly misunderstood concepts. First, avoid legal jargon. As one commentator notes, "Many legal terms are unfamiliar to lay persons or, even worse, have slightly different meanings in the general community."[22] The lament of a juror during deliberations in a California murder trial applies to many trials: "[W]e only just realized that first-degree murder requires 'express' malice, as opposed to 'implied' malice. So then we had to agree on what 'express' means. None of these things legally means what you always thought."[23]

Other drafting rules, too, ought to be followed. Avoid complex sentences. Short, declarative sentences should be the norm. Unusual terms should be minimized. More familiar ones should be used. Avoid abstract terms. For example, replace "defendant" or "plaintiff" with the name of the parties or "the occurrence in question" with a concrete description of what the litigation is about. The active voice should replace passive constructions. Multiple negatives should be banned. Not surprisingly, when existing pattern instructions have been reformulated along such commonsense lines, comprehension of the instructions increases.

The desirability of such reform seems obvious. Incomprehensible instructions undermine the rule of established law. And, according to some jury scholars, "[T]he only reform that consistently improves juror comprehension is to simplify and clarify jury instructions."[24]

With few exceptions, however, courts and legislatures have stood firmly against clarification. There are many reasons for this. Judges and lawyers have developed a tin ear. They have become so accustomed to the instructions that they cannot hear them as jurors do. Appellate courts have also shown remarkably little concern over incomprehensibility. These courts almost always uphold a technically accurate instruction no matter how convoluted its prose. Individual trial judges, faced with the task of clarifying accepted instructions and fearing reversal for their effort, continue to use the long and confusing ones because they have been accepted by the higher courts. Stephen Saltzburg, who with others has successfully written instructions in plain language for federal criminal trials, states: "[E]ven when we have been able to convince some judges that our instructions are clearer and more likely to be understood than others, in several circuits the existence of pattern instructions (those approved by the federal courts) discourages federal judges from taking a chance on new ones. We also found that some judges stick with instructions that have withstood appeal, even if the judges acknowledge that jurors have trouble understanding the language."[25]

Saltzburg also found another problem. Simplified instructions were often resisted because the law itself was ambiguous. The drafting process forces "courts and lawyers to confront the meaning of legal doctrines which the old instructions, embedded in jargon, leave unconfronted. An amazing number of times, we found that the law was unclear to the judges and lawyers themselves. . . . [N]o one could be sure whether these [new] instructions changed anything because no one knew what the old ones meant."[26]

When lawyers and judges cannot agree on what the law is, we can hardly expect a clear instruction. Any attempt, for example, to clarify the requirement that a person can be convicted of a crime only if guilt is proved "beyond a reasonable doubt" founders because lawyers and judges do not agree on the exact meaning of the phrase. "Most trial judges and attorneys probably understand that 'beyond a reasonable doubt' means 'nearly certain.' Many members of the public have the same understanding, or can be educated quickly on the subject. However, agreement breaks down at the point of calibrating and explaining just *how* close to certain 'beyond a reasonable doubt' requires."[27]

One survey of federal judges disclosed that a slim majority said that reasonable doubt required 80 to 90 percent certainty. Most of the others required at least 95 percent certainty, and 12 percent required 100 percent certainty. Another survey found federal judges spread out relatively evenly across a 76 to 95 percent range. Such variability "represents a stunning lack of consensus among judges. In other words, the apparent agreement on 'near certainty' hides a substantial disagreement over how much certainty is required."[28] When the law-givers cannot agree on what the law means, a vague instruction is sure to follow.

A better jury system requires better instructions. Their drafting should not be left solely to lawyers and judges. The writing should include laypeople, and reformulated instructions should be pretested on the jury pool. This is hardly news. The problems with instructions have been clear for a long time, but meaningful reform is not imminent.

REFORMING THE INSTRUCTION PROCESS

Studies show that jurors comprehend clarified instructions better than existing ones, but even improved instructions are not always understood. Routinely, jurors are given too many instructions—far too many to be fully grasped in a short time. People learn new subjects by repeated exposure and persistent attempts to master them, and a trial, concentrated as it is, may simply not allow enough opportunities for the necessary learning to occur. Some legal concepts are difficult no matter how clear the language. I can teach a course for a term, and at the end of it, many of my students fail to comprehend principles presented through lectures, discussions, and readings. It is not surprising that jurors hearing complex legal concepts for the first time do not fully comprehend them.

Traditionally, instructions have been delivered orally. This, too, may affect the jurors' ability to learn. All of us receive a great deal of information through the spoken word—college lectures, campaign speeches, business meetings, television news. Usually, however, oral delivery is supplemented with written or other illustrative materials—textbooks, business reports, newspaper articles, slides, on-screen graphics. We seldom expect people to learn new, complex matters by hearing them recited once, and yet that is what we expect from jurors.

Such difficulties in the instruction process have prompted suggestions for other reforms beyond the mere clarification of language. The first concerns the timing and frequency of instructions. The traditional practice presents the bulk of the instructions after the jury has heard the evidence. Jurors are thus forced to hear evidence without knowing the relevant legal concepts. Some have suggested that it would be beneficial if jurors were given instructions before hearing the evidence as well as after. "First, pre-instruction may give jurors a framework that helps them make sense of the testimony, alerting them to important factual and legal issues whose significance they otherwise might not recognize.

As a result, they may be more likely to encode and be able to recall evidence that otherwise might seem of little importance. Second, pre-instruction may also increase jurors' comprehension of the legal rules simply because the rules are heard twice."[29]

Pre-instruction is resisted because it will make trials longer and because judges may not know what substantive instruction to give until after the evidence is heard, a rare situation in civil cases because typically the relatively complete civil discovery makes the issues clear in advance of trial. Nevertheless, issues that can be anticipated could be addressed in pre-instructions while other instructions could be presented at a more appropriate time. Even so, critics of pre-instruction argue, giving instructions before the evidence is presented may encourage premature decisions by jurors, who will then engage in a hypothesis-confirming, selective analysis of the evidence.

As with other suggested reforms, however, research shows that the effects of change are minor. Most studies show that fears of premature judgments are unfounded. Some research indicates that pre-instructed jurors understand instructions better, but only minimally so, and other studies do not confirm that pre-instruction leads to any significant increase in comprehension. Jurors favor pre-instruction, and lawyers and judges see no harmful or disruptive effects from them. In short, there are no drawbacks, but only a few benefits.[30]

Another suggested reform includes giving instructions in writing to supplement the traditional oral delivery. Many people absorb information better when it is written, and providing copies of the instructions in the deliberation room may help jurors to efficiently settle differences about them. Some contend, however, that with written instructions present in the deliberations, jurors may spend too much time discussing those instructions at the expense of discussions of the evidence. This might needlessly extend deliberation time.

Once again, studies show few consequences—positive or negative—from written instructions. They have affected neither the length nor the quality of deliberations. Some research has suggested that comprehension increases with written instruction, but most studies have discovered no improvement. As with pre-instructions, however, jurors feel that written instructions are helpful, and judges and lawyers who have used them generally approve of them. When judges have been using pattern instructions already, the burden of providing written ones is minimal. An increasing number of courts, in fact, have been supplying jurors with written instructions. There seems to be no reason why that practice should not expand.

Indeed, further experimentation extending the practice is worth a try. Comprehension might increase somewhat not only if jurors were handed the written instructions after the oral presentation, but if they were also given time to read them, perhaps overnight, and then allowed to ask clarifying questions before deliberations begin. This might make jurors more active in learning the instructions, which could improve comprehension. The downside is that trials could take longer, not only because of the time necessary for jurors to read the instructions, but also because this process might provoke needless, extensive questions. More studies are needed to weigh the benefits and disadvantages of this practice.

JUDICIAL CLARIFICATIONS

Jurors are routinely told that if they are unsure of an instruction they can seek clarification from the judge. Research has shown that such requests can sometimes lead to a better understanding of the instruction, but, in fact, the process of judicial clarification too often fails.[31]

Jurors are usually required to write out their requests. When jurors do not completely understand the instructions in the first place, however, their questions are imprecise at best, garbled at worst. As a result, the judicial response can be unhelpful or misleading. Jurors are not encouraged to have a direct conversation with the judge to help explain why a difficulty still exists. Instead, jurors are sent back to the jury room to formulate another written request. Because many judges show exasperation when jurors do not grasp the explanation, this process is hardly conducive to seeking clarification. Jurors are "often too intimidated by the judge to ask questions."[32]

Furthermore, the request for clarification is frequently met not with a true attempt to explain, but merely with a recitation of what has already been said. Surveys also show that when the jury makes such a request, "fearing reversal, the judge often responds to these questions by either rereading the already misunderstood instructions or by telling the jury to rely on their best recollections of them."[33] One Supreme Court case, *Weeks v. Angelone,* illustrates this practice. In the sentencing phase of a capital murder trial, the trial court first read the instruction and then later gave the jury a copy of it. Put yourself in the place of the juror trying to understand the instruction. You are told to determine whether the sentence will be death or life imprisonment. You are then told:

> Before the penalty can be fixed at death, the Commonwealth must prove beyond a reasonable doubt at least one of the following two alternatives:

1. That, after consideration of his history and background, there is a probability that he would commit criminal acts of violence that would constitute a continuing serious threat to society; or

2. That his conduct in committing the offense was outrageously or wantonly vile, horrible or inhuman, in that it involved depravity of mind or aggravated battery to the victim beyond the minimum necessary to accomplish the act of murder.

If you find from the evidence that the Commonwealth has proved beyond a reasonable doubt either of the two alternatives, and as to that alternative you are unanimous, then you may fix the punishment at death or if you believe from all the evidence that the death penalty is not justified, then you shall fix the punishment of the defendant at life imprisonment. . . .

If the Commonwealth has failed to prove beyond a reasonable doubt at least one of the alternatives, then you shall fix the punishment of the defendant at life imprisonment.[34]

During deliberations, you ask for clarification:

If we believe that Lonnie Weeks, Jr., is guilty of at least one of the alternatives, then is it our duty as a jury to issue the death penalty? Or, must we decide (even though he is guilty of one of the alternatives) whether or not to issue the death penalty . . . ? What is the rule? Please clarify.[35]

The question has a definite legal answer. The jury did not have to issue a death sentence just because it found one or both of the alternatives existed. The jurors could still find from all the evidence that death was not warranted. Was that clear to you? The defense attorney asked the trial judge to tell the jury that they could still impose a life sentence. The judge did not do that; instead he merely told the jury to read the instruction again. A few hours later, the jury returned a death sentence, with the court reporter noting that "a majority of the jury members [were] in tears" when they returned the verdict.[36]

It might seem obvious that when jurors say they do not understand an instruction, something more is needed than a simple rereading of it, but for many courts the mere repetition is sufficient. The Supreme Court in *Weeks v. Angelone* found that rereading the charge sufficed for this disputed death penalty instruction, concluding that the condemned prisoner had "demonstrated only that there exist[ed] a slight possibility that the jury had precluded itself from considering mitigating evidence." After all, the instruction was formally correct. It told the jurors that under one of two circumstances they "may" sentence to death, not that they had to. Careful reading should also have revealed that they could consider mitigating evidence because they could sentence to life "if you believe from all the evidence that the death penalty is not justified."[37]

This case captures an essential facet of much of the instruction process. The overriding consideration for the courts is whether an instruction formally states the law correctly. Courts have shown little concern for whether juries actually understand. Instructions are too often a rite that legally satisfies as long as proper forms are followed. A lower federal court has captured the stance of many judges. "Instead of inquiring what juries actually understood, and how they really reasoned, courts invoke a 'presumption' that jurors understood and follow their instructions."[38] Judges may recognize the obvious fact that instructions can be hard to comprehend, but they remain hopeful that the present process works. "Difficulty in coping with abstract concepts (most jurors spend their lives in the world of the concrete) explains why we have lengthy arguments, why judges give instructions orally as well as in writing (and reinstruct juries that ask questions), why juries deliberate. Jurors who 'don't get it' on first hearing may do better as the process continues."[39]

This unrealistic notion persists despite the many studies showing that jurors frequently do not "get it." A study attempting to replicate the *Weeks* case found that about half the mock jurors did not understand the instruction and that simply directing them to reread it did not improve their comprehension. A simple clarifying instruction, however, improved comprehension "dramatically."[40]

IMPORTANCE OF INSTRUCTIONS

Even with better methods of presenting jury instructions, they will not be completely understood. Surely this is a weakness in our jury system, but its detrimental effects can be overstated. Often the unclear instruction will not be at the heart of the deliberations because it concerns a peripheral issue or the evidence will be so clear that the misunderstanding does not matter. For example, researchers studying *Weeks v. Angelone* discuss the confusion over the death penalty instruction:

> Does a juror's belief that she must return a death sentence if she finds heinousness have any influence on the sentence she imposes? The answer will undoubtedly depend on the strength of the case at hand. Where the evidence in favor of death is extremely weak or extremely strong, improved comprehension probably wouldn't change the verdict of most jurors. In extremely weak cases, many jurors wouldn't find an aggravating factor in the first place and thus would never even reach the death-selection question; in extremely strong cases, most jurors would probably vote for death whether or not they believed the law required them to do so.[41]

It is worth repeating that judges generally agree with juries' verdicts, and when they differ, judges usually ascribe the conflict to differing views of the evidence. Whatever conceptions of the law jurors use to decide cases, their notions typically coincide with those of the judges.

This is partly because jurors do not act randomly when instructions are unclear. Instead, they appear to interpret them to be consistent with their commonsense notions of what the law is, and this usually leads to satisfactory results. The law is meant to regulate all of us, and it does this best when it articulates accepted community norms. Not surprisingly, the conceptions of the law held by jurors (who are, after all, representatives of the community) generally coincide with the law or at least are not antithetical to the law. In fact, jurors seem to have the most trouble following instructions that do not comport with their commonsense intuitions about the law. A group of researchers note, "[C]omprehension of the law and legal rules will be maximized when the legal instructions require an understanding that is compatible (rather than at odds) with intuitive reasoning."[42] When these counterintuitive directives are hard to follow, we should be concerned, but not because of what they tell us about limitations of the jury system. They should raise concerns that this particular law does not embody community norms.

Sometimes the juror's inability to comprehend the law stems from the failure of the law itself to be clear. If the law cannot be stated simply and clearly, not only will juries have trouble applying the legal principles, so, no doubt, will judges. One commentator opines, "Although it would be very surprising if their comprehension levels were not higher than those of jurors who hear them delivered, it would be useful to find out whether judges fully understand their own words. This would be useful not only for its titillation value, but as potential ammunition in the effort to persuade judges to present their instructions in language which is more accessible to lay jurors."[43]

Judges, in fact, may not understand their own instructions all that well. In the past, when judges drafted their own instructions, they had to have knowledge about the law being articulated. But with the introduction of pattern instructions, that knowledge is no longer absolutely necessary. Indeed, as we have seen, reiterating the instruction rather than clarifying it is a common judicial response to jury questions. That judges cannot simply and clearly answer queries about instructions may indicate that they are not confident that they can interpret the law without making mistakes. Part of the problem with instructions may be that judges simply do not know the law.

OBSCURE INSTRUCTIONS AS AN OBSTACLE
TO LEGAL REFORM

If we all knew just how indeterminate or ambiguous some laws are, public confidence in the law might erode. Instructions that are hard to understand hide the fact that the law itself is sometimes unclear. The unintended result is that criticism gets deflected from the law and those who create it or articulate it to the jury, thus leaving the authoritativeness of the law more intact. A consequence is that these areas of ambiguity can remain.

Even when all agree on what the law is, the nature of the instruction process tends to hide from the public the applicable legal principles. Instructions are long. Their language makes them hard to follow. They lack drama. Movie and television scripts seldom if ever focus on the instructions. Many consider them boring. Even in trials that have gained extensive public attention, media coverage rarely focuses on the instructions that define the applicable law for the jury. Because the public learns little about the controlling substantive law, criticism surrounding a verdict seldom focuses on application of the law that may have compelled the outcome. Instead, it is much more likely to center on the jury— its ethnic composition, its manipulation by the attorneys, its prejudice, its limited ability to reason. The instruction process tends to obscure the fact that sometimes a "wrong" verdict is the law's fault, not the jury's.

On occasion, criticized jurors point this out. A juror defensive about a verdict that acquitted Bernhard Goetz of the most serious offenses pleaded:

> To you who have read this book and believe in Goetz's guilt on the assault and attempted murder charges, I suggest that the fault in failing to convict him lies not with the jury nor the judge nor the prosecutor, but with a deficiency in the justification laws. The law, I think, is not specific enough about the alternatives Goetz should have been required to seek before being allowed to fire his gun as a legitimate act of self-defense.
>
> According to the law, explained by Justice Crane, once the implied threat of deadly force is present a person can shoot to defend himself if he cannot retreat "with complete safety." When a person is confronted by two or more persons within the close confines of a moving subway car, a strong argument can always be made that the person's safety is not ensured. I believe that a truly reasonable person with a proper respect for the sanctity of human life should do more than Goetz did to try to avoid shooting preemptively. Nothing more, however, is required by the law.[44]

The public reaction, however, did not center on New York's justification law. Instead, the verdict was interpreted in racial terms, with critics maintaining that a black man shooting four white youths on a subway train would not have been acquitted. Others praised the verdict as a proper step in "a modern morality play in which right and order triumph over the forces of evil and disorder."[45] Race and the struggle between good and evil—those social or philosophical issues—drew discussion, but few discussed what role the instructions played in the outcome.

Notorious civil cases have drawn similar reactions. One of the most famous is the McDonald's case in which the jury awarded millions to a woman who was scalded after spilling hot coffee purchased from the restaurant. Many cited the verdict as a failure in the torts system. Few put the verdict in its full context. Editorialists and columnists were quick to blame "greedy lawyers" or the jury. One stated, "It's just another in a long line of irresponsible awards made by emotionally-manipulated jurors with someone else's money."[46]

No one discussed the instructions given to the jury. The spotlight did not fall on this part of the process. Had it done so, the nature of the debate might have changed. Rather than focusing on lawyers or jurors, criticism might have focused on the imprecision of the laws that govern liability and awards. What Harry Kalven said a generation ago still applies: "When one speaks . . . of the merits of the jury trial in personal injury cases, the objection is usually not to the jury trial as a distinctive mode of trial but to the . . . systems of negligence and damages. . . . The serious arguments for substantive change would remain the same had the jury never been involved in these cases. The target of reform is the uneven incidence of . . . compensation."[47]

The instruction process often obscures important facts about the jury system. A jury may be the focus of criticism even when the instructions have made the law incomprehensible. Needlessly difficult instructions do not always affect the outcome of a case, but they do some of the time. A jury may be the focus of criticism when the substantive law should be at the heart of the discussion. Instructions using legal jargon, abstract terms, and complex syntactical formulations shroud the governing legal principles, shielding the law itself from needed reconsiderations. Clearer instructions will not only produce better verdicts in some individual cases, they might lead to better law in the long run.

Chapter 16 Jury Verdicts and
the Primacy of Evidence

It is not easy to determine how and why juries reach their verdicts. Jury deliberations, after all, are secret. Outsiders who could record the proceedings are not privy to this process. Furthermore, trials themselves cannot be subjected to controlled experiments. We need other methods to analyze how and why juries make their determinations.

We can have access to certain kinds of information once verdicts are recorded. We can know conviction rates or how conviction rates differ between murder and robbery cases. We can find out what percentage of medical malpractice trials finds doctors liable or what awards are given in differing kinds of civil cases. This kind of information is important, but it has limitations: it does not show how or why juries reach their decisions. Furthermore, making generalizations from such data is difficult because the methods of classifying trials and their outcomes vary so much around the country.

Judicial surveys, pioneered by Kalven and Zeisel, have been useful, but these, too, have limitations. Practicalities tend to restrict the amount of information that can be obtained from judges; the more lengthy the questionnaire, the fewer the number returned. The complexity of the data sought is also limited. If, for example, researchers wish to determine whether the rate of disagreement within juries varies according to their ethnic composition, there would have to be some uniform method for defining that diversity. Such definitions are difficult to construct; consequently, judicial surveys do not touch many topics of interest. The data collected are also further limited by the variability in the judges' abilities to respond to questionnaires thoughtfully and completely. John Guinther notes, "[W]e have no way of knowing from the published results anything about the abilities of the judges who were passing on the abilities of their jurors."[1]

Interviews of jurors after the verdict have provided insight into modes of jury deliberations, but these, too, have limitations. Interviews are rarely conducted immediately after a verdict has been delivered, and even a short lapse of time can cloud memories of the deliberations. In addition, anyone who has interviewed jurors discovers the "Rashomon problem." In the classic film *Rashomon,* the participants all describe an event differently, making it difficult to discern what actually happened. Similarly, seldom do all the jurors on a case recount deliberations in the same way. Some will find one factor crucial, while others will not. Unless all, or at least most, of the jurors from a particular trial are interviewed, a mistaken impression of the deliberations can result. In addition, the information gleaned from these interviews tends to be focused on the issues that were the subjects of discussion in the jury room. Rarely do we gain insights into the effect of unarticulated or unconscious influences.

In addition to social scientists, the media has conducted and published a growing number of juror interviews and memoirs. These accounts have even more limitations. They may yield information about how a particular jury proceeded, but we must be careful about using that information to make generalizations about the larger jury system. These interviews by the media, unlike those conducted by social scientists, do not collect data systematically, but rather seek to present anecdotal material about a specific trial. The cases that elicit such media attention may be atypical, and jurors willing to endure the spotlight may not be representative of other jurors. Finally, these jurors may have special reasons for being less than candid. Norman Finkel notes, "[J]urors' statements may . . . be suspect, particularly after controversial trials . . . in which the public may have been critical of the verdict. . . . Are we hearing what really happened, or are jurors' selected statements self-serving, aimed at justifying what happened?"[2]

Much of the information about jury deliberation comes from studies using mock jurors. The basic technique is to present trial-like information to people who are eligible for jury service and ask them how they would decide the case. Such a method, unlike other sources of information about jury verdicts, allows a particular variable of interest to be studied by controlling what is presented to the mock jurors. If, for example, researchers would like to know whether the gender of a party affects verdicts, mock jurors can be divided into two groups and given exactly the same information except that one is told the party is male and the other female. The resulting "verdicts" can then be analyzed to see if differences emerge. This method can also allow for deliberations to be studied directly, because mock jurors can be observed while they consider their verdicts.

How much can be learned from this method, however, is disputed. A mock trial is not a real one, and a mock juror is not a real juror. No matter what is done to induce mock jurors to take the situation seriously, the stakes are always different in a real trial. Also, mock jurors almost always know that they are being studied, and such knowledge could make them act differently from real jurors. A further concern is that jury studies by academics often rely on college students as mock jurors, and some people question whether information from this restricted pool can be generalized to the wider jury population.[3]

Mock trials are also unlike real trials because the presented evidence seldom comes from live witnesses. Instead, written descriptions of trials or videotapes simulating trials are used. Not only is the method of presenting information different, the mock trials are almost always truncated versions of what a trial would be, and the mock jurors do not experience the same depth and richness of information—or the fatigue—that real jurors do. Many jury studies have the further limitation that the mock jurors are asked for their individual decisions without any group deliberation, and group deliberation is one of the salient features of the jury system. These limitations notwithstanding, research seems to indicate that mock jurors in well-designed studies do not appear to reach their decisions in significantly different ways from real jurors.

Although all methods of learning about how juries operate have limitations, crucial insights can be gained from them, especially if they are used in conjunction with one another. Perhaps the most important methodological lesson to be grasped is that explained by Michael Saks: "Every type of study, and every individual study, inevitably will be imperfect. The basic solutions to these imperfections are replication and triangulation. Replication: If different studies produce similar results under varying circumstances, we gain increasing confidence in the basic tale the data tell. Triangulation: If studies employing different methodologies produce similar results, again we gain increasing confidence in the conclusions."[4]

Replication and triangulation from all the methods of study converge on a crucially important point: *the factor that overwhelmingly determines jury verdicts is the evidence presented to the jury.* Other things may affect jury decisions—the attorneys' performances, characteristics of the jury and the parties—but all other factors pale when compared to the influence of the evidence. This fact, which is contrary to many popular assumptions, is so crucial to understanding the jury system that it bears repeating: the various methods of examining jury deliberations converge on the inescapable conclusion that the evidence is the prime determinant of a jury's verdict.

WHAT JURORS AND NONJURORS SAY
ABOUT THE PRIMACY OF EVIDENCE

Jurors often state that the evidence compelled their decisions. Nancy Marder, who analyzed fifteen years of post-verdict interviews in major newspapers and magazines, found that jurors most frequently explained their verdict by pointing out how the evidence supported it. The next most frequent comment stated that the verdict followed the law as given in the judicial instructions. Jurors infrequently referred to race and gender, and when they did, most often it was to comment that those factors had no effect on the verdict.[5]

Although jurors report using the evidence and the law in making their decisions, many of us choose not to believe them. We seek other explanations. Michael Saks summarizes the common perception: "When people who served as jurors are asked why they decided a matter as they did, they tend to explain their decisions in terms of the characteristics of the evidence and arguments placed before them. When we ask observers of juries . . . why those decision-makers decided a matter as they did, the observers tend to explain the decisions in terms of the characteristics of the decision-makers." Marder's media survey, for example, reveals that while the jurors made strikingly few comments about race and gender, 71 percent of the news articles presented the case as having a race or gender component, and the press often included the gender or racial composition of the jury. The belief that juror characteristics and attitudes drive verdicts more than the evidence is an enduring, longstanding misperception. James Fenimore Cooper identified it well over a century ago when his novelistic alter ego states, " 'Who is on the jury?' is the first question asked now-a-days; not 'What are the facts?' "[6]

Critics contend that if factors other than the evidence and law produced verdicts, jurors would be unlikely to confess that to others because this would be akin to admitting irrationality or lawlessness. Moreover, our true motivations may be hidden from ourselves, and while jurors may honestly ascribe their actions to the evidence and the law, the ascription may simply be wrong. But such critics may be succumbing to the "fundamental attribution error": "In explaining the actions of another, particularly untoward actions, we attribute more responsibility to the person's characteristics and less to the person's circumstances than we should. If the attribution error applies when we look at jury verdicts, and there is no reason why it should not, there will be a natural tendency to attribute verdicts more to the supposed dispositions and attitudes of jurors than to their circumstances, which are being in court, hearing a particular case and being instructed in legal rules."[7]

So, the less the outside observer knows about the evidence, the more he will attribute the result to other extraneous factors. Furthermore, ascribing the outcome to factors other than the evidence can lead to a more easily accessible explanation than one that requires mastery of the evidence: "[P]eople tend to stick up for those who are like them with respect to race, gender, or other relevant characteristics. Therefore, if a black inner city jury acquits a black youth charged with distributing drugs, a ready explanation is that this is most likely due to a sense of racial solidarity rather than to the jury's reasonably concluding, after hearing all the evidence, that the arresting officer may have planted drugs on the defendant to help explain the brutality of an arrest. A similar view that likeness has created bias is available to explain any verdict for an individual suing a business. The jurors are, after all, the plaintiff's peers."[8]

Losing attorneys champion such "bias stories." If jury bias did not cause the result, then either poor lawyering or the evidence may have. In taking the case to trial, however, the lawyer probably told the client and convinced herself that the evidence was persuasive enough to win. Consequently, she would quite naturally blame the outcome on the jurors. Others who have a stake in undermining the jury system often focus on factors other than the evidence. Richard Lempert states, "Many organizations that are repeat players in the litigation process seem to believe either that juries are out to get them because of what they are or that juries favor the 'little guys.' They have reason to promote stories of jury bias or incompetence as part of a long term campaign to limit the power of juries and a shorter run effort to influence the votes of citizens who might serve on juries."[9]

SIGNIFICANCE OF LIABILITY VERDICTS
IN CIVIL CASES

A popular image portrays civil juries not as evaluators of the evidence, but as Robin Hoods redistributing wealth. Juries are supposedly biased against defendants such as large companies, the government, and hospitals—any entity having resources to pay large awards.

An analysis of civil verdicts, however, undermines this assertion. In fact, plaintiffs win only about half the time. A study of cases in seventy-five of the country's largest counties during one year found that civil plaintiffs won at a 49 percent rate, with the rate varying slightly depending on the kind of case. Such data indicate that juries do not impose damages on defendants just because they are wealthy, for such defendants often win more than they lose. Indeed, research shows that corporate defendants actually win at about the same rate or at an even higher rate than do individual defendants. The popular notion that civil verdicts are driven primarily by the depth of the defendants' pockets is not borne out by the data.[10]

Another popular impression is that juries, because of a natural sympathy, automatically find in favor of severely injured plaintiffs. Analyses of actual verdicts, however, indicate that if such a jury bias exists, it is complex and subtle. Research has found that juries do not find corporations liable more often than they find other defendants liable in ordinary tort cases. But if plaintiffs have suffered severe permanent injuries, juries do find corporations liable more often than they do other defendants. Other data, however, suggest that juries are not generally biased in favor of the severely injured plaintiff. A review of ten years of product liability cases found no statistically significant connection between the plaintiff's claimed economic loss and the liability finding. An analysis of New Jersey medical malpractice trials also failed to find a significant correlation between severity of injury and the liability verdict. As has been noted by others, however, correlating injury severity and win rates is complicated by modes of litigation and reporting practices. But what emerges from this research is that jury bias in favor of the severely injured, if it exists, is slight. The severely injured do not automatically win.[11]

If plaintiffs win about half the time and defendants win about half the time, factors other than resentment toward the rich or sympathy for the plaintiff must be coming into play. Jurors may react with sympathy and anger to an accident, but the adversarial nature of a trial means that jurors will hear competing versions of the events. This dynamic discourages jurors from blindly accepting one version of events and encourages them to pay more attention to what is presented at trial. Neal Feigenson has observed that jurors "do not simply yield to the melodrama often offered by plaintiffs' attorneys. One possible reason is that the sheer amount of attention that jurors devote to trial information and the seriousness with which they undertake their duties . . . may tend to supersede superficial understandings of the case."[12]

While juries do not automatically find against civil defendants or for severely injured plaintiffs, decisions concerning damages present a somewhat different picture. When corporate entities are found liable, juries do give higher awards than when individuals are found liable. Interviews with jurors suggest they do not automatically award excess damages against corporations. Instead, the jurors are concerned about the impact of damages on an individual defendant, and tend to discount the damages when the defendant is an individual while imposing full damages on corporations. Corporations do not pay excess damages; instead, individual defendants pay less than they should.[13]

Sympathy factors, however, might more easily affect the damages decision than the liability determination. Because liability is a yes or no decision, jurors would have to sympathize quite powerfully in order to reverse a "no" to a "yes." "In contrast, damages are more like a dial that requires very little effort to fine tune the results. In this way it is relatively easy for a juror to modify a damage award based on the sympathy factors involved."[14]

Extralegal factors may affect the damages decision more than other jury determinations because juries are given few guidelines in awarding damages, and consequently they rely heavily on their own experiences and outlook. Research shows little correlation between the characteristics of the jurors and liability decisions, but more of a correlation between those characteristics and damages assessments: "One explanation . . . might be that in a task as undefined as awarding general damages, people rely on the only reference scale with which they are familiar, namely their own. Those who are accustomed to dealing in larger amounts fit the cases onto a mental reference scale that runs into higher numbers. This would explain not only the finding that wealthier individuals give higher awards, but also that on average men give higher awards than women. Another explanation might be more cultural: that something in their value system leads people of higher socioeconomic status to place a higher monetary value on personal injuries and their sequela."[15]

Even so, the effects of extralegal factors on damages awards can be overstated. Evidence presented at trial seems to trump other considerations. One example is a study that ranked cases according to the severity of the plaintiffs' injuries using a scale devised by the National Association of Insurance Commissioners. In these cases the damages awards were not random, but increased as the severity of the injuries increased. A summary of similar research concludes, "Severity of injury, its permanence, and age of the victim are consistent and potent predictors of awards." These legally relevant characteristics not only correlate with damages, they outrank other correlates. Thus, the severity of the injury is by far the strongest determinant of the damages award.[16]

This is yet another way of saying that the evidence is the strongest determinant of the verdict: "[T]here is little evidence that winning a liability verdict or obtaining a big damage award predictably results from selecting a jury with particular characteristics. Research on decisionmaking about damages indicates *that the strongest predictors of jury damage awards are characteristics of the case rather the attributes of the jurors.*"[17] "Characteristics of the case" emerge solely from the evidence at trial.

SIGNIFICANCE OF CONVICTION RATES

Unlike what happens in civil trials, in criminal trials convictions significantly outnumber acquittals. This suggests, as was discussed earlier, that attorneys are not the prime determinants of verdicts; conviction rates are high regardless of personnel changes in the prosecutors' office and the defense bar. Conviction rates are high primarily because only strong cases for the prosecution are brought to trial. The prosecutor controls the charging process, and she will not bring criminal charges in weak cases or dismiss or plea bargain those cases. Juries, then, generally hear strong prosecution cases, that is, cases in which the admissible evidence strongly supports a conviction. The high conviction rate indicates further that juries are generally convinced by that evidence.

Some have suggested that juries in criminal trials are returning an increasing number of acquittals caused by factors other than the presented evidence: "Various authors have blamed the use of the 'abuse' excuse, which appeals to the natural sympathies and gullibility of jurors, the ability of jury consultants to stack juries with persons who are defense-prone, and the greater representativeness of juries, which has resulted in jury panels with less educated and less intelligent members who can be more easily swayed by defense lawyers. Others have ascribed the problem to racial politics, which leads minority juries to acquit even in the face of overwhelming guilt."[18]

The fact is, however, that there has not been an increase in the rate of acquittals. Those rates have remained stable or dropped. So, for example, the jury conviction rate for non-drug-related federal offenses, which stood at 63 percent from 1945 to 1960, has actually climbed since. In 1995 it stood at 82 percent. Conviction rates for federal drug offenses are even higher.

States' conviction rates are generally quite stable. In North Carolina, the felony jury conviction rate remained level from 1985 to 1996, averaging 68 percent. In Florida, an average 59 percent conviction rate showed no decline over a ten-year period. In California the 82 percent conviction rate remained steady from 1980 to 1995. New York, too, showed no decline in convictions, averaging 72 percent from 1986 through 1995. In those same years, Texas showed a steady rate at 84 percent.[19]

The data, thus, refute assertions of increasing acquittal rates. They show further that conviction rates are quite high. Why? Because prosecutors bring strong cases to trial, and juries respond to the strong evidence with convictions. All those other extraneous factors—gender, race, sympathy, education, manipulative jury consultants—take a backseat when jurors are confronted with compelling evidence.

JUDGE–JURY AGREEMENT AND
THE PRIMACY OF EVIDENCE

As we have seen, trial judges generally agree with juries' verdicts. Kalven and Zeisel report that judges concurred with juries in 78 percent of both criminal and civil cases. More recent studies have confirmed this: "In a 1991 survey of Georgia judges, 87% of the respondents indicated that their experience in civil negligence cases was substantially the same as the Kalven and Zeisel respondents while another 10% reported even higher levels of judge-jury agreement. A 1998 evaluation of jury reform initiatives in Arizona revealed an 84% judge-jury agreement among judges indicating their preferences in civil verdicts." Marc Galanter reports on another survey that found that only 6 percent of judges thought jury awards were excessive "in many cases."[20] Such agreement is notable:

> When compared to other human decisionmakers, the rate of agreement is more impressive than it first appears. This 78% agreement rate [reported by Kalven and Zeisel] is better than the rate of agreement between scientists doing peer review, employment interviewers ranking applicants, and psychiatrists and physicians diagnosing patients, and almost as good as the 79% or 80% rate of agreement between judges making sentencing decisions in an experimental setting. So although theory

plausibly suggests some judge/jury differences—such as that juries, because of a need for compromise to produce a unanimous verdict, would tend to give plaintiffs more wins but less money—the significance of any such differences seems to fade in actuality. Apparently, judge trial and jury trial combine to operate a decisionmaking system that is, at least in one sense, highly reliable.[21]

Such judge–jury agreement yields an important insight. If, as some contend, juries are deciding cases on whim or prejudice or in disregard of the evidence or the law, then judges, too, must be deciding cases on similar whim or prejudice or with a similar disregard of the evidence or the law. The data indicate that similar forces do, in fact, drive the verdicts of both judge and jury, but not similar whims or prejudices. What judge and jury share are not their demographic or attitudinal characteristics; these almost always differ significantly. They share knowledge of the presented evidence and the relevant law. The strong agreement between judge and jury indicates yet again that evidence strongly influences the decisions of each.

Judicial evaluations of jury verdicts were about the same whether a civil defendant was an individual or a business, poking yet another hole in the theory that juries rely on the depth of defendants' pockets in assessing liability. In addition, judge–jury agreement remains the same whether the case is rated easy or difficult, suggesting that juries comprehend difficult cases as well as judges do. Indeed, Kalven and Zeisel noted that when trial judges were polled for the reasons they sometimes differed with the jury, "they virtually never offered the jury's inability to understand the case as a reason." Instead, "issues of evidence" was the reason most often given for judge–jury disagreements. Kalven and Zeisel concluded that their results established two basic propositions: "The first is simply that, contrary to an often voiced suspicion, the jury does by and large understand the facts and get the case straight. The second proposition is that the jury's decision by and large moves with the weight and direction of the evidence."[22]

The jury's competence in following the evidence is also suggested by comparisons with nonjudicial professionals: "[I]n a study in North Carolina, the same medical malpractice injuries were presented to eighty-nine jurors and to twenty-one arbitrators. The average award made by the jurors as well as the arbitrators came quite close to what had been awarded by the arbitrator in the actual case. The authors note, further, that because jurors work as a group and the arbitrators work as individuals, the jury awards would in practice probably have less variation and be more stable and predictable than arbitration awards."[23]

Other studies have compared jury decisions on medical malpractice with doctors' assessments of negligence done for the insurance companies involved in the cases. The jury verdicts were in line with the medical ratings of negligence.[24]

MOCK JURIES AND THE PRIMACY OF EVIDENCE

Mock jury studies provide the best method for studying how juror demographics—such as race, gender, and age—affect verdicts. These studies address how the characteristics of the case, such as the race or gender of the parties, correlate with the outcomes; and how the evidence, such as whether one or two eyewitnesses testify, influences the determinations. Such research is extensive, and the results are consistent. Franklin Strier has reviewed findings from these studies and concludes, "[N]early every study of jury decision making indicates that the evidence presented is the primary determinant of jury verdicts."[25] He gives an example of a typical finding: "In a study of 340 jurors in actual sex assault trials, [a researcher] found evidence factors accounted for 34% of the variance in jury verdicts, victim and defendant characteristics accounted for 8% of the variance, and jurors' characteristics accounted for a mere 2% of the variance."[26] These results are typical in finding that the evidence is by far the most important correlate to the verdict. This fact comes as a surprise to many, but not to those who study influences on jury decisions—here, of influences on civil liability: "[W]hile the core attributes of injuries accounted for the lion's share of variance in severity judgements, the sociodemographic variables played essentially no role. Because a finding that the background characteristics of the decisionmakers have little or no impact on their decisions may surprise readers unacquainted with the relevant literature, it may be worth mentioning that this merely extends a finding now well established elsewhere in the jury decisionmaking literature. Though most of that research has been on criminal trials, juror sociodemographic characteristics also have been found to play only a modest role in their civil liability verdicts, certainly compared to the dominant impact of evidence and arguments presented in the cases."[27]

Even a jury consultant concedes that verdict predictions based on the gender of jury members are ineffective, and others report, "Several researchers who have studied the correlations between verdicts and various characteristics of defendants, victims, jurors, and cases have concluded that juror race was not significant in predicting the verdict or sentence outcomes of the actual or mock juries they studied."[28]

Predictions from juror demographics are difficult if not impossible to make. This is so not only because the effects are small, but also because they are unstable; a correlation in one case does not always yield a similar correlation in another. Jurors respond to the evidence in each sort of case. Thus, for example, two researchers found that a particular demographic group seemed pro-plaintiff in one case but pro-defendant in another and came to "the heartening conclusion that, rather than simply voting prejudices, jurors respond to the specific facts of the case they hear. In many cases, it will be a grave mistake to simplistically rely on generalizations about the tendencies of demographic groups; a group may be plaintiff oriented on one set of facts but defense oriented on another."[29] Sometimes, however, the demographic characteristics or particular attitudes of the jurors do come into play.

INTERPLAY BETWEEN JUROR CHARACTERISTICS
AND THE EVIDENCE

Jurors try very hard to make sense of the evidence presented to them. As discussed earlier, they try to organize the evidence into a narrative that is complete and comprehensible to themselves and their fellow jurors. The attempt to form narratives out of a mass of information is such a basic human process that it cuts across demographic lines. Almost everyone does this, and because the mechanism is nearly universal, the fruits of it can be shared with others in an understandable way. The formation of stories requires jurors to attend carefully the evidence. In an important way, this process unites jurors.

Not everyone, however, forms the same summary from the same information. If all initially agreed on the import of the evidence, all juries would reach instant agreement, and that is not the case. Only about one-third of juries are unanimous on the first ballot. Because all the jurors have heard the same trial, something more than just the evidence must account for this lack of immediate agreement. Here the differences among the individuals who make up the jury do matter. The presented information is not the sole source of the juror's personal narrative of the contested events, for the evidence is viewed through the prism of each juror's background. Reid Hastie tells us: "Virtually all of everyday human knowledge is based on stories constructed from past experiences. New experiences are interpreted in terms of 'old stories.' A prime example is the jury decision process; these decisions are the result of a story construction and evaluation process. Verdicts are heavily dependent on the 'old stories' that we bring to bear on the current decision and on the ease of constructing story summaries of the trial events and evidence."[30]

According to some observers, "Rather than the mythical blank slates who wait until the close of a trial to decide a verdict, jurors bring a host of attitudes and assumptions with them to the jury box and actively construct explanations for the evidence."[31] Those preexisting attitudes and assumptions are not the same for everyone. Because some groups are more likely to have had certain experiences than are others, the filtering of trial information that leads to differing explanations for the events may tend to cluster according to juror characteristics. For example: "Recent studies investigating juror decisionmaking have concluded that each juror, using her own life experiences, organizes the information she receives about a case into what for her is the most plausible account of what happened and then picks the verdict that fits that story best. Jurors may interpret the same evidence differently depending on which stories they choose. Because racial background may influence a juror's judgment of whether any given story is a reasonable explanation of events, black and white jurors may reach different conclusions after evaluating the same evidence."[32]

The explanations for the evidence can sometimes vary along demographic lines, but that does not mean that these variations will determine outcome. Jurors do not vote as representatives of a demographic group; they vote as individuals trying to make their assessment of the evidence comport with the assessment of others. The focus is still on the evidence.

This is not to say that particular attributes of jurors never matter, for in some cases juror characteristics and attitudes become larger factors in the decision making process: "Juror differences appear to make significant differences in some contexts. These basically amount to situations where the evidence is highly ambiguous. Jurors then look to their assumptions and biases in order to fill the informational gap. This finding is what Kalven and Zeisel referred to as the 'liberation hypothesis'—close, ambiguous cases liberated jurors from the discipline of evidence. Thus, in particularly close cases, juror differences are likely to increase in importance."[33]

In these cases, although evidence is still the driving force, factors that are otherwise insignificant can have a crucial influence on the verdict. Also, because judges have seldom consented to participate in studies investigating the influences on their decision making processes, we do not know how extralegal influences might affect their verdicts in such cases. There is no reason to believe, however, that judicial determinations would not also be affected by nonevidentiary factors when the evidence is close or ambiguous.

Those who assume that factors other than the evidence drive jury verdicts tend to have lost sight of the similarities and overstate the dissimilarities among us. They underplay and underestimate our common beliefs, thoughts, and actions. In fact, in much of the thinking and assessments that are important to the trial process, people are much more alike than they are different.

For example, a study assembled people from diverse demographic groups to see how potential jurors might set punitive damages. They were given differing scenarios in which a person was hurt and a defendant had been held liable for the injuries. The respondents were asked to rank the moral outrage at the defendant's actions and their willingness to impose punitive damages. The researchers found extraordinary agreement across demographic lines. "The correlations were remarkably high for judgments of outrage and of punitive intent. In particular, there was essentially perfect agreement among groups in the ranking of cases by punitive intent: the median correlation was .99. Men and women, Hispanics, blacks and whites, and respondents at very different levels of income and education produced almost identical orderings of the twenty-eight scenarios used in the study. Judgments of intent to punish in these personal injury scenarios evidently rest on a bedrock of moral intuitions that are broadly shared in society."[34]

Given the same facts, people often respond similarly. What becomes important, then, are the facts themselves.

DELIBERATIONS AND THE PRIMACY OF EVIDENCE

A verdict is a group decision, requiring unanimity or at least a strong consensus. Jurors with diverse attributes must find common ground. The deliberative process that precedes the verdict diminishes the differences produced by juror characteristics and increases the likelihood that the decision will be based on the evidence.[35]

Others disagree that deliberations play a valuable role in determining verdicts, pointing to data showing that nine out of ten juries that failed to reach agreement on the first ballot ultimately decided in the direction of the initial poll. Kalven and Zeisel found that when the majority first voted for an acquittal, 91 percent of the time the jury eventually returned a not guilty verdict. If the initial majority was for conviction, 86 percent of the time a guilty verdict resulted. If verdicts follow the first ballot, it is easy to conclude that deliberations do little to affect the result. Kalven and Zeisel concluded that "*the real decision is often made before the deliberations begins*. . . . [The deliberation process] does not so much decide the case as bring about the consensus, the outcome of which has been made highly likely by the distribution of first ballot votes. The deliberation process might well be likened to what the developer does for exposed film: it brings out the picture, but the outcome is pre-determined."[36]

Even when deliberations precede the first votes, the research showing that the first ballot is the best indicator of the verdict is still something of an embarrassment "for proponents of the jury as the embodiment of the 'deliberative ideal.'"[37]

Or is it? The importance of jury deliberations should not be summarily dismissed. The *prospect* of jury deliberations itself is important. Jurors' memoirs and diaries commonly reveal nervous speculation about anticipated deliberative discussions and debates. They expect them to be important. They know they will have to take a stand. They expect that they will have to justify their position and perhaps try to persuade others. Some of those others will be from different demographic groups, and few jurors, if any, contemplating deliberations think that the anticipated justification and persuasion can be based on appeals to status, gender, economic standing, or ethnicity. No one expects to defend his position by maintaining, "I am a white male and we white males tend to think. . . ." Jurors know that what they have in common is the evidence, arguments, and the law. What jurors share is the trial itself, and they anticipate that the deliberations will be about the trial itself. Jurors envision having to justify and defend based upon the evidence. To do this, they must pay attention to the evidence, which helps give the evidence primacy.

In contrast, imagine a system where jurors are told that after the evidence is taken, they will have a secret ballot and the majority vote will determine the verdict. Jurors would have only to decide how they were going to vote. They would not have to prepare themselves to justify their decision or persuade others to endorse it. Surely jurors' behavior would be different under such a system. Because they would not have to construct defensible and convincing positions from the evidence, they would not have to pay much attention to it. The evidence would have less primacy, allowing extralegal factors more play. Thus, the *expectation* of deliberations brings a critical focus on the evidence. As Robert Burns puts it, "For the trier of fact, the undeniable reality is the trial itself. The trial's the thing."[38]

Chapter 17 Jury Trials of Complex Cases

The fictional barrister Sir Ethelred Rutt, K.C., captures the views of many who believe that juries cannot decide complex cases well. He describes the complications of the case to the jurors: "[It has been a]ll about debentures and mergers and mortgages and subsidiary companies—twenty-five subsidiary companies on one side alone! Not to mention the expert evidence about the scientific stuff—all that fandango about the magnesium alkaloid and the patent vapour-feed. The chemists on the two sides flatly contradicted each other, and so did the accountants. I don't believe there is an accountant on either side who really knows what some of the figures mean."[1]

In the face of such complexities, Sir Ethelred asserts, it was unfair to expect the jury—"Decent fellows, I dare say, some of you, but with no particular intelligence or financial training, and wildly divergent in character and opinion"—to come to a unanimous decision "about questions that baffle the wisest brains of the Bench and Bar." He concludes:

> I consider it quite idle to discuss this difficult case with you at all. Though I spoke with the tongues of men and of angels and for as long as me learned friend, it would still be a complete gamble which side you came down on.

For all I know, the gentleman with the strongest personality in that box may particularly dislike me or have a warm admiration for Sir Humphrey Codd. One of us two is right in this case and represents truth and honesty; the other does not; and all I propose to tell you is that I am the one who is right. But I will fortify that bald assertion with the reminder that I have at least, to your knowledge, told the truth about me learned friend, about the jury system, and about yourselves. Which is more than Sir Humphrey can say. And I ask you to argue that if I am demonstrably truthful and right about so much I am probably truthful and right about the rest. Good afternoon.

Whereupon the jury without retiring to deliberate found for Sir Ethelred's client and proposed three cheers for the barrister in the bargain.[2]

EXTENT OF COMPLEX CASES

A case can be complex because of its length, the number of witnesses, the number of parties, or the number of issues to be decided. Most often, however, when juries' abilities are questioned in complex cases, the critics are referring to trials where technical, scientific, or mathematical issues outside the normal experience of jurors, often presented by competing experts, are crucial to the outcome. The concern about such cases has heightened because of the perception that the number of trials containing complex issues is increasing:

> An ever-increasing number of facts of importance for the legal process can now be established only by sophisticated technical instruments. . . .
>
> Associated with the use of technical instruments is growing reliance on technical expert opinion. . . . Common sense and conventional means of proof thus compete with scientific data in establishing the factual predicate for the court's decision. These data are often conceptually sophisticated, punishingly copious, and occasionally even counterintuitive. With increasing frequency, then, courts are confronted with complex scientific and technical information that only persons with highly specialized knowledge or rare skills have no trouble in comprehending.[3]

The extent of this growth has not been measured. Perhaps the most that can be said about the increase, if any, is the answer that Graham Lilly provides to his own question: "Can it be shown persuasively that, on average, cases tried to a jury today are more complicated than those presented to juries during the middle decades of the last century? Certainly both intuition and anecdotal evidence suggest an affirmative answer."[4]

The level of complexity in modern trials, however, can be overstated. Many trials have no expert witnesses, and most trials with experts do not meet most definitions of "complex." A routine trial concerning a contract usually requires no essential expert testimony nor does a robbery case. It is true that in a drug case an expert may confirm that a substance is cocaine; in a murder case an expert may say the cause of death was a gunshot to the head; in a personal injury case an expert may state that the plaintiff suffered a broken leg. Most often, this expert testimony goes uncontested. The defendant does not contend that the substance was not cocaine or that a gunshot did not cause the death or that a broken leg was not suffered. Much more often the defendant maintains that he was not part of the drug-selling conspiracy, or that someone else shot the victim, or that the plaintiff fell from her own clumsiness.

Only rarely is technical evidence crucial to the outcome. Rarity, however, does not equal insignificance. Although complex cases may constitute only a fraction of all trials, many such cases do come before the courts each year. Furthermore, their significance extends beyond their numbers because complex cases often affect society more broadly than do other trials. For example, with claims that the dumping of toxic substances into waterways has caused illness or that a product or a workplace practice is unreasonably dangerous or that companies have violated antitrust laws have far-reaching effects on society, such cases often hinge on difficult and highly contested technical issues.

Jurors do have trouble with complex cases partly because such trials often present much evidence. Research shows "that jurors do have significant difficulty with large volumes of data, especially when the evidence is not about a topic with which the jurors are already familiar."[5]

Ultimately, however, jury performance in such cases is better than many critics suggest. Studies show that, as with other, more routine cases, jury verdicts in complex cases tend to follow the evidence. The outcomes correlate positively with outside expert analyses of the evidence. What we are to conclude from these findings, however, is not quite clear: "The results of these studies are, of course, open to various interpretations. They indicate that jury verdicts are not random events with respect to the quality of the evidence, but they also suggest that many errors are made. What we do not know is exactly how to assess this result. We do not know, for example, whether jurors did better or worse on 'hard' cases, or whether another fact-finder (a trial judge or even another insurance company evaluator) would do better than the jury."[6]

JURORS AND COMPLEX EXPERT TESTIMONY

Because jurors have trouble evaluating difficult expert testimony, they sometimes employ "peripheral processing" to assess it: "[I]n peripheral or heuristic processing people do not attend to the quality and validity of the arguments. Rather, they adopt shortcuts to determine the value of a message. People rely on factors such as the number of arguments (rather than their quality), the attractiveness of the communicator, and the communicator's credentials. Peripheral processing is more likely to occur when there is a lack of motivation to attend to an argument or the ability to process a message is not present."[7]

Various studies support the conclusion that the more complex the case, the more likely that jurors will use peripheral processing to assess it. For example, jurors often downplay the importance of complex scientific testimony in their decisions, indicating a "lack of motivation of some jurors to fully attend to the testimony of party experts."[8] Nonetheless, jurors do take seriously the job of trying to understand expert testimony. Two researchers state:

> The responses to expert testimony we observe . . . suggest that jurors play an active role in assimilating and assessing testimony. Jurors did not simply adopt the view of a witness they rated high on expertise, using apparent expertise as a peripheral cue to conclude that the expert must be correct. Rather, consistent with deeper processing of information which produces attitude change when the listener is highly involved, the jurors appeared to consider and evaluate the content of what the expert was presenting, and were less likely to be persuaded if they did not feel they understood it. This approach not only suggests active evaluation and perhaps even subtlety in dealing with expert testimony, but it also indicates the care jurors use in evaluating evidence to reach their decisions.[9]

This has also meant that the way in which experts testify makes a significant difference in the way jurors assimilate the information:

> Jurors were impressed by an expert's reputation and educational credentials, but clarity of presentation was the most important factor. . . . [E]xperts who conveyed information in a nontechnical fashion and were willing to reach a firm conclusion were more readily believable than other expert witnesses. Communicative skills and decisiveness were seen as the two most important characteristics of believability while educational background, pleasant personality, and attractiveness were rated as less important. . . . [T]he ability to convey technical information in a non-technical manner was the most important consideration for jurors, followed by a willingness to draw firm conclusions.[10]

Jury deliberations can also be crucial in helping jurors navigate through complex testimony. Although jurors who have had the most difficulty understanding the expert testimony are likely to be tentative in their initial assessments of the case, they benefit from the abilities of their fellow jurors. They rely on more knowledgeable jurors, who end up being the most influential leaders of the deliberations. Most important, research suggests, these leaders often do understand the evidence and help guide these less competent, less knowledgeable jurors to make correct verdicts.[11]

JUDGE VERSUS JURY AND COMPLEX CASES

Assessment of jury competence in complex cases must be considered in comparison to the judicial alternative. A common assumption is that judges will perform better than juries when technical evidence is involved. Mirjan Damaska, for example, asserts: "Professional judges in the role of fact finders, albeit also novices in science, are in a somewhat better position to cope with novel, technically difficult evidentiary material: being repeat players, they can gradually accumulate the requisite technical understanding and can even undergo training in the basics of forensic science."[12]

This, however, is merely an article of faith; examples of judges who have made mistakes in complex cases are legion.

> The anecdotal evidence does mean that just as there are no guarantees that juries will understand the technical evidence in a complex case or decide such cases correctly, so there are no guarantees that judges will get everything right. Nor do we have any firm empirical basis for deciding whether judges will in some sense decide complex cases better than juries do over the long run. The best evidence we have on this count is [the] finding that judges are no more likely to disagree with jury verdicts when cases are complex than when they are not. This suggests that jury and judge verdicts are not likely to differ over the long run because of factors that distinguish complex cases from simpler ones.[13]

Some reformers have suggested withdrawing complicated cases from jurors and having judges adjudicate them, but this would apparently have little effect on verdicts. A suggestion for a more fundamental change comes from United States Court of Appeals Judge Patrick Higginbotham:

> [A] question we ought to ask, when we conclude that a case is beyond the ken of a jury, is whether it belongs in a court at all.
>
> Except for those cases, which I suppose to be few in number, that are understandable by a judge but not by a jury, the answer must be that they do not belong in court at all, at least not a court with all the current trappings of fairness. . . . My point, and I wish to stress it, is that the debate over the capacities of juries is part of a much larger issue. That larger issue is whether the judicial model constructed for party-ori-

ented and defined issues is affordable in the behemoths such as mass tort and other multiparty, multi-issue cases. Are they truly "cases," or are they social ills, better addressed by processes more akin to those of a legislature than by judicial models?[14]

Such cases, perhaps, do not belong in court, but they will be removed only if some other system is set up to deal with them. This takes legislative study, creativity, and will, and when that is lacking, trials remain the method for handling such matters. And it should not simply be assumed that trials will resolve these problems less well than the possible alternatives. Jeffrey Stempel, for example, who has studied trial complexity and competency, concludes, "[C]ourts appear to continue to be distinctly more competent as the default option for adjudication than their current competitors—broad-based legislation, administrative agencies, arbitration, mediation, and variant hybrids."[15]

Within this default option, it may seem useful to debate whether judges or juries should decide complex cases, but we simply lack the information to decide which will be the better choice in a particular case. As Richard Lempert maintains, in some complex cases judges may do better than juries, but in others juries will do better, and seldom can we know in advance of trial who will perform more ably.[16]

COMPLEX EVIDENCE:
PROBABILITIES AND STATISTICS

We do know that complex cases often include testimony about probabilities and statistics and that jurors frequently misunderstand and misuse such information. Reform efforts in this area have not been heartening. One summary of the research concludes, "Attempts to improve jurors' use of probabilistic evidence have not met with much success."[17] Such findings only confirm the broader, well-established proposition that people in general have trouble assessing probabilities and statistics. Consider a famous problem:

> A cab was involved in a hit-and-run accident at night. Two cab companies, the Green and the Blue, operate in the city. You are given the following data: (i) 85% of the cabs in the city are Green and 15% are Blue. (ii) A witness identified the cab as a Blue Cab. The court tested his ability to identify cabs under the appropriate visibility conditions. When presented with a sample of cabs (half of which were Blue and half of which were Green) the witness made correct identifications in 80% of the cases and erred in 20% of the cases. Question: What is the probability that the cab involved in the accident was Blue rather than Green?[18]

Few of us, whether juror or judge, could answer the question accurately, because few of us know how to use probabilities or draw conclusions from them:

What little research has been done to compare judge and jury decision making [about probabilities] suggests that judges, too, can be influenced by errors and expectancies. For instance, Kalven and Zeisel . . . found that the rate of disagreement between the judge and jury verdicts was not attributable to an inability of the jury to understand the evidence—the rate was the same whether the judge characterized it as "easy" or "difficult" to understand. In a similar vein, [another study] found that judges and jury-eligible undergraduates were equally reluctant to find in favor of a plaintiff in a civil case when presented with naked statistical evidence. Furthermore, a substantial proportion of judges who chose not to apply statistical evidence gave weak or flawed reasons for discounting it. Finally, [another study] found that judges and jurors who were exposed to information that had been ruled inadmissible were influenced by that information to a similar extent.[19]

There is little reason to believe that judges are more likely than juries to arrive at the correct answer when a problem like the one involving the Green and Blue cabs is being considered.[20] Most of us—judges included—are not competent to assess probabilistic data. With a jury, however, especially a twelve-person jury, there is a reasonable chance that at least one juror would know how to assess such information and be able to explain the approach to her colleagues on the jury.

COMPLEX EVIDENCE AND NARRATIVES

Jurors, as we have seen, comprehend and assess evidence by organizing it into narratives or stories. As far as we know, judges do the same. Jurors—and no doubt judges as well—often have difficulty integrating technical evidence into commonsense narratives. This is part of the reason they have difficulty with such evidence. This is particularly true of probabilistic information. Let us say, for example, that the evidence indicates that DNA found at a crime scene matches the defendant's DNA. We learn further that one in a thousand other people also have such DNA and, furthermore, that the laboratory mischaracterizes DNA once every five hundred times. Or the evidence might establish that birth defects occur ten times in every ten thousand births, but when pregnant women take a certain drug, the birth defect rate is thirteen out of every ten thousand births. What are we to conclude about who was at the crime scene or what role that drug played in causing a particular birth defect?

Incorporating the probability into a coherent, complete, satisfying narrative is difficult. Jurors, like the rest of us, are uncomfortable with the uncertainties inherent in probability data. We all seek certainty. In trials, stories told with certitude can be assessed to see how fully and plausibly they account for the evidence, but stories based on probabilities are not so easily weighed. Indeed, this helps explain why jurors tend to find experts who state definite conclusions more persuasive than those who do not.

Testimony leading to an incomplete narrative is often unpersuasive even when it is based on reliable science. The case against the pharmaceutical company Merrell and its morning sickness drug Bendectin provides an example. Plaintiffs claimed the drug caused birth defects and that Merrell had negligently tested and marketed the drug. The evidence that the drug actually caused birth defects was weak. Nevertheless, the plaintiffs presented a complete, coherent story allowing the jurors to develop a logical connection between taking Bendectin and production of a birth defect. The drug company, however, did not present such a full narrative. Although it presented strong evidence that the drug did not cause birth defects, it failed to explain a glaring and undisputed fact—the plaintiff had a birth defect. The failure to provide a complete, alternative narrative proved damaging:

> Providing a specific reason for the plaintiff's injury is an attractive defense because it creates a story that competes with the plaintiff's. A complete story would be: Merrell was careful in the testing and marketing of this drug, and as a consequence it marketed a safe product that had nothing to do with the plaintiff's injury. Moreover, we know what did cause the plaintiff's injury; her injury has a genetic basis.
>
> The value of such specific causation can be appreciated more fully by considering Merrell's relatively unpersuasive alternative story: Unfortunately, we have no way of knowing what caused the plaintiff's injury, but Bendectin didn't cause the injury. . . . This truncated story failed to cover all of the evidence [and] decreased the likelihood that a jury would accept Merrell's case.[21]

BETTER-EDUCATED JURORS

Given the fact that both judges and juries are limited in their ability to assess complex testimony, are there ways to improve performance? One way might be to enhance the collective education of juries in such cases. The juries that have the most trouble with complex cases are the ones with few or no members with a college education or other valuable background to help them to decide the difficult matter. Data show that juries in complex cases often include a disproportionately small number of educated jurors. There are a number of reasons for this. Sometimes attorneys try to exclude such jurors, fearing "that educated jurors will see through a weak case or use their education to sway other jurors."[22] Also, because of the length of these trials, a disproportionate number of educated and professional jurors seek and get excusals for hardship. Furthermore, some jurisdictions provide exemptions from jury service that disproportionately allow educated people to avoid service.

Ameliorative steps can be taken. The trend to eliminate exemptions for professionals such as doctors and lawyers should continue. Shorter trials might mean fewer hardship excusals for the better-educated. Methods to decrease the duration of trials should be tried, including "imposing deadlines on the parties for the presentation of evidence, allowing jurors to take exhibits, videotaped depositions and other evidence to view at home over a weekend, and segregating discrete issues for trial by different juries. Scheduling trials after working hours would also enhance the availability of highly-paid individuals." Furthermore, "highly capable juries may be seated if the lawyers, perhaps urged on by the judge, cooperate and do not routinely exercise their peremptory challenges on those jurors most likely to understand the case."[23]

Experimentation with blue-ribbon juries might also be useful. "Notwithstanding the obvious dangers of elitism and class bias, the notion of impaneling a jury with minimum educational or experiential qualifications relevant to the subject matter of factually or legally complex cases is worthy of experimentation."[24] The whole jury would not have to meet the requirement, because research shows that the presence of a few highly qualified members can raise the quality of the entire jury. Some who advocate requiring a college degree for jurors in some cases suggest that "the ideal college-educated component of the proposed special jury would be the lowest number (or fraction) generally necessary to obtain the desired advantages. . . . [I propose] half of the jury as an initial, and admittedly, tentative baseline fraction. Accompanying this proposal, however, is an exhortation for further research in this area so that, given the 'lowest number necessary' criterion, commensurate refinements to the minimum college education component can be made in the future."[25]

MORE ACTIVE INVOLVEMENT WITH WITNESSES

Clarification of complex issues could be facilitated if jurors were permitted direct questioning of expert witnesses. Moreover, the normal trial procedure that requires one side to present its entire case before the other side proceeds might be changed in complex cases. This traditional approach leads to a disjointed presentation of scientific and technical evidence, making the evidence harder to grasp. Mirjan Damaska states: "The adversary system's fission of proof-taking activities into two evidentiary cases further bedevils the smooth presentation of scientific information. Witnesses testifying to the same issue—when called by different parties—cannot normally be examined back to back. In most ordinary trial circumstances, the resulting loss of temporal focus is not a serious impediment to understanding. But when complicated scientific subjects are involved, the two-sided structure of the trial makes the comprehension of information more difficult."[26]

Some judges have occasionally altered the standard procedures in complex cases and segregated the disputed technical issues from the rest of the trial to provide a more continuous stream of scientific evidence. Further experimentation along these lines should be encouraged.

BETTER EVIDENCE IN COMPLEX CASES

These changes might improve jury performance in complex cases, but they do not address one central issue in such cases: the nature and quality of the presented evidence. Complex cases prompt discussions of juries' abilities to decide technical and scientific issues, but such debate, as Joseph Sanders points out,

> implicitly assumes that juries receive an unbiased translation of science. In fact, a jury must reach a verdict on the basis of the trial evidence, not on the basis of the underlying science.
>
> Evidence is filtered fact. Ideally, litigation provides a relatively benign purifying filter that removes prejudice and unwarranted inference while maintaining evidence's probative force. . . . [But h]ow does the legal filter affect the capacity to reflect fairly the changing and growing body of scientific knowledge . . . ? In turn, how does expert testimony affect the ability of the factfinder to reach a verdict consistent with the weight of scientific opinion?[27]

Expert witnesses are selected by the parties, who choose them because their views support the parties and because they are expected to be persuasive testifiers. The chosen experts are often on the spectral ends of the discipline, giving the impression that a field has less consensus than it does. Furthermore, because of trial constraints, each side tends to call about the same number of experts on a disputed topic, giving the impression that the scientific opinions within the discipline are equally split about an issue even when they are not. In the end, "All experts appear similarly qualified, all evidence of equal value and relevance."[28]

Although cross-examination of ordinary witnesses may illuminate the strengths and weaknesses of the testimony, the cross-examination of experts often does little to clarify the complex issues. First, expert witnesses are often experienced testifiers, projecting an image of competence and confidence that is difficult to penetrate. Second, the lawyers themselves may not have the degree of understanding that is necessary for an enlightening cross-examination, or the lawyers may believe that the jurors cannot grasp the technical material. Consequently, "[i]n typical cross-examinations, much of the lawyers' energy is spent in attempts to undermine a witness' credibility. While lawyers routinely deny that their own experts are hired guns, they just as routinely design their cross-examination to show that opposing experts are. As a result, cross-examination becomes a ritual that does little to clarify the strengths and weaknesses of a witness' testimony."[29]

Juries cannot do a good job without information that can be meaningfully assessed, and often in complex cases such information is not presented. We may strive to have more educated and active jurors in complex cases, but this by itself will not lead to better decisions, for, as Joseph Sanders has concluded, "If the evidentiary inputs and trial procedures remain unchanged, . . . these jurors may be no better at judging between experts or determining the weight of scientific opinion. . . . Changing the factfinder cannot solve problems created by the presentation of a case unless the factfinder possesses the very knowledge that the evidence fails to provide."[30]

Many critics have suggested that a good way to present better information to the jury in complex cases is to have the court appoint experts to testify. Such appointments, however, have been rare. Few judges can spare the time and effort to secure qualified experts. Furthermore, such court appointments might erode the traditional adversary system. Attorneys often oppose them because they lessen the lawyer's control. Attorneys also contend that court-appointed experts will have too much power because juries will merely follow the court's experts, who will appear neutral and infallible, without considering other information. What little research exists on whether juries slavishly adopt the view of court-appointed experts is mixed, but it is clear that attorneys stand firmly opposed to these appointments.

Although court appointments have been infrequent, experimentation with them should be encouraged. Differing schemes for finding these experts should be tried, and different limitations on their testimony might usefully be studied.

Certainly courts could appoint experts as educators to explain the state of the discipline. Jurors as a result might learn where consensus does and does not exist, giving them a better perspective on the claims of partisan experts.

Test we should, but we need, as in all possible areas of jury reform, to experiment in ways we can learn from those efforts. Richard Lempert states it well:

> With regard to the management of complex cases and the conduct of jury trials, we live in a world of constantly experimenting judges. The problem is that the experimentation most judges do is uncontrolled, hardly visible, and unsystematic, so we learn almost nothing from it except what we learn from the fact that great outcries over various novel procedures seem not to have arisen. Given this, I have suggested that we should apply the little we have learned from systematic experimentation, consider what social science theory suggests, add a good dose of common sense, and make those limited changes we think will improve the jury system. We should, however, resolve to study the changes we make so that we will learn if our hunches are right.[31]

Chapter 18 Jury Nullification

Juries have the power to disregard the law and acquit a guilty defendant, a power commonly labeled "jury nullification." Jury nullification has produced fierce and frequent debate. Everyone agrees that juries have the ability to acquit a guilty defendant. Everyone does not agree whether juries have the right to do so or whether juries should be informed of this power. The roots of this debate extend back to earlier times when juries determined the law for themselves.

THE RISE AND FALL OF THE JURY
AS ARBITER OF THE LAW

When this country was founded, juries were not required to apply the law as the judge gave it to them; instead, they could define it for themselves. Thus, juries decided the law as well as the facts. This power predated the Constitution, acting as a check on unjust colonial laws and royally appointed judges. Juries could not serve as a bulwark against oppression if they had to follow an oppressive judge's instructions about the law.[1]

Practical reasons also impelled juries to decide the law. In many trials, more than one judge presided, and each told the jury his views of the applicable law. These legal interpretations did not always coincide, partly because judges had little formal legal training.[2] Early juries often had to make a choice among competing views.

Prevalent antihierarchical religious views also dovetailed with the belief that jurors should determine the law. "One argument was the Puritan belief that just as the people have the right to interpret Scripture, so, too, do they have the right to interpret the law. Since many people accepted that Scripture was the 'principal basis' of the law, . . . this claim was likely to strike a responsive chord in a sizable segment of the populace." Indeed, the law was seen as generally accessible to all. The belief was that the law was not something that took years to study and understand, but rather that it emerged naturally from the common sense and conscience that everyone possessed. By extension, then, anyone could determine and interpret the law.[3]

Even the United States Supreme Court recognized a jury's right to determine the law. In the 1794 case of *Georgia v. Brailsford*, an unusual case in which the United States Supreme Court presided over a jury trial, Chief Justice John Jay told the jurors that the justices all agreed on the applicable law, but continued: "It may not be amiss, here, Gentlemen, to remind you of the good old rule, that on questions of fact, it is the province of the jury, on questions of law, it is the province of the court to decide. But it must be observed that by the same law, which recognizes this reasonable distribution of jurisdiction, you have nevertheless a right to take upon yourselves to judge of both, and to determine the law as well as the fact in controversy. On this, and on every other occasion, however, we have no doubt, you will pay that respect, which is due to the opinion of the court: For, as on the one hand, it is presumed, that juries are the best judges of fact; it is, on the other hand, presumable, that the court are the best judges of the law. But still both objects are lawfully within your power."[4]

Soon, however, judges sought to restrict the jury's power to determine the law. Several factors were at work. Both bench and bar became more professional. Judges became convinced that they knew the law better than the jury. Judges may also have come to fear what they perceived as populist tendencies of jurors. The sense that judges needed greater control of juries deepened as increased immigration and expanding jury rolls brought a greater social division between judges and jurors. In addition, many businessmen and bankers who had the ears of judges sought greater legal stability in commercial matters. To plan transactions, these men needed to know what the law was, a difficult determination when juries could decide it.

As a result, judges increasingly concluded that juries should be required to decide cases upon settled law defined by judges. The judges' job became "to instruct the jury on the principles of law already established and guide it in bringing forth a verdict consistent with them." The transfer of power in civil cases was swift and largely accomplished by 1820.[5]

Judicial control over the law in criminal cases took longer, but it was well established in most American jurisdictions by 1895 when the Supreme Court considered the matter in *Sparf and Hansen v. United States*. Herman Sparf and Hans Hansen had been two seamen on watch on an American ship at sea. At the end of their duty, the second mate could not be found, but much blood on the deck, a broomstick, and a wooden bludgeon were. In the subsequent murder trial, jurors, apparently concerned that a murder conviction would bring the death penalty, asked during deliberations whether they could convict Sparf and Hansen of manslaughter. The trial court replied that if the two had committed a crime, the law required a murder conviction, and the jurors had to follow the law as it was given to them: "[I]f a felonious homicide has been committed, the facts of [this] case do not reduce it below murder. Do not understand me to say that manslaughter or murder has been committed. That is for you gentleman to determine from the testimony and the instruction I have given you. . . . [A]s one of the tribunals of the country, a jury is expected to be governed by law, and the law it should receive from the court."[6]

Sparf and Hansen objected to these instructions, maintaining that the jury had the authority to determine the law in a criminal case. In the appeal that followed the murder conviction, the Supreme Court rejected this position and held that the jury had to follow the law given by the court. Justice John Harlan, writing for the Court, concluded: "Upon the court rests the responsibility of declaring the law; upon the jury, the responsibility of applying the law so declared to the facts as they, upon their conscience, believe them to be. Under any other system, the courts, although established in order to declare the law, would for every practical purpose be eliminated from our system of government as instrumentalities devised for the protection equally of society and of individuals in their essential rights. When that occurs our government will cease to be a government of laws, and become a government of men. Liberty regulated by law is the underlying principle of our institutions."[7]

This opinion generally settled the issue for the courts—juries do not have the right to decide the law. They are instead under an obligation to accept and apply the law as the court defines it.

The 1895 decision, however, did not end the debate. Some saw this as an unwarranted action that violated the original constitutional meaning of the right to a jury trial. Moreover, the Supreme Court decision did not end the practice of jury nullification, for even if a jury does not have the right to determine the law, it has the absolute power to disregard judicial instructions and acquit an otherwise guilty defendant. The dissenters in *Sparf and Hansen* correctly stated, "It is universally conceded that a verdict of acquittal, although rendered against the instructions of the judge, is final, and cannot be set aside; and, consequently, that the jury have the legal power to decide for themselves the law involved in the general issue of guilty or not guilty."[8] The jury derives this power from a number of sources, but it stems chiefly from the constitutional right against double jeopardy.

DOUBLE JEOPARDY

The Fifth Amendment to the United States Constitution states: "Nor shall any person be subject for the same offense to be twice put in jeopardy of life or limb." This protection against double jeopardy means that a person charged with a crime can be tried only once for the offense. If the accused is convicted of killing Billy Smith, she cannot be tried again for killing Billy Smith. If the accused is acquitted of killing Billy Smith, she cannot be tried again for killing Billy Smith. She can be tried but once for a single crime. (A hung jury is neither a conviction nor an acquittal. The protection against double jeopardy does not prevent another trial when the jury cannot agree on a verdict.)

The accused, however, may appeal her conviction, and in doing so, she, in effect, waives part of her double jeopardy protection. By appealing, she consents to the possibility that if she wins the appeal a new trial can be ordered, and she can be tried a second time for the same offense. If, however, she accepts the first judgment of conviction and does not appeal, that conviction will be final, and she cannot be tried again.

An acquittal, on the other hand, is absolutely final. The same jurisdiction is prohibited from prosecuting the accused again for the same offense. (If, however, the accused's actions potentially violated the laws of more than one jurisdiction, double jeopardy does not prevent the second jurisdiction from also trying her.) The double jeopardy protection checks governmental oppression. Supreme Court Justice Hugo Black gave the classic justification: "The underlying idea, one that is deeply ingrained in at least the Anglo-American system of jurisprudence, is that the State with all its resources and power should not be allowed to make repeated attempts to convict an individual for an alleged offense, thereby subjecting him to embarrassment, expense, and ordeal and compelling him to live in a continuing state of anxiety and insecurity, as well as enhancing the possibility that even though innocent he may be found guilty."[9]

As a result, the prosecution cannot appeal in a criminal case if a successful appeal would lead to a second trial for the same offense. An acquittal is, therefore, final even if it is based on misguided or erroneous conceptions of law. Perhaps if the trial judge had not incorrectly excluded important prosecution evidence, the jurors would not have acquitted. This does not matter. The government cannot appeal; the acquittal is final. Perhaps the not guilty verdict was irrational or against the weight of the evidence. Once again, this does not matter. The acquittal is final.

The same finality applies to an act of jury nullification. Perhaps the jury disregarded or violated the law to return an acquittal. Even if that could be irrefutably established, the acquittal is final, and the defendant cannot be tried again on those charges. Consequently, even if juries do not have the right to determine the law, they do have the power to disregard the law and free an otherwise guilty defendant. An acquittal is final.

LEGAL ACCOUNTABILITY OF JURORS

The doctrine that jurors cannot be held legally accountable for their decisions—that they cannot be legally rewarded or punished for their verdict—protects juries if they acquit in disregard of the law. This principle grew out of ancient struggles for religious freedom.

In 1670 the Quaker religion was illegal in England. A Quaker meetinghouse had been locked by the authorities, and in response, William Penn and William Mead held a meeting of Quakers in the street. For this action, Penn and Mead were tried for the capital offenses of unlawful assembly, disturbance of the peace, and riot.

The offenses being clear to the trial judge, he instructed the jury to convict. The jury, however, refused to do so, eventually acquitting the pair. The court then held the jurors in contempt, fined them, and imprisoned the twelve until the fine was paid. Four, including Edward Bushell, refused to pay and were jailed, with another court subsequently considering the legality of the incarceration. In that decision, known as *Bushell's Case,* the court found that the jailing was improper. There was little point to a jury trial, the reviewing court noted, if the jury could be judicially commanded to reach a specific result: "To what end must they undergo the heavy punishment of the villainous judgment, if after all this they implicitly must give a verdict by the dictates and authority of another man, under threats of fines and imprisonment, when sworn to do it according to the best of their own knowledge? A man cannot see by another's eye, nor hear by another's ear, nor more can a man conclude or infer the thing to be resolved by another's understanding or reasoning."[10]

From this case came the legal understanding that jurors cannot be punished (or rewarded) for their verdict.

GENERAL AND SPECIAL VERDICTS

At the end of a trial, juries usually render a general verdict that announces the outcome without disclosing the reasoning that led to the result. The jury may pronounce, for example, that a doctor is liable for malpractice or that an accused is not guilty of murder, but they do not reveal the basis of their decision. The verdict does not disclose what evidence the jury found persuasive; it does not reveal what inferences the jurors made; it does not indicate whether the judicial instructions were understood. Consequently, a general verdict does not disclose whether the jurors followed the law. The general verdict, then, protects the jury's ability to acquit in disregard of the law. For example, jurors may conclude that the evidence does not quite persuade them that a defendant caused a plaintiff's injuries. If so, the law commands that the defendant be found not liable. The jury, however, might find for the plaintiff but award lesser damages. This compromise violates the law, but the general verdict would not reveal the improper basis of the verdict. A juror might acquit not because he believes that the wrong person has been identified as a drug dealer, but because he believes that marijuana should be legal. The general verdict, once again, would not reveal that the juror disregarded the law as defined by the judge.

Because general verdicts hide whether a jury followed the law, they have been lambasted. Federal Judge Jerome Frank, a strong critic of much of our trial structure, had this to say: "[T]he general verdict . . . confers on the jury a vast power to commit error and do mischief by loading it with technical burdens far beyond its ability to perform, by confusing it in aggregating instead of segregating the issues, and by shrouding in secrecy and mystery the actual results of its deliberations. . . . In short, the general verdict is valued for what it does, not for what it is. It serves as the great procedural opiate . . . draw[ing] the curtain upon human errors and sooth[ing] us with the assurance that we have attained the unattainable."[11]

Special verdicts provide an alternative. With them, the jury does not actually decide who wins, but instead only resolves specified factual issues. After doing so, the judge applies the law to the jury's factual findings. The judge then announces the trial's outcome. In a variant, the jury renders a general verdict but also answers special interrogatories, which disclose the grounds for the verdict. "Advocates of the use of these forms emphasize that the jury's exclusive function is finding facts. Further, the special verdict in particular is seen as a useful device in making the jury process more scientific. Because special verdicts allow the jury to make only findings of fact and the court is not required to instruct the jurors on how the law will be applied to their findings, the judge can control any tendencies the jury might have to be swayed by sympathy."[12]

Special verdicts see only limited use. Trial judges seldom conclude that special verdicts are useful or necessary in the straightforward cases that make up the overwhelming bulk of trials. Furthermore, for special verdicts to work well, judges must give the "jury a small number of simply worded, unambiguous questions, each limited to one issue."[13] In the complex cases where special verdicts are most often used, however, the formulation of such questions is often contentious and difficult, restricting their use.

Special verdicts are also resisted because they shift power from the jury to the judge. They strip away the jury's authority to apply legal rules to the facts. According to one federal judge, this is not how the jury system should work: "The jury is not to be set loose in a maze of factual questions to be answered without intelligent awareness of the consequences. One of the purposes of the jury system is to temper the strict application of law to facts, and thus bring to the administration of justice a common sense lay approach, a purpose ill-served by relegating the jury to a role of determining facts *in vacuo,* ignorant of the significance of their findings."[14]

These factors have dampened enthusiasm for the use of special verdicts in civil cases; they have virtually doused it for their use in criminal cases. Federal and state courts usually do not allow special verdicts or special interrogatories if the criminal defendant objects to their use. Because special verdicts and interrogatories can give the judge power to channel the jury's decision making, some see their unconsented use as violating the Sixth Amendment right to a criminal jury trial. The federal Court of Appeals for the First Circuit has stated that special verdicts in criminal cases are suspect because of "the subtle, and perhaps direct, effect that answering special questions may have upon the jury's ultimate conclusion. There is no easier way to reach, and perhaps force, a verdict of guilty than to approach it step by step. A juror, wishing to acquit, may be formally catechized." The court continued that a strictly logical conviction is not the goal of the criminal trial system: "[T]he principle [is] that the jury, as the conscience of the community, must be permitted to look at more than logic. . . . The constitutional guarantees of due process and trial by jury require that a criminal defendant be afforded the full protection of a jury unfettered, directly or indirectly."[15]

Criminal juries, thus, render general verdicts. If jurors have disregarded the law in reaching their decision, they will not announce that fact. This makes jury nullification easier.

THE MISNOMER OF JURY NULLIFICATION

"Jury nullification," however, is a misnomer. No jury action ever actually nullifies the law. Even if a jury acquits the guilty, the law remains in effect. A jury may understand from the evidence, for example, that an adult daughter yielded to the insistent and agonized entreaties of her aged father, who was suffering terribly from a terminal disease, and killed him. Even though the statute may define her actions as murder, the jury might still acquit. But that verdict does not abrogate the murder statute. The prohibition on homicide stays in effect. That law can, and will, be used to punish other people. The jury has not nullified, or even altered, the law.

Similarly, it is not accurate to say that the jury was "determining" the law. The jury's action is not akin to legislation that enacts a rule of general applicability. Neither is it like a court decision, which can affect future cases. A jury's decision affects but one case, and the law itself goes unaltered.

Finally, branding an acquittal in disregard of the law as "illegal" involves a strained use of that word. Illegality implies that such an action can be punished or overturned, but legal doctrine clearly allows verdicts of this kind. There is nothing illegal about them.

Instead, "jury nullification" allows juries unreviewable discretion in refusing to apply the law to a particular person. This grant of discretionary authority may seem aberrational, but is in fact similar to the discretionary power allowed others in the justice system. Juries that acquit the guilty are acting no more illegally than are law enforcement officers who choose not to prosecute the guilty. The prosecutor who does not charge someone she could charge or who accepts a guilty plea to a lesser offense than the one actually committed is not acting illegally. Neither is she nullifying or determining the law. She is merely exercising the discretion that the system grants her. Jury nullification offers similar discretion to juries and, in the process, serves as a check on the broad discretionary power of the prosecutor.

JURY NULLIFICATION AS A CHECK
ON GOVERNMENTAL POWER

The government's power to bring charges is extensive. The Supreme Court has stated, "In our criminal justice system, the Government retains broad discretion as to whom to prosecute. So long as the prosecutor has probable cause to believe that the accused committed an offense defined by a statute, the decision whether or not to prosecute, and what charge to file . . . , generally rests entirely in his discretion."[16]

The jury's absolute authority to acquit acts as a check on this discretion. When the jury refuses to apply the criminal law in a particular case, the jury, in essence, is using its power to find that the prosecutor should not have used his discretionary power to bring the case.[17]

The jury's absolute power to acquit also acts as a safety valve for and a check on legislatures. Indeed, legislators, perhaps without much reflection, intuitively depend on this jury power, for without it the process of legislating would often become impossibly difficult. Charles Curtis explains:

> Logically an exception to any rule can be only the intrusion of another rule. Thou shalt not kill, for example, has obvious exceptions, not only in battle but at the bedside, for example, as some argue, a mother in order to save the child; but they are dictated by other rules, which we profess to recognize, but which are so hard to express that they are impossible to apply. Practically, and ignoring pretensions to logic, there are exceptions, and the law looks to the jury to make them, because it does not feel able to make intelligible rules to cover them; nor does it want to admit that the law is less than a complete system.
>
> Euthanasia is one example of exceptional cases. The law recognizes that it is incapable of dealing with euthanasia directly and candidly. . . . Lacking itself the genius to cope with them, the law turns them over to a jury.[18]

The jury has the power in such situations to personalize an otherwise too broad and rigid statute. Jury nullification also acts as a roadblock to inequitable laws. Colonial juries, for example, acquitted when the English tried to enforce what were regarded as unjust tax, trade, and seditious libel laws. Indeed, the attempt to limit jury discretion in such cases was one of the stated grievances leading to the Revolution.

Early American juries also reacted against overly harsh laws. In an 1815 South Carolina case, for example, a defendant was acquitted of grand larceny and found guilty of only petty larceny because the grand larceny conviction would have required the death penalty. Similar instances were widespread.[19]

By some accounts, however, the need for juries to act as a check on politically repressive and overly harsh laws declined or disappeared with the birth of the new country and the adoption of increasingly just laws: "Americans no longer had unjust law foisted on them by a foreign power across the sea. American legislators were elected by the people. . . . The Revolutionary power of the musket had given way to the electoral power of the ballot. The intervening power of the jury was considered to be less imperative, now that Americans were free to 'vote the rascals out.'"[20]

Even so, American juries continued to react against American law when it was perceived as unjust. The response to the Fugitive Slave Act of 1850 is an example. The law provided that those who aided slaves to escape could be fined and imprisoned and were liable to the owner for the value of the slave. In some parts of the country, juries simply disregarded the law, refusing to convict those who helped slaves. They found the law so unjust that they would not enforce it.

The Prohibition laws provide a similar example. While all juries in the 1920s may not have been "totally at war" with the national ban on alcohol, juries in some portions of the country seemed to be engaged in serious battle. In Kansas, Nebraska, and Oklahoma, the acquittal rate for liquor violations was 13 percent; in New England it was 48 percent; in New York it was 60 percent. Juries seemed to be voting with their verdicts.[21]

INFORMING JURORS OF THEIR POWER

Jury nullification is akin to the law enforcement power not to prosecute, but it differs in an important way. Police and prosecutors are aware of their discretion. Studies have shown, however, that few people in the jury pool are aware of the jurors' powers. This situation has fostered a debate over whether jurors should be informed of their power to acquit the legally guilty. The conflicting positions on this issue tend to mirror the broader debate about nullification itself:

> Proponents of instructing the jury argue that: 1) the jury's right to an instruction existed from colonial times through the early 1800's; 2) the jury's use of its power to ex-

tend mercy is needed to do justice in specific, unanticipated cases and fact situations; 3) the power places a curb on the power of judges, legislators, prosecutors, and police; and 4) the jury's knowledge of this power allows it to apply community standards to the law.

On the other hand, courts and commentators opposed to instructing the jury of its absolute right to acquit argue that such an instruction will 1) lead to anarchy; 2) defeat the will of the people; 3) violate the defendant's rights; 4) lead to unjust verdicts; and 5) place too great a burden on jurors' psyches.[22]

This matter has largely been settled by the seemingly contradictory position taken by almost all courts. While conceding that jurors have the absolute and often valuable power to acquit, courts have concluded that jurors should not be informed of this power. The jury does not have to be informed about its ability to acquit in disregard of the law.[23]

NULLIFICATION AS A REFLECTION OF SOCIETY

So, jury nullification is controversial. "Of course, one person's jury nullification is another's tempering of justice with equity. Such behavior can be condemned as an inappropriate usurpation of legislative authority by juries that have run amok. Or it may be viewed as an example of the democratic and populist role of the jury in shaping the application of legal rules to the living norms of the community."[24]

Defenders have suggested that nullification has been a compelling force for changing unpopular laws and policies. Some suggest, for example, that acquittals of 1920s liquor violations helped end Prohibition. Such claims, however, often confuse the causes and effects of nullification. The nullifying jury is often following public opinion, not creating it. Certainly Prohibition had produced wide disdain that existed apart from and in advance of any jury action. Such disdain may have made it easier for juries to acquit violators, but it was the disdain, not the jury action, that led to the laws' demise. In fact, jury nullification scholar Andrew Leipold states, there are few or "no examples in which frequent nullifications *created* dissatisfaction with the law; at best, nullification has *reflected* discontent that was already in place."[25]

Just as praise for jury nullification has been overblown, criticism, too, has been excessive. Critics have focused largely on the potential for abuse that is inherent in unexplained verdicts and the power to render acquittals that do not follow the law. Jurors can acquit a guilty defendant for any reason, but there is no guarantee that those reasons are just or noble. Jurors could, for example, return a rape or murder acquittal simply because the accused was white and the victim black. It is widely assumed that juror racism has led to many such verdicts, but confirming examples are, in fact, rare. For one reason, jurors seldom had to decide such cases. Racist society did not approve of the prosecution of white people for violence against black individuals, and law enforcement generally chose not to bring such prosecutions. Members of lynch mobs, for example, were almost never prosecuted.[26] Furthermore, trials of white citizens accused of racist violence typically had lackadaisical prosecutions and lacked forthright witnesses. The resulting acquittals simply followed from the presented evidence.

We may have hoped for more stalwart jurors when the few racist acquittals did occur, but with the pressures of the prevailing culture we could not really expect them. Neither, however, can we presume that government officials were oblivious to the same forces. The judges were drawn from the same society, and no reason exists to believe that judges, especially elected ones, would have performed any differently had they been charged with rendering a verdict. Certainly, the same societal forces that produced racist acquittals also produced racist convictions of black defendants, and the state courts did little to prevent or overturn those verdicts. No matter what the region of the country, history does not "show the jury as being more racist than other decision-makers in the criminal justice system—prosecutors, judges, police, attorneys."[27] Curbing the jury's power would have changed little.

Some changes have occurred since the racist acquittals preceding and during the civil rights movement. Those racist verdicts almost always came from juries that were not drawn from a fair cross section of the community. The juries were further skewed because peremptory challenges were allowed on racial grounds. Consequently, those juries were (almost) all white. Today, of course, jury pools must be drawn from a representative sample of the population, and potential jurors cannot be peremptorily challenged legally simply because of their race. The result is that the composition of juries is significantly different from those of only thirty or forty years ago in many places in this country, and the likelihood of race-based acquittals of white defendants charged with violence against black citizens has decreased drastically.

THE "NEW" RACE-BASED JURY NULLIFICATION

The situation has changed so dramatically that some feel the problem has been reversed. Their concern is not white juries acquitting white people in disregard of the law, but rather minority juries acquitting minority defendants in disregard of the law. Assertions of a new wave of "race-based" nullifications were fueled in part by Paul Butler's controversial *Yale Law Journal* article urging black jurors to acquit some black defendants despite the evidence.[28] Butler's incendiary remarks were fanned by statistics originally published in a *Wall Street Journal* article the day after the 1995 acquittal of O. J. Simpson for the murder of his white wife. Roger Parloff summarizes: "Bronx juries, it is asserted, acquit minority defendants at a 47.6 percent rate—nearly three times the national acquittal rate of 17 percent for all races. Hispanics in the Bronx are acquitted 37.6 percent of the time, the argument continues. There are similarly elevated acquittal rates in the heavily black jurisdictions of Washington, D.C.—about 28.7 percent—and Wayne County, Michigan, which includes Detroit—about 30 percent. . . . Thus, the reader is invited to infer that the largely minority jurisdictions may be acquitting inappropriately high numbers of minority defendants out of, at least in part, race-based jury nullification."[29]

National statistics on such issues are hard to come by, but Parloff could find almost no evidence for the cited acquittal rate of 17 percent. The data, inconclusive as they are, tended to point to a nationwide rate of closer to 28 percent, making the so-called elevated rates in Washington and Detroit merely average. Parloff concedes that the rates in the Bronx are high, but reminds us that these statistics alone do not prove the existence of widespread race-based nullification. He reports: "The nine experienced trial-level judges in the Bronx who agreed to talk with me . . . did not appear to be aware of a jury nullification crisis in their courts, nor did two prosecutors or two defense lawyers interviewed. . . . 'I consider [jury nullification] a rare bird indeed,' says William Hrabsky, first trial assistant in the Bronx, and an assistant district attorney for 24 years. He believes that inexperienced prosecutors blame jury nullification for their own 'bad prep' or for serious problems with their own witnesses. . . . Many of the judges volunteered that jurors in the Bronx are far more skeptical of police officers' testimony than suburban jurors probably would be, since the qualities of their experiences with police are so different."[30]

Although the suggestion of increased race-based nullifications by black juries has generated much publicity and speculation, examples are few, if any. The jeremiads are similar to those, discussed earlier, that claim the number of hung juries has increased because lone black jurors simply refuse to convict. The data do not prove the assertions.

THE RATE OF JURY NULLIFICATION

Even without the controversy surrounding race-based nullifications, jury nullification generates enormous interest. Although jury nullification is rare in actuality, hundreds, perhaps thousands, of articles and books have been written about the topic, with no end in sight. Indeed, novelists as diverse as John Grisham and Ayn Rand have relied on jury nullification to advance or resolve their stories.[31]

Juries do render unreasonable verdicts. They do sometimes acquit the guilty or convict the innocent. A wrongheaded acquittal, however, is not necessarily nullification. Jury nullification implies that the jurors know the accused is guilty and render an acquittal anyway. A sincere but mistaken verdict is not nullification any more than a sincere but mistaken decision by a judge is. If the jury believes an accused is innocent when he is not, an acquittal is not decided in disregard of the law. "[M]istake and nullification are not synonymous."[32] Identifying and separating "mistake" from "nullification" is difficult, making accurate assessment of data on the incidence of either difficult.

Jury nullification, however, simply cannot be a routine matter, for, as we know, criminal juries convict in the vast majority of cases. Moreover, polled judges, whether they agree with the jury verdict or not, almost always think that acquittals are reasonable. The incidence of nullification cases seems confined to the small percentage of acquittals that trial judges label unreasonable, but even within this fraction, at most only some of the verdicts could be true instances of jury nullification, for a judge's assessment of an acquittal as "unreasonable" may simply be wrong.

The affirmative evidence of widespread jury nullification is slender. Juries seldom proclaim that they acted in disregard of the law. Of course, they do not give reasons for their verdicts, but in interviews after verdicts have been handed down, jurors overwhelmingly justify their decisions by citing the evidence and the law. Nancy Marder's analysis of such interviews found that no jurors claimed to have disregarded the law. Jurors rendering acquittals consistently maintain that the prosecution's evidence left them with reasonable doubts and that the law required them to acquit.[33]

Nullification claims come primarily from people who are not jurors, and these assertions should be treated warily. Norman Finkel explains: "A nullification claim rests on two tenuous assumptions: that we know what the 'true' verdict should have been, and the jury likewise knew it but consciously chose to reject it. The first assumption is theoretically problematic; the second is pragmatically so. If we know a priori what the correct verdict should be, the trial would be purposeless, for the jurors would not serve as finders of truth but merely as window dressing."[34]

Sometimes people conclude a verdict is a nullification by relying on information not presented to the jury. Gerard Petrone's examination of the nineteenth-century trial of Frank James for committing two murders during a train robbery labels the acquittal nullification, maintaining that James's guilt was clear. But Petrone reaches his conclusion by relying on the confession of a co-conspirator that was not introduced into evidence. At the trial no eyewitness to the robbery was presented; contradictory evidence was presented about aspects of the crime; James presented an alibi; and the prime witness was a proclaimed accomplice who could charitably be described as sleazy.[35] Perhaps Frank James was truly guilty, but in light of the evidence, a jury surely could have had a reasonable doubt. Many claims of nullification are like this one. The assertions do not stem from an analysis of the evidence the jury was legally instructed to consider. Rather, they assume the existence of information not available to the jury.

Nullification claims also arise from the natural human difficulty of accepting decisions with which we disagree as reasonable or right. Not surprisingly, losing attorneys often cry nullification. Unsuccessful attorneys are unlikely to concede that their cases were not good or that their own performance was problematic. Often, as a result, the lawyer proclaims or suggests that the jury did not follow the law. After the 1995 acquittal of O. J. Simpson, Los Angeles District Attorney Gil Garcetti spoke like many losing advocates when he "described the verdict as one that 'many people' would look at as jury nullification and that the jury had based its decision 'on emotion. Not reason.'"[36]

Was the verdict nullification? Proving a negative is always difficult, and it is almost impossible to prove that it was not nullification. But the evidence that the verdict was an act of jury nullification is slight. Jeffrey Abramson states: "There is no concrete evidence that the jury responded to the call for nullification—one of the two white jurors has said she found the argument ludicrous." Those two were not alone. Nancy Marder notes: "The most compelling reason for concluding that the Simpson verdict was not the result of a nullifying jury is that the jurors who explained their reasoning said that they reached their verdict based on reasonable doubt. All of the jurors who were interviewed after the verdict said that they voted for acquittal because they believed the prosecution had failed to establish its case beyond a reasonable doubt."[37]

Of course, those who believe the verdict was nullification may believe the jurors did not wish to confess to disregarding the law and entered into and carried out effectively a conspiracy to lie about what happened. On the other hand, jury scholars who have analyzed the evidence in the Simpson trial noted that this was a difficult case because the murky term "reasonable doubt" was crucial; the case was complex and long; and the core of the proof was technical circumstantial evidence, which is difficult to "comprehend because the conclusions of the analysis are probabilistic, there is controversy among the experts about how to analyze and report conclusions, and bloodstain evidence can be 'planted' or contaminated much more easily than fingerprints, ballistic traces, or other comparable evidence."[38]

After studying the *Simpson* case, Reid Hastie and Nancy Pennington concluded that it was justifiable for jurors to have had a reasonable doubt: "[I]t seems plausible that the defense was effective enough to create genuine reasonable doubt. Even with our exposure to incomplete and biased media reports of the evidence, several of the reasonable doubts cited in jurors' post-trial interviews were the same issues that had made us doubt the prosecution's case: the time interval (approximately six minutes) for Simpson to clean up, change clothes, and appear at his door to board the airport limousine seemed implausibly short; the possibility of some evidence contamination seemed convincing; and some of the most incriminating bloodstains were questionable."[39]

Jurors denied nullification and gave evidentiary explanations for the outcome. Serious students of the trial found the verdict reasonable and perhaps right. But still the media preferred to label the verdict as one that disregarded the law. "[T]he mainstream press did not credit the jurors' explanation that their verdict was based on reasonable doubt, as demonstrated by many writers' labelling of the verdict as nullification."[40]

This controversy is understandable. When press and commentators differ over a verdict, it is simpler to claim nullification than to undertake a difficult, perhaps boring, recital of the evidence. The *Simpson* case exemplifies a wider pattern and indicates why jury nullification may seem much more prevalent than it is. Even when support for the assertion is slight, claims of nullification emerge. In the popular imagination, verdicts are often ascribed to factors other than the presented evidence. People seek a simple explanation when the actual issues of the trial are controversial or difficult to grasp. These "simpler" explanations focus on racial bias or other external factors that tend to slight the most important fact about jury verdicts: juries strive mightily to grasp and analyze the significance of the evidence, and because they do, *the overriding determinant of the verdict is the evidence itself.* Almost always everything else recedes into the background.

IMPORTANCE OF JURORS' SENTIMENTS
ABOUT THE LAW

Kalven and Zeisel found that when judge and juries disagreed, the disagreement was caused by either differing views of the facts, differing values, or a combination of both. Kalven and Zeisel concluded that the differing views about values had the most influence when the evidence was close.

> [T]he evidentiary doubt provides a favorable condition for a response to the sentiment. The closeness of the evidence makes it possible for the jury to respond to sentiment *by liberating* it from the discipline of the evidence. . . .
>
>   We know . . . that the jury does not often consciously and explicitly yield to sentiment in the teeth of the law. Rather it yields to sentiment in the apparent process of resolving doubts as to evidence.[41]

Suggesting that evidentiary doubt "liberates" juries so that values and sentiments can dominate is somewhat misleading. In most cases, whether the evidence is close or not, jurors hold no special values that will affect the outcome. In a close robbery case with seemingly credible eyewitnesses and a seemingly credible alibi, for example, it is unlikely that jurors will have strong sentiments about either the robbery statute or this particular prosecution that will shape the result. Robbery is bad; convicting an innocent person is bad. The closeness of the case will not provide liberation; instead, the jury will just have to grapple with difficult evidence.

Even when values and sentiments are involved in deciding a verdict, jurors do not ordinarily feel freed from considering the evidence even if it is close. Their values shape how they see and interpret that evidence, but it is still the evidence that dominates. If I watch a football game between the Chicago Bears and the Green Bay Packers with a Chicago fan and a Packer receiver catches a pass near the sidelines, our conflicting sentiments may come into play. I will hope that the receiver's feet came down in-bounds, while my friend will wish otherwise. Most of the time we will agree with the official's call because the receiver will have so obviously been in or out that the result is clear. No matter what our sentiments, we will concur on what happened. Sometimes, however, the second foot will be very near the boundary line, and now, not surprisingly to anyone, how the two of us see the play varies according to our loyalties. I "know" he was in; my friend "knows" he was out. These differing calls do not arise because we are "liberated" from the evidence; both of us claim to "know" what happened. We see ourselves as faithful to the evidence. But, of course, we tend to see what we want to see, and, being human, we have a tendency to interpret the evidence consistently with our sentiments.

Similarly, in cases that tap into jurors' values, those sentiments can influence how those jurors see the evidence, and in close cases those feelings can, in effect, decide the verdict. Such results, however, are not nullifications. The jury is not disregarding the law in order to reach a result. Instead, the jury is diligently trying to apply a given law to a set of contested facts. English jurist Patrick Devlin came close to capturing the situation when he said: "I do not mean that [juries] often deliberately disregard the law. But if they think it is too stringent, they sometimes take a very merciful view of the facts." For example, a study has shown "that when a war becomes less popular, juries convict draft evaders at a lower rate than when the public supports the war." These sentiments, however, do not prevent all such convictions; they only lower the rate. The views about the conflict have an effect, but only in some cases, and those will most often be the ones with evidentiary doubt. In other words, a key fact is that the evidence was close, and even when jury values come into play, the presented evidence still has a dominant role.[42]

There is a reverse side to this. Jury sentiments are sometimes offered as a reason why acquittal rates increase in certain circumstances. Such a dynamic, however, will produce not only "extra" acquittals, but also "extra" convictions. So, for example, the data indicate that when a war is popular, convictions for draft evasion increase. Once again, in close cases, jury sentiments may tip the balance, in this case producing more convictions. Students of this phenomenon suggest that when crime seems rampant juries convict "at higher rates . . . because of their expressed indignation at high crime rates."[43] It is extremely doubtful, however, that such juries are consciously disregarding the law in order to produce more convictions. Jurors do not wish to convict innocent people. Instead, their feelings affect how they see the evidence, and in close cases, that can matter.

IMPORTANCE OF JURY NULLIFICATION

Scholars and critics discuss and debate jury nullification much more than jurors practice it. In fact, as we have seen, few verdicts involve nullification. Its importance may be largely symbolic. It speaks to our conflicting feelings about the power and judgment of ordinary people, the people just like you and me. Part of America's mythic foundation proclaims that ordinary citizens can and should be able to take actions to promote justice in spite of the established order. This is why we honor Zenger's jury, the Boston Tea Party, *Shane,* and the civil rights freedom riders. These are "ordinary" people who defied the established order, and by doing so served justice. In our collective mythology, their sheer ordinariness is key. We like to think that we, too, could have acted as nobly.

On the other hand, we also know that while we might trust our ordinary selves, we do not completely trust the good sense and judgment of all those others, especially when those others seem different from us in some significant way. We want not an unconstrained democracy but a controlled one. We do not want people to act in ways that fly in the face of established order. We do not want people "taking the law into their own hands." Jury nullification speaks to all these conflicting feelings.

The debates over nullification, however, can give the impression that nullification is more prevalent than it is, and this can be harmful. "False claims of nullification contribute to a sense that nullification happens frequently, and there is a problem that needs to be fixed. Judges and legislatures then feel the need to step in and figure out how to limit juries' opportunities to engage in nullification, which usually results in limitations on jury power. False claims of nullification can be used to undermine a verdict by questioning its legitimacy. Even more insidiously, false claims can be used to cast aspersions on the integrity and competence of the jury that rendered the verdict."[44]

Claims of nullification can also obscure needed reforms. If we reach the conclusion that a jury's failure to follow the law stems primarily from the jury's unreviewable discretion to acquit, we might overlook the fact that the jury received unclear judicial instruction. And yet, as Michael Saks explains: "[T]he inescapable conclusion [is] that judges themselves routinely nullify the law by not communicating the law intelligibly to jurors. Judges who rail against jury nullification and then offer incomprehensible instructions are kidding someone, perhaps including themselves. Organizations trying to promote a right of juries to be informed of their power to decide the law as well as the facts are trying to accomplish something that already exists by virtue of the fact that jurors have little choice but to make up much of the law on their own."[45]

The debates over jury nullification are misleading about another aspect of the jury system. Defenders of nullification often paint it as a benign safeguard that only allows a jury to ignore the law to acquit. They stress that the jury does not have the power to ignore the law in order to convict or to decide civil cases. "Proponents view the power as one-sided and limited to acquittals in criminal cases. A judge can set aside a jury verdict of guilty, but not an acquittal. In civil cases, the judge has the power to set aside or prevent a verdict for plaintiff or defendant on the grounds that it has no legal basis."[46]

Put this way, the spotlight falls on the jury's power to acquit in disregard of the law because it is implied that convictions and civil verdicts in disregard of the law will somehow be prevented or fixed by the judiciary. Debates over nullification deflect a more serious consideration of judicial control in those other situations. That oversight is not what is implied. As discussed in Chapter Nineteen, judicial control does only a little to prevent either wrongful convictions or incorrect civil verdicts. For the most part, it is legal doctrine that operates to make verdicts, whether right or wrong, final.

Chapter 19 The Finality
of Verdicts

An acquittal, even if rendered in disregard of the law, is final. All other verdicts, however, can be appealed. Nevertheless, few appeals are successful for any reason, and even fewer win because the jury did not properly apply the law. Appellate court doctrines generally act to preserve the decisions made in the trial court, whether right or wrong, especially jury determinations. As a result, the jury's verdict is almost always final.

PRESERVATION, DEFERENCE,
AND HARMLESSNESS

Only some erroneous trial court rulings can be raised as issues on appeal. Only rulings that were promptly and properly objected to at trial—that is, were "preserved"—can normally be presented to an appellate court. Prompt objections are required to bring errors to the trial court's attention so that they can be immediately corrected, thus obviating the need for appellate review and a possible new trial. In the hurly-burly of a trial with many split-second decisions, errors often do not elicit a prompt objection and therefore go unpreserved, and trial rulings become final, even if wrong.

Furthermore, many trial court decisions stand because an appellate court reviews them only to determine whether an abuse of discretion occurred. We have seen, for example, that appellate deference is extended to a trial judge's determination of the reasons for a peremptory challenge. The abuse of discretion standard also applies to evidentiary and many other rulings. Appellate courts determine not whether the trial ruling was correct, but whether the trial judge's decision was reasonable. Few are found to be unreasonable.

Appellate courts do sometimes find that trial court rulings were erroneous and that the errors were properly preserved. Such congruence, however, does not lead automatically to a reversal. Appellate courts have repeatedly held that few, if any, trials can be expected to be error-free: a party is entitled only to a fair trial, not a perfect one. It is not enough to convince an appellate court that a preserved error was committed; it must be shown further that the error probably affected the trial's outcome. An error will not lead to a reversal if it is "harmless"—if it has not "prejudiced" the losing side.

Determining whether an error is harmless depends on the kind of error. Constitutional errors involving a "structural defect affecting the framework within which the trial proceeds, rather than simply an error in the trial process itself"—and these are few—require an automatic reversal.[1] Other constitutional errors are harmless, though, if the appellate court is convinced beyond a reasonable doubt that the error did not affect the trial's outcome. The harmless error formulation for nonconstitutional errors varies among jurisdictions, but generally they will lead to reversal only if the mistake was likely to have affected the jury's verdict.

No matter what the test, however, judges may not be particularly good at distinguishing "harmless" from "prejudicial." Norman Finkel gives an illustration:

In *Brooks v. Kemp*, . . . the appellate court found that the prosecutor made twelve specific statements deemed erroneous and in violation of the defendant's constitutional rights. These included statements indicating the prosecutor's own belief in the death penalty, reminding the jurors of the cost of imprisoning Brooks, suggesting that Brooks, not the jury, would be pulling the switch at the execution, and so on. Yet the Court of Appeals deemed these "harmless errors." When researchers tested this notion by presenting subjects with the original case (incorporating the twelve errors) and another version that lacked the twelve errors, they found that 67.5 percent voted for the death sentence under the former condition but only 40.4 percent voted for it in the latter condition. The errors weren't so harmless after all.[2]

Moreover, differences in harmless error formulations do not seem to affect outcomes as much as do other factors. Francis Allen, who studied appellate courts' harmless error analyses in criminal cases, reports:

> One detects little evidence that differences in the tests of harmless error produce corresponding differences in case outcomes. Most often the appellate court announces its conclusion of harmless error in language that is terse and conclusory. . . . The one factor common to a great number of opinions affirming criminal convictions on harmless error grounds is the staunch belief of the reviewing courts in the guilt of the appellants seeking reversals of their criminal convictions. This belief appears to transcend all variations of formula and all problematic calculations about what juries might have done had the error complained of been avoided.[3]

While the apparent overuse of the harmless error doctrine in criminal cases may stem from the appellate courts' hostility to those who come before them convicted of crimes, the standard also applies in civil cases. And civil attorneys, too, complain of the appellate courts' frequent invocation of harmless error, suggesting that an institutional force may also be at work. Society has assigned the judiciary the job of resolving disputes. When a new trial is ordered it means that a dispute has not been resolved, and an institutional goal has not been met. Consciously or not, appellate judges are prompted to find errors harmless in order to make the trial's determination final.

Appellate courts exist to correct trial errors, but these appellate principles— preservation of error, deference to trial judges, the harmless error doctrine—all tend to ensure that only the most egregious errors will be corrected. Not surprisingly, then, successful appeals are rare. More than 90 percent of the cases decided by appellate courts uphold the trial court determinations. This does not mean, however, that 90 percent of trials proceed without error. Put another way, the appellate system generally operates to preserve the verdict, thus making the jury's decision final.

INSUFFICIENT EVIDENCE IN CRIMINAL CASES

Few appeals focus on a jury's error in determining facts; claims of prejudicial error are more often against some other actor—police, lawyer, judge, or other official. The appeal may assert, for example, that the jury was not properly selected, that evidence was improperly admitted or excluded, that the attorneys' arguments and behavior were not within legal bounds, or that the trial court incorrectly stated the law.

Appellate courts can review any verdict but an acquittal to see if there was sufficient evidence to support it, yet the standards for overturning jury determinations on these grounds are so rigid that few verdicts are affected. The United States Supreme Court in *Jackson v. Virginia* gave the generally accepted test for insufficient evidence in criminal cases: "[T]he relevant question is whether, after viewing the evidence in the light most favorable to the prosecution, any rational trier of fact could have found the essential elements of the crime beyond a reasonable doubt." Such a construction requires the reviewing court to assume that, in the face of competing conclusions, the jury accepted those favoring the prosecution. "[A] court faced with a record of historical facts that supports conflicting inferences must presume—even if it does not affirmatively appear in the record—that the trier of fact resolved any such conflicts in favor of the prosecution, and must defer to that resolution."[4] Furthermore, any conflicts in testimony must be assumed to have been resolved by the jury in favor of the prosecution. The reviewing court then asks: With the evidence viewed this way, could a rational juror have rationally and lawfully convicted? Because the credibility conflicts and the competing inferences must all be assumed to have been resolved for the prosecutor, the answer as to whether a rational juror could have reached the verdict is almost always yes. The verdict will be sustained as long as the prosecutor has produced some evidence that supports all the elements of the crime. And prosecutors, knowing these precepts, seldom go to trial without presenting at least a modicum of evidence on every issue.

The presumption that the jury has viewed the evidence in the most favorable light for the prosecution does not mean, of course, that the jury has done so. This is merely an assumption that the reviewing court is required to make. It is possible that in fact the jury actually determined the facts much differently and that the conviction is irrational or in disregard of the law. Even so, however, the stacked deck created by the reviewing court almost always leads to affirmation of the verdict.

The trial in Harper Lee's novel *To Kill a Mockingbird* furnishes an example. Atticus Finch defends Tom Robinson against the charge that he raped Mayella Ewell in Maycomb, Alabama, in the 1930s. Robinson denies the charge. He maintains that he often did little chores for Mayella without payment and that one day she asked him to do one in her house. When he entered, however, she grabbed and kissed him. Tom Robinson, a poor black laborer, tried to flee from the white Mayella. She barred the door, but then her father appeared and yelled through the window, "You goddamn whore, I'll kill ya."[5] Robinson, seizing the moment, fled.

Mayella's trial testimony, however, is that she had offered Robinson some money for a minor job when he jumped her. She fought back, but failed. She remembers little about what followed until her father was standing over her demanding to know who did it. She states that Robinson "done what he was after."[6]

Mayella has bruises and contusions on the right side of her face and body. The beating, we readers are led to conclude, was delivered by a left-handed man. Her father is left-handed. Robinson has a shriveled, useless left arm—an arm so deficient it slides off the Bible as he takes the oath.

Atticus Finch forcefully cross-examines Mayella and her father, but their stories remain the same—Robinson is a rapist. They deny that the father beat her. When Finch confronts her with the impossibility of Tom's crippled left arm inflicting the damages, she maintains, "I don't know how he done it, but he done it."[7]

The defense succeeds with the novel's readers, but not with the fictional jury. Steven Lubet comes to this conclusion about Finch's efforts: "His defense was doomed to failure by the very nature of Southern life, but Atticus nonetheless succeeded in demonstrating both the innocence of his client and the peculiar sickness of Jim Crow society. Through his deft, courtly, and persistent cross examination, Atticus made it apparent to everyone that Tom Robinson was being scapegoated for a crime that had not even occurred. He even made Tom's innocence apparent to the all-white jury, which deliberated for an unprecedented several hours even though the judgment of conviction was a foregone conclusion."[8]

In the novel, this wrongful conviction does not get appealed or otherwise challenged, because Robinson is killed as he tries to scale the jailyard fence shortly after the trial. But what if this had been a verdict in a real case? Would the appellate court have overturned the obviously biased result because the evidence was legally insufficient? Although shocking, the answer is clear. Robinson's conviction would have been affirmed by a court following the accepted review standards.

The law requires the appellate court to assume that the prosecution witnesses were telling the truth, and Mayella maintains throughout that she was raped by Robinson. Although the cross-examination of her and her father might seem effective to any rational person, they never waver in their stories. Father and daughter adamantly maintain that Robinson is a rapist, and that would be enough for the conviction to stand. Furthermore, although the physical evidence convinces us that her father, not Robinson, hit her, the standards for reviewing evidence require the court to presume that the jury resolved any competing inferences in the prosecution's favor. It is not irrational to resolve the evidence by concluding that Robinson beat his daughter. Steven Lubet notes: "But it does not strain credulity to conclude that he could have used his right hand to hit her right eye—either as her head was turned or perhaps with a backward slapping motion. Tom was a physical laborer, a powerful man who admitted that even with his damaged arm he was 'strong enough to choke the breath out of a woman and sling her to the floor.' For Mayella, the shock of being attacked might make it difficult for her to fight back effectively, or to remember the precise timing of the blows."[9]

Nor does the father's beating preclude a rape. Lubet reasons: "Rape victims are regularly blamed for what happened to them. It is easily imaginable that Bob Ewell, living in Maycomb, Alabama in the 1930s, might have taken out his anger on the victim of the crime. So the fact that Mayella protected her father does not mean that she lied about being raped."[10]

The point, of course, is not that Tom Robinson was guilty. Surely he was not. He was convicted because he was black and a white woman accused him of rape in the Jim Crow South. Even so, an unbiased court reviewing the conviction for sufficiency of the evidence would have to uphold the result. The reviewing court is not authorized to make a searching inquiry into whether the jury was right, or even whether it rationally evaluated the evidence. The Supreme Court in *Jackson v. Virginia* makes this clear. "The question whether the evidence is constitutionally sufficient is of course wholly unrelated to the question of how rationally the verdict was actually reached. Just as the standard announced today does not permit a court to make its own subjective determination of guilt or innocence, it does not require scrutiny of the reasoning process actually used by the factfinder—if known."[11] The court only determines whether, when the evidence is viewed most favorably to the prosecution, the jury *could* have convicted.

The jury in *To Kill a Mockingbird* did not act reasonably. Atticus Finch describes what happened: "Those are twelve reasonable men in everyday life, Tom's jury, but you saw something come between them and reason."[12] The jury, as in jury nullification, returned a verdict that did not follow the law. Nevertheless, a reviewing court would have had to defer to this unreasonableness and affirm.

It is true that only an acquittal is an absolutely final verdict. The courts have some power to reverse convictions because of insufficient evidence, but that power is remarkably limited. Although statistics on this point are not kept, only the rare verdict is so egregiously wrong that it cannot be rationally defended. Almost always, the courts have to accept the irrational verdict that convicts even when jurors should have had reasonable doubts. The primary effect of the rules for reviewing the sufficiency of a conviction is not to weed out bad or wrong decisions, but rather to preserve verdicts and make them final.

INCONSISTENT VERDICTS

Even when a conviction is made in clear disregard of the law, legal doctrine can allow it to stand. This happens when multiple verdicts are returned that are in conflict with one another. A jury is asked to return a number of verdicts when the trial has multiple parties or multiple charges. Sometimes those verdicts are irreconcilable. The law and evidence may, for example, indicate that a defendant is guilty of either two crimes or no crimes, but the jury finds him guilty of one and not guilty of the other. Prohibition-era gangster Al Capone's trial provides an example. Capone was charged with various federal tax crimes. The jury, among other verdicts, found Capone guilty of failing to file tax returns in 1928 and 1929, but not guilty of tax evasion for those two years, a result that seemed logically impossible given the evidence.[13]

There are several possible causes of inconsistent verdicts. The jury may not have understood the instructions, and as a result, not properly applied the law. The jury may reach an inconsistent verdict to overcome an impasse. Eric Muller, who has examined inconsistent verdicts, states, "A jury returns a compromise verdict, when after reaching a deadlock and dividing into two (or more) camps unable to achieve unanimity for either acquittal or conviction, the jury splits the difference, and achieves unanimous support for some negotiated mix of convictions and acquittals." If so, the instructions have been disregarded. "By reaching a compromise verdict, the jury dishonors the reasonable doubt standard, because each faction on the jury surrenders its honestly held beliefs on the question of proof beyond a reasonable doubt. To be sure, compromise verdicts are undoubtedly quite common, and they help to resolve cases, avoid retrials, and clear crowded dockets. But useful as they may be, compromise verdicts are lawless verdicts."[14] Finally, inconsistent verdicts could be caused by jury nullification—acquittals of some charges in disregard of the law.

An inconsistent verdict thus happens because the jury did not properly follow the law. A general verdict, however, does not reveal the jury's path to the verdict, and the inconsistent results by themselves do not indicate whether they were caused by confusion, compromise, or leniency. The Supreme Court has noted, "Inconsistent verdicts therefore present a situation where 'error,' in the sense that the jury has not followed the court's instructions, most certainly has occurred, but it is unclear whose ox has been gored."[15]

Even though it is clear that the jury has not followed the court's instructions, the typical judicial response has been to affirm the resulting convictions. This approach is taken partly because of the imbalance that allows only the accused to appeal. The Supreme Court has stated, "[I]n such situations the Government has no recourse if it wishes to correct the jury's error; the Government is precluded from appealing or otherwise upsetting such an acquittal by the Constitution's Double Jeopardy Clause." Given that the cause of the inconsistency is uncertain, "and the fact that the Government is precluded from challenging the acquittal, it is hardly satisfactory to allow the defendant to receive a new trial on the conviction as a matter of course."[16]

Moreover, in the Supreme Court's view, overturning inconsistent verdicts would be "hardly satisfactory" because those jury decisions frequently benefit the accused—"such inconsistencies often are a product of jury lenity. Thus, [affirming inconsistent verdicts] has been explained by both courts and commentators as a recognition of the jury's historic function, in criminal trials, as a check against arbitrary or oppressive exercises of power by the Executive Branch."[17]

The courts, however, have no reason to assume that inconsistent verdicts result from leniency more than other causes. Because jurors often have difficulty understanding instructions, juror confusion is, no doubt, a frequent cause. Furthermore, a compromise to reach unanimity may seem appropriate to some juries. The odds are high that most inconsistent verdicts are not nullifications. Affirming inconsistent verdicts indicates a willingness to accept findings of guilt that do not follow the law.

When a civil jury produces verdicts or special factual findings that are inconsistent, the trial judge returns those findings to the jury for reconciliation, and if that fails, a new trial is ordered. This can be done because the civil jury can reexamine all determinations, increasing the likelihood that the conflict will be resolved. Furthermore, inconsistent civil verdicts are harder to accept than criminal ones because the courts have no convenient presumption to reconcile them as they do when they assume that acquittals are an act of jury leniency. Permitting inconsistent verdicts in civil cases would be a public acknowledgment that we allow irrational jury decisions.

Because an acquittal is final, however, it cannot be resubmitted to the jury even if it is inconsistent with convictions rendered at the same time. Furthermore, criminal law can indulge the presumption that the acquittal was an act of leniency. Thus, the verdicts are allowed to stand even when the odds are good that the conviction was unlawful. The criminal law chooses a doctrine that obscures possible irrationalities and promotes the preservation and finality of the rendered verdicts.

OFFICIAL CONFIDENTIALITY OF VERDICTS

An obvious solution to the problem of inconsistent verdicts would be to establish some means for determining the basis of the jurors' decision. We could then ascertain whether confusion, compromise, or leniency operated and take appropriate action. This suggestion, however, runs afoul of another doctrine, the shorthand version of which states that jurors may not impeach their verdicts. The law does not allow a juror to reveal to the court anything about a juror's statements or evaluations during deliberations. Federal Rule of Evidence 606 states this generally prevailing prohibition: "Upon an inquiry into the validity of a verdict . . . , a juror may not testify as to any matter or statement occurring during the course of the jury's deliberations or to the effect of anything upon that or any other juror's mind or emotions as influencing the juror to assent or dissent from the verdict . . . or concerning the juror's mental processes in connection therewith."

Attorneys, neighbors, or the press may ask about the nature and content of deliberations, but the law forbids any formal inquiry into this matter. Jurors are not allowed to describe to the court why they believed one witness but not another. They cannot recount how they calculated damages or why an apparently compromise verdict was reached. Perhaps more important, the court cannot quiz the jurors after the verdict as to their understanding of the instructions or collect their testimony about whether the law was followed.

Several reasons have been given for this proscription. Early in the twentieth century the United States Supreme Court stressed that without such a rule, losing attorneys and litigants would badger jurors to try to find flaws in how they reached their decision. If deliberations were routinely made public, the full and frank discussion needed to reach the best verdicts might be chilled.[18] Toward the end of the twentieth century, the Court added:

> There is little doubt that postverdict investigation into juror misconduct would in some instances lead to the invalidation of verdicts reached after irresponsible or improper juror behavior. It is not at all clear, however, that the jury system could survive such efforts to perfect it. Allegations of juror misconduct, incompetency, or inatten-

tiveness raised for the first time days, weeks, or months after the verdict seriously disrupt the finality of the process. Moreover, full and frank discussion in the jury room, jurors' willingness to return an unpopular verdict, and the community's trust in a system that relies on the decisions of laypeople would all be undermined by a barrage of postverdict scrutiny of juror conduct.[19]

The drafters of the Federal Rules of Evidence further suggested that jury determinations would be too unstable without the rule: "The mental operations and emotional reactions of jurors in arriving at a given result would, if allowed as a subject of inquiry, place every verdict at the mercy of jurors and invite tampering and harassment."[20]

Of course, if juror privacy is truly a primary goal, then many voir dire practices ought to be banned. Harassment by losing litigants may be an important concern, but the rule forbids juror testimony even if the willingness to testify is voluntary and not prompted by contact from the losing side. Preserving the confidentiality of deliberations may seem desirable, but while jurors are prevented from making formal testimony, they are free to tell the public about them. Because only some jurors do so, a view of the deliberations is likely to emerge that is more distorted than one that might result from an official inquiry. Moreover, such selective disclosures about deliberations would seem to be at least as chilling of future full and frank discussions as would court-ordered probings.

The legal prohibition seems based predominantly on the fear that if we learn too much about how juries reach their verdicts, we will no longer accept those verdicts. A sausage-making value seems at work: I love bratwurst, but I do not want to know how they are made.

By guaranteeing official ignorance, the proscription against jury interrogation inhibits discovery of faulty decisions and advances the finality and public acceptance of verdicts, whether good or bad. Mark Cammack notes, "Whatever the truth of the matter, the fear that allowing impeachment by juror testimony would result in an unacceptable disruption of the litigation of disputes is frequently expressed, and secrecy is thought necessary to 'preserve public confidence in a system which more intimate knowledge might destroy.'"[21] The doctrine operates alongside many others that primarily preserve a verdict, whether it be right or wrong.

JUDICIAL CONTROL OF CIVIL VERDICTS

Just as in criminal cases, appellate courts seldom reverse civil trial court decisions. As with criminal cases, trial errors have to be properly preserved; many trial rulings are reviewed only for an abuse of discretion; and the harmless error doctrine applies. The standards for overturning civil liability verdicts are basically the same as those for reviewing the sufficiency of the evidence of a criminal conviction. Consequently, the percentage of civil verdicts reversed by appellate courts is about the same as it is for criminal cases, and this means that verdicts are almost always as final in civil cases as they are in criminal cases.

On the other hand, trial judges may be more willing, through various procedural devices, to take cases away from juries in civil cases than in criminal cases, with federal judges being more activist in this regard than state judges. Legal doctrine, however, allows the judge to act only when it is clear that there are no factual issues for the jury and that some legal issue to be decided by the judge will determine the case. In fact, this sort of judicial action occurs in only a tiny fraction of civil cases. Jack Friedenthal explains, "Because the result . . . is to take a case away from the jury, courts exercise great care in deciding when any of these motions can and should be used so as not to intrude improperly into the jury's domain."[22]

JUDICIAL OVERSIGHT OF DAMAGE AWARDS

Although few liability decisions are overturned by the courts, judges, through additur and remittitur, do have greater oversight of damages decisions. If the trial judge or appellate court agrees that a damage award was erroneously set, the court can grant a new trial unless the opposing party agrees to a judicially specified increase (additur) or decrease (remittitur) in the damages. Thus, the opposing party has the choice of accepting the judicial figure or taking on the risks and expenses of a new trial.

Remittitur is available in almost all jurisdictions. Additur, however, exists in only some. It is not available, for example, in federal court. The Supreme Court has noted that remittitur was available at the time the Constitution was adopted, but additur was not. Furthermore, the Court has reasoned, when the judge offers the choice between a new trial and the reduction in damages, for example, from $100,000 to $80,000, he accepts the jury decision that the plaintiff was entitled to at least the lesser amount. If, however, the choice is between a new trial and increased damages from, say, $100,000 to $120,000, this, in effect, decides facts that the jury has not found. The jury, after all, had not found that damages in excess of $100,000 were appropriate. Not all states accept this logic, and many have adopted additur as well as remittitur.

These devices are infrequently employed. For example, researchers have found that only 5 percent of surveyed judges had reduced jury awards more than five times in a three-year span. "A Rand Corporation study of post-trial adjustments to jury awards in Cook County (Illinois) and California found that 80 percent of the jury verdicts were unchanged after trial. While post-trial processes led to lower awards in about 15 percent of the cases, two-thirds of these reduced payments resulted from settlements between the parties, not court orders. Many reductions were made because of a defendant's inability to pay the full amount rather than judicial concern over unfair awards; courts reduced awards in just 6 percent of the cases overall."[23]

Data do indicate, however, that the larger the award, the more likely it is to be reduced. A study found that 33 percent of verdicts over $1 million and 44 percent of verdicts over $20 million were reduced. Other research reveals that "on average, about 70 percent of dollars awarded were paid out. In cases where punitive damages were awarded [which occurs in less than four percent of verdicts], slightly less than 60 percent of the amount awarded was paid."[24] This does not mean, however, that 70 percent of the cases saw a decrease in damages. Instead, most of the reduction came in a small number of cases with large awards.

Courts have no precise standards for ascertaining whether awards are excessive or inadequate. Judges determine "whether the award is reasonable given the court's conception of a proper award. In reviewing an award for excessiveness, for instance, the question is commonly phrased as whether the amount of the award shocks the court's conscience or is manifestly unreasonable." The judge's greater experience supposedly allows him to develop instincts that jurors do not have for setting appropriate awards. Still, the remittitur and additur decisions produce little more consistency than do jury verdicts, for the law "relies principally on the court's intuition and normative judgment concerning the correct quantum of damages in the review case. The court's valuation is as highly individualized as the jury's initial assessment." Comprehensive databases correlating the size of damage awards to the nature of the injury and the age and sex of the injured person could be developed that would better guide judges on the use of their adjustment discretion, but just as schedules of damages have not generally been presented to juries for use in setting awards, neither have they been widely sought or used by judges.[25]

Some legislatures, perceiving a problem of excessive damages, have stepped in not to make the adjustment process better, but rather to impose caps on the amount of damages. These caps decree that damages cannot exceed predetermined amounts in certain kinds of cases. The schemes vary among the states that have adopted them, with a few states limiting all awards but most states restricting damages only when certain parties, such as health care providers or the government, are sued. Some plans limit only nonpecuniary damages, such as pain and suffering, while others restrict only punitive damages, sometimes by setting a dollar limit and sometimes by limiting punitive damages to some multiple of the nonpunitive damages.

At least one study has found that caps affect only large awards and therefore few cases (7 percent on average), but that when caps have been applied, they have had a huge effect, producing a 70 percent reduction in the awards (more than $1.4 million on average). While such caps have the obvious goal of restraining runaway awards, they have also been severely criticized on ethical and policy grounds:

> With respect to both general and special compensatory damages, the dollar limits selected cannot be morally justified because they are arbitrary and completely unrelated to the level of compensable harm suffered by the plaintiff. The burden of legislative caps is borne almost entirely by seriously injured plaintiffs, many of whom are infants or relatively young and are confronting long-term, very expensive health care. . . . In skewing this burden, caps may unduly impair the deterrent effect of the tort system that is achieved in part through award of damages for nonpecuniary harms. . . . [T]hey offer no relief at all to plaintiffs whose damages awards are unreasonably low, given the nature of their injuries.[26]

Legislative limits have been challenged in various states as a denial of state constitutional rights of access to the courts and a jury trial. Courts have split on these arguments, with the majority upholding the caps.

THE FINALITY OF VERDICTS

Although formally only acquittals represent absolutely final verdicts, in fact the jury's verdict is almost always final. The doctrines for reviewing verdicts tend to ensure that verdicts are preserved. This should not be surprising: "It is incongruous as well as irrational to entrust a complex fact determination to a body, to expend vast sums of money on a long trial, and then to accord the findings of the trier of fact not even the slightest presumption of correctness."[27]

But more than efficiency is at stake. We count on juries to act as a check on judges; they generally determine facts better than do judges; and their decisions are accepted as final by the public and litigants. If judges can easily substitute their fact-finding for that of a jury, the strengths of the jury system are undermined. While judges occasionally override jury fact-finding, legal doctrine makes this rare. This is as it should be.

Jury verdicts are almost always final. This is a crucial fact in understanding the American jury system. It is especially essential for understanding the focus of the most important reforms of the jury system. Because the jury's decision is likely to be final, the focus should be on aiding the jury to get it right the first— and only—time the matter will be considered. Because the prime determinant of jury verdicts is the information presented to it, the most important way to make the jury system better is to improve the quality of that information.

Chapter 20 Reform

Many who look at the American jury system see an ungainly institution in dire need of reform, if not replacement. As this exploration attempts to demonstrate, however, the jury system works surprisingly well. Juries are quite able in finding facts; they inject community values into broad legal mandates; they act as a restraint on the powers of judges and prosecutors; their determinations are almost always accepted by disputants and society. That our jury system performs well, however, does not mean that reform efforts should stop. Surely the system can be improved, and many possible reforms and areas for experimentation have been discussed throughout this book.

Mistaken impressions of juries, however, often drive reform efforts, obscuring important areas of reform. Extralegal factors—such as the composition of the jury in terms of race or gender, attorneys' theatrics, the social or economic status of the parties—have been assumed to be greatly influential in jury decisions, but the data suggest otherwise. Although we must not overlook the possible importance of jury consultants and questionnaires or the effects of jury members' race, gender, and level of education on how they make their determinations, reform efforts should focus on the crucial fact that the evidence is the prime determinant of a jury's verdict. Because jurors are most influenced by the quality of information presented to them, *the best way to improve jury verdicts is to improve the information the jury receives to consider. The better that evidence is, the better the resulting verdicts are likely to be.*

A JURY OF HER PEERS

Susan Glaspell's 1917 short story "A Jury of Her Peers" illustrates why reform efforts should be concentrated on producing better evidence for juries. A man on an isolated farm has been strangled in his bed with a knotted rope. His wife, Minnie Foster Wright, has been arrested after claiming that she slept by his side through the attack. The sheriff, the county attorney, and the neighbor who reported the death, accompanied by two of their wives, go to the farm. The officials, convinced that Mrs. Wright is the killer, are looking for a motive. The county attorney announces, "It's all perfectly clear, except the reason for doing it. But you know juries when it comes to women. If there was some definite thing—something to show. Something to make a story about. A thing that would connect with this clumsy way of doing it." Coming out to the farm, he had told the party, "What was needed for the case was a motive. Something to show anger—or sudden feeling."[1]

The sheriff looks around the kitchen, "with a little laugh for the insignificance of kitchen things." Mrs. Peters, the sheriff's wife, notes that after her arrest Mrs. Wright voiced concern about the state of her preserves. "'Oh, well,' said Mrs. Hale's husband, with good-natured superiority, 'women are used to worrying over trifles.'" As the men are about to quit the kitchen to look around the rest of the house, the county attorney asks the sheriff's wife to keep an eye out for any clues to the motive. Mr. Hale asks rhetorically, "But would the women know a clue if they did come upon it?"[2]

With the men gone, the women observe signs of interrupted work—a sugar bucket uncovered, a paper bag half filled, a dish towel on a table wiped only partially clean. They find a quilt sewn well except for one square that "looks as if she didn't know what she was about!" They discover a broken birdcage, and Mrs. Hale reflects on Mrs. Wright's life. Without children it was "'a quiet house—and Wright out to work all day—and no company when he did come.'" She concedes that he was "'a good man. . . . He didn't drink and kept his word as well as most, I guess, and paid his debts. But he was a hard man, Mrs. Peters. Just to pass the time of day with him—.' She stopped, shivered a little. 'Like a raw wind that gets to the bone.' Her eye fell upon the cage on the table before her, and she added, almost bitterly: 'I think she would've wanted a bird!' "[3]

The women then discover a sewing basket containing a canary with its neck wrung. After a few moments' reflection, Mrs. Hale states:

> "No, Wright wouldn't like the bird, . . . a thing that sang. She used to sing. He killed that too." Her voice tightened.
>
> Mrs. Peters moved uneasily.
>
> "Of course we don't know who killed the bird."
>
> "I knew John Wright," was Mrs. Hale's answer.
>
> "It was an awful thing was done in this house that night, Mrs. Hale," said the sheriff's wife. "Killing a man while he slept—slipping a thing round his neck that choked the life out of him."
>
> Mrs. Hale's hand went out to the bird cage.
>
> "His neck. Choked the life out of him."
>
> "We don't *know* who killed him," whispered Mrs. Peters wildly. "We don't *know*."
>
> Mrs. Hale had not moved. "If there had been years and years of—nothing, then a bird to sing to you, it would be awful—still—after the bird was still."[4]

The women replace the bird in the sewing basket. Upon their return, the men reveal that they still have not found anything to indicate a motive. After the men leave again for a few moments, Martha Hale looks at the "basket in which was hidden the thing that would make certain the conviction of the other woman."[5] After Mrs. Peters tries and fails to push the basket into her handbag, Mrs. Hale forces it into her coat pocket. They say nothing to the men about the bird.

Not surprisingly, legal academics have used "A Jury of Her Peers" as a springboard for discussing the changing role of women on juries. Indeed, the story highlights a prime strength of the jury system—people with different backgrounds will bring different ways of seeing and interpreting information. A diverse jury will more thoroughly consider the implications of the evidence than will a homogeneous body and, as a consequence, is more likely to produce a right result.[6]

Glaspell's story, however, while suggesting the importance of juror diversity, also indicates the relative insignificance of jury composition reform compared to the need for high-quality evidence. The men search for a motive, assuming—apparently correctly—that all-male juries were reluctant to convict women for murder, believing that women by their natures were unlikely to kill, especially without a strong, discernible reason for doing so.[7] Male myopia, however, prevented the men from perceiving the revealing farmhouse signs. A jury, no matter what its composition, stood little chance of determining what had happened if the only trial evidence were that collected by the men. Only the women in the story find and correctly interpret crucial information. This evidence is not to be presented to the jury, but what if it had been? Crucial to the story is the implication that even the all-male jury would understand the significance of the evidence *had it been presented.* The hidden canary "would make certain the conviction" of Mrs. Wright.

It is not that the local officials could not grasp the importance of the crushed neck; it is rather that they had been too arrogant and inattentive to the possibilities and disappointments in women's lives to discover the evidence. The officials in the story and ultimately the all-male jury are unable to accurately determine the facts not because they do not understand the evidence, but because they do not have the important evidence in the first place. Without the appropriate information, a jury—no matter its composition—is less likely to determine the facts accurately than is a jury with that information.[8]

Because the most important determinant of a jury verdict is the evidence presented to that jury, ways should be sought to improve that information. This is not simply a question of changing the doctrines and rules that control courtroom evidence. Rules of evidence pertaining to Mrs. Wright's bird do not matter if that creature is not discovered and revealed. Rather, reforms are needed to improve the generation, collection, and preservation of information. The crucial time for this is well before the trial has begun.

This reform topic is so broad that entire books could be devoted to it. I can only suggest here examples of reforms that might assure that better evidence is presented to the jury.

THE TOO-FREQUENT FAILURE OF THE ADVERSARY SYSTEM

By allowing the presentation of competing claims, the adversary system, when implemented correctly and responsibly, should lead by presenting and challenging evidence to the most accurate and complete accounting of the facts. But the system is not always implemented correctly and responsibly. A survey of over 5,750 death sentences imposed in the United States from 1973 to 1995 found that on appellate and postconviction review, 68 percent of the capital judgments were found to have a serious error. The most common fault found at the state postconviction stage was "egregiously incompetent defense lawyering (accounting for 37% of the state post-conviction reversals)." Another study found poor defense lawyering to be a prime factor in more than a quarter of the convictions later proved wrongful by DNA technology not available at the time of trial. Indeed, anecdotal evidence of sleeping or tipsy attorneys, witnesses not interviewed, ill-prepared testimony, and incoherent summations abounds.[9]

The problem has a number of causes. The Constitution requires the appointment of attorneys for criminal defendants too poor to hire their own. Nationwide more than 80 percent of those charged with felonies are represented by publicly financed lawyers.[10] Study after study establishes that the quality of these lawyers' performances varies from excellent to abysmal. Poor performance is partly due to the fact that fees and support for publicly appointed attorneys are often shockingly low. Low pay inexorably leads to heavy caseloads and slapdash preparation.

In addition, the best and brightest often prefer to do other legal work than defending those charged with crimes. Although there are many good defense attorneys, some, regrettably, are not of the highest quality. For example, Alan Berlow reports in the *Atlantic Monthly:* "In Kentucky an investigation by the Department of Public Advocacy found that 25 percent of death-row inmates had been represented at trial by attorneys who had since been disbarred or had resigned to avoid disbarment. A 1990 study found that 13 percent of the defendants executed in Louisiana had been represented by lawyers who had been disciplined, a rate sixty-eight times as great as for the state bar as a whole."[11]

The adversary system depends upon committed, able attorneys working hard for their clients. In criminal trials at least, this is not always the case. Under these circumstances we can have little confidence that the best information is being presented to juries. When defense attorneys are not doing their job, evidence suffers. Such a failure came to light in a series of wrongful convictions that occurred when a West Virginia forensic scientist repeatedly faked laboratory results. That such a "scientist" was "able to thrive for years is a backward tribute to the anemic work of defense attorneys. . . . As Public Defender George Castelle of West Virginia points out, if even one defense lawyer had challenged [the scientist] to present his notes during his ten-year reign of error, the charade would have come to an end."[12] But none did.

Deficient defense counsel would seem to run afoul of the Sixth Amendment guarantee that all criminal defendants have *effective* assistance of counsel. The Supreme Court's test for effective assistance of counsel, however, has done little to remedy the situation: "[Deficient performance] requires showing that counsel made errors so serious that counsel was not functioning as the 'counsel' guaranteed the defendant by the Sixth Amendment. Second, the defendant must show that the deficient performance prejudiced the defense. This requires showing that counsel's errors were so serious as to deprive the defendant of a fair trial, a trial whose result is unreliable."[13]

The Court went on to state that reviewing courts should be "highly deferential" to an attorney's performance and therefore, "counsel is strongly presumed to have rendered adequate assistance and made all significant decisions in the exercise of reasonable professional judgment." This presumption means that courts usually find a "reasonable" explanation for lapses in an attorney's representation. According to most commentators, these constitutional standards have occasionally required reversals because of outrageously incompetent performances, but their influence has been minimal.[14]

IMPROVED DISCOVERY

Even dedicated, skilled advocates cannot present what they cannot find. Because the discovery process in criminal cases is so restricted, too often the adversaries in criminal cases do not know, and have no way of finding out, what information in their opponents' possession remains undisclosed. The result is that too often juries do not learn about important evidence. An investigation by the *Chicago Tribune* found 381 homicide convictions that had been overturned because the prosecutor either presented evidence known to be false or did not disclose exculpatory evidence. A study of wrongful convictions established by DNA typing found that in about 40 percent of those trials, prosecutors had behaved similarly. The problem, however, is no doubt bigger than these surveys indicate. Undisclosed evidence tends to remain hidden, and we simply cannot know how many other cases have been affected by the failure to disclose pertinent information.[15]

The jury system would operate better if discovery in criminal cases for both the defense and the prosecution were improved. Although there are some problems in expanding the scope of such discovery, they are solvable. After all, almost every other civilized country provides for significantly more criminal discovery than we do in the United States.

PRESERVATION OF EVIDENCE

A good jury system depends on good advocates and ways for them to discover information and present it at trial. Such information, however, can be presented to the jury only if it has been preserved. If the dead bird gathered from the farmhouse disappears before trial, it cannot be presented to the jury.

There is little focus on methods to preserve evidence, possibly because the importance of unpreserved evidence is difficult to evaluate. If the evidence is not available, we cannot assess its value.

Larry Youngblood's case, however, provides a sobering example of the importance of preserving evidence. Youngblood was charged in the 1980s with a sexual assault on a ten-year-old boy. Shortly after the attack, semen samples were collected from the boy and his clothing. Ten days later, the biological specimens were examined by a police criminologist to determine whether sexual contact had occurred, but not to see if the attacker's blood type could be discerned. Afterward, the clothing was simply placed in room-temperature storage. A month later, blood-typing tests were tried unsuccessfully. The unrefrigerated biological samples had by then degraded, preventing accurate typing.

Youngblood was convicted. The United States Supreme Court rejected his claim that his constitutional rights had been violated when the government failed to properly preserve evidence, thus preventing tests that might have revealed his innocence. The Court held "that unless a criminal defendant can show bad faith on the part of the police, failure to preserve potentially useful evidence does not constitute a denial of due process."[16] Bad faith, the Court held, occurs only if the police lose or destroy evidence knowing that it is exculpatory, not simply, as it may have been in the *Youngblood* case, through negligence.

Some of the victim's clothing, however, remained in storage, and DNA tests that were not available when the crime occurred were done on them years later. They exonerated Larry Youngblood. He had not assaulted the child, and he was released from prison more than a decade after his conviction.

The sorts of blood tests that were available when Youngblood was arrested were not as discriminating as the later DNA tests, and we do not know that the earlier tests would have exonerated him. We do know that without the tests an innocent man was sent to prison, and the search for the real child rapist stopped.

The system failed in the *Youngblood* case. The jury convicted an innocent person, but the error was not the jury's. The jurors probably did as well as they could given the evidence they had. They simply did not have all the evidence.

CRITICAL MOMENTS IN A TRIAL

As with many other cases, the most crucial moments of Larry Youngblood's jury trial came not when the jury was selected, not when witnesses were examined and cross-examined, not when the judge gave instructions, and not even when the jury deliberated. The most important moments came when evidence was, or should have been, collected, generated, or analyzed. If evidence is not gathered early on, it often becomes irretrievably lost. If investigators do not discover a dead bird or collect dried blood samples or note the direction and length of skid marks, the jury will never have that information to consider. Without good and thorough collection of the pertinent evidence, the jury's decision will be based on less than the best evidence.

The law says little about the collection of possible evidence, and if it did, whatever strictures it imposed might have little effect beyond the hortatory. Well-meaning investigators already assume that they effectively gather all the relevant evidence. The men in Susan Glaspell's farmhouse felt certain that they had found everything that bore on the killing, and a rule requiring them to collect and preserve all the pertinent information would not have changed their behavior.

Even so, evidence collection can be improved. The starting point is not a legal edict, but study of information-gathering methods and training of those who do it. The possibilities for improvement are vast, and so are the difficulties. A spotlight needs to be cast on this truly fundamental issue of how well we collect, generate, and analyze evidence. The interviewing and preparation of witnesses is a crucial component of this evidence-gathering process.

WITNESS PREPARATION

Witnesses do not simply walk into court unbidden and tell the jury what they know. Witnesses have to be discovered. People have to be interviewed. Information has to be assessed. Witnesses are not then simply left alone to be called at trial. They may be interviewed again and again, perhaps to see if additional information can be elicited, but also to prepare them for testifying. Such preparation can produce better evidence by helping witnesses organize their information and present it cogently in a useful framework. Professor Robert Burns gives an example: "[C]onsider a case in which an attorney is sure that his opponent will attempt to show that his client, the owner of a small business, hired his employees without regard to their qualifications. In preparing the client for testimony, the lawyer asks his client why he hired his vice president, Peter Jones. The client responds, 'Because he was my friend.' A competent American lawyer will not remain content with that answer. Further inquiry may well lead the client to respond the next time, 'Because I have known and respected him for a long time, and I knew that he had many qualities that the job required.' Is the less considered answer the 'truer' answer? . . . Recall that the client will be cross-examined. His friendship will be exposed at that time, when the comparative fairness of the two answers can be evaluated."[17]

All witness preparation, however, is not beneficial or even benign. Advocates seeking a particular outcome interview and prepare witnesses. This affects the collection of evidence. The dynamics that affect criminal matters infect all cases:

> Criminal investigations do not proceed like English drawing-room mysteries in which every conceivable person remains suspect until the investigator impartially amasses all the evidence concerning each of them. In the real world, all the evidence is not gathered before it is decided who did it. Even if the investigator could operate with such suspended belief, limited resources make it impractical. Instead, at some point before the evidence about all the possibilities has been collected, the investigation focuses on a suspect. In effect, the investigator quickly "determines" who is guilty. He then seeks evidence, not to learn about all conceivable suspects, but to confirm his conclusion that a particular person is guilty. At a crucial point in every investigation, therefore, the information gathering shifts from an impartial inquiry as to who did it to the building of a case against a specific person. What results is a natural tendency to acquire all the evidence that inculpates the person selected as guilty while all the other evidence is ignored.[18]

Legal interviewers usually have an idea what they would like witnesses to say and often try, consciously or not, to get them to say it. Such bias can affect the information elicited. So, for example, the mode of posing a question can affect its answer. Subjects asked about cars when they "smashed," for example, were more likely to mistakenly remember broken glass than those asked about cars when they "hit." Similarly, half the people in a group were asked how "tall" a person was and gave an average of 79 inches. The other half were asked how "short." The average then became 69 inches. Also, information included in the question can find its way into a witness's testimony. In one study a group of people watched a film of a moving automobile and were then asked, "How fast was the white sports car going while traveling along the country road?" Another group who saw the same movie were asked, "How fast was the white sports car going when it passed the barn while traveling along the country road?" No barn was in the film. A week later, all the subjects were asked whether they remembered seeing a barn in the movie. Of those given the misinformation, 17 percent remembered the nonexistent structure, while only 3 percent who had been asked the neutral question said they had seen it.[19]

An interviewer might be even more direct in supplying answers. For example, a witness may tell the interviewing lawyer that the robber was wearing a brown coat. The attorney might then respond, "Are you sure it was a brown coat? The other four eyewitnesses are all positive it was a blue coat. Think about the color again, and if you are not sure, it's all right to say that you don't know." Such questioning can have important consequences at trial: "Attorneys can suggest 'better' answers that insidiously corrupt the truth and attorneys can orchestrate a common story among the client and all friendly witnesses. . . . [T]he more a witness is rehearsed, the more confident and detailed she becomes in her recollections. And the more confidence displayed by the witness, the more accurate juries treat her testimony as being, notwithstanding the absence of any relationship between confidence and accuracy."[20]

It is astonishing to many—particularly to foreign observers—that in America today extensive witness preparation is one of the hallmarks of the diligent, successful trial attorney.[21] With our tradition and constitutional protection of partisan advocacy, we will not end pretrial contact between advocates and witnesses. We should be concerned, however, about how this practice affects the quality of information that results.

One possible remedy to lessen pretrial influences would be to require that police interrogations of suspects be taped, which "is either commonplace or mandatory in countries as far flung as England, Australia, and Canada."[22] This practice is not required in most parts of the United States. Only Alaska and Minnesota have compelled police to record custodial interrogations of suspects. Such taping, it is hoped, will inhibit bad interrogation practices, thereby increasing the reliability of any resulting statements. In addition, recordings provide jurors with more accurate information than do oral descriptions of an event.

Police interrogations of suspects, of course, are but a small fraction of the contact attorneys and investigators have with witnesses. A rule requiring all such interviews to be taped and those tapes to be available for trial could produce enormous changes in preparation practices and would certainly yield valuable information not now available to juries. Indeed, few reforms affecting juries are as important as this one.

The Queens, New York, murder trial in which Melvyn Zerman was a juror provides a glimpse of the potential importance of having recordings available at trial. The final prosecution witness had testified that the accused was at the scene shortly before the murder, but this witness became ill during the lunch break and could not return to complete her testimony. In lieu of her presence, the prosecution and defense agreed to permit a tape of her interview with the district attorney to stand for her testimony. The jurors noticed that on the tape she stated that when she saw the accused, many police were also present. Realizing that the police presence came only after the murder had been committed, the jury concluded that she was describing events after the murder, not before. The tape, Zerman concluded, "turned out to be the most important piece of evidence."[23]

Of course, such a taping requirement would engender costs and difficulties, but studies of jurisdictions where recording is required could indicate how such a mandate could be satisfied most efficiently. Yet, the taping requirement is a far less popular jury reform proposal than other such proposals that would produce only marginal improvements in trials. This is partly because reformers seldom focus on the crucial importance of evidence, but it also bespeaks an unwillingness on the part of attorneys to have their methods of witness preparation scrutinized. In this way, lawyers are bound in a kind of covert conspiracy. They may want to know how their opponent is conducting witness interviews, but not if that means divulging their own practices.

Although the importance of witness interviews can hardly be overstated, very little thought is given to what constitutes, and how to institutionalize, good interview practices. Information not elicited from witnesses is information that a jury will not hear, and information elicited in a distorted form may retain that shape when it is presented to a jury. Lawyers and other legal interviewers may not be consciously seeking distorted or incomplete information, but because they rarely receive meaningful training in interviewing methods that is often what they get. This seems unnecessary in the face of an increasing number of studies that point to better interviewing techniques and to the unfortunate fact that these are not used. For example, "analysis of American police interviews of cooperative witnesses revealed that police make systematic, avoidable errors that limit the amount of information they elicit. . . . Some of the more flagrant errors are (a) asking too many closed-ended questions and too few open-ended questions, (b) frequently interrupting eyewitnesses in the middle of narrative responses, and (c) asking questions in a predetermined inflexible order. In hindsight, it is not surprising that police interviewing procedures are poor, given that officers receive little or no formal training in conducting interviews with cooperating witnesses."[24]

Institutionalizing better interviewing techniques is no small task. Recent developments trying to improve another form of evidence, eyewitness identifications, indicates how hard it can be to establish better methods of collecting information.

IMPROVING IDENTIFICATIONS

More than 75,000 people a year become criminal defendants based on eyewitness identifications. The resulting testimony of an eyewitness is often crucial. Data show that juries overwhelmingly convict even when the only evidence against the accused is identification by one or more eyewitnesses.[25]

Because of their importance, eyewitness identifications have generated much study. The research consistently confirms two key points. First, many mistakes are made in eyewitness identifications. Second, jurors are not good at distinguishing incorrect identifications from correct ones. Indeed, one researcher has concluded that "jurors . . . believed inaccurate witnesses just as often as they did accurate ones."[26]

Because they are often pivotal, often wrong, and often mistakenly evaluated by jurors, eyewitness identifications cause wrongful convictions. In cases where DNA testing has led to exoneration, 84 percent of the wrongful convictions rested at least in part on mistaken identifications. This finding is consistent with those of many studies conducted over more than seventy years. E. M. Borchard's classic 1932 study of convictions of innocent people concluded, "Perhaps the major source of these tragic errors is an identification of the accused by the victim of a crime of violence."[27]

These facts should lead inexorably to the conclusion that eyewitness identifications and their evaluations should be improved. But how? Changing the composition of the jury will not change the situation. Nothing indicates that such factors as juror education, race, or gender correlate with mistaken eyewitness identifications. Eliminating the jury is not the answer either; judges are apparently no better than juries at evaluating identifications.

One possible improvement would involve the use of expert testimony to inform jurors about conditions that correlate with increased misidentifications. For example, jurors could be told about the research that correlates stress with misidentification; the greater the stress, the greater the chance of making an incorrect identification. Thus, those robbed at gunpoint are more likely to misidentify the robber than are those robbed without a gun. This reform, however, would have limited value. Jurors might gain new insights into identifications, but general information does little to determine whether a specific identification in a particular case is accurate.

Instead, reforms are needed in the pretrial process. Juries tend to be impressed by eyewitness identifications. The better the identifications presented to the jury, the better the resulting verdicts will be. This can be done not by changing what happens in the courtroom but by reforming what happens when identifications are made. The most important change that could be made would be to improve the quality of eyewitness evidence itself.

A great many studies have focused on the procedures employed during a lineup. So, for example, lineups typically present the suspect and "fillers." It is not surprising, of course, that mistaken identifications increase when the fillers are obviously dissimilar from the suspect. Too much similarity, however, may confuse the witness so that accurate identifications decrease. In the ideal lineup "fillers should fit the verbal description of the perpetrator (which is given by the eyewitness prior to viewing the lineup), but additional similarity should not be sought. Physical similarity between the suspect and the fillers beyond the level of the description provides no additional protection to the innocent suspect and can actually harm the eyewitnesses's ability to identify the perpetrator."[28]

Decades of research also indicate that witnesses at lineups too often assume the perpetrator is present and pick out the person who most resembles the criminal. This problem can be avoided by simply telling the witnesses that the criminal might or might not be in the lineup. "Failure to warn the witness that the perpetrator might not be in the lineup leads to very high rates of mistaken identification in perpetrator-absent lineups. [A] meta-analysis, which included 22 tests of the hypothesis using 2,588 participants and witnesses, shows a 42% reduction in mistaken choices from perpetrator-absent lineups when the instruction was included versus not included. Importantly, the 'might or might not be present' instruction has little effect on correct identification rates when the perpetrator is present (a mere 2%)."[29]

Such research indicates that even simple changes can increase the accuracy of identifications. Amazingly, the changes are not always instituted. Legal doctrine does not require these more accurate procedures. Evidence law says nothing about how identifications should be elicited, and while constitutional law does require an attorney for the accused to be present at a postindictment, live-person lineup, the Supreme Court has also permitted identifications from even highly suspect procedures to be presented at trial if the totality of the circumstances indicates that the identification was trustworthy. The result has been that "courts almost never suppress identification evidence prior to trial, even when egregiously biased lineup [and other identification] procedures are used." So it is that identification procedures of widely varying quality all pass constitutional muster. And wrong verdicts sometimes result. A recent event, however, hints at possible avenues for improvement.[30]

In 1999 the Department of Justice's National Institute of Justice published a report, *Eyewitness Evidence: A Guide for Law Enforcement.* This guide reflects the efforts of a Technical Working Group for Eyewitness Evidence on which prosecutors, defense attorneys, law enforcement officials, and researchers were represented. The chief purpose of the project was to recommend "best practices and procedures . . . in investigations involving eyewitnesses [because] eyewitness evidence, in general, can be improved and made more reliable through the application of currently accepted scientific principles and practices."[31]

The report, however, highlighted how difficult it is to change procedures when present methods are perceived by one constituency to serve them well. Gary Wells, a scientist who was a member of the group, noted that "prosecutors were . . . the most reluctant members . . . to accept the premise that there is an eyewitness problem." Wells suggested two reasons for this. "Prosecutors win almost all of their cases. . . . They are understandably concerned about any change, because it is unlikely to increase any further their already high rate of success. [Moreover, w]hereas police routinely encounter cases in which an eyewitness has mistakenly identified a known-innocent filler, prosecutors rarely learn of such instances. Prosecutors' eyewitnesses cases are based on 'hits,' instances in which an eyewitness has identified the suspect in the case."[32]

The fact that resistance to reform has been strong among a specially convened group committed to exploring changes bodes ill for other areas of evidentiary procedure that could use reform.

Resistance to change prevented the working group from recommending even those improvements supported by a large body of research. So, for example, the standard lineup presents all the lineup members together at one time. Eyewitnesses viewing such an array too often simply make a comparative judgment and pick the member who most resembles the criminal. This leads to mistakes. With another procedure, the witness views lineup members one at a time and decides whether the presented person is the criminal before another person is brought forth. Research shows that this sequential process reduces the likelihood of a relative judgment and encourages the witness to focus on whether each separately viewed person is the perpetrator, more than halving the rate of mistaken identifications. These results have been duplicated in experiments in at least six countries, "making this one of the most replicated effects in the eyewitness area. The simplicity and robustness of the sequential-superiority effect has made it one of the most important of all the practical contributions of eyewitness . . . research."[33]

Even so, the Department of Justice guide on identifications, while discussing the advantages of the sequential process, does not recommend it. Bureaucratic inertia is partly the cause. "Many of the law enforcement members of the working group were concerned that they could not simply on their own use the sequential method, because the simultaneous method is the traditional method." The lack of a recommendation, Wells states, was also fueled by the "underlying concern . . . that an explicit declaration that the sequential procedure is superior to the simultaneous procedure would lead to new trials for those who had been convicted in the past using simultaneous procedures. Because the simultaneous procedure has been the standard across the country, this would be very disruptive to the courts."[34]

Similarly, the police officers and prosecutors who were members of the Technical Working Group for Eyewitness Evidence, which drafted the guide, successfully excluded from it language that would endorse double-blind testing, which requires that the official conducting the identification procedure not know who the suspect is. According to Gary Wells: "The police were quite concerned that their peers would be insulted by a requirement for double-blind testing, because it would be construed as a statement the police are not to be trusted to conduct their own investigations. This was something that took us by surprise, because double-blind testing is a familiar precaution against inadvertent, rather than intentional, influence in psychological research."[35] What this all illustrates is a simple but important point: the path to evidentiary improvement is littered with obstacles.

It boils down to this: improving the evidence is the best way to improve jury verdicts. The American jury system currently fulfills its functions—not perfectly, but very well. It could serve them even better if the evidence presented to juries were improved. Make the evidence better, and jury verdicts will be better. Yet, despite this truth, reform is resisted. As the efforts to improve witness identification procedures indicate, entrenched attitudes and practices interfere with an objective consideration of reform and hinder the adoption of necessary improvements. Methods for institutionalizing reforms need to be found. And more research needs to be undertaken into the myriad areas of evidence that might be improved.

Notes

INTRODUCTION

1. Harry Kalven, Jr., "The Dignity of the Civil Jury," *Virginia Law Review* 50(1964): 1066, 1068.

2. Fred R. Shapiro, ed., *Oxford Dictionary of Legal Quotations* (Oxford: Oxford University Press, 1993), 223.

3. Charles A. Boston, "Some Practical Remedies for Existing Defects in the Administration of Justice," *University of Pennsylvania Law Review* 61 (1912): 11–13.

4. Albert W. Alschuler, "Explaining the Public Wariness of Juries," *DePaul Law Review* 48 (1998): 408.

5. Shapiro, *Oxford Dictionary of Legal Quotations,* 226; Matthew P. Deady, "Trial by Jury," *American Law Review* 17 (1883): 409; J. C. McWhorter, "Abolish the Jury," *American Law Review* 57 (1923): 57.

6. Alschuler, "Explaining the Public Wariness of Juries," 410; Adela Rogers St. Johns, *Final Verdict* (Garden City, N.Y.: Doubleday, 1962), 131.

7. Deady, "Trial by Jury," 402.

8. J. Anthony Lukas, *Big Trouble: A Murder in a Small Western Town Sets Off a Struggle for the Soul of America* (New York: Simon and Schuster, 1997), 525–26.

9. Deady, "Trial by Jury," 399; Shapiro, *Oxford Dictionary of American Legal Quotations,* 226; Chester Mirsky, "Diallo Jury Did Its Best, But . . . ," *National Law Journal,* March 13, 2000, A23.

10. Marc Galanter, "Jury Shadows: Reflections on the Civil Jury and the 'Litigation Explosion,'" in *The American Civil Jury* (Washington: Roscoe Pound–American Trial Lawyer Foundation, 1987): 16; Boston, "Some Practical Remedies," 15; Morton J. Horwitz, *The Transformation of American Law, 1780–1860* (Cambridge, Mass.: Harvard University Press, 1977), 141, 84.

11. David Ray Papke, "The American Courtroom Trial: Pop Culture, Courthouse Realities, and the Dream World of Justice," *South Texas Law Review* 40 (1999): 919–20.

12. Quoted in Jerome Frank, *Courts on Trial: Myth and Reality in American Justice* (Princeton, N.J.: Princeton University Press, 1949), 325.

13. Boston, "Some Practical Remedies," 18.

14. McWhorter, "Abolish the Jury," 54.

15. Mirsky, "Diallo Jury Did Its Best," A23.

16. Deady, "Trial by Jury," 399.

CHAPTER ONE. OVERVIEW

1. *Baldwin v. New York,* 399 U.S. 66 (1970) and *Blanton v. City of North Las Vegas, Nevada,* 489 U.S. 538 (1989). A jury trial was not required to find a union in contempt and fine it $10,000. *Muniz v. Hoffman,* 422 U.S. 454 (1975). A jury trial is required, however, when a person is held in contempt after a trial for actions during the trial, and when the sentences aggregate to more than six months even though each individual sentence is less than six months. *Codispoti v. Pennsylvania,* 418 U.S. 506 (1974).

2. Samuel R. Gross, "The Risks of Death: Why Erroneous Convictions Are Common in Capital Cases," *Buffalo Law Review* 18 (1996): 489.

3. Randolph N. Jonakait, "The Ethical Prosecutor's Misconduct," *Criminal Law Bulletin* 23 (1987): 553.

4. Gross, "The Risks of Death," 493.

5. Ibid., 489.

6. Albert W. Alschuler, "Plea Bargaining and Its History," *Columbia Law Review* 79 (1979): 27–28.

7. *Singer v. United States,* 380 U.S. 24 (1965).

8. Sean Doran, John D. Jackson, and Michael Siegel, "Rethinking Adversariness in Nonjury Criminal Trials," *American Journal of Criminal Law* (1995): 9–11.

9. William C. Smith, "Empowering Prosecutors: Movement to Allow Equal Right to Jury Trial Has Judges Fearing Overload," *ABA Journal,* March 1999, 28.

10. *Ring v. Arizona,* 122 S.Ct. 2428 (2002).

11. Jack H. Friedenthal, Mary Kay Kane, and Arthur Miller, *Civil Procedure,* 3d edition (St. Paul, Minn.: West Group, 1999): 387.

12. Paula L. Hannaford, B. Michael Dann, and G. Thomas Munsterman, "How Judges View Civil Juries," *DePaul Law Review* 48 (1998): 256.

13. Stephen E. Chappelear, "Jury Trials in the Heartland," *University of Michigan Journal of Law Reform,* 32 (1999): 262–63.

14. Marc Galanter, "An Oil Strike in Hell: Contemporary Legends About the Civil Justice System," *Arizona Law Review* 40 (1998): 736.

15. Marc Galanter, "The Regulatory Function of the Civil Jury System," in Robert E. Litan, ed., *Verdict: Assessing the Civil Jury System* (Washington, D.C.: Brookings Institution, 1993): 90.
16. Ibid., 66.

CHAPTER TWO. CHECKING ABUSES OF POWER

1. *Duncan v. Louisiana,* 391 U.S. 145 (1968).
2. Glen Jeansonne, *Leander Perez: Boss of the Delta,* 2d edition (Lafayette: University of Southwestern Louisiana, 1995), xiii.
3. Ibid.
4. Ibid., xxi.
5. *Sobol v. Perez,* 289 F. Supp. 392 (E.D. La. 1968); *Duncan v. Perez,* 321 F. Supp. 181 (E.D. La. 1970), *affirmed Duncan v. Perez,* 445 F.2d 557 (5th Cir. 1971).
6. Chicago, B. & Q. R. Co. v. City of Chicago, 166 U.S. 226 (1897).
7. *Duncan v. Louisiana,* 391 U.S. at 154.
8. Ibid.
9. Ibid., 155, 156, 149.
10. James Alexander, *A Brief History of the Case and Trial of John Peter Zenger, Printer of the New York Weekly Journal,* ed. Stanley Nider Katz (Cambridge, Mass.: Belknap Press of Harvard University Press, 1972).
11. William Smith, Jr., *The History of the Province of New-York,* ed. Michael Kammen (1757: reprint, Belknap Press, 1972), 14–15.
12. James Alexander, *A Brief History of the Case and Trial of John Peter Zenger,* 75.
13. Eben Moglen, "Consider *Zenger:* Partisan Politics and the Legal Profession in Provincial New York," *Columbia Law Review* 94 (1994): 1520.
14. Carl Ubbelohde, *The Vice-Admiralty Courts and the American Revolution* (Chapel Hill: University of North Carolina Press, 1960), 15.
15. Jack N. Rakove, *Original Meaning: Politics and Ideas in the Making of the Constitution* (New York: Vintage Books, 1997), 293.
16. Edmund S. Morgan, "The American Revolution Considered as an Intellectual Movement," in Morton White and Arthur M. Schlesinger, Jr., eds., *Paths of American Thought* (Boston: Houghton Mifflin, 1963), 26; Alexander, *A Brief History of the Case and Trial of John Peter Zenger.*
17. John Philip Reid, *Constitutional History of the American Revolution: The Authority of Rights* (Madison: University of Wisconsin Press, 1986), 50.
18. *Ex parte Milligan,* 71 U.S. 2, 64–65 (1866).
19. Arthur O. Lovejoy, "The Theory of Human Nature in the American Constitution and the Method of Counterpoise," in *Reflection on Human Nature* (Baltimore, Md.: Johns Hopkins Press, 1961), 38–39; *Ex parte Milligan,* 71 U.S. at 123.
20. Joan Jacoby, *The American Prosecutor: A Search for Identity* (Lexington, Mass.: Lexington Press, 1980), 10.
21. *Duncan v. Louisiana,* 391 U.S. at 156.
22. Mary K. Bonsteel Tachau, *Federal Courts in the Early Republic: Kentucky 1789–1816* (Princeton, N.J.: Princeton University Press, 1978), 108–9.

23. Charlie LeDuff, "Corruption Indictment Called Political," *New York Times,* June 8, 2000, B5.

24. Myron Moskovitz, "The O. J. Inquisition: A United States Encounter with Continental Criminal Justice," *Vanderbilt Journal of Transnational Law* 28 (1995): 1164.

25. Thomas Jefferson, *Thomas Jefferson on Democracy,* ed. Saul K. Padover (New York: Mentor Book, 1939), 62.

26. James Gould Cozzens, *The Just and the Unjust* (New York: Harcourt, Brace, 1942): 242–43.

27. Sean Doran, John D. Jackson, and Michael Siegel, "Rethinking Adversariness in Nonjury Criminal Trials," *American Journal of Criminal Law* 23 (1995): 25.

28. Quoted in Alan Feuer, "2 Brooklyn Lawyers, Ex-Insiders, Outline a Court Patronage System," *New York Times,* Jan. 5, 2000, B1.

29. Daniel W. Shuman and Anthony Champagne, "Removing the People from the Legal Process: The Rhetoric and Research on Jury Selection and Juries," *Psychology, Public Policy, and Law* 3 (1997): 244, 247.

30. Gordon Van Kessel, "Adversary Excesses in the American Criminal Trial," *Notre Dame Law Review* 67 (1992): 427.

    Van Kessel continues:

    "English High Court judges, on the other hand, are appointed for life and can only be removed by both Houses of Parliament. Even English judges of lesser status, such as recorders sitting as Crown Court judges, are appointed by senior judiciary and are not subject to the elective process.

    "Continental judges are career civil servants and cannot claim the same distinguished status as English judges, or possibly even the status of our federal and senior state judges. However, the Continental system generally focuses on merit, rather than on an elective process when choosing its judges, and Continental judges are promoted using a hierarchical system which rewards meritorious performance. After a probationary period, Continental judges ordinarily gain tenure which they hold until retirement" (427–28).

    The Continental European judicial path starts at the end of legal studies when graduates choose to be lawyers or judges. Those picking the judiciary must pass a highly competitive state examination. Acceptance to the judiciary is on the merits, without consideration of political beliefs or affiliations. The career begins with an apprenticeship to an experienced judge, and follows with assignments to relatively minor matters. Promotions are based upon performance.

31. *Ring v. Arizona,* 122 S.Ct. 2428; Fred B. Burnside, "Dying to Get Elected: A Challenge to the Jury Override," *Wisconsin Law Review* (1999): 11.

32. William Glaberson, "Fierce Campaigns Signal a New Era for State Courts," *New York Times,* June 5, 2000, A1.

33. Richard Lempert, "Why Do Juries Get a Bum Rap? Reflections on the Work of Valerie Hans," *DePaul Law Review* 48 (1998): 461–62.

34. Harry Kalven, Jr., and Hans Zeisel, *The American Jury* (Boston: Little, Brown, 1966), 58.

35. *Duncan v. Louisiana,* 391 U.S. at 157.

36. *Colgrove v. Battin,* 413 U.S. 149, 157 (1973).

37. Max Farrand, ed., *Records of the Federal Convention of 1787* (New Haven: Yale University Press, 1966), 3: 101.

38. Charles W. Wolfram, "The Constitutional History of the Seventh Amendment," *Minnesota Law Review* 57 (1973): 675–76.

39. Ibid., 679.

40. Leonard Levy, *The Palladium of Justice: The Origins of Trial By Jury* (Chicago: Ivan R. Dee, 1999): 92.

41. Wolfram, "The Constitutional History of the Seventh Amendment," 664.

42. Akhil Reed Amar, "Fourth Amendment First Principles," *Harvard Law Review* 107 (1994): 775–78.

43. Farrand, *Records of the Federal Convention of 1787*, 3: 221.

44. Kalven and Zeisel, *The American Jury*, 63–65.

45. Paula L. Hannaford, B. Michael Dann, and G. Thomas Munsterman, "How Judges View Civil Juries," *DePaul Law Review* 48 (1998): 249–50.

46. Richard Lempert, "Juries, Hindsight, and Punitive Damage Awards: Failures of a Social Science Case for Change," *DePaul Law Review* 48 (1999): 884.

CHAPTER THREE. HAMMERING OUT FACTS

1. Victor Villaseñor, *Jury: The People vs. Juan Corona* (Boston: Little, Brown, 1977), 40.

2. Melvyn Bernard Zerman, *Call the Final Witness: The People v. Darrell R. Mathes as Seen by the Eleventh Juror* (New York: Harper & Row, 1977), 133.

3. Reid Hastie, Steven D. Penrod, and Nancy Pennington, *Inside the Jury* (Cambridge, Mass.: Harvard University Press, 1983), 236.

4. Villaseñor, *Jury*, 78.

5. Hastie, Penrod, and Pennington, *Inside the Jury*, 236.

6. Robert P. Burns, *A Theory of the Trial* (Princeton, N.J.: Princeton University Press, 1999), 192.

7. David Rohde, "Do Diplomas Make Jurors any Better? Maybe Not," *New York Times*, April 10, 2000, B1.

8. Hazel Thornton, *Hung Jury: The Diary of a Menendez Juror* (Philadelphia, Pa.: Temple University Press, 1995), 76, 148.

9. Zerman, *Call the Final Witness*, 152.

10. Mark Lesley with Charles Shuttleworth, *Subway Gunman: A Juror's Account of the Bernhard Goetz Trial* (Latham, N.Y.: British American Publishing, 1988), 280.

11. Villaseñor, *Jury*, 75.

12. Zerman, *Call the Final Witness*, 159.

13. Paul D. Carrington, "Law as 'The Common Thoughts of Men': The Law—Teaching and Judging of Thomas McIntyre Cooley," *Stanford Law Review* 50 (1997): 545.

14. Richard Lempert, "Civil Juries and Complex Cases: Taking Stock After Twelve Years," in Robert E. Litan, ed., *Verdict: Assessing the Civil Jury System* (Washington, D.C.: Brookings Institution, 1993), 214.

15. Michael J. Saks, "What Do Jury Experiments Tell Us About How Juries (Should) Make Decisions?" *Southern California Interdisciplinary Law Journal* 6 (1997): 43.

16. Kenneth M. Hoyt, "What Juries Know: A Trial Judge's Perspective," *South Texas Law Review* 40 (1999): 911.

17. Gerald Bullett, *The Jury* (London: J.M. Dent & Sons, 1935), 385.

18. A recent summary of such research concluded, "Many top-notch lie catchers seem to possess an inherent skill that is independent of any training. 'I'd like to know how they do it,' Dr. [Paul] Ekman[, a leading researcher on lying,] said. 'Is this somehow in their constitution?'" Erica Goode, "To Tell the Truth, It's Awfully Hard to Spot a Liar," *New York Times* May 11, 1999, F1; Aldert Vrij, *Detecting Lies and Deceit: The Psychology of Lying and the Implications for Professional Practice* (Chichester: Wiley, 2000), 68–69.

19. Vrij, *Detecting Lies and Deceit*, 7, 54.

Virj continues: "Some behaviors, while not invariably occurring during the telling of lies, do increase during the act." "It is more likely that liars show a decrease in illustrators, movements of legs and feet and subtle hand finger movements . . . , differences in speech fluency and speech rate or microfacial expressions (which last less than one-twenty-fifth of a second) of emotions. These cues are more likely to occur when the liar experiences emotions of fear, guilt or delight, and when the lie requires a lot of mental effort." "All other non-vocal characteristics (e.g., gaze aversion, smiling, self-manipulations, shifting position and eye blinks) do not consistently seem to be reliable indicators of deception. This is a striking finding, as it contradicts the stereotypical beliefs that many people hold about non-verbal indicators of deception" (54. 38).

20. Ibid., 210.

21. Goode, "To Tell the Truth," F1.

22. Vrij, *Detecting Lies and Deceit*, 95–96.

23. Ibid., 77.

24. Ibid., 88, 79.

25. Bernard Botein and Murray A. Gordon, *The Trial of the Future* (New York: Simon and Schuster, 1963), 112.In Pg Wyal's floridly written science fiction story "A Jury Not of Peers," in Joseph D. Olander and Martin Harry Greenberg, eds., *Criminal Justice Through Science Fiction* (New York: New Viewpoints, 1977), a worker on another planet killed his boss. It was decided that the world was too complex for humans to comprehend, so an infallible judging machine was built. "It could not lie. It could not feel. It had no selfish interests against which to balance its decisions, to intrude upon the cold process of reason." Although people were not sure how the device worked, "The machine's decisions were always abided" (59).

26. W. Lance Bennett and Martha S. Feldman, *Reconstructing Reality in the Courtroom: Justice and Judgment in American Culture* (New Brunswick, N.J.: Rutgers University Press, 1981), 7.

27. Burns, *A Theory of the Trial*, 222, quoting Barbara Hardy, "Toward a Poetics of Fiction," which is in turn quoted in Alasdair MacIntyre, *After Virtue* (Notre Dame, Ind.: University of Notre Dame Press, 1984), 211.

28. Norman J. Finkel, *Commonsense Justice: Jurors' Notions of the Law* (Cambridge, Mass.: Harvard University Press, 1995), 66.

29. Ibid., 67.

30. Reid Hastie and Nancy Pennington, "The O.J. Simpson Stories: Behavioral Scientists'

Reflections on the People of the State of California v. Orenthal James Simpson," *University of Colorado Law Review* 67 (1996): 968.

31. Ibid., 961.
32. Ibid.
33. Ibid.
34. Lesley and Shuttleworth, *Subway Gunman,* 275–76, 306–9.
35. Ibid., 299.
36. Zerman, *Call the Final Witness,* 8, 113.
37. Villaseñor, *Jury,* 73, 81, 227–28.
38. G. K. Chesterton, *Tremendous Trifles* (New York: Dodd, Mead, 1909), 85–87.
39. Reginald Rose, *Twelve Angry Men,* adapted by Sherman L. Sergel (Woodstock, Ill.: Dramatic Publishing, 1955), 44–45.
40. This was the instruction in a case in which I was involved.
41. Villaseñor, *Jury,* 241–43.
42. Ibid., 259.
43. The persuasive measures placed on a juror in Robert O'Neil Bristow's short story "Beyond Any Doubt," in Elizabeth Villiers Gemmette, ed., *Law in Literature* (New York: Praeger, 1992), are certainly the exception. In the story, one juror "feels" that the defendant is guilty, but still has doubts. He is the only exception as his eleven colleagues vote for conviction. Another juror, a powerful person in the small community where the trial is held, approaches the holdout and states that if he changes his vote he will get a badly needed bank loan. After internal turmoil, the holdout still votes not guilty on the next ballot, but now someone else has joined him. As the story ends, the implication is that the jury will eventually acquit.
44. Harry Kalven, Jr., "The Jury, the Law, and the Personal Injury Damage Award," *Ohio State Law Journal* 19 (1958): 176.

CHAPTER FOUR. JURIES AND COMMUNITY VALUES

1. Richard Epstein, *Torts* (Gaithersburg, Md.: Aspen Business and Law, 1999), 69.
2. Quoted in Harry Kalven, Jr., "The Dignity of the Civil Jury," *Virginia Law Review* 50 (1964): 1071, n. 35. (Emphasis added.)
3. Harry Kalven, Jr., "The Jury, the Law, and the Personal Injury Damage Award," *Ohio State Law Journal* 19 (1958): 159, 160.
4. *Railroad Co. v. Stout,* 84 U.S. 657, 664 (1874).
5. Alexis de Tocqueville, *Democracy in America* (New York: Vintage Books, 1945), 294; Kalven, "The Jury, the Law, and the Personal Injury Damage Award," 161; George L. Priest, "Justifying the Civil Jury," in Robert E. Litan, ed., *Verdict: Assessing the Civil Jury System* (Washington, D.C.: Brookings Institution, 1993), 109.
6. Priest, "Justifying the Civil Jury," 117, 124.
7. Shari Seidman Diamond, Michael J. Saks, and Stephan Landsman, "Juror Judgments About Liability and Damages: Sources of Variability and Ways to Increase Consistency," *DePaul Law Review* 48 (1998): 316.
8. *Ward v. James,* Court of Appeal [England] [1966] 1 Q.B. 273.

9. Neil Vidmar and Jeffrey J. Rice, "Assessments of Noneconomic Damage Awards in Medical Negligence: A Comparison of Jurors with Legal Professionals," *Iowa Law Review* 78: (1993), 884–85.

10. W. Page Keeton, Dan B. Dobbs, Robert E. Keeton, and David G. Owen, *Prosser and Keeton on the Law of Torts,* 5th edition (St. Paul, Minn.: West Publishing, 1984), 574.

11. Colleen P. Murphy, "Determining Compensation: The Tension Between Legislative Power and Jury Authority," *Texas Law Review* 74 (1995): 409–10.

12. Laurie Levenson, "Change of Venue and the Role of the Criminal Jury," *Southern California Law Review* 66 (1993): 1553.

13. Gary Goodpaster, "On the Theory of American Adversary Criminal Trial," *Journal of Criminal Law and Criminology* 78 (1987): 146.

14. Paul D. Carrington, "The Seventh Amendment: Some Bicentennial Reflections," *University of Chicago Law Forum* (1990): 42; Levenson, "Change of Venue and the Role of the Criminal Jury," 1556.

15. Villaseñor, *Jury,* 231.

16. Ibid., 235.

17. Villaseñor, *Jury,* 230–37.

18. Harry Kalven, Jr., and Hans Zeisel, *The American Jury* (Boston: Little, Brown, 1966), 189.

19. Levenson, "Change of Venue and the Role of the Criminal Jury," 1556.

CHAPTER FIVE. ABIDE THE ISSUE

1. Stephen Vincent Benet, *The Devil and Daniel Webster* (New York: Dramatists Play Service, 1938), 27.

2. Benet did not indicate such faith in all parts of our judicial system. Before the trial, Webster and Scratch duel over precedents, with the devil getting the upper hand. Webster hesitatingly concedes, "You seem to have an excellent acquaintance with the law, sir." Scratch responds, "Sir, that is no fault of mine. Where I come from, we have always gotten the pick of the Bar." Ibid., 25.

3. Matthew Deady, "Trial by Jury," *American Law Review* 17 (1883): 399.

4. Zechariah Chafee, Jr., *Free Speech in the United States* (Cambridge: Harvard University Press, 1964).

5. Chafee, *Free Speech in the United States,* 337–42. Similar concerns about the use of injunctions and contempt power led to an unusual provision in the federal Clayton Anti-Trust Act of 1914. This law gave labor unions some basic rights, limited the federal courts' injunctive powers in labor disputes, and provided for trial by jury in federal contempt cases. The jury trial "provision was intended as a remedy against the arbitrary conduct of many federal judges who indiscriminately issued federal injunctions in labor disputes and then convicted strikers in summary contempt procedures." Alfred H. Kelly and Winfred A. Harbison, *The American Constitution: Its Origins and Development,* 3d edition (New York: Norton, 1963), 655.

For example, an injunction against the workers was issued in the 1890s strike against the Pullman Company. Enforcement of that injunction, which had placed almost all strikers in contempt, escalated the violence in an already violent situation. President Cleveland called out the army, and "[u]ltimately more than 16,000 troops were used to break the strike." Eugene Debs and other union leaders were charged with criminal offenses and were also cited for contempt. At the contempt hearing, the judge found Debs guilty of every charge and sentenced him to six months in prison. In the criminal case, "the Government's case collapsed and with the jury reportedly poised to acquit, the prosecutors sought delay and ultimately dismissed the case." Charles A. Wright and Kenneth W. Graham, Jr., *Federal Practice and Procedure: Evidence,* vol. 30A (St. Paul, Minn.: West Group, 2000), 293–95.

The *Debs* contempt conviction went to the Supreme Court, which held that Debs had not been entitled to a jury trial in that proceeding because "The power of a court to make an order carries with it the equal power to punish for disobedience of that order. . . . To submit the question of disobedience to another tribunal, be it jury or another court, would operate to deprive the proceeding of half its efficiency." In re Debs, 158 U.S. 564, 598 (1895).

6. James Gould Cozzens, *The Just and the Unjust* (New York: Harcourt, Brace, 1942).

7. Cozzens, *The Just and the Unjust,* 427–28.

8. George P. Fletcher, *A Crime of Self Defense: Bernhard Goetz and the Law on Trial* (Chicago: University of Chicago Press, 1988), 82.

9. Neil Vidmar and Jeffrey J. Rice, "Assessments of Noneconomic Damage Awards in Medical Negligence: A Comparison of Jurors with Legal Professionals," *Iowa Law Review* 78 (1993): 900.

10. Norman J. Finkel, *Commonsense Justice: Jurors' Notions of the Law* (Cambridge, Mass.: Harvard University Press, 1995), 21, quoting T. R. Tyler, *Why People Obey the Law* (New Haven: Yale University Press, 1990).

11. These results, however, do not compare the relative satisfaction of judge and jury verdicts, because 96 percent of the trials in the survey were jury trials. But we do see that jury trials can have a value for getting litigants to accept outcomes.

12. T. J. Davis, *Rumor of Revolt: The "Great Negro Plot" in Colonial New York* (New York: Free Press, 1985), 56.

13. Michael J Saks, "Public Opinion About the Civil Jury: Can Reality Be Found in the Illusions?" *DePaul Law Review* 48 (1998): 240.

14. Paula L. Hannaford, B. Michael Dann, and G. Thomas Munsterman, "How Judges View Civil Juries," *DePaul Law Review* 48 (1998): 249–50.

15. Valerie P. Hans, "Attitudes toward the Civil Jury: A Crisis of Confidence," in Robert E. Litan, ed., *Verdict: Assessing the Civil Jury System* (Washington, D.C.: Brookings Institution, 1993), 265.

16. Peter Schuck, "Mapping the Debate on Jury Reform," in Robert E. Litan, ed., *Verdict: Assessing the Civil Jury System* (Washington, D.C.: Brookings Institution, 1993), 328.

17. Saks, "Public Opinion About the Civil Jury," 235.

18. *People v. Guzman,* 125 Misc.2d 457, 466, 478 N.Y.S.2d 455, 462 (N.Y. Co. 1984).

19. Alexis de Tocqueville, *Democracy in America* (New York: Vintage Books 1945), 295–96.

20. George L. Priest, "Justifying the Civil Jury," in Robert E. Litan, ed., *Verdict: Assessing the Civil Jury System* (Washington, D.C.: Brookings Institution, 1993), 120–24; Lisa Kern

Griffin, "'The Image We See Is Our Own': Defending the Jury's Territory at the Heart of the Democratic Process," *Nebraska Law Review* 75 (1996): 333; George P. Fletcher, *With Justice for Some: Protecting Victims' Rights in Criminal Trials* (Reading, Mass.: Addison-Wesley, 1996), 223.

21. Saks, "Public Opinion About the Civil Jury," 231; Diamond, "What Jurors Think: Expectations and Reactions of Citizens Who Serve as Jurors," in Robert E. Litan, ed., *Verdict: Assessing the Civil Jury System* (Washington, D.C.: Brookings Institution, 1993), 287.

22. Cozzens, *The Just and the Unjust*, 313.

23. Melvyn Bernard Zerman, *Call the Final Witness: The People v. Darrell R. Mathes as Seen by the Eleventh Juror* (New York: Harper and Row, 1977), 159–61.

24. Ibid., 158–63.

CHAPTER SIX. JURY SIZE AND JURY PERFORMANCE

1. *Cheff v. Schnackenberg*, 384 U.S. 373 (1966).

2. *Thompson v. Utah*, 170 U.S. 343, 353 (1898).

3. *Williams v. Florida*, 399 U.S. 78, 99 (1970).

4. Ibid., 100.

5. Ibid., 100–101.

6. *Colgrove v. Battin*, 413 U.S. 149, 159 (1973).

7. *Ballew v. Georgia*, 435 U.S. 223, 233 (1978).

8. Ibid., 236.

9. Ibid., 239.

10. Michael J. Saks, "What Do Jury Experiments Tell Us About How Juries (Should) Make Decisions?" *Southern California Interdisciplinary Journal* 6 (1997): 14; Neil Vidmar, "The Performance of the American Civil Jury: An Empirical Perspective," *Arizona Law Journal* 40 (1998): 897.

11. Robert MacCoun, "Inside the Black Box: What Empirical Research Tells Us About Decisionmaking by Civil Juries," in Robert E. Litan, ed., *Verdict: Assessing the Civil Jury System* (Washington, D.C.: Brookings Institution, 1993), 162.

12. Paul D. Carrington, "The Seventh Amendment: Some Bicentennial Reflections," *University of Chicago Law Forum* (1990): 54.

13. Saks, "What Do Jury Experiments Tell Us," 15.

14. Robert MacCoun, "Inside the Black Box," however, maintains: "Although some studies have found differences in the verdicts rendered by smaller or nonunanimous juries, these results typically may be explained by other factors. For example, some archival studies have failed to account for differences in the types of cases brought to traditional or nontraditional types of juries. More carefully controlled studies have not found differences in the rates of criminal conviction, although there may be effects on civil-jury awards. It is quite possible that the reduction in jury size has made awards more variable and therefore less predictable" (161).

15. Vidmar, "The Performance of the American Civil Jury," 897.

16. Carrington, "The Seventh Amendment," 55.

17. Ibid, 52.

18. Peter Schuck, "Mapping the Debate on Jury Reform," in Robert E. Litan, ed., *Verdict: Assessing the Civil Jury System* (Washington, D.C.: Brookings Institution, 1993), 321.

CHAPTER SEVEN. UNANIMITY AND HUNG JURIES

1. Leonard Levy, *The Palladium of Justice: The Origins of Trial by Jury* (Chicago: Ivan R. Dee, 1999), 43.
2. Majority rule is so ingrained that we seldom think about all its potential costs. In Barbara Kingsolver's *The Poisonwood Bible* (New York: HarperFlamingo, 1998), the Congo is becoming independent and struggling with western ideas of democracy. An American narrator states that the educated native

"Anatole has been explaining to me the native system of government. He says the business of throwing pebbles into bowls with the most pebbles winning an election—that was Belgium's idea of fair play, but to people here it was peculiar. To the Congolese (including Anatole himself, he confessed) it seems odd that if one man gets fifty votes and the other gets forty-nine, the first one wins altogether and the second one plumb loses. That means almost half the people will be unhappy, and according to Anatole, in a village that's left halfway unhappy you haven't heard the end of it. There is sure to be trouble somewhere down the line.

"The way it seems to work here is that you need one hundred percent. It takes a good while to get there. They talk and make deals and argue until they are pretty much all in agreement on what ought to be done" (265).
3. *Apodaca v. Oregon,* 406 U.S. 404, 410–11 (1972).
4. Ibid., 366.
5. *Burch v. Louisiana,* 441, 130, 137 (1978).
6. Roger Parloff, "Race and Juries: If It Ain't Broke," *American Lawyer* (June 1997), 5.
7. H. Lee Sarokin and G. Thomas Munsterman, "Recent Innovations in Civil Jury Trial Procedures," in Robert E. Litan, ed., *Verdict: Assessing the Civil Jury System* (Washington, D.C.: Brookings Institution, 1993), 394.
8. *Apodaca v. Oregon,* 406 U.S. at 377.
9. Michael J. Saks, "What Do Jury Experiments Tell Us About How Juries (Should) Make Decisions?" *Southern California Interdisciplinary Law Journal* 6 (1997): 33–34; Neil Vidmar, "The Performance of the American Civil Jury: An Empirical Perspective," *American Law Review* 40 (1998): 872.
10. "The List of Justice," *Los Angeles Times,* Sept. 13, 1998, B2. This figure did not include the money jurors lose from their occupations while they serve.
11. In some cases, the jury itself is concerned that its short deliberations might be perceived negatively. In the 1920s, Samuel Insull was the genius of the utility companies. His pyramiding holding companies had more than a half million bondholders and even more shareholders, so many were hurt when the corporations collapsed in the Great Depression. The federal government indicted Insull and others in a fifty-page, twenty-five-count indictment. After a lengthy trial with eighty-three witnesses, however, the jury saw no merit in the prosecution. Robert Grant and Joseph Katz, *The Great Trials of the Twenties: The Watershed Decade in America's Courtrooms* (Rockville Center, N.Y.: Sarpedon,

1998), describe the end of the trial: "Two hours after the jury began its deliberations, it found all the defendants innocent of all charges. Actually, it took the jury only five minutes to reach a verdict. But given the importance of the case, the great sums spent on investigation and prosecution, and the worldwide publicity generated, five minutes of deliberation seemed quite inadequate. Besides, [one juror] pointed out, might not so quick a verdict give rise to suspicions of bribery? So the jurors made small talk and marked time while the world waited. Two hours seemed long enough" (243).

12. Notable hung juries include the heavily reported first trial of the Menendez brothers for killing their parents and Special Prosecutor Ken Starr's trial of Susan McDougal and Julie Hiatt Steele.

In 1995 the California district attorneys reported that the rate of jury deadlocks exceeded 15 percent in parts of the state, and the next year courts in the District of Columbia reported a hung jury rate of 11 percent, higher than normal.

Jeffrey Rosen's investigation found little to support claims of increased race-based acquittals, but District of Columbia judges and prosecutors suggested to him "that they had observed a rise in hung juries, in which a lone hold out—often an African American woman—refused to convict over the furious objections of eleven black and white fellow jurors who were convinced of guilt beyond a reasonable doubt." Rosen wrote an attention-getting article in *The New Yorker* entitled "One Angry Woman" (Feb. 23 and March 3, 1997), which discussed four such cases.

13. Paula Hannaford, Valerie P. Hans, and G. Thomas Munsterman, "How Much Justice Hangs in the Balance: A New Look at Hung Jury Rates," *Judicature* 83 (1999): 61, 62, 63.

14. As quoted in ibid., 63.

15. A research summary concludes that "the overall data suggest that the number of hung juries increase with jury size." Ramon Arce, Francisca Farina, Mercedes Novo, and Delores Seijo, "In Search of Causes of Hung Juries," *Expert Evidence* 6 (1998/99): 244.

16. As quoted in Hannaford, Hans, and Munsterman, "How Much Justice Hangs in the Balance," 66.

17. Ibid.

18. Ibid., 67.

19. Kalven and Zeisel seemingly confirmed their conclusion about how much ten-to-two verdicts would reduce deadlocked juries by calculating the frequency of hung juries in jurisdictions where unanimity was required, which was 5.6 percent, with the rate in places that then permitted majority verdicts, which was 3.1 percent. They concluded, "The jurisdictions that allow majority verdicts have 45 per cent fewer hung juries than those that require unanimity. This result is very close to the 42 per cent measure we derived above for this difference by a different route." Harry Kalven, Jr., and Hans Zeisel, *The American Jury* (Boston: Little, Brown 1966), 461.

Five of the states Kalven and Zeisel surveyed then permitted majority verdicts in criminal cases, although only two required a ten-to-two, or five-sixths, majority, while one required a two-thirds vote, and the other two required three-fourths. The hung jury rate, then, in these jurisdictions does not truly indicate the rate where the decision rule required a ten-to-two majority. Furthermore, that rate was derived from only sixty-four trials that produced but two hung juries. Numbers this small may not be stable. Obviously, just one fewer hung jury or two more would have greatly changed the percentages.

20. Parloff, "Race and Juries," 5. Although the hung jury rates for California often appear to be much higher than the 5.5 percent rate Kalven and Zeisel found, Kalven and Zeisel's data show a 1.3 percent rate of hung juries nationwide split eleven to one for conviction, a statistic close to the California number.

21. Kalven and Zeisel, *The American Jury,* 462–63.

22. It does happen, however. Hans Zeisel and Shari Seidman Diamond, "The Jury Selection in the Mitchell-Stans Conspiracy Trial," *American Bar Foundation Research Journal* (1976): 151, describe the Watergate-era trial of Mitchell Stans as being as close to *Twelve Angry Men* as any case where one person convinced the other eleven jurors to acquit.

In real life the initial lone holdout almost never convinces the others and hardly ever even maintains his own views to the end of deliberations, forcing a hung jury. It is a recurrent theme, however, in popular culture. In Robert O'Neill Bristow's short story, "Beyond Any Doubt" in Elizabeth Villiers Gemmette, ed., *Law and Literature: Legal Themes in Short Stories* (Praeger: New York, 1992), for example, the first jury vote is eleven to one for conviction, but at the end of the story the reader sees that eventually the jury will acquit. In Gerald Bullett's excellent British mystery *The Jury* (London: J.M. Dent & Sons, 1935), on the initial vote only one juror is against conviction, but the jury ends up acquitting the defendant of murdering his wife. The situation is different in William Faulkner's 1940 short story "Tomorrow" (reprinted in William Faulkner, *Knight's Gambit* (New York: Vintage Books, 1978)), where only one juror throughout votes for a conviction.

In addition to *Twelve Angry Men,* other movies have used the device of one juror standing firm against eleven. Indeed, Faulkner's "Tomorrow" is one of them. It was adapted for a 1972 movie, after first appearing as a television movie in 1960 and being written as a stage play in 1963.

The theme of one holdout juror in American movies dates back to at least 1927. In the comedy *Ladies of the Jury,* one juror convinces the rest of the jury to acquit. In a movie from 1937, *We're on the Jury,* another character holds out and eventually gets an acquittal. In the previous year, a British movie, *Jury's Evidence,* saw the foreman trying to persuade the rest of the jury that the defendant did not kill his wife, and Gildersleeve held out for an acquittal in the 1943 movie, *Gildersleeve's Bad Day,* as did Miss Marple in 1964 in *Murder Most Foul.* In a less dignified manner, Pauly Shore also is the initial lone holdout in *Jury Duty,* made in 1995.

In variations on this theme, *Trial by Jury* (1994) and *The Juror* (1996), jurors sitting on organized crime trials are terrorized into voting for an acquittal and trying to convince their fellow jury members to acquit.

Kalven and Zeisel's data indicate that, in fact, in only 7 out of 146 instances was the initial minority's preference reflected in a verdict. This works out to 4.8 percent. Kalven and Zeisel, *The American Jury,* 488. See also Nancy J. King, "Postconviction Review of Jury Discrimination: Measuring Effects of Jury Race on Jury Decisions," *Michigan Law Review* 92 (1993), 98.

Civil cases, on the other hand, may have more fluidity in juror movement. Shari Seidman Diamond, "What Jurors Think: Expectations and Reactions of Citizens Who Serve as Jurors," in Robert E. Litan, ed., *Verdict: Assessing the Civil Jury System* (Washington, D.C.: Brookings Institution, 1993), notes, "Thirty percent of jurors questioned in . . . [a] survey, for example, reported that the verdict reached by the jury was not the one favored by a majority at the start of deliberations. Deliberations may play a larger role in civil cases in part because a variety of viewpoints and extensive avenues for compromise are available when damages are involved; an initial majority may exist only on the issue of liability" (297).

23. Reid Hastie, Steven D. Penrod, and Nancy Pennington, *Inside the Jury* (Cambridge, Mass.: Harvard University Press, 1993), 228–29; Saks, "What Do Jury Experiments Tell Us ," 4041; Robert MacCoun, "Inside the Black Box: What Empirical Research Tells Us About Decisionmaking by Civil Juries," in Robert E. Litan, ed., *Verdict: Assessing the Civil Jury System* (Washington, D.C.: Brookings Institution, 1993), 161.

24. Hastie et al., *Inside the Jury,* 229; Saks, "What Do Jury Experiments Tell Us," 41.

25. Hastie et al., *Inside the Jury,* 229.

26. Lisa Kern Griffin, "'The Image We See Is Our Own': Defending the Jury's Territory at the Heart of the Democratic Process," *Nebraska Law Review* 75 (1996): 375.

27. Parloff, "Race and Juries," 74.

CHAPTER EIGHT. THE VICINAGE

1. Remnants of the ordeal system sprang up in colonial America. Benjamin Franklin wrote in 1730 about a Mount Holly, New Jersey, witch trial. Some people had been accused of "making their Neighbours' Sheep dance in an uncommon manner, and with causing Hogs to speak and sing Psalms, etc., to the great Terror and Amazement of the king's good and peaceable Subjects in this Province; and the Accusers, being very positive that if the Accused were weighed in Scales against a Bible, the Bible would prove too heavy for them; or that, if they were bound and put into the River they would swim." Those accused agreed to the tests if the accusers would undergo the same ordeals. The supposed "Wizard was first put in the Scale, and over him was read a Chapter of the Books of Moses and then the Bible was put in the other Scale, (which being kept down before) was immediately let go; but, to the great Surprize of the Spectators, Flesh and Bones came down plump, and outweighed that great good Book by abundance." Gravity had a similar effect on the rest, and trial by water ensued. All but one floated, and the one sinker remained mostly on the surface. An accused who did not sink, "being surpriz'd at his own Swimming, was not so confident of his Innocence as before, but said, 'If I am a Witch, it is more than I know.'" An accuser who floated claimed that the accused had bewitched her to make her so light, but Franklin concluded, "The more thinking Part of the Spectators were of Opinion that any Person so bound and placed in the Water (unless they were mere Skin and Bones) would swim, till their breath was gone, and their Lungs fill'd with Water." Benjamin Franklin, *Autobiography and Selected Writings,* ed. Larzer Ziff (New York: Holt, Rinehart and Winston, 1959), 192–94.

2. For the early adoption of the jury and its change from an active to a passive group, see Frederick Pollock and Frederic W. Maitland, *The History of English Law,* vol. 2, 2d edition (Cambridge: Cambridge University Press 1968 [1895]), 595–602, 616–27; A. T. Carter, *A History of English Legal Institutions* (Littleton, Colo.: Fred B. Rothman 1986

[1902]), 199–221; Harold Potter, *An Historical Introduction to English Law and Its Institutions* (London: Sweet and Maxwell 1932), 218–25, 255–61; R. C. Van Caenegem, 2d edition (Cambridge: Cambridge University Press 1973), 62–84.

3. Quoted in William Wirt Blume, "The Place of Trial of Criminal Cases: Constitutional Vicinage and Venue," *Michigan Law Review* 43 (1944): 65–66.

4. Julius Goebel, Jr., and T. Raymond Naughton, *Law Enforcement in Colonial New York: A Study in Criminal Procedure (1664–1776)* (Montclair, N.J.: Patterson Smith, 1970), 603–4; Arthur P. Scott, *Criminal Law in Colonial Virginia* (Chicago: University of Chicago Press, 1930), 87.

5. Such a broad notion of vicinage worked a hardship and may have damaged accurate verdicts in some early trials. In the 1790s, for example, many in western Pennsylvania refused to pay a federal excise tax on whiskey. "[H]istorians agree that the tax threatened the economic survival of small farmers on the frontier who brewed for themselves and their neighbors, and this tax was supported by large Eastern distillers who could afford the tax and its attendant record-keeping requirements with greater ease. . . . [A] notable grievance was the provision for trials for violations of the excise in the federal court in Philadelphia. The notion that westerners were being denied a trial of the vicinage was heightened when the U.S. Attorney refused to stipulate that violators could use depositions in their defense rather than go to the expense of dragging their witnesses clear across the Alleghenies to testify." Charles A. Wright and Kenneth W. Graham, *Federal Practice and Procedure: Evidence,* vol. 30A (St. Paul, Minn.: West Group, 2000), 9.

6. Drew L. Kershen, "Vicinage," *Oklahoma Law Review* 33 (1977): 79.

7. Martha Minow, "Stripped Down Like a Runner or Enriched by Experience: Bias and Impartiality of Judges and Jurors," *William and Mary Law Review* 33 (1992), 1205, quoting Lon Fuller, "The Forms and Limits of Adjudication," *Harvard Law Review* 92 (1978): 391.

8. Concern that parties try to affect the attitudes of potential jurors predates the growth of the modern public relations industry. J. Fenimore Cooper's last novel, *The Ways of the Hour* (Phoenix Mill, U.K.: Alan Sutton Publishing, 1996 [1850]), centers on a criminal trial in a rural New York town where the pool of potential jurors is known and small. A local practitioner explains "horse-shedding" and "pillowing" to the defense lawyer, a Manhattan attorney:

"'Horse-shedding . . . explains itself. In the country most of the jurors, witnesses, &c, have more or less to do with the horse-sheds, if it's only to see their beasts are fed. Well, we keep proper talkers there, and it must be a knotty case indeed into which the ingenious hand cannot thrust a doubt or an argument. . . .'

"'But how is that done?—do you present your arguments directly, as in court?'

"'Lord bless you, no. In court, unless the jury happen to be unusually excellent, counsel have to pay some little regard to the testimony and the law; but, in horse-shedding, one has no need of either. A skillful horse-shedder, for instance, will talk a party to pieces, and not say a word about the case. That's the perfection of the business. It's against the law . . . to talk of a case before a juror—an indictable offense—but one may make a case of a party's general character, of his means, his miserly qualities, or his aristocracy; and it will be hard to get hold of the talker for any of them qualities' " (84).

"Pillowing" was the comparable activity undertaken in inns where a number of beds were placed in the same room. "'The conversation is the most innocent and nat'ral in the world; not a word too much or too little, but it sticks like a bur. The juror is a plain, simple-minded countryman, and swallows all that his room-mates say, and goes into the box next day in a beautiful frame of mind to listen to reason and evidence!' " (88).

After this education lesson, the country practitioner working for the defense pays members of the press for writing paragraphs favorable to the client, but he does not stop there: " *Talkers* was what he wanted; and well did he know where to find them. . . . A few he paid in a direct, business-like way. . . . These confidential agents went to work with experienced discretion but great industry, and soon had some ten or fifteen fluent female friends actively engaged in circulating 'They says,' in their respective neighbourhoods" (96).

See also *Richmond Newspaper, Inc. v. Virginia,* 448 U.S. 555 (1980); *Waller v. Georgia,* 467 U.S. 39 (1984), which stated that for a hearing or trial to be closed to the press or public: (1) the party seeking to close the hearing must advance an overriding interest that is likely to be prejudiced; (2) the closure must be no broader than necessary to protect that interest; (3) the court must consider reasonable alternatives to closure; and (4) the court must make findings adequate to support the closure.

The Supreme Court has never held that the media have a right to broadcast court proceedings, but it has held that states may permit televised trials even if an accused objects. *Chandler v. Florida,* 449 U.S. 560 (1981). Judges who have conducted televised trials generally conclude that the broadcasting has little effect on the trial and its participants. On the other hand, televising has not had the educative value that many judges had hoped for, because the coverage usually contains few explanations about legal processes. Ralph E. Roberts, "An Empirical and Normative Analysis of the Impact of Televised Courtroom Proceedings," *Southern Methodist University Law Review* 51 (1998).

9. *Mu'Min v. Virginia,* 500 U.S. 415 (1991).
10. Michael J. Saks, "What Do Jury Experiments Tell Us About How Juries (Should) Make Decisions?" *Southern California Interdisciplinary Law Journal* 6 (1997): 18.
11. Victor Villaseñor, *Jury: The People vs. Juan Corona* (Boston: Little, Brown, 1977), 187.
12. Seymour Wishman, *Anatomy of a Jury* (New York: Penguin, 1986), 91.
13. Lawrence S. Wrightsman and Amy J. Posey, "Psychological Commentary on the Diary," in Hazel Thornton, ed., *Hung Jury: The Diary of a Menendez Juror* (Philadelphia, Pa.: Temple University Press, 1995), 112.
14. Laurie Levenson, "Change of Venue and the Role of the Criminal Jury," *Southern California Law Review* 66 (1993): 1539, n. 27.

CHAPTER NINE. THE MOST DIVERSE OF OUR DEMOCRATIC BODIES

1. Albert W. Alschuler and Andrew G. Deiss, "A Brief History of the Criminal Jury in the United States," *University of Chicago Law Review* 61 (1994): 886.
2. *Strauder v. Virginia,* 100 U.S. 303 (1880).
3. Linda K. Kerber, *No Constitutional Right to Be Ladies: Women and Obligations of Citizenship* (New York: Hill and Wang, 1998), 144.
4. Quoted in Kerber, *No Constitutional Right to Be Ladies,* 137. Quoted in Alschuler and Deiss, "A Brief History of the Criminal Jury," 900.

5. Quoted in Kerber, *No Constitutional Right to Be Ladies*, 142.

6. *Glasser v. United States*, 315 U.S. 60 (1942).

7. *Thiel v. Southern Pacific*, 328 U.S. 217 (1946).

8. *United States v. Ballard*, 329 U.S. 187 (1946).

9. *Hoyt v. Florida*, 368 U.S. 57, 62 (1961).

10. *Taylor v. Louisiana*, 419 U.S. 522 (1975).

11. Ibid., 531.

12. Ibid., 535–38.

13. Ibid., 538.

14. *Duren v. Missouri*, 439 U.S. 357 (1979).

15. Laura Gaston Dooley, "Our Juries, Our Selves: The Power, Perception, and Politics of the Civil Jury," *Cornell Law Review* 80 (1995): 325 n. 3.

16. See, e.g., Boynton Merrill, Jr., *Jefferson's Nephews: A Frontier Tragedy* (New York: Avon, 1976), 152.

17. Gerard S. Petrone, *Judgment at Gallatin: The Trial of Frank James* (Lubbock, Tex.: Texas Tech University Press, 1998), 76.

18. Seymour Wishman, *Anatomy of a Jury* (New York: Penguin, 1986), 28.

19. Kerber, *No Constitutional Right to Be Ladies*, 154.

20. Nancy J. King, "Juror Delinquency in Criminal Trials in America, 1796–1996," *Michigan Law Review* 94 (1996): 2692 n. 73.

21. James Oldham, "The History of the Special (Struck) Jury in the United States and Its Relation to Voir Dire Practices, the Reasonable Cross-Section Requirement, and Peremptory Challenges," *William and Mary Bill of Rights Journal* 6 (1998): 626, quoting *Rex v. Gasciogne*, 7 State Trials 959, 963 (K.B. 1680).

22. *Fay v. New York*, 332 U.S. 261 (1947); *Moore v. New York*, 333 U.S. 565 (1948).

23. Oldham, "The History of the Special (Struck) Jury," 627.

24. Jonathan D. Casper, "Restructuring the Traditional Civil Jury: The Effects of Changes in Composition and Procedures," in Robert E. Litan, ed., *Verdict: Assessing the Civil Jury System* (Washington, D.C.: Brookings Institution, 1993), 431.

25. Ibid., 432.

26. Peter Aranson, David E. Rovella, and Bob Van Voris, "Jurors: A Biased Lot," *National Law Journal*, Nov. 2, 1998, 1.

27. Douglas Greenberg, *Crime and Law Enforcement in the Colony of New York: 1691–1776* (Ithaca, N.Y.: Cornell University Press, 1976), 172; Leo Hershkowitz, *Tweed's New York: Another Look* (Garden City, N.Y.: Anchor Books, 1978), 235; King, "Juror Delinquency in Criminal Trials in America," 2688.

28. Wishman, *Anatomy of a Jury*, 12.

29. Dooley, "Our Juries, Our Selves," 325–26; Robert P. Burns, *A Theory of the Trial* (Princeton, N.J.: Princeton University Press, 1999), 8–9.

CHAPTER TEN. CHALLENGES FOR CAUSE

1. Hans Zeisel and Shari Seidman Diamond, "The Jury Selection in the Mitchell-Stans Conspiracy Trial," *American Bar Foundation Journal* (1976), explain, "The French name

seems to mean 'see them talk' but in fact means 'truth talk,' *voir* being a corruption of the Latin *verus*" (172 n. 28).

2. James Gobert, *Justice, Democracy and the Jury* (Brookfield, Vt.: Ashgate Publishing, 1997), 144–45.

3. *Mu'Min v. Virginia*, 500 U.S. 415 (1990); *Ham v. South Carolina*, 409 U.S. 524 (1973).

4. *Ham v. South Carolina*, 409 U.S. 524 (1973); *Ristaino v. Ross*, 424 U.S. 589 (1976). Capital cases provide a narrow exception. The Court has held that the sentencing jury in a capital case must be asked about racial prejudice when the accused is charged with an interracial crime. *Turner v. Murray*, 476 U.S. 28 (1986). In that case, where such questions were not asked, the conviction was allowed to stand but the sentence was vacated.

5. At one time it was common in civil cases for the voir dire to be conducted by the attorneys in the absence of the judge. This process generally resulted in a longer jury selection process because without a judge present to push the proceedings along, the attorneys often questioned for longer periods of time. In addition, the parties often jointly agreed to excuse certain jurors, in effect expanding the number of available peremptory challenges. Voir dire without the trial judge is less common today.

6. Albert W. Alschuler, "The Supreme Court and the Jury: Voir Dire, Peremptory Challenges, and the Review of Jury Verdicts," *University of Chicago Law Review* (1989), 158. Lengthy jury selections have occurred regularly throughout our history. For example, it took three days to pick the jury in the 1880s trial of Frank James [Gerard Petrone, *Judgment at Gallatin: The Trial of Frank James* (Lubbock, Tex.: Texas Tech University Press, 1998), 82]; two weeks and the examination of 502 prospective jurors to pick the jury in the 1899 murder trial of Roland Molineux [Samuel Klaus, ed., *The Molineux Case* (Holmes Beach, Fla.: Gaunt Reprint, 1997 [1929]), 24]; and three weeks in 1907 to select the jury for the trial of Big Bill Haywood and others for the murder of Idaho Governor Frank Steunenberg [J. Anthony Lukas, *Big Trouble: A Murder in a Small Western Town Sets off a Struggle for the Soul of America* (New York: Simon and Schuster, 1997), 539]. Interestingly, the 1931 jury that convicted Al Capone of income tax evasion was selected in less than a day. John Kobler, *Capone: The Life and World of Al Capone* (New York: Fawcett Crest, 1971), 317.

7. Stephen Phillips, *No Heroes, No Villains: The Story of a Murder Trial* (New York: Vintage Books, 1978), 137.

8. Neil Vidmar, "Generic Prejudice and the Presumption of Guilt in Sex Abuse Trials," *Law and Human Behavior* 21 (1997): 18.

9. Lukas, *Big Trouble*, 528.

10. Nancy J. King, "Juror Delinquency in Criminal Trials in America, 1796–1996," *Michigan Law Review* 94 (1996), 2690; Seymour Wishman, *Anatomy of a Jury* (New York: Penguin, 1986), 80–81.

11. Newton N. Minow and Fred H. Cate, "Who Is an Impartial Juror in an Age of Mass Media?" *American University Law Review* 40 (1991): 651. Minow and Cate conclude, "Potential jurors are influenced by a desire to get the 'right' answer, find approval from the judge, and be in the majority. . . . The fact that fewer jurors admit to bias as the voir dire questioning process continues suggests that potential jurors learn from their colleagues the 'right' answers to the voir dire questions." Ibid.

12. John Guinther, "The Jury in America," in *American Civil Jury* (Washington, D.C.: Roscoe Pound–American Trial Lawyers Association, 1996), 49.

13. Alschuler, "The Supreme Court and the Jury," 206.

14. Morris B. Hoffman, "Peremptory Challenges," *The Green Bag* 3 (2000), 139.

15. Minow and Cate, "Who Is an Impartial Juror in an Age of Mass Media?." report that "Repeated studies have concluded that jurors tend not to speak out during voir dire, nor admit to their true prejudices and preconceptions" (650).

16. Wishman, *Anatomy of a Jury*, 84.

17. Hans Zeisel and Shari Seidman Diamond, "The Effect of Peremptory Challenges on Jury and Verdict: An Experiment in a Federal District Court," *Stanford Law Review* 30 (1978): 512.

18. Phillips, *No Heroes, No Villains*, 132–33.

19. *New York Criminal Procedure Law*, Sec. 270.20.

20. Canada has a much different system for determining challenges for cause. Jurors are presumed to follow their oath of impartiality and are not questioned in the same way potential jurors are in an American voir dire. Normally all that is known about a juror is age, gender, demeanor, and perhaps occupation. If, however, the attorney can convince the judge that there are reasons to question the impartiality of the juror, a few questions may be put to the witness about her state of mind regarding her ability to impartially weigh the evidence. "Unlike the practice in the United States, the judge does not decide which jurors are not impartial! Rather, two lay 'triers' selected from the jury pool are sworn to hear the prospective juror's answers. These triers actually deliberate as a sort of mini-jury and render a verdict on whether the juror is or is not impartial." Vidmar, "Generic Prejudice and the Presumption of Guilt," 9.

21. *Witherspoon v. Illinois,* 391 U.S. 510 (1968); *Wainwright v. Witt,* 469 U.S. 412 (1985).

22. *Lockhart v. McCree,* 476 U.S. 162 (1986).

23. Ibid., 174.

24. Ibid., 178.

25. Ibid., 180.

26. William J. Bowers, Marla Sandys, and Benjamin D. Steiner, "Foreclosed Impartiality in Capital Sentencing: Jurors' Predisposition, Guilt-Trial Experience, and Premature Decision Making," *Cornell Law Review* 83 (1998): 1506–7.

27. Charles H. Whitebread and Christopher Slobogin, *Criminal Procedure: An Analysis of Cases and Concepts* (New York: Foundation Press, 2000), 737.

CHAPTER ELEVEN. PEREMPTORY CHALLENGES

1. Paul R. Lynd, "Juror Sexual Orientation: The Fair Cross-Section Requirement, Privacy, Challenges for Cause, and Peremptories," *UCLA Law Review* 46 (1998): 233–34.

2. *Swain v. Alabama,* 380 U.S. 202 (1965).

3. Steven Phillips, *No Heroes, No Villains: The Story of a Murder Trial* (New York: Vintage Books, 1978), 133.

4. Melvyn Bernard Zerman, *Call the Final Witness: The People v. Darrell R. Mathes as Seen by the Eleventh Juror* (New York: Harper and Row, 1977), 46.

5. *Batson v. Kentucky,* 476 U.S. 79 (1986); *J.E.B. v. Alabama,* 511 U.S. 127 (1994); *Georgia v. McCollum,* 502 U.S. 1056 (1992).

6. *Purkett v. Elem,* 514 U.S. 765 (1995).

7. Ibid.; *Hernandez v. New York,* 500 U.S. 352 (1991).

8. *People v. Randall,* 671 N.E.2d 60, 65–66 (Ill. App. Ct. 1996).

9. *Purkett v. Elem,* 514 U.S. 765 (1995).

10. Ibid.

11. Leonard I. Cavise, "The Batson Doctrine: The Supreme Court's Utter Failure to Meet the Challenge of Discrimination in Jury Selection," *Wisconsin Law Review* (1999): 527–28; Susan Hightower, "Sex and the Peremptory Strike: An Empirical Analysis of J.E.B. v. Alabama's First Five Years," *Stanford Law Review* 52 (2000); Jean Montoya, "The Future of the Post-Batson Peremptory Challenge: Voir Dire by Questionnaire and the 'Blind' Peremptory," *University of Michigan Journal of Law Reform* 29 (1996); 1004; Cavise, "The Batson Doctrine," 501.

12. Mark Cammack, "In Search of the Post-Positivist Jury," *Indiana Law Journal* 70 (1995): 455–56.

13. J. Anthony Lukas, *Big Trouble: A Murder in a Small Western Town Sets off a Struggle for the Soul of America* (New York: Simon and Schuster, 1997), 527.

14. F. A. MacKenzie, *The Trial of Harry Thaw* (London: Geoffrey Bles, 1928), 210.

15. Ludovic Kennedy, *The Airman and the Carpenter: The Lindbergh Kidnaping and the Framing of Richard Hauptmann* (New York: Viking, 1985), 246.

16. Ibid., 246–47.

17. Wayne R. LaFave, Jerold Israel, and Nancy J. King, *Criminal Procedure* (St. Paul, Minn.: West Group, 2000), 1040.

18. Douglas D. Koski, "Sex Crime Jury Selection: A Social Scientific Analysis," *Criminal Law Bulletin* 35 (1999): 51; Dale W. Broeder, "Voir Dire Examinations: An Empirical Study," *Southern California Law Review* 38 (1965): 503.

19. Koski, "Sex Crime Jury Selection," 42; Broeder, "Voir Dire Examinations," 505.

20. Tracy Kennedy and Judith Kennedy with Alan Abrahamson, *Mistrial of the Century: A Private Diary of the Jury System on Trial* (Beverly Hills, Calif.: Dove Book 1995), 28–33.

21. *Brandborg v. Lucas,* 891 F.Supp. 352, 355 (E.D. Texas 1995).

22. Ibid., 360–61.

CHAPTER TWELVE. "SCIENTIFIC" JURY SELECTION

1. Franklin Strier and Donna Shestowsky, "Profiling the Profilers: A Study of the Trial Consulting Profession, Its Impact on Trial, Justice, and What, If Anything, to Do About It," *Wisconsin Law Review* (1999), 443.

2. Gerry Spence, *O. J.: The Last Word* (New York: St. Martin's Press, 1997), 136.

3. Strier and Shestowsky, "Profiling the Profilers," 450–51.

4. Franklin Strier, "Whither Trial Consulting? Issues and Projections," *Law and Human Behavior* 23 (1999): 98.

5. James W. Loewen, *Lies My Teacher Told Me: Everything Your American History Textbook Got Wrong* (New York: The New Press, 1995), 297–302.

6. Reid Hastie, Steven D. Penrod, and Nancy Pennington, *Inside the Jury* (Cambridge, Mass.: Harvard University Press, 1983), 127.

7. Strier and Shestowsky, "Profiling the Profilers," 459.

8. Ibid., 459.

9. Jonathan Harr, *A Civil Action* (New York: Random House, 1995), 284–85.

10. Reid Hastie, "Is Attorney-Conducted Voir Dire an Effective Procedure for the Selection of Impartial Juries?" *American Law Review* 40 (1991): 724.

11. Strier, "Whither Trial Consulting?" 102.

12. Harr, *A Civil Action*, 268.

13. Robert MacCoun, "Inside the Black Box: What Empirical Research Tells Us About Decisionmaking by Civil Juries," in Robert E. Litan, ed., *Verdict: Assessing the Civil Jury System* (Washington, D.C.: Brookings Institution, 1993),151; Hastie, Penrod, and Pennington, *Inside the Jury*, 128.

14. Hastie, Penrod, and Pennington, *Inside the Jury*, 129–30; Reid Hastie and Nancy Pennington, "The O.J. Simpson Stories: Behavioral Scientists' Reflections on *People v. Orenthal James Simpson*," *University of Colorado Law Review* 67 (1996), 975.

15. John Grisham, *The Runaway Jury* (New York: Island Books, 1996), 4.

16. Jessica L. Cadorine, "A Novel Look at Juries: Representations of Juries in Six Works of Contemporary Popular Fiction" (unpublished manuscript, 2000).

17. Laurence H. Geller and Peter Hemenway, *Last Chance for Justice: The Juror's Lonely Quest* (Dallas, Tex.: NCDS Press, 1997), 296.

18. *Hamer v. United States,* 259 F.2d 274 (9th Cir. 1958).

19. See Strier and Shestowsky, "Profiling the Profilers," 494.

20. Ibid., 488.

21. Hastie and Pennington, "The O.J. Simpson Stories," 975.

22. *Lewis v. United States,* 146 U.S. 370, 378 (1892); *Ross v. Oklahoma,* 487 U.S. 81, 89 (1988).

23. H. Lee Sarokin and G. Thomas Munsterman, "Recent Innovations in Civil Jury Trial Procedures," in Robert E. Litan, ed., *Verdict: Assessing the Civil Jury System* (Washington, D.C.: Brookings Institution, 1993), 384.

24. Morris B. Hoffman, "Abolishing Peremptory Challenges," *Judicature* 82 (1999): 203.

25. Morris B. Hoffman, "Peremptory Challenges," *Green Bag* 3 (2000): 135–36; Toni M. Massaro, "Peremptories or Peers?—Rethinking Sixth Amendment Doctrine, Images, and Procedures," *North Carolina Law Review* 64 (1986): 525; Hoffman, "Peremptory Challenges," 139.

26. Hoffman, "Peremptory Challenges," 140.

27. Michael J. Saks, "What Do Jury Experiments Tell Us About How Juries (Should) Make Decisions?" *Southern California Interdisciplinary Law Journal* 6 (1997): 12.

28. Barbara Allen Babcock, "A Place in the Palladium: Women's Rights and Jury Service," *University of Cincinnati Law Review* 61 (1993):1176.

29. Ibid., quoting William Blackstone, Commentaries 1714 (3d edition, 1894), 3.

30. Albert Alschuler, "The Supreme Court and the Jury: Voir Dire, Peremptory Challenges, and the Review of Jury Verdicts," *University of Chicago Law Review* 56 (1989): 206.

31. Ibid.; Gordon Van Kessel, "Adversary Excesses in the American Criminal Trial," *Notre Dame Law Review* 67 (1992): 537–38.

32. Babcock, "A Place in the Palladium," 1175–76.

CHAPTER THIRTEEN. THE ADVERSARY SYSTEM

1. J. M. Beattie, "Scales of Justice: Defense Counsel and English Criminal Trial in the Eighteenth and Nineteenth Centuries," *Law and History Review* 9 (1991): 222.
2. Stephan A. Landsman, "The Rise of the Contentious Spirit: Adversary Procedure in Eighteenth Century England," *Cornell Law Review* 75 (1990): 514; J. F. Stephen, *A History of the Criminal Law in England,* vol. 1 (London: MacMillan, 1883), 424.
3. Beattie, "Scales of Justice," 233–34.
4. Randolph N. Jonakait, "The Origins of the Confrontation Clause: An Alternative History," *Rutgers Law Journal* 27 (1995).
5. See, e.g., *United States v. Cronic,* 466 U.S. 668, 685 (1984), where the Court stated that "the adversarial process [is] protected by the Sixth Amendment." In *Faretta v. California,* 422 U.S. 806, 818 (1975), the Supreme Court stated, "The Sixth Amendment includes a compact statement of the rights necessary to a full defense. . . . [T]hese rights are basic to our adversary system of criminal justice. . . . In short, the Amendment constitutionalizes the right in an adversary criminal trial to make a defense as we know it."
6. Gary Goodpaster, "On the Theory of American Adversary Criminal Trial," *Journal of Criminal Law and Criminology* 78 (1987): 124.
7. Stephen S. Saltzburg, "Lawyers, Clients, and the Adversary System," *Mercer Law Review* 37 (1986): 656.
8. Italy is an exception. In 1989, it modified its traditional civil law methods in criminal cases. After extensive research into different systems, it adopted an American-style adversarial procedure where attorneys for the prosecution and defense control the gathering and presentation of the evidence and conduct direct examination and cross-examination of witnesses. A jury, however, is not used. The trial court consists of a mixed bench of professional and lay judges, which does produce a written judgment.
   Many places in Latin America once used juries. They have been abandoned everywhere, except for some criminal matters in Brazil.
9. Max Frankel, "The Search for Truth: An Umpireal View," *University of Pennsylvania Law Review* 123 (1975): 1036.
10. John Jackson, "Theories of Truth Finding in Criminal Procedure: An Evolutionary Approach," *Cardozo Law Review* 10 (1988), states, "[I]t is hard to see how it could be empirically proved that one system is better at truth finding, for the simple reason that it is impossible to know in any particular system how many truly guilty are convicted and how many truly innocent are acquitted" (485).
11. Franklin Strier, "Making Jury Trials More Truthful," *University of California Davis Law Review* 95 (1996): 104.
12. Stephan A. Landsman, *Readings on Adversarial Justice: The American Approach to Adjudication* (St. Paul, Minn.: West Publishing, 1988), 34.
13. Robert P. Burns, *A Theory of the Trial* (Princeton, N.J.: Princeton University Press, 1999), 78–9.
14. Ibid., 80.
15. Ibid., 80–81.
16. Our trial system of separating functions has another advantage. Aldert Vrij, *Detecting*

Lies and Deceit: The Psychology of Lying and the Implications for Professional Practice (Chichester, U.K.: Wiley, 2000), 70, summarizes research showing that observers are more accurate in detecting lies than are interviewers because the observers can better concentrate on the speakers and what is said than can the interviewers. A judge eliciting testimony and simultaneously assessing credibility is, thus, not as well situated as a jury for detecting falsehoods.

17. Charles A. Wright and Kenneth W. Graham, Jr., *Federal Practice and Procedure: Evidence* 30A (St. Paul, Minn.: West Group, 2000), 730; Nancy Brekke, Peter J. Enko, Gail Clavet, and Eric Seelau, "Of Juries and Court-Appointed Experts: The Impact of Non-adversarial versus Adversarial Expert Testimony," *Land and Human Behavior* 15 (1991): 452.

18. Landsman, *Readings on Adversarial Justice,* 28.

19. George P. Fletcher, *A Crime of Self-Defense: Bernhard Goetz and the Law on Trial* (Chicago: University of Chicago Press, 1988), 7–8.

20. Shari Seidman Diamond, Jonathan D. Casper, Cami L. Heiert, and Anna-Maria Marshall, "Juror Reaction to Attorneys at Trial," *Journal of Criminal Law and Criminology* 87 (1996): 42–43; Strier, "Making Jury Trials More Truthful," 98; Harry Kalven, Jr. and Hans Zeisel, *The American Jury* (Boston: Little, Brown, 1966), 351.

21. Diamond et al., "Juror Reaction to Attorneys at Trial," 43. (Emphasis added.)

22. Ibid., 44.

23. Kalven and Zeisel, *The American Jury,* 354, 371.

24. Edward Connors, Thomas Lundgren, Neal Miller, and Tom McEwen, *Convicted by Juries, Exonerated by Science: Case Studies in the Use of DNA Evidence to Establish Innocence After Trial* (Washington, D.C.: National Institutes of Justice, 1996), xvii, xxx.

CHAPTER FOURTEEN. PRESENTATION OF EVIDENCE

1. *Federal Rules of Evidence* 403.

2. Franklin Strier, "Making Jury Trials More Truthful," *University of California Davis Law Review* 95 (1996): 138–39.

3. Richard Lempert, "Civil Juries and Complex Cases: Taking Stock After Twelve Years," in Robert E. Litan, ed., *Verdict: Assessing the Civil Jury System* (Washington, D.C.: Brookings Institution, 1993), 222.

4. William W. Schwarzer, "Reforming Jury Trials," *Federal Rules Decision* 132 (1991): 591.

5. For example, the Mississippi Supreme Court has stated:

"The most obvious problem with allowing jurors to question witnesses is the unfamiliarity of jurors with the rules of evidence. . . . Other potential problems included (1) Counsel may be forced to either make an objection to a question in front of the juror who asks the question, at the risk of offending the juror, or withhold the objection and permit prejudicial testimony to come in without objection; (2) juror objectivity and impartiality may be lessened or lost; (3) if a juror submits a question in open court, the other jurors are informed as to what the questioning juror is thinking, which may begin the deliberation process before the evidence is concluded and before the final instructions from the court; (4) if the juror is permitted to question the witness directly, the interaction may create tension or antagonism in the juror; and (5) the procedure may disrupt court-room decorum.

"Our prior warnings concerning juror questioning have apparently gone unheeded. Today we hold that juror interrogation is no longer to be left to the discretion of the trial court, but rather is a practice that is condemned and outright forbidden by the Court." *Wharton v. State*, 734 So.2d 985, 990 (Miss. S.Ct. 1998).

6. Schwarzer, "Reforming Jury Trials," 592.
7. Melvyn Bernard Zerman, *Call the Final Witness: The People v. Darrell R. Mathes as Seen by the Eleventh Juror* (New York: Harper and Row, 1977), 65; Victor Villaseñor, *Jury: The People vs. Juan Corona* (Boston: Little, Brown, 1977), 24.
8. Schwarzer, "Reforming Jury Trials," 593.
9. Stephen Phillips, *No Heroes, No Villains: The Story of a Murder Trial* (New York: Vintage Books, 1978), 113.
10. Paula L. Hannaford, B. Michael Dann, and G. Thomas Munsterman, "How Judges View Civil Juries," *DePaul Law Review* 48 (1998): 262; Schwarzer, "Reforming Jury Trials," 593; Lempert, "Civil Juries and Complex Cases," 222.

CHAPTER FIFTEEN. INSTRUCTIONS

1. Victor Villaseñor, *Jury: The People vs. Juan Corona* (Boston: Little, Brown, 1977), 55.
2. Ibid., 176; Reid Hastie, Steven D. Penrod, and Nancy Pennington, *Inside the Jury* (Cambridge, Mass.: Harvard University Press, 1983), 87.
3. Raymond Postgate, *Verdict of Twelve* (Chicago: Academy Chicago Publishers, 1986 [1940]), 149, 168.
4. Melvyn Bernard Zerman, *Call the Final Witness: The People v. Darrell R. Mathes as Seen by the Eleventh Juror* (New York: Harper and Row, 1977), 64.
5. M. Patricia Roth, *The Juror and the General: An Eyewitness Account of the Libel Trial of the Century: Westmoreland v. CBS* (New York: William Morrow, 1986), 27, 37.
6. Paula L. Hannaford, Valerie P. Hans, and G. Thomas Munsterman, "Permitting Jury Discussions During Trial: Impact of the Arizona Reform," *Law and Human Behavior* 24 (2000): 379.
7. Paula L. Hannaford, B. Michael Dann, and G. Thomas Munsterman, "How Judges View Civil Juries," *DePaul Law Review* 48 (1998): 261.
8. Ibid., 262.
9. Hannaford, Hans, and Munsterman, "Permitting Jury Discussions," 379.
10. Ibid., 377.
11. Hazel Thornton, *Hung Juror: The Diary of a Menendez Juror* (Philadelphia, Pa.: Temple University Press, 1995),13.
12. Ibid., 110–11.
13. Robert D. Dodson, "What Went Wrong with Federal Rule of Evidence 609: A Look at How Jurors Really Misuse Prior Convictions Evidence," *Drake Law Review* 48 (1999): 37, 38.
14. Michael J. Saks, "What Do Jury Experiments Tell Us About How Juries (Should) Make Decisions?" *Southern California Interdisciplinary Law Journal* 6 (1997): 26.

15. Neil Vidmar, "The Performance of the American Civil Jury: An Empirical Perspective," *Arizona Law Review* 40 (1998): 865.

16. Saks, "What Do Jury Experiments Tell Us," 28.

17. Walter W. Steele, Jr., and Elizabeth G. Thornburg, *North Carolina Law Review* 67 (1988): 96; Phoebe C. Ellsworth, "Jury Reform at the End of the Century: Real Agreement, Real Changes," *University of Michigan Journal of Law Reform* 32 (1999): 222.

18. Shari Seidman Diamond, "What Jurors Think: Expectations and Reactions of Citizens Who Serve as Jurors," in Robert E. Litan, ed., *Verdict: Assessing the Civil Jury System* (Washington, D.C.: Brookings Institution, 1993), 295.

19. Joel D. Lieberman and Bruce D. Sales, "What Social Science Teaches Us About the Jury Instruction Process," *Psychology, Public Policy, and Law* 3 (1997): 596–97.

20. Diamond, "What Jurors Think," 295.

21. Firoz Dattu, "Illustrated Jury Instructions: A Proposal," *Law & Psychology Review* 22 (1998): 70.

22. Robert C. Power, "Reasonable and Other Doubts: The Problem of Jury Instructions," *Tennessee Law Review* 67 (1999): 98.

23. Thornton, *Hung Juror,* 89–90.

24. Hannaford, Dann, and Munsterman, "How Judges View Civil Juries," 262.

25. Stephen A. Saltzburg, "Improving the Quality of Jury Decisionmaking," in Robert E. Litan, ed., *Verdict: Assessing the Civil Jury System* (Washington, D.C.: Brookings Institution, 1993), 355.

26. Ibid., 356.

27. Power, "Reasonable and Other Doubts," 105.

28. Ibid., 106.

29. Jonathan D. Casper, "Restructuring the Traditional Civil Jury: The Effects of Changes in Composition and Procedures," in Robert E. Litan, ed., *Verdict: Assessing the Civil Jury System* (Washington, D.C: Brookings Institution, 1993), 445.

30. Richard Lempert, "Civil Juries and Complex Cases: Taking Stock After Twelve Years," in Robert E. Litan, ed., *Verdict: Assessing the Civil Jury System* (Washington, D.C.: Brookings Institution, 1993), 221.

31. Lieberman and Sales, "What Social Science Teaches Us," 636.

32. Ibid.

33. Ibid.

34. *Weeks v. Angelone,* 528 U.S. 225, 229 (2000).

35. Ibid., 229.

36. Ibid., 248.

37. Ibid., 226, 229.

38. *Gacy v. Wellborn,* 994 F.2d 305, 313 (7th Cir. 1993).

39. Ibid., 312.

40. Stephen P. Garvey, Sheri Lynn Johnson, and Paul Marcus, "Correcting Deadly Confusion: Responding to Inquiries in Capital Cases," *Cornell Law Review* 85 (2000): 639.

41. Ibid., 640.

42. Dean Morier, Eugene Borgida, and Roger Park, "Improving Juror Comprehension of Judicial Instructions on the Entrapment Defense," *Journal of Applied Psychology* 26 (1996): 1859.

43. Casper, "Restructuring the Traditional Civil Jury," 423.
44. Mark Lesley with Charles Shuttleworth, *Subway Gunman: A Juror's Account of the Bernhard Goetz Trial* (Latham, N.Y.: British American Publishing, 1988), 315.
45. George P. Fletcher, *A Crime of Self-Defense: Bernhard Goetz and the Law on Trial* (Chicago: University of Chicago Press, 1988), 201.
46. Quoted in Marc Galanter, "An Oil Strike in Hell: Comtemporary Legends About the Civil Justice System," *Arizona Law Review* 40 (1998): 732. Galanter summarizes the McDonald's case:

> "The story of the spill, the suit and the $2.9 million award is abstracted from the facts about the extent of the plaintiff's injury (third-degree burns on legs and groin, necessitating skin grafts); the defendant's practice of serving coffee twenty or so degrees hotter [than] the standard in the trade; its earlier encounter with some seven hundred claims of this type, some of which it settled (for a total outlay of more than $500,000); the defendant's refusal of plaintiff's initial request for payment of medical (and attendant) expenses (about $11,000), which it countered with an offer of $800; its rejection of settlement proposals by her lawyer and of a court-appointed mediator's recommendation that the parties settle for $225,000; and the subsequent judicial reduction of punitive award (from the jury's $2.7 million, supposedly an estimation of two days of McDonald's coffee sales, to $480,000, three times the amount of compensatory damages); or the subsequent settlement between the parties" (731–32).

The settlement was confidential, but it was reported that "the parties ended up settling for an undisclosed amount not exceeding $600,000" (732).
47. Harry Kalven, Jr., "The Dignity of the Civil Jury," *Virginia Law Review* 50 (1964): 1057.

CHAPTER SIXTEEN. JURY VERDICTS AND THE PRIMACY OF EVIDENCE

1. John Guinther, "The Jury in America," in *American Civil Jury* (Washington, D.C.: Roscoe Pound-American Trial Lawyers Association, 1996), 47.
2. Norman J. Finkel, *Commonsense Justice: Juror's Notions of the Law* (Cambridge, Mass.: Harvard University Press, 1995), 42.
3. Studies using a wider range of mock jurors indicate that college students may be appropriately representative. Brian Bornstein, "The Ecological Validity of Jury Simulations: Is the Jury Still Out?" *Law and Human Behavior* 23 (1999), reports that research reveals there is "strong evidence that factors at trial affect students and nonstudents in the same way" (80).
4. Michael J. Saks, "What Do Jury Experiments Tell Us About How Juries (Should) Made Decisions?" *Southern California Law Review* 6 (1997): 5.
5. Nancy J. Marder, "Deliberations and Disclosure: A Study of Post-Verdict Interviews of Jurors," *Iowa Law Review* 82 (1997): 483.
6. Michael J. Saks, "Public Opinion About the Civil Jury: Can Reality Be Found in the Illusions?" *DePaul Law Review* 48 (1998): 238; James Fenimore Cooper, *The Ways of the Hour* (Phoenix Mills, U.K.: Alan Sutton Publishing, 1996 [1850]), 173.
7. Richard Lempert, "Why Do Juries Get a Bum Rap? Reflections on the Work of Valerie Hans," *DePaul Law Review* 48 (1998): 455.

8. Ibid., 457.

9. Ibid., 458.

10. Neal Feigenson, *Legal Blame: How Jurors Think and Talk About Accidents* (Washington, D.C.: American Psychological Association, 2000), 7; Valerie P. Hans, "The Illusions and Realities of Jurors' Treatment of Corporate Defendants," *DePaul Law Review* 48 (1998): 338, 339.

11. Marc Galanter, "An Oil Strike in Hell: Contemporary Legends About the Civil Justice System," *Arizona Law Review* 40 (1998): 71; Neil Vidmar, "The Performance of the American Civil Jury," *Arizona Law Review* 40 (1998): 869.

12. Feigenson, *Legal Blame,* 97.

13. Hans, "The Illusions and Realities of Jurors' Treatment of Corporate Defendants," 337.

14. Chris F. Denove and Edward J. Imwinkelried, "Jury Selection: An Empirical Investigation of Demographic Bias," *American Journal of Trial Advocacy* 19 (1995): 333.

15. Roselle L. Wissler, Allen J. Hart, and Michael J. Saks, "Decisionmaking About General Damages: A Comparison of Jurors, Judges, and Lawyers," *Michigan Law Review* 98 (1999): 806.

16. Neil Vidmar, Felicia Gross, and Mary Rose, "Jury Awards for Medical Malpractice and Post-Verdict Adjustments," *DePaul Law Review* 48 (1998): 269; Saks, "What Do Jury Experiments Tell Us," 45.

17. Shari Seidman Diamond, Michael J. Saks, and Stephan Landsman, "Juror Judgments About Liability and Damages: Sources of Variability and Ways to Increase Consistency," *DePaul Law Review* 48 (1998): 301. (Emphasis added.)

18. Neil Vidmar, Sara Sun Beale, Mary Rose, and Laura F. Donnelly, "Should We Rush to Reform the Criminal Jury? Consider Conviction Rate Data," *Judicature* 80 (1997): 287.

19. Ibid., 290.

While the overall North Carolina felony conviction rate was 68 percent, it was 81 percent for murder; 56 percent for rape and first-degree sex offenses; 55 percent for other sex offenses; 72 percent for robberies; 65 percent for assaults; and 75 percent for controlled substance offenses. The conviction rates remained stable in these crime categories over the studied time except for murders. The conviction rate from 1985 to 1988 for murder was 77 percent. From 1993 to 1996, the rate was 86 percent.

Florida had the lowest conviction rate of the studied jurisdictions. It is the only jurisdiction to use six-person juries for felony trials, which Florida uses for all trials except capital murder cases.

20. Harry Kalven, Jr., and Hans Zeisel, *The American Jury* (Boston: Little, Brown, 1966), 58–64; Paula Hannaford, B. Michael Dann, and G. Thomas Munsterman, "How Judges View Civil Juries," *DePaul Law Review* 48 (1998): 249; Marc Galanter, "The Regulatory Function of the Civil Jury," in Robert E. Litan, ed., *Verdict: Assessing the Civil Jury System* (Washington, D.C.: Brookings Insitution, 1993), 72.

21. Kevin M. Clermont and Theodore Eisenberg, "Trial by Judge or Jury: Transcending Empiricism," *Cornell Law Review* 77 (1992): 1153–54.

22. Hans, "The Illusions and Realities of Jurors' Treatment of Corporate Defendants," 341; Harry Kalven, Jr., "The Dignity of the Civil Jury," *Virginia Law Review* 50 (1964): 1067; Kalven and Zeisel, *The American Jury,* 115, 149.

23. Saks, "What Do Jury Experiments Tell Us," 43.
24. Vidmar, "The Performance of the American Civil Jury," 858–59.
25. Franklin Strier, "Whither Trial Consulting? Issues and Projections," *Law and Human Behavior* 23 (1999): 101.
26. Ibid.
27. Wissler et al., "Decisionmaking About General Damages," 805.
28. Molly Stuart, "The Why and How of Using Social Science Research in Jury Selection," *The Trial Lawyer* 22 (1999): 133; Nancy J. King, "Postconviction Review of Jury Discrimination: Measuring Effects of Juror Race on Jury Decisions," *Michigan Law Review* 92 (1993): 82.
29. Denove and Imwinkelried, "Jury Selection," 334.
30. Reid Hastie, "Reflections in the Magic Mirror of Law: Media Effects on Juror Decisions," *South Texas Law Review* 40 (1999): 904–5.
31. Valerie P. Hans, Paula L. Hannaford, G. Thomas Munsterman, "The Arizona Jury Reform Permitting Civil Jury Trial Discussion: The Views of Trial Participants, Judges, and Jurors," *University of Michigan Journal of Law Reform* 32 (1999): 351.
32. King, "Postconviction Review of Jury Discrimination," 78.
33. Saks, "What Do Jury Experiments Tell Us," 10–11.
34. Cass R. Sunstein, Daniel Kahneman, and David Schkade, "Assessing Punitive Damages (With Notes on Cognition and Valuation in Law)," *Yale Law Journal* 107 (1998): 2098.
35. The advantages of the jury as a deliberative body are perhaps most strongly stated by Jeffrey Abramson, *We, the Jury: The Jury System and The Ideal of Democracy* (New York: Basic Books, 1994). For example, Abramson defends "the jury as a deliberative . . . body. . . . No group can win that debate simply by outvoting others; under the traditional requirement of unanimity, power flows to arguments that persuade across group lines and speak to a justice common to persons drawn from different walks of life. By history and design, the jury is centrally about getting persons to bracket or transcend loyalties. This is why, ideally, voting is a secondary activity for jurors, deferred until persons can express a view of the evidence that is educated by how the evidence appears to others" (8).
36. Kalven and Zeisel, *The American Jury*, 488–89. Civil jury verdicts might not as closely track the initial ballot. A survey found that 30 percent of the questioned civil jurors said the ultimate verdict was not one the majority initially endorsed. Shari Seidman Diamond, "What Jurors Think: Expectations and Reactions of Citizens Who Serve as Jurors," in Robert E. Litan, ed., *Verdict: Assessing the Civil Jury System* (Washington, D.C.: Brookings Institution, 1993), 297.
37. Robert P. Burns, *A Theory of the Trial* (Princeton, N.J.: Princeton University Press, 1999), 145.
38. Ibid., 67.

CHAPTER SEVENTEEN. JURY TRIALS OF COMPLEX CASES

1. A. P. Herbert, *Uncommon Law: Being Sixty-Six Misleading Cases Revised and Collected in One Volume* (London: Eyre Methuen, 1977): 346–51.

2. Ibid.

3. Mirjan Damaska, *Evidence Law Adrift* (New Haven: Yale University Press, 1997), 143–44.

4. Graham Lilly, "The Decline of the American Jury," *University of Colorado Law Review* 72 (2001): 57.

5. Joseph Sanders, "Scientifically Complex Cases, Trial by Jury, and the Erosion of Adversarial Process," *DePaul Law Review* 48 (1998): 361, 363.

6. Ibid., 361.

7. Ibid., 363–64.

8. Ibid., 365.

9. Shari Seidman Diamond and Jonathan D. Casper, "Blindfolding the Jury to Verdict Consequences: Damages, Experts, and the Civil Jury," *Law and Society Review* 26 (1992): 558.

10. Daniel W. Shuman, Anthony Champagne, and Elisabeth Whitaker, "Juror Assessments of the Believability of Expert Witnesses: A Literature Review," *Jurimetrics* 36 (1996): 379–80.

11. Richard Lempert, "Civil Juries and Complex Cases: Taking Stock after Twelve Years," in Robert E. Litan, ed., *Verdict: Assessing the Civil Jury System* (Washington, D.C.: Brookings Institution, 1993), 192, 204.

12. Damaska, *Evidence Law Adrift*, 144.

13. Lempert, "Civil Juries and Complex Cases," 216–17.

14. Patrick E. Higginbotham, "Juries and the Complex Case: Observations About the Current Trend," in *American Civil Jury* (Washington, D.C.: Roscoe Pound–American Trial Lawyers Association, 1996), 75.

15. Jeffrey W. Stempel, "A More Complete Look at Complexity," *Arizona Law Review* 40 (1998): 784.

16. Lempert, "Civil Juries and Complex Cases," 235. Emphasis deleted.

17. Jason Schklar and Shari Seidman Diamond, "Juror Reactions to DNA Evidence: Errors and Expectancies," *Law and Human Behavior* 23 (1999): 179.

18. Jonathan Koehler and Daniel N. Shaviro, "Veridical Verdicts: Increasing Verdict Accuracy Through the Use of Overtly Probabilistic Evidence and Methods," *Cornell Law Review* 75 (1990), 255, quoting Amos Tversky and Daniel Kahneman, "Causal Schellas in Judgments Under Uncertainty," in Martin Fishbein, ed., *Progress in Social Psychology* (Hillsdale, N.J.: Erlbaum, 1980).

19. Schklar and Diamond, "Juror Reactions to DNA Evidence," 182.

20. The probability that it was actually Blue is only 12/29, or about 41 percent. Koehler and Shaviro suggest thinking about one hundred cases arising with the stated probabilities. This means that 85 percent of the cabs would be Green.

"Given the witness's 80 percent accuracy rate, in 68 percent of these cases he would correctly state that the cab was Green, and in seventeen cases he would incorrectly state that the cab was Blue. Second, in fifteen cases the cab would be Blue. Given the witness's accuracy, in twelve of these cases he would correctly state that the cab was Blue, and in three cases he would incorrectly state that it was Green.

"In the present case, however, the witness stated that the cab was Blue. Accordingly, the two relevant frequencies above are the twelve cases in which he said it was Blue when it indeed was Blue, and the seventeen cases in which he said it was Blue when it actually was Green. Thus, the probability that the cab in fact was Blue, given that the witness said it was Blue, is only 12/29, or about 41 percent" (256).

21. Joseph Sanders, "From Science to Evidence: The Testimony on Causation in the Bendectin Cases," *Stanford Law Review* 46 (1993): 56–58.

22. Franklin Strier, "The Educated Jury: A Proposal for Complex Litigation," *DePaul Law Review* 47 (1997): 72.

23. Ibid., 74; Lempert, "Civil Juries and Complex Cases," 192.

24. Stempel, "A More Complete Look at Complexity," 839.

25. Strier, "The Educated Jury," 76–77.

26. Damaska, *Evidence Law Adrift*, 146.

27. Sanders, "From Science to Evidence," 3.

28. Ibid., 47.

29. Ibid.

30. Ibid., 82.

31. Lempert, "Civil Juries and Complex Cases," 235.

CHAPTER EIGHTEEN. JURY NULLIFICATION

1. Irwin A. Horowitz and Thomas E. Willging, "Changing Views of Jury Power: The Nullification Debate, 1787–1988," *Law and Human Behavior* 15(1991): 167.

2. Matthew P. Harrington, "The Law-Finding Function of the American Jury," *Wisconsin Law Review* (1999): 378–79.

3. Norman J. Finkel, *Commonsense Justice: Jurors' Notions of the Law* (Cambridge, Mass.: Harvard University Press 1995): 24–25; Harrington, "The Law-Finding Function of the American Jury," 378.

4. *Georgia v. Brailsford*, 3 U.S. (3 Dall.) 1, 3–4 (1794).

5. Harrington, "The Law-Finding Function of the American Jury," 413, 379.

6. *Sparf and Hansen v. United States,* 156 U.S. 51, 61 n. 1 (1895).

7. Ibid., 102–3.

8. Ibid., 171.

9. *Green v. United States,* 355 U.S. 184 (1957).

10. 6 *Howell's State Trials* 999, 1012 (1670).

11. *Skidmore v. Baltimore & Ohio Railroad Company,* 167 F.2d 54, 61 (2d Cir. 1948).

12. Jack H. Friedenthal, Mary Kay Kane, and Arthur R. Miller, *Civil Procedure,* 3d edition (St. Paul, Minn.: West Group, 1999), 550–51.

13. Ibid., 553.

14. *Porche v. Gull Mississippi Marine Corp,* 390 F.Supp 624, 632 (E.D. La. 1975).

15. *United States v. Spock,* 416 F.2d 165 (1st Cir. 1969).

16. *Wayte v. United States,* 470 U.S. 598 (1985).

17. Colleen P. Murphy, "Integrating the Constitutional Authority of Civil and Criminal Juries," *George Washington Law Review* 61 (1993): 750.

18. Charles P. Curtis, "The Trial Judge and the Jury," *Vanderbilt Law Review* 5 (1952): 157–58.

19. Horowitz and Willging, "Changing Views of Jury Power," 168; Julius Goebel, Jr., and T. Raymond Naughton, *Law Enforcement in Colonial New York: A Study in Criminal Procedure (1664–1776)* (Montclair, N.J.: Patterson Smith, 1970), 674.

20. Clay S. Conrad, *Jury Nullification: The Evolution of a Doctrine* (Durham, N.C.: Carolina Academic Press, 1998), 65.

21. Harry Kalven, Jr., and Hans Zeisel, *The American Jury* (Boston: Little, Brown, 1966), 76, 292 n. 10.

22. David C. Brody, "*Sparf* and *Dougherty* Revisited: Why the Court Should Instruct the Jury of Its Nullification Right," *American Criminal Law Review* 33 (1995): 92. The exceptions are Maryland and Indiana. Since 1851, the Maryland constitution has granted criminal juries the right to decide the law. Today that provision states, "In the trial of all criminal cases, the jury shall be the judges of law as well as of fact, except that the court may pass upon the sufficiency of the evidence to sustain a conviction." Indiana's constitution contains comparable language. Court decisions in both jurisdictions, however, have limited the jury's right to decide the law. In Indiana jurors can be instructed that they are not arbitrarily to ignore the law as the judge defines it. The Maryland Supreme Court has held that the jury can decide the law only where there is a good faith dispute about the law, and the jurors cannot disregard the law simply because they have conscientious scruples against it. For a discussion of the Maryland and Indiana constitutional provisions and the court decisions interpreting them, see Conrad, *Jury Nullification,* 88–90, 119–21.

23. Patrick M. Pericak, "Using Rule 23(b) as a Means of Preventing Jury Nullification," *Southern Illinois Law Review* 23 (1998): 179.

24. Jonathan D. Casper, "Restructuring the Civil Jury: The Effects of Changes in Composition and Procedures," in Robert E. Litan, ed., *Verdict: Assessing the Civil Jury System* (Washington, D.C.: Brookings Institution, 1993), 418.

25. Andrew D. Leipold, "The Dangers of Race-Based Jury Nullification: A Response to Professor Butler," *UCLA Law Review* 44 (1996): 126.

26. Conrad, *Jury Nullification,* 173.

27. Ibid., 187.

28. Paul Butler, "Racially Based Jury Nullifcation: Black Power in the Criminal Justice System," *Yale Law Review* 105 (1995): 677.

29. Roger Parloff, "Race and Juries: If It Ain't Broke . . . " *American Lawyer* (June 1997): 5.

30. Ibid., 7.

31. In John Grisham's *A Time to Kill* (New York: Dell, 1989) the nine-year-old daughter of Carl Lee Hailey, a black in the rural South, has been brutally raped and left for dead by two white men. As the two are brought to court for their arraignment, Hailey openly kills them both and wounds their guard. Grisham's jury deliberations indicate that all the jurors know that Hailey committed the killings and only a few jurors accept the defense's contention that Hailey was temporarily insane. One juror then implores the others to imagine that their daughter had been the victim of a similar crime by two black men and to ask themselves whether they would not do the same as Hailey. The jury finds the accused not guilty on the grounds that he was temporarily insane, acquitting him in disregard of the law.

In Ayn Rand's *The Fountainhead* (New York: Signet, 1993 [1943]), architect Howard Roark is criminally tried for dynamiting "his" building, or at least one he designed. Because Roark admits doing the deed, he seems clearly guilty under the terms of the law, but after Roark's impassioned plea for understanding, the jury quickly acquits, apparently convinced that Roark's motive made the destruction justifiable in spite of what the law said.

32. Nancy S. Marder, "The Interplay of Race and False Claims of Jury Nullification," *University of Michigan Journal of Law Reform* 32 (1999): 286.

33. Nancy S. Marder, "Deliberations and Disclosures: A Study of Post-Verdict Interviews of Jurors," *Iowa Law Review* 82 (1997): 480–81.

34. Finkel, *Commonsense Justice*, 41.

35. Gerard S. Petrone, *Judgment at Gallatin: The Trial of Frank James* (Lubbock, Texas: Texas Tech Press, 1998): 180–81.

36. Quoted in Marder "The Interplay of Race," 288–89.

37. Jeffrey Abramson, "Introduction," in Jeffrey Abramson, ed., *Postmortem: The O.J. Simpson Case* (New York: Basic Books, 1996), 15; Marder, "The Interplay of Race and False Claims of Jury Nullification," 290–91.

38. Reid Hastie and Nancy Pennington, "The O.J. Simpson Stories: Behavioral Scientists' Reflections on *The People of the State of California v. Orenthal James Simpson*," *University of Colorado Law Review* 67 (1996): 958.

39. Ibid., 976.

40. Marder, "The Interplay of Race and False Claims of Jury Nullification," 291–92.

41. Kalven and Zeisel, *The American Jury*, 165.

42. Patrick Devlin, *The Enforcement of Morals* (London: Oxford University Press, 1959), 21; Horowitz and Willging, "Changing Views of Jury Power," 174.

43. Horowitz and Willging, "Changing Views of Jury Power," 174.

44. Marder, "The Interplay of Race and False Claims of Jury Nullification," 286.

45. Michael J. Saks, "What Do Jury Experiments Tell Us About How Juries (Should) Make Decisions?" *Southern California Interdisciplinary Law Journal* 6 (1997): 35.

46. Horowitz and Willging, "Changing Views of Jury Power," 166.

CHAPTER NINETEEN. THE FINALITY OF VERDICTS

1. *Arizona v. Fulminante*, 499 U.S. 279 (1991).

2. Norman J. Finkel, *Commonsense Justice: Jurors' Notions of the Law* (Cambridge, Mass.: Harvard University Press, 1995), 100–101.

3. Francis Allen, "A Serendipitous Trek through the Advance Sheet Jungle: Criminal Justice in the Court of Review," *Iowa Law Review* 70 (1985): 332.

4. *Jackson v. Virginia*, 443 U.S. 307, 319 and (1979).

5. Harper Lee, *To Kill a Mockingbird* (New York: Warner Books, 1982 [1960]): 194.

6. Ibid., 181.

7. Ibid., 186.

8. Steven Lubet, "Classics Revisited: Reconstructing Atticus Finch," *Michigan Law Review* 97 (1999): 1339–40.

9. Ibid., 1347.
10. Ibid.
11. *Jackson v. Virginia,* 443 U.S. at 319.
12. Lee, *To Kill a Mockingbird,* 220.
13. John Kobler, *Capone: The Life and World of Al Capone* (New York: Fawcett Crest, 1971), 324.
14. Eric L. Muller, "The Hobgoblin of Little Minds? Our Foolish Law of Inconsistent Verdicts," *Harvard Law Review* 111 (1998): 782, 784.
15. *United States v. Powell,* 469 U.S. 57, 65 (1984).
16. Ibid.
17. Ibid.
18. *McDonald v. Pless,* 238 U.S. 264, 267–78 (1915).
19. *Tanner v. United States,* 483 U.S. 107, 120 (1987).
20. Federal Rule of Evidence 606(b) advisory committee note.
21. Mark Cammack, "The Jurisprudence of Jury Trials: The No Impeachment Rule and the Conditions for Legitimate Legal Decisionmaking," *University of Colorado Law Review* 65 (1993): 78, quoted in Glanville Williams, *The Proof of Guilt* 268 (3d edition, 1963).
22. Joseph Sanders, "From Science to Evidence: The Testimony on Causation in the Bendectin Cases," *Stanford Law Review* 46 (1993): 29; Jack Friedenthal, Mary Kay Kane, and Arthur R. Miller, *Civil Procedure,* 3d edition (St. Paul, Minn.: West Group, 1999), 561.
23. Valerie P. Hans, "Attitudes Toward the Civil Jury: A Crisis of Confidence," in Robert E. Litan, ed., *Verdict: Assessing the Civil Jury System* (Washington, D.C.: Brookings Institution, 1993), 265.
24. Erik K. Moller, Nicholas M. Pace, and Stephen J. Carroll, "Punitive Damages in Financial Injury Verdicts," *Journal of Legal Studies* 28 (1999): 298.
25. David Baldus, John C. MacQueen, and George Woodworth, "Improving Judicial Oversight of Jury Damages Assessments: A Proposal for the Comparative Additur/Remittitur Review of Awards for Nonpecuniary Harms and Punitive Damages," *Iowa Law Review* 80 (1995): 1130–32.
26. Ibid., 1123–25.
27. George C. Christie, "Judicial Review of Findings of Fact," *Northwestern University Law Review* 87 (1992): 50.

CHAPTER TWENTY. REFORM

1. Susan Glaspell, "A Jury of Her Peers," in Elizabeth Villiers Gemmette, *Law in Literature* (New York: Praeger, 1992), 124–28.
2. Ibid., 138–29.
3. Ibid., 135–36.
4. Ibid., 136–37.
5. Ibid., 139.
6. Another fictional piece written during the time that women were being added to juries presented a different view. Arlo Bates's 1893 short story "In the Jury Room" presented women jurors as a topic for humor and derision. Set in a "Western State of recent cre-

ation," the country's first all-woman jury deliberates over a woman's claim that a man borrowed money under pretense of intended marriage. The women, including one who "is by profession a woman's rights orator," discuss sick babies, the appearance of the plaintiff, how husbands had said they should vote, the defendant's handsome countenance, jurors' hairdos, and the effect of their decision on the future of women's suffrage. The women question the sheriff on who the parties are and how they should vote. They address the problem of voting without a hat to drop ballots into. Many things are discussed, but never the evidence. Finally, several jurors announce that they are resigning. After protests from the sheriff, the judge finally agrees to a hung jury and discharges the jurors. The story concludes: "But among the lawyers of that part of the world it is held to be a fact not to be disputed that whatever is the second best story in the world, the best is certainly that which is given by the sheriff of his dealing with the female jury." Bates, "In the Jury Room," in *The Bundle of Time.*

7. The premise of "A Jury of Her Peers," that juries were reluctant to convict women of murder, seems to have been correct. Patricia L. Bryan, "Stories in Fiction and Fact: Susan Glaspell's *A Jury of Her Peers* and the 1901 Murder Trial of Margaret Hossack," *Stanford Law Review* 49 (1997): 1332–33, summarizes a study of many women accused of murder, *Women Who Kill,* by Ann Jones:

"Jones concludes that juries during the time of ["Jury of Her Peers"] were particularly lenient with female defendants, especially those who were extremely feminine in manner and appearance and who behaved as women were expected to behave. Lawyers defending women charged with murder blatantly relied on the sense of chivalry and paternalism imbued in the all-male juries, arguing that the jurors, as men, had a duty to protect the female defendant, typically portraying her as helpless, weak, and fragile.

"As Ann Jones convincingly argues, many guilty women went free during this period, with their freedom being "the price society paid to maintain the illusion that women had no reason to hate their husbands or marriage itself." Jurors, all male and most married, were understandably reluctant to believe that a woman was capable of murdering her husband."

8. Reality is often not as neat as a short story, which was true for the real-life trial that inspired "A Jury of Her Peers." The jury did not divide along gender lines as starkly as the story. In 1900, Susan Glaspell (who would go on to be a Pulitzer prize–winning playwright), was working as a reporter for a Des Moines newspaper when Iowan Margaret Hossack was accused of murdering her husband. (This account of Hossack's case is drawn largely from Patricia Bryan's excellent article.)

John Hossack's skull had been split and then crushed with an axe. According to his wife, he was attacked as she slept by his side, with her awakening only to see the bedroom door closing. She called out to the five of her nine children who still lived at home, but they had heard and seen nothing. Suspicion quickly fell on her. Burglary was easily discounted because readily accessible money and other valuables were undisturbed, and Mr. Hossack had no apparent enemies in town. Meanwhile, many reported that he had been abusive toward his family, and Mrs. Hossack had frequently sought the aid of neighbors.

The trial evidence presented a strong circumstantial case. It seemed to prove that if

Mrs. Hossack had been in bed with her husband when he was attacked, as she claimed, she, too, would have had to have been struck. A bloody ax was found secreted on the property, and Mrs. Hossack apparently knew its location before it was discovered. And so on. But as in the short story, concern that a jury would not think a woman could commit such a crime led the prosecution to focus on motive. On this point, "some of the women neighbors made the strongest witnesses against Margaret Hossack, repeating sometimes in a tone of animosity, her words to them about her husband and his violent threats. According to one newspaper, the women seemed either unaware of the impact of their testimony on the defendant or not averse to making a strong case against her" (1330).

The jury convicted, but rejected the death penalty, and Mrs. Hossack was sentenced to life imprisonment. Glaspell stopped reporting about the case at this point, but the story did not end here. Although public opinion had run against Mrs. Hossack before the trial, after the conviction it quickly shifted. Newspaper accounts and editorials questioned the correctness of the outcome. Prominent citizens called for her parole. Instead, however, one year after the verdict, the conviction was reversed. According to Bryan, "despite the lack of strong precedent . . . , the Iowa Supreme Court decided that technical errors had been made by the trial court [and] that she had been unfairly prejudiced by those two seemingly minor errors" (1347).

A new trial was held. Bryan states:

"In reading about Margaret Hossack's second trial, I cannot help but wonder how Susan Glaspell would have reacted had she been there. Just as at the first trial, she would have seen a courtroom controlled by men, with male lawyers, a male judge, and an all-male jury. She would have heard testimony much the same as that given at the first trial, with the prosecution using the domestic abuse as evidence of Mrs. Hossack's motive and the defense seeking to convince the jury of the evidence's irrelevance. And yet, without doubt, a different attitude toward Mrs. Hossack seemed to prevail, both within and outside of the courtroom. . . .

"[T]he same evidence [of motive and the circumstantial evidence] that had been used so successfully by the prosecution to prove her guilt now seemed to arouse sympathy" (1349–51).

New evidence was presented that an unknown, furiously riding horseman was seen near the house at the time of the murder. This time, after thirty hours of deliberation, the jury hung, nine to three, for conviction. The case was not tried a third time, and Margaret Hossack died thirteen years later, apparently without speaking again of the murder.

9. James S. Leibman, Jeffrey Fagan, Valerie West, and Jonathan Lloyd, "Capital Attrition: Error Rates in Capital Cases, 1973–95," *Texas Law Review* 78 (2000): 1850; Edward Connors, Thomas Lundgren, Neal Miller, and Tom McEwen, *Convicted by Juries, Exonerated by Science: Cases Studies in the Use of DNA Evidence to Establish Innocence After Trial* (Washington, D.C.: National Institutes of Justice, 1996).

10. Fox Butterfield, "Texas Nears Creation of State Public-Defender System," *New York Times,* April 6, 2001, A14.

11. Alan Berlow, "The Wrong Man," *Atlantic Monthly,* November 1999.

12. Barry Scheck, Peter Neufeld, and Jim Dwyer, *Actual Innocence: Five Days to Execution and Other Dispatches from the Wrongly Convicted* (New York: Doubleday, 2000), 125.

13. *Strickland v. Washington,* 446 U.S. 668 (1984).

14. Donald A. Dripps, "Ineffective Assistance of Counsel: The Case for an Ex Ante Parity Standard," *Journal of Criminal Law and Criminology* 88 (1997): 243.

15. Berlow, "The Wrong Man"; Scheck, Neufeld, and Dwyer, *Actual Innocence,* appendix 2.

16. *Arizona v. Youngblood,* 488 U.S. 51 (1988).

17. Robert P. Burns, *A Theory of the Trial* (Princeton, N.J.: Princeton University Press, 1999), 83.

18. Randolph N. Jonakait, "The Ethical Prosecutor's Misconduct," *Criminal Law Bulletin* 23 (1987): 552.

19. Elizabeth F. Loftus, *Eyewitness Testimony* (Cambridge, Mass.: Harvard University Press, 1979): 77–78, 94–95, 60.

20. Franklin Strier, "Making Jury Trials More Truthful," *University of California Davis Law Review* 95 (1996): 179.

21. Paul D. Carrington, "The Seventh Amendment: Some Bicentennial Reflections," *University of Chicago Law Forum* (1990): 68.

22. Wayne T. Westling and Vicki Waye, "Videotaping Police Interrogations: Lessons from Australia," *American Journal of Criminal Law* 25 (1998): 497.

23. Melvyn Bernard Zerman, *Call the Final Witness: The People v. Darrell R. Mathes as Seen by the Eleventh Juror* (New York: Harper & Row, 1977): 141.

24. Gary L. Wells, Roy S. Malpass, R. C. L. Lindsay, Ronald P. Fisher, John W. Turtle, and Solomon M. Fulero, "From the Lab to the Police Station: A Successful Application of Eyewitness Research," *American Psychologist* 55 (June 2000): 582–83.

25. Atul Gawande, "Under Suspicion: The Fugitive Science of Criminal Justice," *The New Yorker* (January 8, 2001): 50; Loftus, *Eyewitness Testimony,* 8.

26. Gawande, "Under Suspicion," 51.

27. Quoted in Loftus, *Eyewitness Testimony,* 179.

28. Wells et al., "From the Lab to the Police Station," 585.

29. Ibid.

30. *United States v. Wade,* 388 U.S. 218 (1967). Defense attorneys are not required to be present at lineups that precede the initiation of postindictment judicial proceedings, *Kirby v. Illinois,* 406 U.S. 682 (1972), nor are they required at any photographic identification. *United States v. Ash,* 413 U.S. 300 (1973); *Manson v. Brathwaite,* 432 U.S. 98 (1977); Wells et al., "From the Lab to the Police Station," 588.

31. U.S. Department of Justice, *Eyewitness Evidence: A Guide for Law Enforcement* (Washington, D.C.: Department of Justice, 1999): 3–5.

32. Wells et al., "From the Lab to the Police Station," 591–92.

33. Ibid., 586.

34. Ibid., 594–95.

35. Ibid., 594.

Index

Bristow, Robert O'Neil, 301n43, 307n22
Broeder, D. W., 151
Brooks v. Kemp, 266
Bryan, Patricia L., 328n7
Bullett, Gerald, 50, 307n22
Burch v. Louisiana, 96
Burns, Robert, 44, 127, 180, 232, 286–87
Bushell's Case, 249–50
Butler, Paul, 257

Cadorine, Jessica, 163
California: conviction rate, 226; criminal syndicalism, 77–88; hung juries, 99, 100, 101–2, 306n12, 307n20; jury instructions, 206; jury pool selection, 122; supermajorities permitted, 96; trial length/cost, 97
California Book of Approved Jury Instructions, 206
Cammack, Mark, 147–48, 274
Canada, 165, 313n20
capital punishment. *See* death penalty
Capone, Al, tax evasion trial, 271, 312n6
Carrington, Paul, 48, 72, 91, 92
Castelle, George, 283
Cate, Fred H., 312n11, 313n15
cause, challenges for. *See* challenges for cause
Chafee, Zechariah, Jr., 77–8
challenges for cause, 16, 134–39, 168. *See also* bias, juror; voir dire
Chesterton, G. K., 59–60
A Civil Action (Harr), 159–61
civil cases: in other countries, 83–84, 176 (*see also* England); resolution without trial, 9–11; right to jury trial, 2, 13–14, 37–39; settlement, 10–14. *See also* civil jury trials
civil jury trials: appeals, 14–15, 274–75; cases taken from jury, 275; compromise verdicts, 96–97; constitutional right to, 2, 13–14, 37–39; criticism of

juries, xxii–xxiii; deliberations and final verdict, 231–32, 307–8n22, 322n36; determination of standards/reasonableness, 65–67; in England, 68–69; fact-finding role of jurors, 36–37; general vs. special verdicts, 17, 251; harmless error doctrine, 267; hung jury rate, 99 (*see also* hung juries); inconsistent verdicts, 272; judge-jury agreement, 227; juries as check/balance, 36–40; jury consultants used, 157 (*see also* jury consultants); length/cost, 97–98; nonunanimous verdicts permitted, 17, 96, 194 (*see also* majority verdicts; unanimity requirement); primacy of evidence in liability verdicts, 223–25; public acceptance of verdicts, 80, 303n11; and settlement, 10–14; standard of proof, 15; statistics, 10. *See also* damage awards; defense attorneys; judges; jurors; liability cases; negligence cases; personal injury cases; plaintiffs and plaintiffs' attorneys; *and specific trials*
civil law countries, trials in, xxiv, 176–78, 316n8
Clayton Anti-Trust Act (1914), 302–3n5
closing arguments (summations), 16
Coates, Charles, 253
Colgrove v. Battin, 36–37, 39, 89
colonial juries, 23–25
community opinion surveys, 157–58, 160, 164
community values, 64–74; in ordinary cases, 67–70; and personal injury law, 65–67; and proof beyond reasonable doubt, 72–74; and trials, 71–72
complex cases, 233–44; expert testimony, 235–40, 323–24n20 (*see also* expert testimony); extent of, 234–35; judicial vs. jury competence, 237–38;